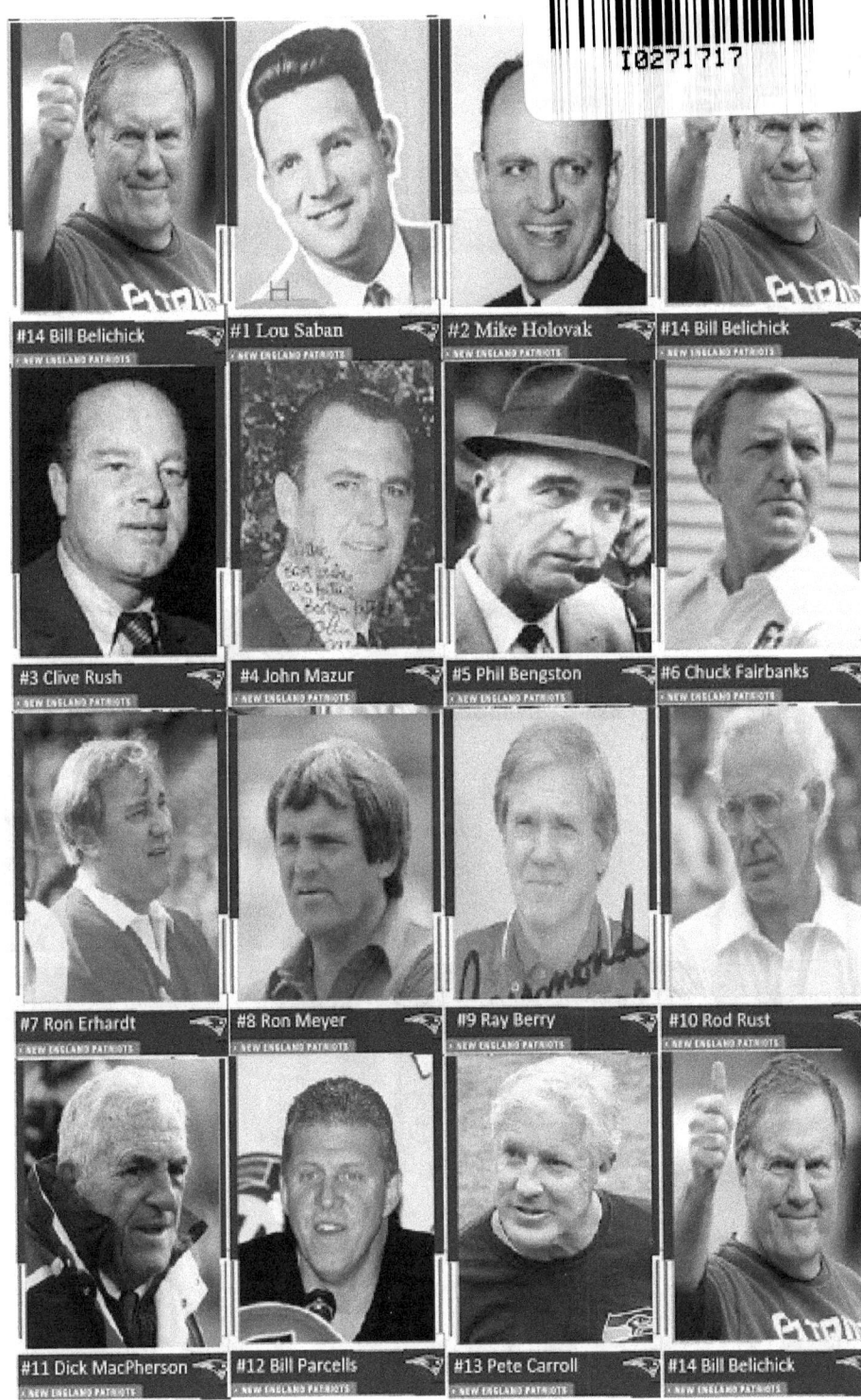

PATRIOTS

Great Moments
in
New England Patriots
Football

This book begins at the beginning of Football and goes to the Bill Belichick era.

This book is written for those of us who love New England Patriots Football. Those who are not the top fans of the Pats will also want this book, so they can try to get a leg up on the facts missing from the bookshelves of those Patriot fans who do not have this book.

The book first tells the story about the founding of the Patriots as a new American Football League (AFL) team from Boston in 1960. But it reaches back even further in history than 1960 to find the precursor professional football teams from the turn of the century when Pro Football was just beginning. This book actually takes the Patriots fan on a journey from when there was no football at all, to where American football was only a dream, and then to where American football was played only by colleges with a mixture of soccer and rugby rules.

After talking about how primitive man played football, this book quickly moves on to describe the beginning of football in the US and it recounts the first "American Football Game" in 1869. From there, the progression includes college football teams that loved the new sport and their football graduates looking for a place to play football after college. Eventually all of this builds up to the NFL, then the AFL, and of course the Boston Patriots first football game in 1960, and the first Patriots coach, Lou Saban. Then of course there are the New England Patriots, and the phenomenal Bill Belichick.

It seems like yesterday but for those pros trying to create a league out of nothing, there would have been nothing without their hard work. And of course, this great book about the Patriots eventually gets a deep look at the great and soon-to-be-immortal-Patriots' coaches including Lou Saban, Mike Holovak, Chuck Fairbanks, Ray Berry, Bill Parcells, Pete Carroll, and of course the greatest living immortal coach in pro football today, Bill Belichick. The Patriots current coach has topped the list of many pundits from his first year as the Patriot head coach in 2000.

This book captures the great moments in Patriots Football even before the Patriots were the New England Patriots. This Patriots-first book takes the reader through stories about the Patriots 14 coaches to great stories about the 58 seasons worth of great games (1018 games) with 523 great wins. The book often stops in time and talks about a particular great player such as John Hannah, Gino Cappelletti, Bob Dee, Vito "Babe" Parilli, Steve Grogan, Bruce Armstrong, Jim Nance, Dont'e Hightower, Drew Bledsoe, Tedy Bruschi, Ty Law, Willie McGinist, Rob Gronkowski, Wes Welker, or the greatest player in football today, Tom Brady. These stops will add substantially to your reading enjoyment.

I dare you to pick up this book. If you are an avid Patriots fan, you will never put it down again. You cannot ever get enough of Patriots' greatness, but we do provide as many stories together in one spot as we can in this can't miss book.

Brian Kelly

Great Moments in New England Patriots Football
Author: Brian W. Kelly
Copyright © 2018 Brian W. Kelly
Publisher/ Editor, Brian P. Kelly

All rights reserved: No part of this book may be reproduced or transmitted in any form, or by any means, electronic or mechanical, including photocopying, recording, scanning, faxing, or by any information storage and retrieval system, without permission from the publisher, LETS GO PUBLISH, in writing.

Disclaimer: Though judicious care was taken throughout the writing and the publication of this work that the information contained herein is accurate, there is no expressed or implied warranty that all information in this book is 100% correct. Therefore, neither LETS GO PUBLISH, nor the author accepts liability for any use of this work.

Trademarks: A number of products and names referenced in this book are trade names and trademarks of their respective companies.

Referenced Material: *The information in this book has been obtained through personal and third-party observations, interviews, and copious research. Where unique information has been provided or extracted from other sources, those sources are acknowledged within the text of the book itself or at the end of the chapter in the Sources Section. Thus, there are no formal footnotes nor is there a bibliography section. Any picture that does not have a source was taken from various sites on the Internet with no credit attached. If resource owners would like credit in the next printing, please email publisher.*

Published by: LETS GO PUBLISH!
Publisher & Editor: Brian P. Kelly
Mail Location: P.O. Box 621, Wilkes-Barre, PA
Email: info@letsgopublish.com
Web site www.letsgopublish.com

Library of Congress Copyright Information Pending
Book Cover Design by Michele Thomas, Editing by Brian P. Kelly

ISBN Information: The International Standard Book Number (ISBN) is a unique machine-readable identification number, which marks any book unmistakably. The ISBN is the clear standard in the book industry. 159 countries and territories are officially ISBN members. The Official ISBN For this book is on the outside cover:

978-1-947402-37-9

The price for this work is : $19.95 USD

10   9   8   7   6   5   4   3   2

Release Date: June 2018

LETS GO PUBLISH!

New England Patriots Season Records from 1960 to 2018

Total 489-386-9 All-time regular season record (1960–2017)
34-20 All-time postseason record (1960–2017)
523-406-9 All-time regular & postseason record (1960–2017)

Total Games   1018
Total Wins 523
Total Losses   406
Total Ties   9   * Prior to Overtime Rules
Stats from   1960   * Through Feb 2018

Boston Patriots

Year	Coach	League	Conf	Div	Pl	Record
1960	Lou Saban	AFL		East	4th	5 9 0
1961	Lou Saban (2–3)	AFL		East	2nd	9 4 1

1960-1961 Lou Saban final record (14-14-1)

Year	Coach	League	Conf	Div	Pl	Record
1961	Mike Holovak (7–1–1)					
1962	Mike Holovak	AFL		East	2nd	9 4 1
1963	Mike Holovak	AFL		East	1st	7 6 1

- Won Divisional Playoffs (at Bills) 26–8
- Lost AFL Championship (at Chargers) 10–51

Year	Coach	League	Conf	Div	Pl	Record
1964	Mike Holovak	AFL		East	2nd	10 3 1
	Gino Cappelletti(MVP)					
1965	Mike Holovak	AFL		East	3rd	4 8 2
1966	Mike Holovak	AFL		East	2nd	8 4 2

- Jim Nance(MVP)

Year	Coach	League	Conf	Div	Pl	Record
1967	Mike Holovak	AFL		East	5th	3 10 1
1968	Mike Holovak	AFL		East	4th	4 10 0

1961-1968 Mike Holovak final record (55-46-6)

Year	Coach	League	Conf	Div	Pl	Record
1969	Clive Rush	AFL		East	3rd	4 10 0
1970	Clive Rush (1–6)	NFL	AFC/	East	5th	2 12 0

1969-1970 Clive Rush final record (5-16-0)

1970 John Mazur [last six games of 1970 (1–6)]

New England Patriots

Year	Coach	League	Conf	Div	Pl	Record
1971	John Mazur	NFL	AFC	East	3rd	6 8 0
1972	John Mazur (2–7)	NFL	AFC	East	5th	3 11 0

1971-1972 John Mazur final record (9-21-0)

1972 Phil Bengtson [last 5 games of 1972 –(1–4)]
1972 Phil Bengston final record (1-4-0)

Year	Coach	League	Conf	Div	Pl	Record
1973	Chuck Fairbanks	NFL	AFC	East	3rd	5 9 0
1974	Chuck Fairbanks	NFL	AFC	East	3rd	7 7 0
1975	Chuck Fairbanks	NFL	AFC	East	5th	3 11 0
1976	Chuck Fairbanks	NFL	AFC	East	2nd	11 3 0

- Lost Divisional Playoffs (at Raiders) 21–24

Year Coach	League	Conf	Div	Pl	Record
1977 Chuck Fairbanks	NFL	AFC	East	3rd	9 5 0
1978 Chuck Fairbanks	NFL	AFC	East	1st	11 5 0

- Lost Divisional Playoffs (Oilers) 14–31[15]

1973-1978 Chuck Fairbanks final record (46-50-0)

1979 Ron Erhardt	NFL	AFC	East	2nd	9 7 0
1980 Ron Erhardt	NFL	AFC	East	2nd	10 6 0
1981 Ron Erhardt	NFL	AFC	East	5th	2 14 0

1979-1981 Ron Erhardt final record (21-27-0)

1982 Ron Meyer	NFL	AFC	East	7th	5 4 0

- Lost First Round (at Dolphins) 13–28 **9 game season w/strike**

1983 Ron Meyer	NFL	AFC	East	2nd	8 8 0
1984 Ron Meyer (5–3)	NFL	AFC	East	2nd	9 7 0
1984 Ray Berry (4-4)					

1982-1984 Ron Meyer final record (18-15)

1984 Ray Berry (4–4)

1985 Ray Berry	NFL	AFC	East	3rd	11 5 0

- Won Wild Card Playoffs (at Jets) 26–14
- Won Divisional Playoffs (at Raiders) 27–20
- Won Conference Championship (at Dolphins) 31–14
- Lost Super Bowl XX (vs. Bears) 10–46

1986 Ray Berry	NFL	AFC	East	1st	11 5 0

- Lost Divisional Playoffs (at Broncos) 17–22

1987 Ray Berry	NFL	AFC	East	2nd	8 7 0
1988 Ray Berry	NFL	AFC	East	3rd	9 7 0

- John Stephens(OROY)

1989 Ray Berry	NFL	AFC	East	4th	5 11 0

1984-1989 Ray Berry final record (47-39)

1990 Rod Rust	NFL	AFC	East	5th	1 15 0

1990 Rod Dust final record (1-15)

1991 Dick MacPherson	NFL	AFC	East	4th	6 10 0

- Leonard Russell(OROY)

1992 Dick MacPherson	NFL	AFC	East	5th	2 14 0

1984-1989 Dick MacPherson final record (8-24-0)

1993 Bill Parcells	NFL	AFC	East	4th	5 11 0
1994 Bill Parcells	NFL	AFC	East	2nd	10 6 0

- Lost Wild Card Playoffs (at Browns) 13–20
- Bill Parcells(COY)[18]

1995 Bill Parcells	NFL	AFC	East	4th	6 10 0

- Curtis Martin(OROY)

1996 Bill Parcells	NFL	AFC	East	1st	11 5 0

- Won Divisional Playoffs(Steelers) 28–3
- Won Conference Championship(Jaguars) 20–6
- Lost Super Bowl XXXI (vs. Packers) 21–35

1993-1996 Bill Parcells final record (32-32-0)

Year	Coach	League	Conf	Div	Pl	Record
1997	Pete Carroll	NFL	AFC	East	1st	10 6 0

- Won Wild Card Playoffs(Dolphins) 17–3
- Lost Divisional Playoffs (at Steelers) 6–7

Year	Coach	League	Conf	Div	Pl	Record
1998	Pete Carroll	NFL	AFC	East	4th	9 7 0

- Lost Wild Card Playoffs (at Jaguars) 10–25

Year	Coach	League	Conf	Div	Pl	Record
1999	Pete Carroll	NFL	AFC	East	5th	8 8 0

1997-1999 Pete Carroll final record (27-21-0)

Year	Coach	League	Conf	Div	Pl	Record
2000	Bill Belichick	NFL	AFC	East	5th	5 11 0
2001	Bill Belichick	NFL	AFC	East	1st	11 5 0

- Won Divisional Playoffs (Raiders) 16–13 (OT)
- Tom Brady(SB MVP)[20]
- Won Conference Championship (at Steelers) 24–17
- Won Super Bowl XXXVI (1) (vs. Rams) 20–17

Year	Coach	League	Conf	Div	Pl	Record
2002	Bill Belichick	NFL	AFC	East	2nd	9 7 0
2003	Bill Belichick	NFL	AFC	East	1st	14 2 0

- Won Divisional Playoffs (Titans) 17–14
- Tom Brady(SB MVP)[21]
- Won Conference Championship(Colts) 24–14
- Bill Belichick(COY)[22]
- Won Super Bowl XXXVIII (2) (vs. Panthers) 32–29

Year	Coach	League	Conf	Div	Pl	Record
2004	Bill Belichick	NFL	AFC	East	1st	14 2 0

- Won Divisional Playoffs (Colts) 20–3
- Deion Branch (SB MVP)[23]
- Won Conference Championship (at Steelers) 41–27
- Won Super Bowl XXXIX (3) (vs. Patriots) 24–21

Year	Coach	League	Conf	Div	Pl	Record
2005	Bill Belichickc	NFL	AFC	East	1st	10 6 0

- Won Wild Card Playoffs(Jaguars) 28–3
- Tedy Bruschi(CBPOY)
- Lost Divisional Playoffs (at Broncos) 13–27

Year	Coach	League	Conf	Div	Pl	Record
2006	Bill Belichick	NFL	AFC	East	1st	12 4 0

- Won Wild Card Playoffs (Jets) 37–16
- Won Divisional Playoffs (at Chargers) 24–21
- Lost Conference Championship (at Colts) 34–38
-

Year	Coach	League	Conf	Div	Pl	Record
2007	Bill Belichick	NFL	AFC	East	1st	16 0 0

- Won Divisional Playoffs(Jaguars) 31–20
- Tom Brady(MVP, OPOY)
- Won Conference Championship(Chargers) 21–12
- Bill Belichick(COY)
- Lost Super Bowl XLII (vs. Giants) 14–17

Year	Coach	League	Conf	Div	Pl	Record
2008	Bill Belichick	NFL	AFC	East	2nd	11 5 0

- Jerod Mayo(DROY

Year	Coach	League	Conf	Div	Pl	Record
2009	Bill Belichick	NFL	A FC	East	1st	10 6 0

- Lost Wild Card Playoffs (Ravens) 14–33
- Tom Brady(CBPOY)[27]

Year	Coach	League	Conf	Div	Pl	Record
2010	Bill Belichick	NFL	AFC	East	1st	14 2 0

Lost Divisional Playoffs (Jets) 21–28

- Tom Brady(MVP, OPOY)
- Bill Belichick(COY)

Year	Coach	League	Conf	Div	Pl	Record
2011	Bill Belichick	NFL	AFC	East	1st	13 3 0

- Won Divisional Playoffs(Broncos) 45–10
- Won Conference Championship(Ravens) 23–20
- Lost Super Bowl XLVI (vs. Giants) 17–21

Year	Coach	League	Conf	Div	Pl	Record
2012	Bill Belichick	NFL	AFC	East	1st	12 4 0

- Won Divisional Playoffs (Texans) 41–28
- Lost Conference Championship(Ravens) 13–28

Year	Coach	League	Conf	Div	Pl	Record
2013	Bill Belichick	NFL	AFC	East	1st	12 4 0

- Won Divisional Playoffs (Colts) 43–22
- Lost Conference Championship (at Broncos) 16–26

Year	Coach	League	Conf	Div	Pl	Record
2014	Bill Belichick	NFL	AFC	East	1st	12 4 0

- Won Divisional Playoffs (Ravens) 35–31
- Rob Gronkowski(CBPOY)
- Won Conference Championship(Colts) 45–7
- Tom Brady(SB MVP)[29]
- Won Super Bowl XLIX (4) (vs. Seahawks) 28–24

Year	Coach	League	Conf	Div	Pl	Record
2015	Bill Belichick	NFL	AFC	East	1st	12 4 0

- Won Divisional Playoffs (Chiefs) 27–20
- Lost Conference Championship (at Broncos) 18–20

Year	Coach	League	Conf	Div	Pl	Record
2016	Bill Belichick	NFL	AFC	East	1st	14 2 0

- Won Divisional Playoffs (Texans) 34–16
- Tom Brady(SB MVP)
- Won Conference Championship(Steelers) 36–17
- Won Super Bowl LI (5) (vs. Falcons) 34–28 (OT)

Year	Coach	League	Conf	Div	Pl	Record
2017	Bill Belichick	NFL	AFC	East	1st	13 3 0

- Won Divisional Playoffs (Titans) 35–14
- Tom Brady(MVP)
- Won Conference Championship(Jaguars) 24–20
- Lost Super Bowl LII (vs. Eagles) 33–41

2000-2017 Bill Belichick final record (214-74-0)

Total 489-386-9 All-time regular season record (1960–2017)
34-20 All-time postseason record (1960–2017)[30]
523-406-9 All-time regular & postseason record (1960–2017)

Dedication

I dedicate this book

To my wife & children and my wonderful brothers and sisters.

Wife—Patricia A. Kelly
Sons & Daughters—Brian P. Kelly, Michael P. Kelly, Katie P. Kelly

Angel Edward J. Kelly, Jr.

Carol & Amelia Kelly

Nancy "Ann" Flannery & Angel Jim Flannery

Mary A. Daniels & Bill Daniels

Joseph A. Kelly & Diane Kelly

I surely am a lucky person to have

Such a great family

Mom & Dad—Angels Edward J Kelly Sr. and Irene McKeown Kelly

Acknowledgments:

I appreciate all the help that I have received in putting this book together as well as all of the other 153 books from the past.

My acknowledgments were so large at one time that readers complained that they had to go through too many pages to get to page one.

And, so I put my acknowledgment list online, and it continues to grow. Believe it or not, it would cost about a dollar more to print my books with full acknowledgments.

Thank you and God bless you all for your help. Please check out www.letsgopublish.com to read the latest version of my heartfelt acknowledgments updated for this book.

In this book, I received some extra special help from many fine American patriots including Dennis Grimes, Gerry Rodski, Wily Ky Eyely, Angel Irene McKeown Kelly, Angel Edward Joseph Kelly Sr., Angel Edward Joseph Kelly Jr., Ann Flannery, Angel James Flannery Sr., Mary Daniels, Bill Daniels, Angel Robert Garry Daniels, Angel Sarah Janice Daniels, Angel Punkie Daniels, Joe Kelly, Diane Kelly, Angel Harry Ashford, Angel Josephine Ashford. Brian P. Kelly, Mike P. Kelly, Katie P. Kelly, Angel Ben Kelly, and Budmund (Buddy) Arthur Kelly.

Thank you all!

Table of Contents

Dedication xi

Table of Contents xv

Chapter 1 Introduction to the Book 1

Chapter 2 History of Patriots Football Stadiums 15

Chapter 3 Patriots Launch First Football Team 31

Chapter 4 The Evolution of Modern Football 45

Chapter 5 The First American College Football Game 49

Chapter 6 Moving Closer Towards American Football 61

Chapter 7 Origin of the Oval-Shaped Sports-Ball 75

Chapter 8 The Birth of Play with Pay 83

Chapter 9 When Pro Football Was Unorganized 89

Chapter 10 NFL's Fast Start from 1920 Set the Stage for Today 97

Chapter 11 Coach Mike Holovak 1961-1968 107

Chapter 12 Coach Clive Rush 1969-1970 133

Chapter 13 Coach John Mazur 1970-1972 141

Chapter 14 Coach Chuck Fairbanks, 1973 to 1978 147

Chapter 15 Coach Ron Erhardt 1979 to 1981 167

Chapter 16 Coach Ron Meyer 1982 to 1984 181

Chapter 17 Coach Ray Berry 1985 to 1989 191

Chapter 18 Coaches Rod Rust & Dick MacPherson, 1990-1992 225

Chapter 19 Coach Bill Parcells 1993 to 1996 233

Chapter 20 Coach Pete Carroll 1997 to 1999 271

Chapter 21 Coach Bill Belichick Part I 2000 to 2005 283

Chapter 22 Coach Bill Belichick Part II 2006-2011 347

Chapter 23 Coach Bill Belichick Part III 2012-2017... 397

Other books by Brian Kelly: (amazon.com, & Kindle) 468

References

I learned how to write creatively in Grade School at St. Boniface. I even enjoyed reading some of my own stuff.

At Meyers High School (HS Diploma) and King's College (BS Data Processing), and Wilkes-University, (MBA Accounting & Finance) I learned how to research, write bibliographies and footnote every non-original thought included in my writings. I learned to hate ibid, and op. cit., and I hated assuring that I had all citations were written down in the proper sequence. Having to pay attention to details took my desire to write creatively and diminished it with busy work.

I know it is necessary for the world to stop plagiarism, so authors and publishers can get paid properly, but for an honest writer, it sure is annoying. I wrote many proposals while with IBM and whenever I needed to cite something, I cited it in place, because my readers, IT Managers, and company management, could care less about tracing the vagaries of citations. I always hated to use stilted footnotes, or produce a lengthy, perfectly formatted bibliography. I bet most bibliographies are flawed because even the experts on such drivel do not like the tedium.

I wrote 153 other books before this book and several hundred articles published by many magazines and newspapers and I only cite when an idea is not mine or when I am quoting, and again, I choose to cite in place, and the reader does not have to trace strange numbers through strange footnotes and back to bibliography elements that may not be readily accessible or available.

Yet, I would be kidding you, if in a book about the great moments in New England Patriots Football, I tried to bluff my way, so you would think that I knew everything before I began to research and write anything in this book. I spent as much time researching as writing. I might even call myself an expert of sorts now for all the facts that I have uncovered.

Without any pain on your part, you can read this book from cover to cover to enjoy the stories about the many great moments in both the Boston Patriots of the AFL and the New England Patriots of the NFL Both generations of New England Teams made their mark on the football world.

This book is not intended for historians per se, but it does teach a lot of history. It is for regular people of all levels of intelligence. It is for people who want to have a fun read, who like smiling when Patriots Football is the topic. It is fun reading about each of New England's 523 wins. This book is for people who love New England Patriots' Football and perhaps it is also for some Patriot's detractors who want to have command of the facts before they defend a point of view.

There are lots and lots of facts in this book. This book is not for sticklers about the mundane aspects of writing that often cause creative writers to lay bricks or paint houses instead of writing. It is for everyday people, like you and I, who enjoy the Patriots because they are the Patriots and who enjoy football because it is football. It is that simple.

When the Patriots play a team and they win or lose, that is a historical fact, but to discover such facts, it does not require fundamental or basic research. The NFL itself as well as the Patriots, copyright their original material but not public facts. They copyright so they can say "no" if somebody else's creativity affects the league or the franchise negatively. Even the NFL does not own publicly well-known facts that are readily available about legacies such as Mike Holovak or Chuck Fairbanks or Bill Parcells or Raymond Berry, or even the more than immortal Bill Belichick and his many championship seasons.

The championships and the coaches and the great players are well known and well defined, though some may think the facts belong to the NFL. Facts are facts, period. So, what? As the author of this book, I care but it is a sports book. I use a judicious approach to assure that I am not throwing the bull when I intend to be presenting the facts.

Nonetheless, this is not a book about heavy math algorithms, or potential advances to the internal combustion engine, or space travel, or the eight elements necessary to find a cure for cancer. So, I refuse to treat this book 100% seriously. It is a sports book. If you find a fault, I will fix it. This is a book about sports and sports legends and stories about sporting events that have been recorded seven million times already someplace else. New Englanders should be pleased. Though I tried for sure to get it all right and I used the work of others to assure so, I bet I made a mistake or two. Tell me about them. Don't

What is my remedy for the *harmed* if I have made a mistake? I did not write this book to harm anybody. If I did not write this book, would the *harmed individuals* from the book be unharmed. So, at the very least, I can *unpublish* those parts of the book. If any reader is harmed, let me know, and I will do whatever must be done for all to be OK.

A Bone to Pick with
The Boston Globe

Ladies and gentlemen: This page of my comments regarding the Boston Globe's business practices was not intended ever to be in this book. But, in life, people, even authors, must fight with the few tools we are given in life. For the people of New England who must deal with the business practices of the Boston Globe on a daily basis, or opt for a new paper, many of you understand why I am doing what I can with my little power of the press against this huge media power from Boston.

I will be as brief as possible. When I was writing this book in April 2018, I was happy when I found a number of stories in the Boston Globe. I was even happier when I found that I could buy a 99 cent a week 4-week deal from the paper. So, I did and it enabled me to see things I had been shut out from. $3.96 was charged to my credit card and I was pleased, and the Globe made the deal so I figured they were pleased too. I live in Pennsylvania, so I did not want a long-term deal.

When I was preparing the initial printing of this book, I found a charge on my credit card for $27.72. from the Boston Globe. I had no time to investigate so I ignored it and figured they got me for something. I have used no services of which I am aware. This week, I got another charge for $27.72. So, I called Customer Service 1-888-694-5623.

They were most cordial and told me I had ordered more than I thought. They promised to cancel the future invoices and after my pleading my case, they reluctantly decided to take off the recent invoice amount. However, they would not remove the initial $27.72. regardless of my urgings.

I asked them to tell me what gave them the authority to steal from my credit card and they said I had signed up for it with the four-week $.99 subscription. I had never seen such a caveat, so I asked them to send me the documentation they said obligated me to pay anything they say I owe. They agreed that I received no benefit for the first invoice, but their policies would not permit a refund. I told them my policies demanded they send me a full refund. Exasperated after several iterations with them holding the upper hand, I took the following action:

I told them I would give them a prominent space in my new book, Great Moments in New England Patriots Football, where they could print their rationale. They were unimpressed. I gave them the opportunity to put their response on the page after my story; but they did not take me up on the offer. When you have a chance, please give them a call and tell them their use of fine print is at the same level that might prompt their investigative team to call on a scam artist for all to know. That is what they acted like in this circumstance

They finally said that there was information about the order on the pages. which constituted my order, and I had agreed to the whole package from them. They were kind enough to send me their fine print. I can say that it was so obvious I missed it and they never sent me a bill or anything to remind me. They simply charged my credit card, hoping I would miss it. I show their fine print below:

BostonGlobe.com digital subscription is a credit card only offer. Your credit card will be automatically charged in advance every four weeks unless a different billing term is specified in the offer. At the end of your introductory period, you will continue to be charged every 4 weeks for $27.72 (99¢/day) unless you cancel your subscription. Offer valid for those who have not had digital access in the last 90 days. Prices are subject to change. Additional terms and conditions may apply.

Response from the Boston Globe:

None received!

Preface:

"Knowing you have a good backup long snapper allows you to sleep good at night" Quote by Bill Belichick, the greatest coach in Patriot Football history. He cannot stand anybody being late, and is known for this famous quote: "Snow is no excuse for being late"

When the 2017 season began, everybody thought the Patriots were going to do well and most thought that Belichick's mastery of the game would have clinched the Pats another Super Bowl. Tom Brady had twenty good games in him from pre-season onward, and few will attempt to deny that Brady is undeniably the best Quarterback who has ever lived—at least in terms of grabbing the most trophies; the most gold medals, and the most kudos from his fellow players.

Tom Brady is a great football player and a great football engineer. He can figure out a solution to a game problem and then more often than not, steer a team out of a game rut, and put them into the victory platform in time for the celebration. This great QB can count on his coach Bill Belichick all the time and Bill Belichick can count on Tom Brady to deliver no matter how difficult the odds. And, oh, by the way, somebody found the Fountain of Youth up there in Foxboro because neither of these guys are aging and Patriots fans just love it. Ponce de Leon would be proud.

Bill Belichick is known for not taking days off, but he is ready to blow out some Eagles' feathers this year as he goes on his regular way to winning all the marbles and then the big Bowl next time around. Belichick had answered the question again and despite the ego bruising loss to the Eagles, he is ready to be on the same sidelines that he has roamed and controlled for the past 18 years.

There had been some reports about a rift between the coach, owner Robert Kraft and QB Tom Brady. All three of the parties have the best deal the cards could deliver and after a few healed wounds, the pundits say the wounds are all healed and the trio are back at making it all better for the Patriots for the 2018 season.

Whoever thought Bill Belichick could look like a crazy kid on a beach?

Just look at the Patriots' full record in the prologue of this book. It shows Bill Belichick as the only long-serving immortal coach in Patriot's history. What owner would give that up? How about the greatest QB in football history looking for a more agreeable trio than the one he is already part of and if you are a sane fan, you gotta say. "What smart, great player would give that relationship up for anything?

So, it looks like the Patriot's will be intact and ready to go in the Fall. Patriot fans are realists and they are most appreciative that in the pre-Kraft, pre-Belichick and the pre-Brady days, nothing compares with today with the "pre" removed and this trio of greats working together for the betterment of New England football. I think that is a Belichick smile on the beach above. I am happy for that for sure.

When Bill Belichick was photographed on the beach with his sweatheart, pictured above, he sure showed no signs of Foxboro or

Gillette anxiety that might force him back to the stadium with an armed escort.

When asked a question about his job security with the Patriots and if he planned on being back next year Belichick said, "Absolutely." Sometimes few words are the best explanation.

Looking back in history as we do in this book, we don't find a ton of great coaches out of the 14 on the Patriot's list. Yes, the Patriots had a lot of losing seasons, but they hit win #500 before any other team that began ignominiously in the AFL.

The Pats have more than an overall big winning record. Why? Well, the excellent coaches over the years, though none comparing to Belichick, had winning percentages that were very good but not every year. The fact is that the poor and so-so coaches could not drag the Pats record downward as the better coaches kept it well above 500 percent. Take a look at the season one-liner summaries at the beginning of the book and you will see what I mean. New Englanders must be proud.

The Boston Patriots were just one of many new AFL teams merged into the NFL when the AFL chose to combine with the NFL. Most NFL teams had been around since long before 1960, when the NFL motley crew entered the realm of real football and they made their mark. It took a lot of years and a tenacious coach named Raymond Berry, well known in the past as a Baltimore Colts receiver for the great Johnny Unitas, to show this AFL set of Patriots that they could win games.

Even before the Boston Patriots existed, Raymond Berry was making pro football history. Check out this picture of one of the most famous passes in NFL history caught by none-other than former Patriots' Coach Raymond Berry. The football thrown by Hall of Fame Baltimore Colts quarterback Johnny Unitas to Hall of Fame split end Raymond Berry for a touchdown in the classic 1958 NFL championship at Yankee Stadium actually sold for $62,140 at a Huggins & Scott Auction. Can you imagine when that night was?

The Patriots had been close to pay-dirt in the past, having had coaches get them into the playoffs. The first Super Bowl appearance of course was in 1986 and the coach that night was Raymond Berry.

After a great season and great playoffs, the Patriots could not keep up the momentum and Berry's Patriots lost their first Super Bowl encounter to the Chicago Bears in SB XX, (10–46).

The infamous great coach Bill Parcells brought the Patriots to their next Super Bowl after the 1996 season in Super Bowl XXXI. Parcells had as much luck as Raymond Berry in 1986. The Patriots showed well but lost the game after a great season and a winning playoff series. Nonetheless, the team still did not win the Super Bowl against the Packers in a 21-35 defeat.

Each of the Super Bowl losses made the team stronger and more prepared to dancing in the big dance. Pete Carroll took over the Patriots for three years and though he was a fine coach, he did not get the Pats into the dance. Then, out of nowhere came the modern beachcomber, Bill Belichick. He changed football forever for New England. He is still there making things OK after five Super Bowl Victories and as many defeats.

Nobody doubts Bill Belichick any more.

After writing about Notre Dame, Penn State, Clemson, Alabama, Florida, Syracuse, and Army, Brian Kelly, your author was moved by the Patriots' great seasons and the work of Tom Brady and Bill Belichick to take a shot at writing a book about one of his favorite pro-teams. Kelly has been rooting for the Patriots in almost every Super Bowl from 1980. Kelly rooted for some Patriots teams that never even made the cut.

And, so, this new book by Brian Kelly, which highlights the Great Moments in New England Patriots Football is one of the items that is expected to be available all 52 weeks and in fact all 365 days each year except in LEAP YEAR where the Patriots add an extra day for your book shopping pleasure.

Amazon, Kindle, Barnes & Noble and other online sites in the US and overseas carry this book and it will add to your year-round football experience especially in the off-season. Once you get this book, it is yours forever unless, of course you give it away to one of the many Patriots fans, who will be in awe of your new possession.

Reading this book is like reliving the last game, the last football season, and / or all the seasons before last season without ever having to get on or off a plane. Seeing a game in Foxboro is an exhilarating adventure. I know of the experience. This book will help you relive the phenomenon over and over. Besides the great read, with this book in your hand at your private venue, there is no limit on the hours for book-tailgating. Moreover, there is no charge, as long as you have stocked up on snack victuals before the read.

The book examines more than just great moments. There are some moments that are not so great in every team's football seasons and the New England Patriots offer no excuses for those times. Your author shows the bad with the good to get the proper perspective for those great moments that we are living now.

Not all New England coaches for example, are named Belichick Berry, Parcells, Carrol, or Holovak, so not all games are in the W column. However, all teams from 1960 to the present, no matter who the coach is, were Patriots tough, nonetheless. That means they all fought hard for wins for the good of the team and the fans.

Opening with its first story at the very beginning of Football as a sport in America, this book goes all the way to Coach Bill Belichick who has stood in time for 18 years changing the record books for New England and pushing the win record over 500.

This book is written for those of us who love Patriots football as played in many of the great American venues over the years. After discussing the origins of football and then the origins of pro-football, the book first tells the story of the first New England Patriots Football Game in 1960. It then advances to the games, the victories and losses, and onward to the great immortal New England coaches of historical fame—Bill Belichick, Ray Berry, Mike Holovak, and Chuck Fairbanks.

Predicting that another future immortal great is already in our midst, the book then takes us up to the last season with Coach Bill Belichick, a present and future immortal.

This book is all about the great moments in New England Patriots Football. It touches every aspect of the historical and mythical Patriots Football Teams. It tells exhilarating stories about the 14 head coaches and the 58 seasons worth of great games. The book stops every now and then, and it takes the reader on a side excursion in time to learn about a particular event or a great player.

The player list always begins with the immortal Gino Cappeletti, Kevin Faulk, Adam Vinatieri, Bruce Armstrong, Tom Brady, Tedy Brischi, Drew Bledsoe, Nick Buoniconti, Tedy Brischi, and John Hannah. These stops will add substantially to your reading enjoyment. These Pro Bowlers have made Patriots Football a bright light experience for the program's many years and many fans.

In my role as Editor in Chief of Lets Go Publish! and a die-hard Patriots' fan, I predict that you will not be able to put this book down

You are going to love this book because it is the perfect read for anybody who loves the New England Patriots and Patriots football, and who wants to know more about one of the most revered professional athletic teams in all of football.

Few sports books are a must-read but my dad, Brian Kelly's Great Moments in New England Patriots Football will quickly appear at the top of Americas most enjoyable must-read books about sports. Enjoy!

Who is Brian Kelly?

Brian Kelly aka Brian W. Kelly, is one of the leading authors in America with this, his 154th published book. Brian continues as an outspoken and eloquent expert on a variety of topics, including the kind of sports that New Englanders love. Moreover, Kelly also has written several hundred articles on other topics of interest to Americans.

Most of my dad's early works involved high technology. Later, Brian wrote a number of patriotic books and most recently, he has been writing human interest books such as The Wine Diet and Thank you, IBM. His books are always well received. If I could get the pen out of Dad's hand for just awhile, I might be able to write a few books of my own, but my editing chores at Lets Go Publish! always come first.

Brian Kelly's books are highlighted at www.letsgopublish.com. They are for sale at Amazon, Kindle, and Barnes & Noble. The link, Amazon.com/author/brianwkelly, is the best but all Kelly books are available at most fine booksellers.

The best!

Sincerely,

Brian P. Kelly, Editor in Chief
I am Brian Kelly's eldest son

About the Author

Brian Kelly retired as an Assistant Professor in the Business Information Technology (BIT) Program at Marywood University, where he also served as the IBM i and Midrange Systems Technical Advisor to the IT Faculty. Kelly designed, developed, and taught many college and professional courses. He continues as a contributing technical editor to a number of technical industry magazines, including "The Four Hundred" and "Four Hundred Guru," published by IT Jungle.

Kelly is a former IBM Senior Systems Engineer. His specialty was problem solving for customers as well as implementing advanced operating systems and software on his client's machines. Brian is the author of 153 other books, including 25 Sports Books, and hundreds of magazine articles. He has been a frequent speaker at technical conferences throughout the United States.

Brian was a candidate for the US Congress from Pennsylvania in 2010 and he ran for Mayor in his home town in 2015. Kelly loves the Patriots and he became a big fan in the 1960's watching AFL games with his dad on Sundays on the 21" Admiral B/W TV.

This is Brian's ninth "Great Moments" book and his second about a professional NFL team. Writing about the New England Patriots has been a special treat.

Chapter 1 Introduction to the Book

The Patriots celebrate 50 years of football

Everybody loves the Patriots!

In 2009, New England celebrated its 50th year of Patriots' football. Fifty is a special number and in November 2009, the team celebrated the formation of the Boston Patriots, soon to be the New England Patriots. The above logo was unveiled to add a special look to the celebration.

This book celebrates New England Patriots Football; its founding; its struggles; its greatness; and football's long-lasting impact on American life. People like me, who love the team from way back when they played tough AFL football, will love this book, as we reach back to the founding and up to the 50th anniversary and now as we approach the 60th anniversary of one of the best organizations that has ever played professional football.

In defining the format of the book, we chose to use a timetable that is based on a historical chronology. Within this framework, we discuss the great moments in New England Patriots Football History, and there are many great moments. No book can claim to be able to capture them all, as it would be a never-ending story, but we sure try. The great moments naturally include a lot of great people, including players and the 14 great coaches that over time would make or break the New England Patriots.

Even before we get into Patriots football, we discuss the beginning of football, the first football game in 1869, the first players paid to play, and then on to the beginning of the NFL.

To know the full story of the New England Patriots, you have to go through Boston.

Boston was always ready to welcome NFL teams. The Patriots were not the first but with their great record, New Englanders are hoping, they are the last pro football team ever needed. The first pro football team welcomed by Boston was the Boston Bulldogs. This adventure lasted only during the 1929 season, but it got the Boston juices flowing.

The next NFL pro team to play was the Boston Braves/Redskins, from 1932 to 1936. In 1933 after the inaugural season, there was a name change to the Boston Redskins. Founder George Preston Marshall named the team the Boston Braves after the city's Major League Baseball team. However, after a financially devastating and poorly attended season in 1932, Marshall abandoned the Braves name in favor of the Redskins.

The Braves / Redskins had played first at Braves Field and then they moved to Fenway Park. Unfortunately for the area, the team did not draw well, even in its final season when they reached the NFL Championship Game. They moved to Washington as the Redskins right after the 1936 season.

The Boston Yanks played from 1944 to 1948 before moving to New York to become the New York Yanks football team. The team, which as noted began as the Boston Yanks, at the time was owned by Kate Smith's manager, Ted Collins. None of the Boston NFL teams that we discussed were the precursor team to the Patriots. In other words, they are not in the ancestry of the Boston Patriots from the AFL. There is no DNA match. The old Boston Yanks folded in 1952.

The AFL formed in 1959 and the Boston Patriots played their first game in the Fall 1960. As you can see, the desire for there to be a Boston or New England presence in professional football goes back a long way. As you can see from the Boston Yanks picture below, players had little choice in those days but to go both ways—O & D.

The Boston Yanks: just a few pro players because they had to be paid

When the AFL was being formed, unlike some other pro-football ventures of the deep past, it looked from the start that it was going to be able to sustain itself and perhaps even surpass the excitement of the NFL. Investors were lining up to become pro-football owners.

It seemed like investors had forgotten the other AFL's that had come before this AFL, and their attempts to out-NFL, the NFL. It was tough slugging. The new upstart AFL clearly operated in direct competition with the more established NFL throughout its ten-year existence.

It was much more successful than earlier rivals to the NFL with the same name, the American Football League (1926), American Football League (1936), American Football League (1940), and the later All-America Football Conference((1944-1950), played in 1946-1949). America had fallen in love with football, and there was a great business out there for a league that could make it.

The Patriots were formed when Boston businessman, William "Billy" Sullivan, an executive of Sullivan Brother Printers, owned by Joseph Sullivan, was awarded the eighth and final franchise of the developing American Football League(AFL) on November 16,

1959. In the next few weeks, locals submitted thousands of ideas for the Boston football team's official name. On February 20, 1960, Sullivan picked "Boston Patriots" from the lot.

First Boston Patriots team picture—more players than the Boston Yanks

"Patriots," of course referred to those colonists of the Thirteen Colonies who rebelled against British control during the American Revolution, and who, in in July 1776 declared the United States of America an independent nation. "Patriots" as the team nickname had been suggested by 74 fans, among them Larry Kepnes, a regular guy whose signature stood out. Immediately thereafter, artist Phil Bissell developed the "Pat Patriot" logo.

There is not much written about Larry other than his recent obituary. I learned that his full name was Lawrence Kepnes, and he was from Swampscott, Massachusetts. He passed away on Friday November 18, 2016, still a devoted Red Sox and Patriots fan. I can tell he was my kind of guy.

Every football fan alive in 1960, including Larry Kepnes loved the AFL as the folks at home got to see more great football—just like that played in the already mature NFL. The only thing they did not see was the great AFL teams playing the great NFL teams. The leagues were 100% separate and they did not share their proceeds or their secrets or their drafted players until they had to. It would take a little time before the NFL begrudgingly realized that the AFL brand of football was here to stay. Rather than trying to beat them, eventually they joined them.

The old NFL Boston Yanks when they played in Boston, claimed Fenway Park as their home spot and got away with it. However, the Patriots' time in the AFL saw them as homeless. They had no regular home stadium. They played wherever they could find a field--Nickerson Field, Harvard Stadium, even Fenway Park sometimes, as well as Boston College's Alumni Stadium. These stadia were all in or near Boston.

The Patriots were quite happy to have these as home fields during their time in the American Football League.

With Coach Lou Saban, the first Boston Coach, and Coach Mike Holovak, the second Boston coach, the Patriots put forth a number of seasons in which the percentage wins were or at least seemed closer to 1000 than to 500. Those were the great start-up days. Many of the player names from the Boston Patriots teams in the 1960's have slipped into oblivion but there are still some of us, who understand oblivion, and who still recall some early Patriots stars.

The great ones include defensive tackles Jim Lee "Earthquake" Hunt and Houston Antwine; quarterback Vito "Babe" Parilli; and flanker-placekicker Gino "The Duke" Cappelletti (no relationship with John from Penn State). These guys were great to watch. Hunt, Parilli and Cappelletti played every year of the existence of the AFL, with Hunt and Cappelletti spending all ten years with the Patriots.

To fans, the AFL was like a big giant never-ending intramural pickup game that would not end. Nobody wanted it to end. Having a named group of guys playing the teams in the AFL in this great pickup game was great football. Everybody loved the AFL. Everybody loved Boston's Patriots.

With all deference to the NFL, the AFL proved that little guys can make it and that's why the league captured the hearts of American football lovers. The fans still loved their Giants, their Eagles, their Steelers, etc. so it was a big gift to fans to have so many other great teams who never played their teams, who had new-name stars gracing the sidelines each week. Football fans from 1960 to 1969 could actually get away with having two favorite pro teams.

Cappelletti was the all-time leading scorer in the AFL. Later the Patriots were joined by such stars as defensive end Larry Eisenhauer, fullback Jim Nance, and middle linebacker and future Hall of Famer Nick Buoniconti. Cappelletti and Nance were AFL Most Valuable Players, Cappelletti in 1964 and Nance in 1966. Buoniconti and Antwine were later named to the American Football League All-Time Team. Who could ask for more?

Boston Patriots in action

Three years into the AFL, we saw the Boston Patriots defeating the Buffalo Bills in an AFL Eastern Division playoff game in 1963, and we saw the Patriots playing in the 1963 AFL championship game. They lost to the San Diego Chargers 51–10 but as always, they took the bad with the good. Just in their third year of existence, Boston was somebody. It was good for morale and it was good for Boston Beer sales, which actually were not too bad before the Patriots.

The Patriots as potential champs would not appear again in an AFL or NFL post-season game for another 13 years, but Boston beer sales were still booming in the Fall as well as all over New England. Additionally, the games were great. Before the AFL delivered its swan-song, the Patriots would often challenge the then dominant AFL Bills for the Eastern Division title. Those of us who remember back then loved those football days.

When the NFL and AFL merged in 1970, I can remember being very disappointed as I had come to like the scrappy, less formal AFL. The Patriots were placed in the AFC East division, where they still play today. Actually, we know that they do more than play. They dominate the AFC East.

It was not long for the Patriots to find a home. They moved to a new stadium in Foxborough, Massachusetts, a suburb of Boston, known as Foxboro Stadium, which would serve as their home for 30 years; the team also changed their name to the New England Patriots to reflect the location change, as well as its following throughout the region. It is the only NFL team (though both New York City teams have substantial followings in parts of Connecticut as well) in New England.

Foxboro Stadium

During the 1970s, the Patriots had some success, eventually earning a berth to the playoffs in 1976. It was not a free ride but a wild card-berth. Then, in 1978, with Chuck Fairbanks as Head Coach, they made it as AFC East champions. They would lose both playoff games.

In 1985, the Patriots, unaccustomed at the time to glory, returned to the playoffs, and made it all the way to Super Bowl XX, which they lost against the Chicago Bears 46–10. Nonetheless, it was a banner year and new Englanders know how to celebrate and so beer sales finally went up again in the city and the suburbs.

Following their Super Bowl loss, the Patriots barreled back into the playoffs in 1986, but were beaten in the first round. The team kept doing its best with non-Bill-Belichicks as coaches, and they would not make the playoffs again for eight more years.

Most fans do not care about ownership changes unless the new owner messes things up. The Pats changed ownership several times in that period, being purchased from the Sullivan family first by Victor Kiam in 1988, who sold the team to James Orthwein in 1992. Orthwein's intention was to move the team to his native St. Louis, Missouri. He chose not to try to do that after visiting some Boston Pubs. OK, his reasons remain a secret.

Nonetheless, he chose to sell the franchise, i.e. the business of the Patriots team two years later to current owner, local businessman Robert Kraft in 1994. Most New Englanders who like football like Kraft because he likes to win.

Orthwein had a short period of ownership and his desire to uproot the team was well-known. Yet he did oversee some major changes to the team. Former New York Giants coach Bill Parcells, who had taken the Giants from misery to stardom was hired in 1993. Nobody could deny Bill Parcells had a unique way of getting the most from any football team he ever coached.

Parcells would bring the Patriots to two playoff appearances, including Super Bowl XXXI, which they lost to the Green Bay Packers by a score of 35–21. Pete Carroll, Parcells' successor, another top NFL coach today with the Seahawks, would also take the team to the playoffs twice. Whodathunk? Would a happy-go-lucky, work-if-you-must kinda guy, like Bill Belichick would out-Parcell and out-Carrol these two great NFL coaches. Yet, he did. Check the record.

Bill Belichick is the Patriots current head coach. He was out hunting one day and was hired in 2000. OK, he may have been doing something else, but he was hired, and it was a great day for the Patriots and for Patriot's fans.

The New England Patriots like Foxborough Mass. However, Foxboro stadium became an old story and the Pats were hoping for a newer, more modern facility. So, the powers that be created a new home field, Gillette Stadium for the Patriots and they opened it in 2002. Coach Belichick was a godsend two-years earlier to those fans in New England who not only liked football but liked to win.

Belichick's teams won five Super Bowls, including three in four years (2001-2004). As a football purist, I happen to love perfect NFL season records almost as much as Super Bowl Wins. Not kidding. For example, in 1972, I loved the perfect season of the Miami Dolphins. Nobody yet, even our famous and fabulous Patriots have outclassed this Dolphins team.

Bill Belichick Loves Winning Super Bowls

The 1972Dolphins still are the only NFL team to win the Super Bowl with a perfect season. Though the Patriots finished the 2007 regular season with a perfect 16–0 record, becoming only the fourth team in league history to go undefeated, and the only one since the league expanded its regular season schedule to 16 games; they did not eclipse the Dolphins challenge: "Be perfect!"

And, so, even after two playoff victories, the 2007 Patriots ended that season with an 18-1 record. There was this unfortunate encounter and a subsequent loss to the New York Giants in Super Bowl XLII that stole away the aura of perfection from the New England Patriots.

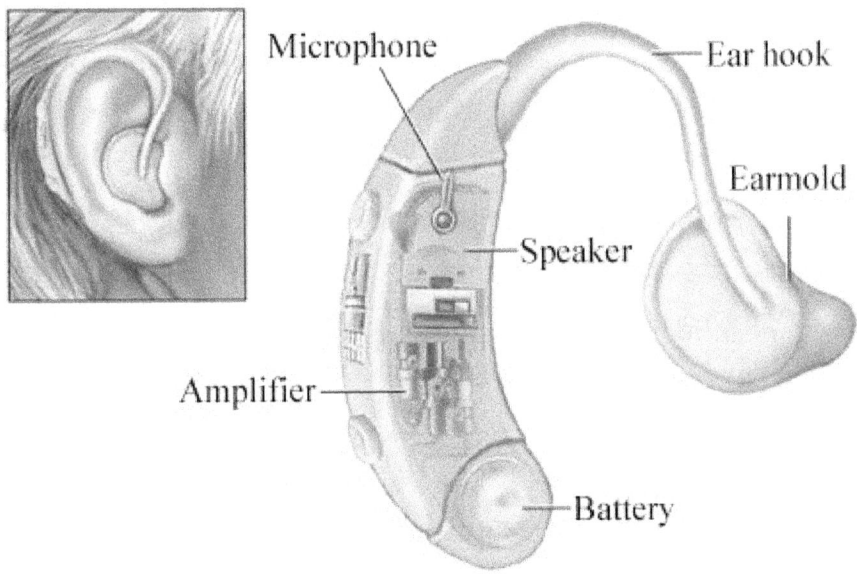

Look above and think of me firing in the commands:

Nobody can argue that the Patriots have made the playoffs in 14 of the 17 seasons that Bill Belichick has been coach, missing them only in 2000 (his first season), 2002, and 2008. They later faced the Seattle Seahawks in Super Bowl XLIX on February 1, 2015, and won by a score of 28-24, and they have won four more times.

I do not count but if I did count, I would miniaturize myself and launch myself from inside a small vessel in Bill Belichick's ear. I would use a miniature loudspeaker that would keep harping to coach Belichick that a perfect season would be a nice way to finish off a miraculous career…Brady too!

Looking at the greats in Patriot's history we find many names we know such as Doug Flutie, Steve Grogan, Babe Parilli, Jim Nance, Gino Cappelletti, Irving Fryar, Stanley Morgan, Wes Welker, Ben Coates, Rob Gronkowski, John Hannah, Mike Haynes, Ty Law, Tedy Bruschi, Nick Buoniconti, Richard Seymour, Houston Antwine, Jim Lee Hunt, Vince Wilfork, Stephen Gostkowski, Adam Vinatieri, and other New England greats from over the years. They all have or have had great reverence for the team for which they played the game of football. That reverence is captured in the subsequent pages of this book.

Looking at the quick snapshot of coaches and seasons at the beginning of the book, it is clear that New England has been able to survive a number of coaches who could not survive themselves, while the Patriots football program has grown both in acceptance, popularity, and sheer dominance.

Look across the Internet with your web browser and you will be reminded that the New England Patriots are runner-up world champions, having barely lost to the Philadelphia Eagles in February 2018 to win the coveted Super Bowl Trophy. The Patriots have their share of Super Bowl rings for sure. If we listed all of the Patriots' accolades individually, we would have to close this book now with no further additions for a too-many-pages violation.

The 2018 Eagles contest marked the 10th Super Bowl appearance for the New England franchise, eighth of which have come since 2001. This year, 2001, was the year in which Tom Brady led the Pats to a 20-17 win over the Rams. It was in Bill Belichick's second year as head coach.

I think as an intro I have done a fine job. I hope you think so also.

In the full book, I do my best to portray an accurate depiction of New England Patriots football history, displayed in a properly summarized format so that none of us are reading this book forever. There are almost 500 pages to this book. However, the many pages are in this book so there is more than enough to accompany you on those cold winter nights after the close of the football season.

There are a ton of great stories for sure. More importantly, none of us should need to search further than this book for the truth about many of the depictions in this book.
.

Chapter 2 History of Patriots Football Stadiums

Boston Patriots had no stadium

In 1970, after a decade of playing at four different sites, including Boston University Field, Harvard Stadium, Fenway Park and Boston College Alumni Stadium, the Patriots selected Foxborough as the new home of the team. In March 1971, the team was renamed the New England Patriots. Let's take a look at these four sites briefly as Patriot fans of the 1960's attended home games at these fields even though the Patriots did not have a home football stadium per se. Having four stadiums to pick from gave the Patriots a better opportunity to have an available stadium for a particular home game.

Harvard Stadium (1970)

The best description of Harvard Stadium is that it looks like a football stadium from early times ought to look. In many ways it has attributes of a coliseum. It is a magnificent structure built in the traditional U-shape of many college football stadiums. It is located in the Allston neighborhood of Boston, Massachusetts.

The stadium has a lot of history, having been built in 1903 when college football was the wave of the country. There were few large stadiums at this time and so the Harvard Stadium was a pioneering execution of reinforced concrete to be used in the construction of large structures.

Harvard Stadium had a major influence on the design of later stadiums. It was designated a National Historic Landmark in 1987. The stadium is the nation's oldest permanent concrete structure dedicated to intercollegiate athletics.

Harvard Stadium – home of Boston Patriots of the NFL in 1970

Today, the stadium is owned and operated by Harvard University and is home to the Harvard Crimson football program. The seating capacity of the stadium is now, though at one time it seated up to 57,166 in the past, as permanent steel stands (completing a straight-sided oval)[7] were installed in the northeast end zone of the stadium in 1929. They were torn down after the 1951 season, due to deterioration and reduced attendance. They can always rebuild if Harvard's squad again reaches national college football prominence. After the demolition, smaller temporary steel bleachers were placed across the open end of the stadium until the building of the Murr Center, which is topped by the fancy new scoreboard, was built in 1998.

Ironically, Harvard Stadium altered the game of football permanently—at least it altered what had been planned for football. And so, it is said that this is a stadium that changed the game. Look at the close proximity of the stands to the field at the Stadium. Think of how difficult with such a strong stadium in place to consider widening the football field. Consequently, Harvard Stadium led to one of the most successful innovations in football history. In 1906, three years after the stadium was built, debate raged about the sport's roughness and several colleges had dropped football in favor of rugby. When the football rules committee met to discuss changes, Walter Camp proposed widening the field by 40 feet. However, that idea would require considerable alterations to the Stadium. Ultimately, the committee adopted the forward pass instead. Where would football be today without the forward pass?

Harvard Stadium hosted just one Boston Patriots season in 1970. It was the Patriots' first season in the NFL after the AFL–NFL merger and their last season before briefly becoming the Bay State Patriots, and then quickly becoming the New England Patriots before the start of the 1971 season. The team moved to Schaefer Stadium in Foxborough, Massachusetts the following season. As we have seen, the Patriots had previously played at Boston College (1969), Fenway Park (1963–68), and Boston University Field (1960–62).

Boston University Stadium Nickerson Field (1960)

The Boston Patriots began their football legacy in 1960 playing home games at Nickerson Field, on the campus of Boston University. Nickerson is an outdoor athletic stadium in the Northeastern United States, in Boston, Massachusetts . The stadium is owned by the university. It was once the home of the Boston University Terriers football team and today is the home field for some other Boston University Terriers athletics programs, including soccer and lacrosse. Football for Boston University was discontinued following the 1997 season.

The Patriots continued to play their home games at Nickerson until 1963.

The stadium has some history as it is located on the site of Braves Field, the former home ballpark of the Boston Braves, a major league baseball team in the National League. The Boston Braves baseball franchise relocated to Milwaukee in March 1953, and relocated again in 1966, to become the Atlanta Braves. Parts of

Braves Field, such as the entry gate and right field pavilion, remain as portions of the current stadium. The old Braves Field ticket office at Harry Agganis Way also remains, now and is used by the Boston University Police Department. The stadium has been the home of BU athletic teams longer (50-plus years) than it was the home of the Braves (parts of 38 seasons).

The field is named for William Emery Nickerson (1853–1930), who was a partner of King C. Gillette during the early years of the Gillette Safety Razor Company.

BU purchased the stadium on July 30, 1953, and in April 1954 renamed it Boston University Field. Lots has happened over the years to the stadium. In 1955, the Braves Field grandstand, left field pavilion, and "Jury Box" (right field bleachers) were demolished. The existing right field pavilion was squared off on the west side and filled in on the east side where a section had been removed to accommodate the Braves Field right field foul pole and bullpens. Three buildings overlooking the field coincidentally suggest the outline of the original main grandstand section.

After being renamed Boston University Field in 1955, the University brought the field back to its naming roots. In February 1956, BU was awarded $391,000 for the Weston field, which had been taken by eminent domain or construction of Massachusetts Route 128. The University used the proceeds, in part, to renovate the former baseball park, and on September 28, 1963, renamed it Nickerson Field, inheriting the name of the prior field in Weston.

In 1968, the University brought a facelift to the stadium and some other innovative changes. The four Braves Field light towers were dismantled. Additionally, that year, BU became the second college in the United States to install Astro-Turf. The following year, not only did the BU football team practice on that field, so did the Boston College Eagles football team and our then Boston Patriots. Both used the field to prepare for away games they would play on AstroTurf fields.

Boston College Alumni Stadium (1969)

Alumni Stadium was the site of Boston Patriot home games during the 1969 season. It was the Boston Patriots 10th season and their final one in the AFL.

Alumni football stadium is located on the lower campus of Boston College in Chestnut Hill, Massachusetts, approximately six miles west of downtown Boston. I've been there; and it is not a pleasant drive in the rain from downtown Boston. The stadium lies within the city limits of Boston, although its postal address is Chestnut Hill. Today it is the home of the Boston College Eagles. Its present seating capacity is 44,500.

Its south façade faces Beacon Street. Keep going towards Boston and you hit Beacon Hill and you can stop for a few quaffs at Cheers. This is Boston College's first stadium and it opened its doors in 1915 and it was located just south of Gasson Quadrangle, on the site of the present Stokes Hall, a newly-built academic buildings for the humanities that opened in 2013.

Before the building of Stokes, the area was known as The Dustbowl, a nickname that originated as a description of Alumni Field in the years when it was intensely used as a practice field, a baseball diamond, and a running track.

It was formally dedicated "as a memorial to the boys that were" on October 30, 1915. Alumni Field and its distinctive "maroon goalposts on a field of green" were hailed in that evening's edition of the Boston Saturday Evening Transcript as "one of the sights in Boston." The original grandstands, which could accommodate 2,200 spectators in 1915, were enlarged over the subsequent years to 25,000. Nonetheless Alumni Field often proved too small for BC football games which were frequently held at Fenway Park, and later Braves Field, beginning in the 1930s.

Alumni Field, precursor to Alumni Stadium, ca. 1920

As time went by, BC knew they needed a new stadium. So, after a period of construction, on September 21, 1957, Alumni Stadium opened on Boston College's lower campus. The complex included a new stadium with a football field encircled by a regulation track. In 1957, it had a max seating capacity of 26,000.

The dedication game for the stadium was a match-up with the Midshipmen of the U.S. Naval Academy, was orchestrated with the help of BC benefactor and then-Massachusetts Senator John F.

Kennedy. Kennedy, who had received his honorary degree at Commencement Exercises in Alumni Field the previous year, would return to Alumni Stadium on a number of occasions over the course of his political career, including a 1963 Convocation Address, one of his last public appearances.

Since then, Alumni Stadium has hosted numerous intellectual and cultural luminaries, religious leaders and heads of state as the venue for Boston College's annual Commencement Exercises since its opening in 1957. In addition to being the permanent home of the Boston College football team, as noted, Alumni Stadium was the home field for the Boston Patriots of the American Football League during the 1969 season.

As the home of the Boston College Eagles, Alumni Stadium has been the site of numerous notable moments in Boston College football history. For example, on September 17, 2005, Alumni Stadium hosted BC's inaugural game as a member of the Atlantic Coast Conference.

Long after the Patriots played before 26,000 fans, the stadium underwent a major renovation before the 1994 season. The renovation eliminated the track and increased the seating capacity to 44,500. Since 1998, a 65-foot (20 m)-high bubble of inflatable vinyl has covered the stadium from December to March, cleverly permitting the field to be used as a winter practice facility.

Alumni Stadium's field surface itself was converted to FieldTurf before the 2004 season. In the summer before the 2005 football season, the $27 million Yawkey Athletics Center opened at Alumni Stadium's north end zone, and the logo of the Atlantic Coast Conference was added to the FieldTurf. For the 2012 season, Alumni Stadium was outfitted with new FieldTurf. As we know, no stadium is ever completed.

Boston's Fenway Park (1963-1968)

The Fenway Ball Park was used for many events in its 100+ year old period serving the greater Boston area. For the purposes of this book, we know that Fenway was the home of the Boston Patriots for six of its ten seasons of existence from 1963 to 1968.

Fenway "Baseball" Park Lined Up for Football

Fenway Park's inaugural year was simply exceptional. After extensive construction in the early months of 1912, Fenway Park hosted its first baseball game on April 9, an exhibition between the Red Sox and Harvard College. Eleven days later, the Red Sox played their first official game at Fenway Park against the New York Highlanders. The club went on to win 105 regular season games, the American League Pennant and a thrilling World Series. During the season, while the Red Sox were on the road, a few amateur baseball games were held at the park and the construction of left-field and right-field bleachers was completed in time for the World Series. In late 1912, Fenway Park hosted the National High School Football Championship Game, concluding an eventful first year in the park's history.

The Red Sox opened the 1912 season with new ownership and a new ballpark. General Charles H. Taylor and his son John I. Taylor had sold controlling interest in the team to James McAleer in September 1911, but the Taylor family stayed on as overseers of construction on the club's new ballpark. After a feverish winter of work, Fenway Park, the new home of the Boston Red Sox, was ready for an April 9 exhibition against Harvard College, a 2-0 contest the Sox won amidst snow flurries. Opening Day of the regular season was scheduled for April 18, 1912 and not only did that day get rained out, but both Patriots Day games on the following day did as well - and the newspaper headlines focused mainly on the sinking of the steamship Titanic, which had sunk on April 15.

When the Sox finally took the field for the first official game on April 20, 1912, some 27,000 fans saw the Red Sox prevail in a 7-6, extra-innings victory over the New York Highlanders (renamed the Yankees in 1913). Boston Mayor John "Honey Fitz" Fitzgerald, a prominent member of the Royal Rooters fan club and grandfather of future President John F. Kennedy, threw out the ceremonial first pitch.

1912, a contest between the Red Sox and New York Highlanders that drew a crowd of 27,000 fans. On May 17, the formal dedication of Fenway Park took place.

Babe Parilli Boston Patriots famed QB tossing a pass at Fenway

Foxboro Stadium

Foxboro stadium filled the void for a great team without a home. After eleven years with no home stadium, Foxboro stadium was built beginning September 23, 1970 while the Boston Patriots were finishing their last season of play using Harvard Stadium as home. It was completed just about a year later and opened up for the 1971 season on August 15, 1971.

It was the home for the New England Patriots for more than 30 years during which the stadium had a unique reputation in the league. Foxboro Stadium, nicknamed from being located in Foxborough Massachusetts, was one of the NFL's worst stadiums for many years which we will explain. As we described earlier in this chapter, during the Patriots first 11 years of existence they played at a number of different stadiums—BU's Nickerson Field (1960-1962)). Fenway Park (1963-1968), BC's Alumni Stadium (1969) and Harvard Stadium (1970).

There were mandates set during the AFL–NFL merger negotiations in 1970 that required that all teams play home games n stadiums with at least 50,000 seats. None of the four stadiums the Patriots had used up to that point were big enough. Moreover, because Boston is one of the oldest and densely packed cities in North America, there was little room in Boston proper for a new stadium—or even a dog coop for that matter.

Nasty rumors began to spread about the team relocating to Tampa, Florida. New England fans today rejoice knowing these rumors ultimately never came to fruition. Tampa, of course, eventually got their Buccaneers in 1976.

In 1971 the Patriots moved into a hastily and inexpensively constructed stadium in suburban Foxborough (also known as Foxboro), on land granted by the Bay State Raceway. The team was renamed the New England Patriots in March 1971, to reflect its new location roughly halfway between Providence and Boston as well as a desire to better position itself as New England's regional NFL team (this would influence the name of the New England Whalers hockey team when they began play in 1972, like the Patriots, labeling themselves a New England team).

About Foxboro: It helps a non-Bostonian to know that "Foxborough" is the official spelling of the town name, although the alternative spelling "Foxboro" is also frequently used. This alternative spelling is used by the United States Postal Service as the correct form by which to address mail to recipients in the town although both can be processed by their system. The sign on the post office reads "Foxboro.

The original choice for a name, *Bay State Patriots*, was rejected by the NFL. The stadium, that would be formally known as Schaefer Stadium, was built at a cost of about $7.1 million in only 325 days. It was one of the first stadiums in the country to be named after a corporate sponsor, as the Schaefer Brewing Company paid $150,000 for naming rights. Additionally, the town of Foxborough was one of the first in the country to assess a surtax on every ticket sold to help pay for the new stadium.

The Patriots naturally wanted a permanent place at which the team could play and "reside." Foxborough, MA was chosen as the site for this first stadium for the Patriots. As noted, having begun the building on September 23, 1970, this one-of-a-kind "rush job" was "ready" in just under a year so it could host the first 1971 NFL season home game.

There was no public funding used to construct the $7.1 million stadium. The Stadium picked up a number of names over the years. Originally named Schaefer Stadium after the Schaefer Brewing Company in 1971, from 1983 until 1989, the stadium was rechristened Sullivan Stadium, after the family that owned the Patriots. Finally, it was renamed Foxboro Stadium in 1989 after the pseudonym for the town in which it was located.

Everything that is new looks new the first time it is used. The New England Patriots were pleased to play their first game at their sparking new stadium against the New York Giants on August 15, 1971. Over 60,000 fans filled the stadium. Foxboro Stadium consisted of one-tier grandstands that were located on both sides of the playing field. Seating areas also extended beyond the end zones. The main scoreboard was located above the seats in the south end zone. Foxboro Stadium was composed of mainly bleachers; but did have some regular seating areas.

THE SNOW BOWL
JANUARY 19, 2002

When Robert Kraft bought the team in 1993, after twenty-two years of aging, he renovated Foxboro Stadium with $10 million in improvements after 1993. In addition to being the home of the New England Patriots, Foxboro Stadium was also the home of the New England Revolution (MLS). Foxboro Stadium also hosted the 1994 World Cup Soccer Championship. The last game at Foxboro Stadium before it was replaced with the modern Gillette Stadium was a snow-covered game vs. the Oakland Raiders on January 19, 2002. The stadium was demolished in the spring of 2002. The Patriots moved into Gillette Stadium the following year.

Gillette Stadium

The Town of Foxborough approved plans for the construction of the new home for the New England Patriots, on December 6, 1999.

The new home for the Patriots would be known as Gillette Stadium. Work began on the stadium three days into the Spring on March 24, 2000. It was to be and in fact is a magnificent structure that, when compared with Schaefer Stadium, would take substantially longer than one year to build. The new stadium cost $350 million to build-- just about $343 million more than Schaefer Stadium.

The first official event at the new facility was a New England Revolution soccer game on May 11, 2002. The Rolling Stones came to town on September 5, 2002 and played at Gillette Stadium on the band's Licks Tour. Grand opening ceremonies were held four days later on September 9 when the Patriots unveiled their Super Bowl XXXVI championship banner before a Monday Night Football game against the Pittsburgh Steelers.

Having opened in 2002, as the replacement for the beat-up Foxboro Stadium, the seating capacity is 65,000 plus 5,876 club seats and 89 luxury suites. The stadium is owned and operated by Kraft Sports Group, a subsidiary of The Kraft Group, the company through which businessman Robert Kraft owns the Patriots and Revolution.

The new Stadium is located in Foxborough (Foxboro), Massachusetts, 28 miles (45 km) southwest of downtown Boston and 20 miles (32 km) northeast of downtown Providence, Rhode Island. It serves as the home stadium and administrative offices for both the NFL's New England Patriots football franchise and MLS's New England Revolution soccer team. In 2012, it also became the home stadium for the football program of the University of Massachusetts(UMass), while their on-campus Warren McGuirk Alumni Stadium was undergoing renovations. Gillette will continue to host higher attended home games for U-Mass.

The new Gillette Stadium was originally known as CMGI Field before the naming rights were bought by Gillette after the "dot-com" bust. Although Gillette has since been acquired by Procter & Gamble, the stadium retains the Gillette name both because P&G has continued to use the Gillette brand name and because the Gillette company was founded in the Boston area.

Gillette and the Patriots jointly announced in September 2010 that their partnership, which includes naming rights to the stadium, will extend through the 2031 season. That's a nice partnership.

You can get there from here. Gillette Stadium can be reached by rail via the Providence/Stoughton and Franklin lines at the Foxboro MBTA station, but only during Patriots games and some concerts. The Patriots are in the playoffs just about every year and they have been the reigning Super Bowl Champions for five recent years. Their popularity has resulted in the stadium being sold out for every football home game since moving to the stadium—preseason, regular season, and playoffs. This streak dates back to the 1994 season, while the team was still at Foxboro Stadium. By the end of the season 2017, this streak was 252 straight games.

Chapter 3 Patriots Launch First Football Team

#1 Coach Lou Saban

Year	Coach	League	Division	Place,	Record
1960	Lou Saban	AFL	Eastern	4th	5 9 0
1961	Lou Saban (2-3)	AFL	Eastern	2nd	9 4 1

1960-1961 Lou Saban final record (14-14-1)

Boston Patriots Early Team

The New England Patriots launched their first football team in 1960 under a different name than we know today. They were the Boston Patriots and they would keep that name until the 1971 season when they would get their own stadium and they would move 25 miles southwest to Foxboro to become the New England Patriots

Most fans understand the Patriots most recent history which includes ten great shots at the big prize --- the Super Bowl. The Patriots have been very successful in all games with the 1-2 combo of Bill Belichick and Tom Brady, putting whatever was necessary together to win five of those ten Super Bowl Outings. And, there is great news for the future beginning in the fall. After his well-deserved vacation with his significant other, Bill Belichick plans to be back in 2018 to take New England to another Super Bowl and another set of those huge rings—making it six in all.

New England's debut in the biggest championship game came against the Chicago Bears in Super Bowl XX. The Patriots looked great all season, but Raymond Berry's Patriots were overwhelmed by Mike Ditka's Chicago Bears when game action began. From the opening kickoff at the Louisiana Superdome, led by quarterback Jim McMahon the Bears had their way that day with a 49-10 big victory.

The Patriots returned to the Super Bowl with Bill Parcells after eleven years for Super Bowl XXXI to face off against Green Bay on January 26, 1997, again at the Louisiana Superdome. It wound up being another big disappointment, but the team looked a lot better than in 1985.

In game action, Desmond Howard returned a kickoff 99 yards for a touchdown and Brett Favre passed for two touchdowns and ran for a score as the Packers won their first Super Bowl in twenty-nine years at the expense of the Patriots. Howard, en-route to garnering the MVP trophy, equaled a Super Bowl record with 244 total return yards.

The Patriots still had not won the big one with this heartbreaking 21 to 35 loss against Green Bay. Finally, after a short wait to Super Bowl XXXVI, the Patriots, with Tom Brady at the close controls and Bill Belichick coaching as he does so well from the sidelines, the New England Patriots broke into Super Bowl Pay dirt and took the gold with their 14th and best head coach ever.

The Patriots found the third time to be the charm. They had lost in their first two appearances, but they won big-time on February 2, 2002 against the stubborn St. Louis Rams, 20-17.

For the rest of the world and all the smart pundits checking on who the Patriots really were with their new second-year coach, this game left no more doubts. The Patriots would get no more disrespect—ever. The New England Patriots had become Champions of the whole World. It was a great game, and it made all the other Super Bowl Victories in the ongoing Belichick/Brady era easier to achieve.

Chapter 3 The Patriots Launch First Football Team

In one of the most exciting Super Bowl finishes ever, in this 2002 encounter, the great Adam Vinatieri booted home a 48-yard field goal with no time left on the clock to give his team of no-name warriors a 20-17 Super Bowl win. This put the final touches on the most amazing season in New England sports history at that point in the Patriots' short life.

The New England Patriots would engage the best of the best in the NFL seven more times. With the mini-team of Tom Brady and Bill Belichick, they would win four more Super Bowls. And, according to Belichick and Brady, it ain't over yet!

Before the New England Patriots were the name of the team, there was already a team in New England playing football in the AFL. The AFL was formed in November 1959 with first games to be played in the fall 1960.

Coach Lou Saban is responsible for molding the players who showed up for the first camp into the Boston Patriots. In 1960 and 1961, Saban did his best to take the raw material and prove to everybody else but the team that the Patriots could win some games. Saban got five wins out of fourteen games in his first season with a bunch of AFL rookies. The NFL was not lending players to the AFL at that time.

In his second season, and the second season for the Boston Patriots, Lou Saban and Mike Holovak together stole nine games from his fellow AFL coaches and gave them back five losses and one tie in return. There was no guarantee at the time that any AFL franchise (they were all new) would be around for a second year. Lou Saban and Mike Holovak set the team up for great things to come with a spectacular two season record of 13-14-1. Actually, Holovak had seven of those wins after taking over for Saban in year two following a 2-3 Saban start.

The most critical time for a new team is in its first several seasons. The Patriots were very lucky they had the mastery of Lou Saban to guide them. By the way, there are reports that at his death Lou Saban's wife Joyce confessed that Nick and Lou Saban may have been second cousins. That explains a lot. Both are of Croation descent.

How did the AFL get its players?

Just like the NFL, the AFL had to draft players for the eight teams that made up the league. Why would any player go with the AFL if they had a shot at the NFL? There are two answers to that question!

#1. Every player after college wants to make as much money in their lifetime as they can as a pro.

#2 Marketing, Marketing, Marketing

It helps to have salesmen selling the product (AFL) like as if they had a shot at selling ice cream to Eskimos. Marketing ultimately gave the AFL its players. The marketers had to have NFL-sized prize money when one of the top college players was ready to go AFL v NFL. There were a lot of guarantees. A lot of rich people ran the NFL teams and they were getting richer. A lot of rich people were about to run the AFL Teams and they had no problem meeting the salary demands of potential AFL players. It was not a given, but the group with the better marketers were destined to win as the money was not an issue.

How the players would be divvied up in the AFL was just as much an issue as in the NFL. But, the NFL had already solved the how-to!

And so, it was quite legitimate before the league even began playing to conduct a draft to help stock the AFL teams with great players who could win ball-games. You may recall that when the College All Stars played the NFL champs for years during this same time period, sometimes the College All Stars actually beat the pros. They were younger and faster and just as strong. The AFL with money and marketing were a sure thing. And so, came the first AFL draft before the AFL played game # 1.

The 1960 American Football League (AFL) draft was held on November 22–23, 1959, in Minneapolis, shortly after the organization of the AFL league. The fact that there was a league meant the money and the marketing were in place. The first AFL draft lasted 33 rounds, enough to fill a team. To make sure it was enough, an additional draft of 20 rounds was held by the AFL on December 2. Considering all of the senior football players graduating from so many colleges, there would be no shortage of qualified players to be picked.

Let's take a look now at the team selected by Boston Patriots coaches did under coach Lou Saban in their first year as a united squad.

1960 Lou Saban, Coach #1

The 1960 Boston Patriots football team competed in their first season of Professional American Football League (AFL) football. They were led by Lou Saban in his first of two as head coach. In this first year in which a Patriots team took the field in a pro game, this Patriots team finished with a losing season record of 5-9-0, winning five games, losing nine, and tying none. They failed to qualify for the playoffs for the first time

By the time July came Lou Saban had the Patriots ready to play football at home in the season opener at Nickerson Field. Let me caution you before we move ahead that you will not find team names such as the New York Giants, Philadelphia Eagles, Pittsburgh Steelers, etc., because they were not in the AFL They were in a league that had been well established known as the NFL.

The AFL had a great model at the time, the NFL so many of their rules and standards were already well known and implemented first in the NFL. One of these notions was a preseason. The first preseason game in American Football League history was played on July 30, 1960. It featured our Boston Patriots and they played the Buffalo Bills at Buffalo.

I marvel at how in such short order, after coming together in November 1959 as a grand idea and a plan, that by July, there were teams on the field playing the first AFL preseason game ever. It sure was a monumental accomplishment in that the league was formed less than a year prior to the first kickoff. In fact, so much work had gone into the preparation for the new league that many of the founders had not even had the time to assess the magnitude and success of their efforts. For example, one of the famous Hunt Brothers, League co-founder Lamar Hunt was driving home from his office in late-July and he was "tickled pink" when he heard a sports radio program running down the odds of the AFL's first weekend of action.

Many US cities had taken a shot at pro football before 1960. Some did not make it. Buffalo, NY was one of those that had been there and done that and now were ready to do it again. They were fully excited about the AFL and a chance to have a pro-team in Buffalo again.

Ironically, this was not the first AFL and so some cities such a Buffalo had once had pro football teams in the NFL, the old AFL, as well as the All-America Football Conference. The city was excited when the Bills were part of the new AFL in 1960.
Such was also the case in Buffalo when team founder Ralph Wilson, Jr. watched more than 100,000 fans gather at a rally the night before the preseason opener. The following evening 16,474 curious fans arrived at the newly renovated and renamed War Memorial Stadium.

Though it was just a pre-season game, and would not counted, it counted for Buffalo and it counted for Boston as the two teams clashed. The Patriots overcame the Bills' home field advantage and the extremely hot temperatures. The Pats defeated Buffalo 28-7. The teams featured a bunch of no-name players who played their hearts out. The star for the evening was Patriots quarterback Butch Songin who tossed two touchdowns to lead the Pats to victory. Head Coach Lou Saban was so ecstatic that it is reported that he shook hands with every member of the Patriot team and asked them to sign an official AFL ball. Ask yourself: Did this game count? You bet it did.

And so, began the long journey of the very successful America Football League that would eventually and forever change the landscape of professional football.

Lou Saban was Boston's first coach. He was no kid and he knew what he as doing in football. His career had spanned 53 years and included 27 different stops. He was one of the "most traveled coaches" in the history of football. Affectionately dubbed "Much Traveled Lou," the Indiana University graduate compiled a record of 95-99-7 in 16 seasons as a pro football head coach. Lou Saban's record probably would have been much better if he was not always so ready to take a shot at something that was not a sure thing.

Saban started his head coaching career after his four-year playing career as a linebacker with the Cleveland Browns ended in 1949. His first job began the very next season at the Case Institute of Technology in Cleveland. Five years later, Saban was at Northwestern for two years and then moved to Western Illinois University in 1957. Eventually he came to Boston and his expertise helped launch the Boston Patriots into a permanent spot in the hearts of New Englanders. Everything starts with something. Lou Saban gave the Patriots their start.

After an unsuccessful bid at retirement, Saban's last stop as head coach was at Chowan University in North Carolina in 2001 and '02. Lou Saban, a fine and gracious man and great coach, died on March 29, 2009 at the age of 87 but his lasting legacy and influence can still be seen on the football field today.

The team he led played teams that were unrecognizable in their day. All have survived but not under their 1960 names. That does not mean that you may not recognize the names of all of the teams that played the Patriots in their first year. The League's idea was to play each team twice providing a fourteen-game season in year 1. There was a bye week for a rest. You may recognize some nicknames but not always the City/Nickname combo such as the Los Angeles Chargers who became the San Diego Chargers, but who strangely enough are again the Los Angeles Chargers. Yes, it is the same team.

You may wonder who the New York Titans might be when you see that the Boston Patriots played them in the inaugural 1960 season. They simply changed their last name from Titans to the Jets in 1962. Then there were the Dallas Texans, who the Patriots also played in 1960.

The American Football League (AFL) had a 1960 charter member named the Dallas Texans. However, after the first season, they chose to become the Kansas City Chiefs. In 1997, the Houston Oilers became the Tennessee Titans. The Oakland Raiders left to become the LA Raiders but came back after the 1994 season and have been the Oakland Raiders ever since.

Now, with that AFL team genealogy straightened out, there should be no team in the AFL schedule for the Boston Patriots in 1960 that you do not recognize. Of course, don't expect to find the New England Patriots.

As a point of note, the Dallas Cowboys joined the NFL, not the AFL, as an expansion team in 1960 so there was a lot of good football stuff happening at this time in football history.

Here are the opposing teams in the sequence of the games played in 1960. Check out the team names because for the next ten years, these, for the most part, are the teams that the Boston Patriots played until they joined the NFL with the rest of the AFL in 1970

1 Denver Broncos
2 New York Titans
3 Buffalo Bills
4 Los Angeles Chargers
5 Oakland Raiders
6 Denver Broncos
7 Los Angeles Chargers
8 Oakland Raiders
9 New York Titans

10 Dallas Texans
11 Houston Oilers
12 Buffalo Bills
13 Dallas Texans
14 Houston Oilers

The AFL was as wild as the old west when it began. They were looking to survive and to eventually be wildly successful. Many of the players could not survive on their AFL salaries and so they tended bar and served other tasks when they got a break from practice and playing. Eventually, it would all come together and like the NFL, a lot of fortunes were made.

One of the first ways the AFL showed their lack of orthodoxy in their methods was in scheduling games. When you look at the Pats schedule for 1960, for example, their first game was a Friday, then a Saturday then back to Friday and Saturday before their first Sunday match came to be. The Patriots played just five Sundays out of a fourteen-week season. That's what you call thinking out of the box. The AFL was so wildly successful that the NFL merged with them just ten years later.

Many did not consider the impact of attendance at high school football games on Friday and college football games on Saturday as being affected by the AFL or pro-football at all. Nonetheless, our Congress, apparently looking for work, having nothing to do, was so concerned about AFL style football becoming dominant on Friday and Saturday, that they passed some laws prohibiting regular season pro games from being played on Fridays and Saturdays.

And you, like me, probably thought the reason Colleges do not play on Sunday is because of some seedy deal with the NFL. Nope. The seedy deal was not a deal at all. It was Congress protecting attendance at HS and college football games. One would think they could have spent their time more wisely but now you know the *rest of the story*.

In the Patriot's first ever season and "home" opener on Friday, Sept 9, the Patriots lost in a close match to the Denver Broncos L (10-13) at Nickerson Field before 21,597. At the NY Titans the following Saturday, Sept 17, the Patriots got their first AFL win W (28-24) in a game played at the Polo Grounds before 19,200. On Sept 23 at home (Nickerson Field), the Pats were shut out by the Buffalo Bills L (013) before 20,732. After a bye on Sept 30, on Saturday Oct 8, Boston traveled to LA Memorial Coliseum to play the Chargers. Thy crushed LA in a 35-0 shutout before 18,226. On the West Coast again on Sunday Oct 16, the Oakland Raiders beat the Patriots L (14-27) before 11,500.

At Denver on Sunday, Oct 23, the Broncos got by the Patriots by one score at Bears Stadium before 12,683. On Friday, Oct 28, at home, the LA Chargers whooped the Patriots L (16-45) before 13,988. At home on Friday, Nov 4, Boston beat Oakland W (34–28) at home before 8,446. Then at home again on Friday November 11, the Patriots outplayed the New York Titans W 38-21) before 11,653

On Friday, Nov 18 at home, the Patriots pounded the Dallas Texans W (42–14) before 14,721. At home on Friday, Nov 25, the Houston Oilers defeated the Boston Patriots L (10-24) before a nice crowd of 27,123. At Buffalo on Sunday Dec 4, the Patriots were defeated by the Bills L (14-38) at War Memorial Stadium before 14,335. At Dallas, on Sunday Dec 11 , the Dallas Texans shut out the Patriots L (0-34) in the Cotton Bowl before 12,000. Wrapping up the inaugural season at Houston on Sunday, Dec 18, the Oilers spoiled the Patriots finale L 21-37) at Jeppesen Stadium before 22,352.

Top Patriot Players Jim Lee Hunt, DT

Jim Lee Hunt played great football for the Boston Patriots from 1960-71. He carried the complimentary nickname, "Earthquake," for obvious reasons.

Hunt played in 141 games at defensive tackle. He was voted to four AFL All-Star games and named "best pass rushing tackle in the AFL" by AFL scouts in 1967.

For a big man, Hunt possessed great speed. One time he intercepted a pass and out-ran two running backs for a 79-yard touchdown return. An award for the best Patriots lineman was named in his honor and John Hannah won it in 1981. In 1993, Hunt was inducted into the Patriots Hall of Fame. He fits in quite well.

1961 Lou Saban, Coach #1
1961 Mike Holovak, Coach #2

The 1961 Boston Patriots football team competed in their second season of Professional American Football League (AFL) football. They were led by Lou Saban in his last of two as head coach. After assuring the team's viability through 14 games, in 1960, Saban began the 1961 season with a 2-3 record and was fired after the fifth game of the season. He was replaced by Mike Holovak who came in with 7-1-1 helping the Patriots finish with a fine record of 9-4-1 for the whole season. We include both the Saban games and the Holovak games in this chapter. upped the ante and brought forth a fine 9-4-1 winning season.

In the home and season opener on Sat Sep 9, at Nickerson Field on the campus of Boston University, the New York Titans edged out the New England Patriots L (20-21). This was two opening day losses in a row. On Sat Sep 16, the Patriots crushed the Denver Broncos at home W (45 17). Then, at Buffalo the next week, again on Saturday, the Patriots defeated the Bills in a close match W (23-21). At New York on Sunday, Oct 1, the Titans nosed out the Patriots L (30 37)

On Sat Oct 7 at home, the San Diego Chargers neutralized the Patriots L (27 38). That was it for coach Lou Saban. Mike Holovak took over immediately when Lou Saban got his notice. He began his successful tenure with the Pats with a tie. On Fri Oct 13, at home, the Boston Patriots tied Houston Oilers T (31 31). At home on Sun Oct 22, the Boston Patriots lambasted the Buffalo Bills W (52 21). At Dallas on Sun Oct 29. The Patriots prevailed by one point over the Texans W (18-17).

At Houston, on Sun Nov 12, the Oilers beat the Patriots L (15 27). Then, at home on Fri Nov 17, the Patriots beat the Oakland Raiders W (20 17). Wrapping up the season with three away game wins, the first was at Denver as the Pats beat the Broncos W (28-24). The next was at Oakland as Boston beat the Raiders W (35-21). And then, at San Diego in the season finale, the Patriots shut out the Chargers W (41-0).
-

Top Patriots Players Vito "Babe" Parilli

Vito "Babe" Parilli played quarterback for the Patriots from 1961-67 and threw for more than 20,000 yards during his career. Parilli was voted to three American Football League All-Star teams and was named the AFL Comeback Player of the Year in 1966 when he threw for 3,441 yards and 31 touchdowns.

In addition to his skills as a quarterback, Parilli became known as an excellent kick holder and earned the nickname "Gold Finger." The combination of holder/quarterback Parilli and kicker/wide receiver Gino Cappelletti came to be known as the "Grand Opera." In 1993, Parilli was inducted into the Patriots Hall of Fame. In 1982, Parilli was inducted into the College Football Hall of Fame for his collegiate career under Bear Bryant at the University of Kentucky. The Kentucky native lives his in home state. Inducted 1993.

Top Patriot Players Houston Antwine, DT

Houston Antwine was unmatched as a sack man for the Boston Patriots. He played all of 11 seasons for the Patriots, appearing in 142 games from 1961-1971. He was the sack leader for the Patriots in three consecutive seasons from 1967-69. His 39 career sacks are tied for 10th (with Richard Seymour) on the Patriots all-time career sacks list.

Antwine was well respected, earning six consecutive American Football League (AFL) All-Star selections from 1963-68. His six all-star appearances are tied for the fourth highest total in franchise history.

He came to the Patriots via a trade from the Houston Oilers in exchange for a fourth-round pick in the 1962 AFL Draft on April 1, 1961. He is one of the good guys, a member of the Patriots 50th Anniversary Team and a member of the 1960s All-Decade Team.

Now that we have whet your appetite with two seasons of Boston Patriots football, before we come back to the rest of the seasons, let's talk about the origins of football and how the NFL/AFL came to be.

You may continue to the 1962 season after you enjoy the origins of pro football. It is in Chapter 11, page 107.

Chapter 4 The Evolution of Modern Football

Lots of playing before playing became official

The official agreed upon date for the first American-style football game is November 6, 1869. It would be ninety-one years after this that the Boston Patriots would win their first game ever in the AFL against the New York Titans. It would be more than one hundred thirty-three years after the game in 1869 for the New England Patriots to beat the St. Louis Rams for their first Super Bowl win.

From the first game to the first NFL season in 1920, American football kept changing for the better. If you can find a replay of a game from the early era someplace in the heavens, you would find its replay would not look much like football as we know it. But, it was not completely soccer or rugby either.

Before the first "football" game, teams were playing a rugby style "fuszball" similar to that played in Britain in the mid-19th century.

At the time in the US, a derivative known as association football was also played. In both games, a football is kicked at a goal or run over a line. These styles were based on the varieties of English public-school football games. Over time, as noted, the style of "football" play in America continued to evolve.

On November 6, 1869, the first intercollegiate formal football game in America featured Rutgers and Princeton. Before the teams were even on the field it was being plugged as the first college (intercollegiate) football game of all time. Most of the popular NFL teams of today were being formed after the turn of the century.

The first game of intercollegiate football was a sporting battle between two neighboring schools on a plot of ground where the present-day Rutgers gymnasium now stands in New Brunswick, N.J. Rutgers won that first game, 6-4. Even the scoring was different back then.

There were two teams of 25 men each and the rules were mostly rugby-like, but different enough to make it very interesting and enjoyable.

Like today's football, there were many surprises; strategies needed to be employed; determination exhibited, and of course the players required physical prowess.

1st Game Rutgers 6 Princeton 4 College Field, New Brunswick, NJ

Before we begin to focus solely on the Patriots, the next several chapters will describe the origins of football, the origin of the football, and how the NFL grew out of something that became known as American football that was first played on college campuses.

Chapter 5 The First American College Football Game

Early American Football

We can all read Walter Camp's books about how the rules of American football came about. We can also learn a lot from the writings of the day. However, since nobody alive today was alive way back when, it is safe to say that nobody actually knows. But from all the accounts, we do have a pretty good idea.

There are a lot of guessers and some wrong readers out there because nobody from November 1869, of which I am aware can refute anything via an eye-witness account. So, there are a lot of great stories, some duplicated many times over. Some are right on the money and others are inexact. We'll do our best to bring you the story as it really happened in this book.

Once the first College football game was played, the next major game to be played was the first professional football game. Though there were dribs and drabs of pro football being played by a number of famous coaches such as Knute Rockne, it took a while for professional football to take off.

In these pre-Patriots football chapters that eventually get us to the first pro-football game, it helps to know that the facts in this section come from a book written by your author that sells much better in England than it does in the US. Its title is *The Birth of American Football*. The modified excerpts within this book help set the stage for a proper introduction of professional football, the NFL, the AFL, and the road to Super Bowl LXI, a game won by our very own Patriots.

It has been almost 150 years since the first American College Football game. Therefore, it helps to recall the old schoolroom exercise of whispering into a person's ear a little passage and thirty students later seeing what comes back. The good news is that the further back that you get from the time of Walter Camp, the stories are all similar and there are fewer and fewer of them.

Camp had all the future rules in his head!

Eventually, in the 1870's, shortly after the very first recognized collegiate football game in America, the great Walter Camp began to get really interested and he wrote a lot of football history and football rule books. These are trusted implicitly today by most experts as the defining moments in American football.

One of the few things about early football that we do know with reasonable certainty is that professional football as we understand it, was non-existent until long after collegiate football was established. It can also be said with certainty that if it were not for the colleges and Walter Camp, in particular, there probably would be no American football today at any level. Of course, more than likely there would still be rugby and soccer.

We also know that there was a great gifted athlete who played every sport imaginable including soccer and rugby, and then American football. His name is Walter Camp. He is universally recognized as the Father of American Football.

There is some irony in putting this out as a two plus two equals four story, however. You see, Walter Camp, as noted, widely considered the most important figure in the development of American football, was not playing organized football when the first football game took place in 1869. So, who gave them their football rules. Voila, a conundrum!

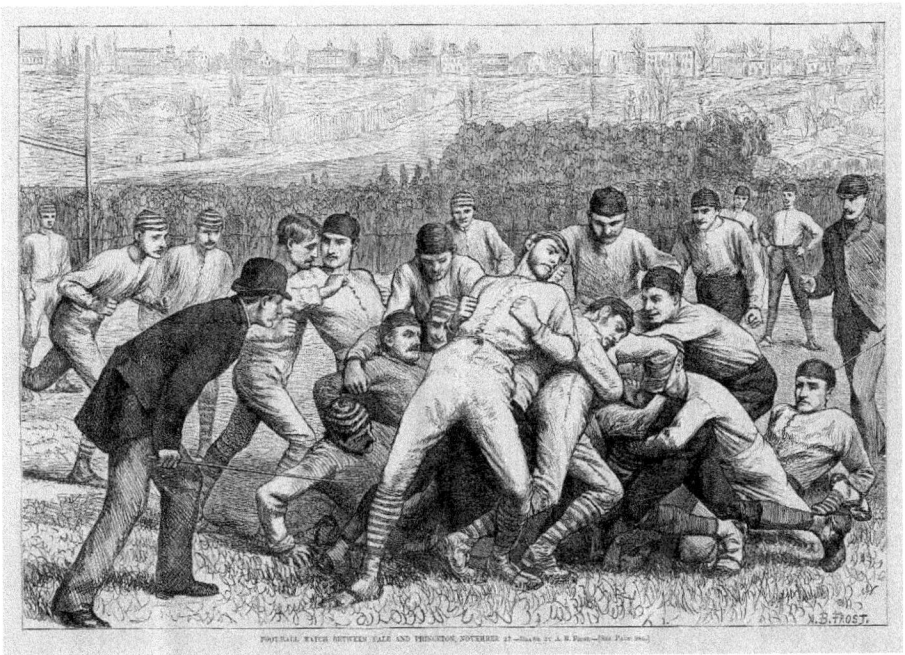
1879 Football Game Depiction

As a youth, we know that Camp excelled in sports such as track, baseball, and association football, and after enrolling at Yale in 1876, he earned varsity honors in every sport the school offered. But, what about 1869, which is the consensus origin date for the beginning of American football in the US?

Many apologists have written about this period from 1869 onward as if it were the beginning of American football that, at the time was played only at the collegiate level. In essence, the true beginning of college football was in fact, the beginning of American football. However, the rules of the game began more as rugby rules than football rules but over the years, changes were made. Today, no other country plays the type of football played in America. America created its own game of football and it is unique.

There were other rough games out there at the time and they still exist across the world. One might conclude that football was unnecessary as those who played soccer and rugby could be maimed or killed in a contest without needing Camp's American football rules.

Scenes from one of first football games

Considering that the centennial of the US was approaching in 1869, the year of the first game, some feel there was a need to create a game besides the American past-time of baseball, that was a cool-weather sport. Yes, there was soccer and rugby, but these have a European or English heritage, from whom America had declared independence about 100 years prior. England for the most part owned the rules of soccer and rugby for some time.

Nonetheless, historians trace the roots of American football to early versions of rugby football and association football. Both games have their origin in varieties of football played in Britain in the mid-19th century, in which a football is kicked at a goal or kicked over a line. These varieties of style in England were based on the various English public school football games.

It helps to be reminded in this story that our nation's birth date is July 4, 1776 and so 1869 was just 93 years from the founding.

There are lots of stories about the evolution towards American football, and this part of this discusses many ideas supplied by Walter Camp for the transition. American football resulted from several major modifications from association football and rugby football, most notably the rule changes instituted by Camp at Yale University and as a Hopkins School graduate. To repeat Camp is significant as he is attributed as being the designated "Father of American Football."

One of the changes not attributed to Walter Camp was the shape of the ball. As you will see, the forward pass did not become legal until 1906 and so the spherical shape of modern footballs was not required until passing became a bigger part of the game.

The football was evolving steadily from the first game. But, it was not completely perfected until 1935. The ball used in the very first game was round, like a soccer ball and like early rugby balls. It was tough to carry, and awkward to throw. In 1874, in a McGill and Harvard game, they used a ball that looked like a watermelon. Over time, balls became more plum-like and easier to throw. The problem was that pigs' bladders, not balloons were used and they by definition were inexact. We refine this study of the ball later in this section before we look at Patriot's season summaries, so please hang on. For now, know that Walter Camp was not involved in determining the ball per se.

Among these important changes to rugby that Camp brought into American football were the introduction of the line of scrimmage, and the down-and-distance rules. He also introduced the notion of legal interference, which today is called blocking. Camp was the rules guy but before he went to Yale, like most New Englanders of the day, he played soccer, which was the preferred cool-weather fall sport of the day. He did not play much rugby football until his time at Yale University from 1876 to 1881.

Camp was not the first person to play football—any kind of football—be it soccer, rugby, or Harpastum. Some joke that Adam and Eve may have played football with a round fruit. Most of us would hope it was an orange or a grapefruit.

A sport called Harpastum and others

You can go back through history and find sports that had some of the roughness and rudiments of soccer, rugby, and American football but the games they played were not very rule-based.

In a "sport" called *Harpastum*, a form of ball game played in the Roman Empire, for example, the Romans enjoyed their own form of football.

There have been many forms of traditional football that have been played throughout Europe and beyond since the beginning of mankind.

We have already discussed the possibility that there may have been nicht-verboten round or oval fruits in the Garden of Paradise used for football.

From the beginning of antiquity, knowing man's propensity to exercise, have fun and use various shaped balls in so doing, if not in the garden, then one can bet it was not long after Paradise that ancient forms of football abounded. See pic of *Harpastum* next page.

Many of these ancient matches would involve handling of a ball and scrummage-like formations. Several of the oldest examples of football-like games include the Greek game of *Episkyros* and the Roman game of *Harpastum* (both pictures on opposite side of page).

Over time many countries across the world developed their own national football-like games. For example, New Zealand has Ki-o-rahi, Australia has Marngrook, Japan has Kemari, China has Cuju, Georgia has Lelo Burti, and the Borders have Jeddart Ba' and Cornwall Cornish have Hurling.

The pictures in this section of balls and balls in play are interesting and make the point. Left to right, Ki-o-rahi ball, Marngrook ball, and a snap of a game of Kemari in process. None of these forms appear to have a direct link to American football but they surely are forerunners.

A traditional kī-o-rahi ball. Marngrook (possum skin football). A game of Kemari.

In football-story-telling, there is also an often-told story about a ship in 1586, almost 100 years after Columbus, in which the men from the ship wanted to play a little sport. The ship was reportedly commanded by an English explorer named John Davis. The young crew would go ashore to play a form of football with the Inuit (Eskimo) people in Greenland. There are other later accounts of an Inuit game played on ice, called Aqsaqtuk.

This game had a similarity to football in that each game, which was called a match, began with the two teams facing each other in parallel lines. The objective was to kick the "ball" through each other team's line and then kick it at a goal. Moving along in time, it is recorded from 1610 that William Strachley from Jamestown Virginia, an English Colonist, wrote the account of a game played by **Native Americans**. They called the game Pahsaheman.

Though there are stories of **Native Americans** playing games, a variety of American football historians agree that the game has its roots from the traditional football games played all over Europe in villages, towns, and schools for centuries before Columbus.

The scuttle on those is that the early games appear to have had much in common with what has been called "mob football" from England. There were typically no uniforms or coaches nor hard and fast rules.

In the 19th century, intramural games of rugby, soccer, and association football began to be played on American college campuses. There were no rules committees and no Walter Camp at the time and so each school played its own variety of football with its own rules.

Princeton University students, for example, are reported to have played a game called ball-own, as early as 1820.

Harvard had its own tradition known as "Bloody Monday," which began in 1827. This was all about a mass ballgame between the freshman and sophomore classes. In 1860, both the town police and the college authorities agreed the Bloody Monday had to go. There was too much blood for the good of the game.

The gendarme would not permit "football" for well over twelve years. Then the game was played again. Dartmouth had its own version, which they called "Old division football." Its rules were first published in 1871, though it is said they played the game from the 1830's.

There were commonalities in all these games Yet, they remained largely "mob" style games, with huge numbers of players on the "field" or whatever makeshift was available. All players were on the field at the same time. There was a little rhyme and some reason as the objective seemed always to be to advance the ball into a goal area, quite often by any means possible and necessary.

There were no complicated rules as the games were played for sport—just for fun. Rules were simple, and so without protection by rules, violence and injury were common. There was supposedly no beer drinking at the games, but plenty was consumed shortly thereafter by the young adult participants.

Yes, to be sure, the games were often heated as no group wanted to lose. Some games were actually violent. Yet, afterwards, sometimes after beating each other to a pulp, both squads normally would choose to gather together from their rivalry for some post-game revelry that often included the singing of songs, awarding of small prizes, and of course lots of beer-drinking.

There is an old football / rugby saying that parallels the US Las Vegas slogan: "What happens on the pitch, stays on the pitch. "This is an oft-quoted rugby truism.

Take away the violence!

The brutality and frequent bloodshed of these mob-style games led to widespread protests and there were many separate decisions from cities and schools to abandon the games. Yale, for example, under pressure from the city of New Haven, banned the play of all forms of football in 1860. Eventually, because of popular pressure, the games would be brought back in one form or another.

From 1854 to 1882, there was a variant of the mob football style that was once again played at Yale in the form of bladderball. The objective, of this "game" was to gain control of an oversized inflatable ball and bring it through the gates of the residential college represented by another on-campus intramural team.

As one would expect, this game was eventually banned by school authorities for a number of reasons, not the least of which was alcohol fueled violence. The violence and the alcohol were most often precipitated by the game. Revival games were played in 2009 and 2011, and very briefly, in 2014. The revivals are most often scripted though the grog surely flows.

Eventually, the informality of the matches gave way to formality as bona fide institutions began to sponsor collegiate level teams. The 1869 college football season is recognized as the first season of intercollegiate football in the United States, though at the time, there were only two teams in the league – Rutgers and Princeton.

The rules were not refined and so the teams used "agreed-upon improvised rules" resembling soccer and rugby as much as the modern American sport. 1869 is considered by historians as the inaugural college football season.

This 1869 football season consisted of only two total games and as noted, there were just two teams – Rutgers University and Princeton University; The first game was played on November 6 at Rutgers' campus, and the second was played on November 13 on the Princeton's campus.

1869–1875

As noted, the November 6, 1869 football game between Rutgers and Princeton, which by the way was then known as the *College of New Jersey,* was played with a round ball. The rules were provided by Rutgers captain William J. Leggett. They were based on the Football Association's first set of American football rules.

Rutgers Scarlett Knights practice 1869

Walter Camp did not write the first set of rules, but he made them all better. These rules were an early attempt by those who had studied football in England's public schools, to codify the rules and create what hopefully would become a universal and standardized set of dictates for the game. Let me posit an analogy of the *evolution* of American Football Rules.

I remember back in the late 1980's when Windows 2.0 came out and it was a major improvement on DOS and the prior Windows. I am sure if the hardware were capable then, the Bill Gates led Microsoft team would have built Windows 10 or Windows 11 instead of going through all the iterations to make the program better over the next thirty years. But, for lots of reasons, they could not.

Rules changes work well through an iterative process of testing new rules, introducing them to the "game," and then removing objectional parts. In the process, some rules are enhanced; others eliminated; while still other rules are added.

The 1869 football games bore little resemblance to the American game, which would be developed slowly in the following decades through the continual work of Walter Camp and others. Nonetheless, it is still regarded as the first game of Intercollegiate American Football.

Think of the mob playing this first game at a Rutgers field. It could have been worse. Two teams of 25 players lined up and attempted to score by kicking the ball into the opposing team's goal. Throwing or carrying the ball was not allowed, but there was plenty of physical contact between players. The first team to reach six goals was declared the winner. Rutgers won by a score of six to four.

A rematch was played at Princeton a week later under Princeton's own set of rules. There was a major difference in the rules of this game as a team was awarded a "free kick" when any player caught the ball on the fly. This feature had been adopted from the Football Association's rules. The fair catch kick rule has survived through our modern American game.

Princeton won the second game with home field advantage by a score of 8-0. More teams began to play each other in 1870. Columbia was next to join the series and then by 1872 several other schools began to field intercollegiate teams, including Yale and the Stevens Institute of Technology.

Yale vs. Columbia

Chapter 6 Moving Closer Towards American Football

Nothing happens overnight

Soon after the early football changes, in the late nineteenth and into the early twentieth centuries, more game-play type developments were introduced by college coaches.

The list is like a who's who of early American College Football. Coaches, such as Eddie Cochems, Amos Alonzo Stagg, Parke H. Davis, Knute Rockne, John Heisman, and Glenn "Pop" Warner helped introduce and then take advantage of the newly introduced forward pass.

In later chapters, we will look at the enhancements attributed to these football greats.

We have learned that American College football as well as professional football, were introduced prior to the 20th century. Pro football remained ragtag until 1920 when the American Professional Football Association was formed. Fans were lured into watching again and again once they saw the game played. How could we not love American football?

American college football grew in popularity even after the beginning of professional football. It became the dominant version of the sport of football in the United States. It was this way for the entire first half of the 20th century. For many fans, it still is this way.

There are pro football fans who do not enjoy college football and vice versa.

Bowl games made the idea of football even more exciting in the college ranks. Rivalries grew and continued, and the fans loved it! This great football tradition brought a national audience to college football games that still dominates the sports world today.

Edgar Allan Poe – No kidding!

In researching this section, I found that some players with some great names played football in the early years. For example, Edgar Allan Poe was an All-American for Princeton in 1889. Additionally, in 1889, first-year players were permitted to wear numbers representing their names in college football games.

This particular Edgar Allan Poe was also a great historical figure. He served as Attorney General of the State of Maryland from 1911 to 1915. Born in Baltimore, Poe was named for his second cousin, twice removed, the celebrated author & poet, Edgar Allan Poe, who died in 1849.

What number is he?

Another interesting tidbit on the formation of football is that teams played without uniform numbers. Nonetheless somehow the players were identified. Just two years after Penn State as well as Notre Dame formed their teams and played their first official football games in 1887, the first All-America team was named in 1889.

There is some scuttle about that, for Walter Camp and some others with mostly Eastern College roots were accused of picking players from the big Eastern Colleges almost exclusively and so there were few All Americans at Notre Dame or Penn State or Alabama in the early years.

Seventeen years after the first all-American for example, W. T. (Mother) Dunn was Penn State's first All-American in (1906). He was named by Walter Camp. He was both a linebacker and a center. The next All-American for PSU was Bob Higgins, the long-time PSU football coach who, as an End, gained the honor both in (1915 & 1919). The PSU football program has produced 88 consensus all-Americans in total. Notre Dame has 90. Alabama has 68.

Notre Dame had two All-Americans in 1913—Knute Rockne, an End, and Gus Dorais, a quarterback. By 1913, the forward pass was legal and that is how ND was winning its games in this undefeated season.

As touched on briefly in this section. in 1889, numbers to identify individual players were permitted but not recommended. It took until 1915 that they were recommended. But, it wasn't until 1937 that numerals were required on both the front and back of game jerseys. In 1967 this rule was further modified to require numbering according to position, with offensive players ineligible to receive forward passes if they were assigned numbers in the 50-79 range.

Pro football came from American college football

There is no denying that the greatest college football players more often than not eventually find their fortunes in professional football. Pro football can be traced back to 1889, just a few years after Penn State and Notre Dame rolled out their programs, and just before Alabama got in the game.

It was 1892, when William "Pudge" Heffelfinger signed a $500 contract to play for the Allegheny Athletic Association against the Pittsburgh Athletic Club. He is reportedly the first player to be paid for playing football.

Twenty-eight years later, the American Professional Football Association was formed. This league changed its name to the National Football League (NFL) just two years later.

Eventually, the NFL became the major league of American football. Originally, pro football was just an unaffiliated sport played in midwestern industrial towns in the United States. Yet, professional football eventually became a national phenomenon.

We all know this because from August to February, in America, every year, many of us are glued to our TV sets or chained to our seats in some of the most intriguing pro-football stadiums in America—mostly on Sundays.

The end of football?

Football was never a game for the light of heart. You had to be tough physically and tough mentally to compete. Way back in 1906, for example complaints were many about the violence in American football. It got so bad that universities on the West Coast, led by California and Stanford, replaced the sport with rugby union rules.

At the time, the very future of American college football, a very popular sport enjoyed by fans nationwide was in doubt. The schools that eliminated football and replaced it with Rugby Union believed football would be gone and Rugby Union would eventually be adopted nationwide.

Soon other schools followed this travesty and made the switch. Eventually, due to the perception that West Coast football was an inferior game played by inferior men when compared to the rough and tumble East Coast, manhood prevailed in the West over the inclination to make the game mild.

The many tough East Coast and Midwest teams had shrugged off the loss of the few teams out West and they had continued to play American style football.

And, so the available pool of Rugby Union "football" teams to play remained small. The Western colleges therefore had to schedule games against local club teams and they reached out to Rugby Union powers in Australia, New Zealand, and especially, due to its proximity, Canada. America at the time was almost exclusively playing American football.

American football OK without the West

The famous Stanford and California game continued as rugby. To make it seem important. The winner was invited by the British Columbia Rugby Union to a tournament in Vancouver over the Christmas holidays. The winner of that tournament was rewarded with the Cooper Keith Trophy. Nobody in the American football America cared. Eventually the West Coast came back to American-style football ala Walter Camp.

Nonetheless the situation of injury and death in football persisted and though there was a lot of pushback, it came to a head in 1905 when there were 19 fatalities nationwide. Nobody wanted this.

President Theodore Roosevelt, a tough guy himself, is reported to have threatened to shut down the game nationwide if drastic changes were not made. Sports historians however, dispute that Roosevelt ever intervened with any wielded power.

What is certified, however, is that on October 9, 1905, the President held a meeting of football representatives from Harvard, Yale, and Princeton. The topic was eliminating and reducing injuries and the President, according to the record, never threatened to ban football.

The fact is that Roosevelt lacked the authority to abolish football but more importantly, he was a big fan and wanted the game to continue. The little Roosevelts also loved the sport and were playing football at the college and secondary levels at the time.

This was over 110 years ago, a century plus. That is why they say football was an even more brutal sport then, than some believe it is today. There are accounts of games that left dozens of dead on college and prep school gridirons. Though I have the reference, I cannot find any of the games in which such carnage may have occurred.

Many in the country were asking for action from politicians. With the very existence of the sport in jeopardy, President Theodore Roosevelt, who actually loved the sport, entered the fray and urged the schools noted above to institute some radical reforms that according to observers at the time saved the sport and gave another birth to the modern game of American football.

On the next page is a picture of a Teddy's Nephew being carried off the field after an injury in the brutal game of football.

There are those who went as far as calling the turn of the 20th century America's football gridirons killing fields. College games drew tens of thousands of spectators and had even more fan appeal than professional baseball, the national pastime.

Baseball was a gentle sport compared to football. American football in the early 1900s was lethally brutal. It was a grinding, bruising sport that required major physical contact on each play. In 1905, the forward pass was still illegal and, so it was sheer brute strength that was required to move the ball.

One of the Roosevelt offspring carried off after injuring his ankle.

Huge players were permitted to lock their arms in mass formations and they would use their unprotected helmetless heads as battering rams. Gang tackles routinely buried ball carriers underneath a ton and a half of "tangled humanity."

Football players fought like gladiators

There was little in the way of protective equipment. Apparently, nobody had ever thought of pads and helmets. Players would often sustain gruesome injuries such as wrenched spinal cords, crushed skulls and broken ribs that were sometimes so severe they pierced their hearts. It did not go unnoticed.

The Chicago Tribune wrote a piece that in 1904 alone, the year before Roosevelt's involvement. there were 18 football deaths and 159 serious injuries, mostly among prep school players. It was sad.

A look at tangled humanity

TR as a college undergraduate; Theodore Roosevelt Collection, Harvard College Library

There were obituaries of young pigskin players on a near-weekly basis during the football season. The carnage appalled America. Everybody loved the sport but not the maimings. The Newspapers did not take it easy on the game. Editorials called for the outright banishment of college and high school football.

Football was often compared to the Roman Gladiators: "The once athletic sport has degenerated into a contest that for brutality is little better than the gladiatorial combats in the arena in ancient Rome," opined the Beaumont Express. The sport had reached such a crisis that one of its biggest boosters—President Theodore Roosevelt—got involved.

Roosevelt's glasses gave away his nearsightedness. But, as a youth in college he did not wear them. This, however, was more than enough to keep this tough man from making the Harvard varsity squad, Yet, he was always a vocal exponent of football's contribution to the "strenuous life," both on and off the field.

When "Teddy" was New York City police commissioner, he helped bring back the old Harvard-Yale football series after it had been canceled for two years following the violent 1894 clash that was labeled "the bloodbath at Hampden Park."

He believed that the football field was more or less a proving ground for the battlefield. This was validated by the performance of his fellow Rough Riders who were mostly former football standouts. "In life, as in a football game," he wrote, "the principle to follow is: Hit the line hard; don't foul and don't shirk but hit the line hard!"

Teddy Roosevelt liked football

In 1903, the president told an audience, "I believe in rough games and in rough, manly sports. I do not feel any particular sympathy for the person who gets battered about a good deal so long as it is not fatal." Unfortunately, in 1904-1905, football injuries were too often fatalities, and it was not improving.

Yes, even the President knew that football had become fatal, and he acknowledged that it needed reform if it were to be saved. With his son, Theodore Jr. who had begun to play for the Harvard freshman team, he had a major league paternal interest in reforming the game as well.

Roosevelt was the guy to negotiate with the foot-ballers for sure. He was straight from having negotiated an end to the Russo-Japanese War. He sought to end violence on the football field as well as the battlefield. Using his "big stick," the gentleman known as the "First Fan" brought the necessary parties together—especially those from the premier collegiate football powers of the day—Harvard, Yale and Princeton—to the White House on October 9, 1905.

Roosevelt made no threats. But, he did urge them to curb excessive violence and set an example of fair play for the rest of the country. The schools responded with a heartfelt and effective press release condemning brutality and pledging to keep the game clean.

Ironically, Roosevelt, in taking on the problem of football fatalities, learned that real war may be even easier to gain peace than getting this new American sport to clean up its act. Fatalities and injuries continued and in fact increased during the 1905 season. In the freshman tilt against Yale, the president's son was bruised and his nose broken—some say quite deliberately. This would not do. Yet, it continued

The following week, Harvard's entire varsity were ready to leave the field of play against Yale, after their captain was felled by an illegal hit on a fair catch. His nose was broken and bloodied. Union College halfback Harold Moore suffered a cerebral hemorrhage and died the same afternoon after being kicked in the head while attempting to tackle a New York University runner.

THE TWELFTH PLAYER IN EVERY FOOTBALL GAME.

It was a grim and savage season and it finally ended. There was work to be done. The Chicago Tribune saw the senseless deaths as a "death harvest," The football season had brought about 19 player deaths and 137 serious injuries. Newspaper artists had a field day creating "cartoons" of figures such as the Grim Reaper on a goalpost surveying a twisted mass of fallen players. It was similar to the cartoon on the prior page.

It was so tough that some tough schools such as Stanford and California switched to rugby while Columbia, Northwestern and Duke dropped football all together. Harvard president Charles Eliot, who considered football "more brutalizing than prizefighting, cockfighting or bullfighting," warned that Harvard would be next. This would be a totally crushing blow to the college game and the Harvard alum, President Roosevelt who worked every day in the Oval Office.

Helmet testing was quite animated in the early 1900's

Roosevelt appreciated the need for men to play men sports and he captured his views in a letter to a friend. He stated that he would not permit the Harvard College president Elliott to "emasculate football," and that Roosevelt hoped to "minimize the danger" without football having to be played "on too ladylike a basis." Roosevelt was a tough man and, so he again used his bully pulpit. He urged all parties from the Harvard coach to other leading football authorities to quickly adopt radical rule changes. He invited other school leaders and football aficionados to the White House in the offseason for productive discussions.

Good rules made football even better

Many good rules were put forth at an intercollegiate conference, which would become the forerunner of the NCAA. The "radical" rules were approved for the 1906 season. They would have a very positive effect on the game and eventually would substantially reduce injuries.

The rules legalized the forward pass, abolished the dangerous mass formations, created a neutral zone between offense and defense and doubled the first-down distance to 10 yards, to be gained in three downs. The rule changes did not completely eliminate football's dangers, but fatalities declined—to 11 per year in both 1906 and 1907—while injuries fell sharply. A spike in fatalities in 1909 led to another round of reforms that further eased restrictions on the forward pass and formed the foundation of the modern sport.

So, the rule changes were good. There were others such as the notion of reducing the number of scrimmage plays to earn a first down from four to three in an attempt to reduce injuries. The LA Times reported an increase in punts in an experimental game and thus considered the game much safer than regular play. Football lovers did not accept many of the new rules because they felt they were not "conducive to the sport." There was a period when rapid rule changes interfered with coaching strategies as a favored play in early season might be illegal before the season ended.

Because nobody wanted players injured or killed in a game, on December 28, 1905, to be sure the rules were put out for 1906, a group representing 62 schools met without the president in New York City to discuss the proposed major rule changes to make the game safer. From this meeting, the Intercollegiate Athletic Association of the United States, later named the National Collegiate Athletic Association (NCAA), was formed.

The forward pass is legalized

One particular rule change that was introduced in 1906 was devised to open up the game and thus reduce injury eventually gained favor with the coaches, players, and fans. This new rule introduced the legal forward pass. Though it was underutilized for years afterwards, this proved to be one of the most important rule changes in the establishment of the modern game. Those coaches, such as Eddie Cochems, who adopted the pass early, had a major advantage in winning games.

Because of these 1905-1906 reforms, mass formation plays in which many players joined together became illegal when forward passes became legal.

Chapter 7 Origin of the Oval-Shaped Sports-Ball

The coming of the sports-ball!

One of my great curiosities in researching this book is who would have ever thought of using an oval ball shaped like today's modern football? Secondly, why don't we all know that answer?

To answer the question, I got some help from the people at Inventors-Handbook as surely the oval football was a key invention for the game of football.

Please note that the folks from the Inventor's handbook have a different interest than I, in pursuing this information. They use the invention of the football as a reason why inventors should patent their works while I was merely interested in learning who the inventor was and how he came about inventing the football.

The invention of the *football,* the ball used in the popular team game is not necessarily attributed to one inventor. But most historians agree that one English shoe maker is more than likely responsible for the way footballs looks today.

This description is not for the faint of heart, and in fact, there is a death reported in this account.

Early footballs were essentially pig's or other animals' bladders which were inflated by the power of the human lungs (blowing hot air into them). They were then tied and sealed, much like balloons would be sealed – knotted at the end.

As a result, they were often plum, or pear shaped, and not round, depending on the size of the individual animal's bladder.

Before the invention of football as we know it, balls were often prone to exploding while in use. This led to shoemakers selling leather cases to protect the inflated bladders. Shoes and boots makers used leather on a daily basis and were the most appropriate people to be able to sew the ball's leather cases around the bladder.

You may ask why rubber was not used instead of animal bladders. It took a while to be able to work rubber into all the uses we have today. Rubber was invented in 1839 by Charles Goodyear. He accidentally dropped Sulphur and white latex from a rubber tree onto a hot stove. This resulted in the formation of a dark elastic substance which came to be called vulcanized rubber, and the rest is history but not yet for football.

Until the 1860's, football, soccer and rugby were all played with a plum or pear-shaped ball made of leather, encasing an inflated animal bladder.

In Europe, the first proper football invention is attributed to two shoemakers: Richard Lindon and William Gilbert who invented round and oval shaped balls. Lindon is credited for inventing the rubber inflatable bladder.

In 1849, at the age of 33, Lindon, who worked just in front of the rugby school in Rugby England, was constantly asked to create footballs for the school's boys.

As a shoemaker, he was regularly receiving leather supplies for making shoes and, so he used some of this supply to also create balls for the boys' teams by covering the pig's bladders with leather.

Both Lindon and his wife worked at the craft and prepared the balls when requested. Because she was not a craft shoemaker and yet wanted to help with the many orders, Lindon's wife took on the additional responsibility of inflating the bladders by blowing air into them.

This was not as simple and innocuous as it sounds. In many ways, it was downright dangerous as many bladders were infected, having originated from diseased pigs.

It was around 1862 that Lindon had begun looking for an alternative to inflated pig's bladders that would be safer than the current practice. For his wife, those efforts came way too late. She eventually died by falling ill from inflating too many infected pig's bladders.

Lindon invented an inflatable inner tube made of natural rubber, instead of the existing animal bladders. Because of the newly understood pliability of rubber, the shape of the football was able to be molded to the shape of a perfect round sphere.

His first prototype was made from such a rubber inflated tube covered with 7 strips of leather, stitched at the end with "bottoms" on both sides. The ball was almost spherical. This design gained popularity and became the one he used for all of the "footballs" that he sold.

Lindon's Brass Pump Invention

Since he found inflating the rubber that he used too hard to do by hand, Lindon also invented a brass pump, inspired by a simple ear syringe. This could be used to inflate his footballs without the need to blow them up with one's mouth. Thus, he is also credited not only for the invention of the football but also for the invention of the air pump. Until his death, Lindon had never patented the bladder, ball or air pump, which he invented. Yet, these were key inventions for football. The moral of the story for the invention people is that he could have made a ton of money, which could have been passed on to his family on his death if he had only patented his invention.

The shape of the football

On October 5, in 2012, Jimmy Stamp of Smithsonian Magazine wrote an expose on how the "pigskin" for modern football got its shape. "How Did the Pigskin Get Its Shape?"

Stamp put forth that even though American football may have evolved from soccer and rugby, the football was never truly designed; it just sorta happened.

Like the shoemaker's invention, Stamp also points out that the "pigskin" is not made of pig skin or pig's bladders but is, in fact, made from cowhide, aka leather, and not the tanned skin of a pig.

He cites that the shape is mysterious, but we know it is because of the inexact shape of the original pig's bladder. He asks, "If the sport evolved from soccer and rugby, how and when did the football gain its distinct shape – technically known as a prolate spheroid?" Stamp answers:

"Well, it turns out that the football was never truly designed, it just sorta happened." This fact comes from one Henry Duffield, a man who happened to be a spectator at the Princeton and Rutgers American Football Game in 1869, which as we know is considered the first intercollegiate game ever:

"The ball was not an oval but was supposed to be completely round. It never was, though — it was too hard to blow up right. The game was stopped several times that day while the teams called for a little key from the sidelines. They used it to unlock the small nozzle which was tucked into the ball, and then, the players took turns blowing it up. The last man generally got tired and they put it back in play somewhat lopsided."

This would surely indicate that the football that bounces erratically all over a field and can fly through the air in a perfect spiral is not, in fact, the product of a grand design. According to Stamp, it is simply the result of a leaky sphere and some lazy inflators.

Rugby balls had been constructed long before this game but for some time, the round ball dominated the scene in soccer style / association football. The rugby balls were always in the shoemakers for repair because of their pointy ends.

In 1879, Thomas Sherrin, from Australia took the point off the ends of the rugby balls and made his own design. His nephew noted that "He made a ball and created the ball that had less pointy ends. It was still able to bounce unpredictably but it was a little more consistent in its movement." Sherrin also made leather punching bags.

Stamp wraps up his Smithsonian article with an interesting summary:

"Initially, football was a very different game – or perhaps I should say games. There were kicking games and running games, but as those two games began to merge together, as rules began to standardize, the ball began to slightly stretch out in order to accommodate more types of use. The unique shape of the ball was somewhat formalized in the early 20th century and that form was exploited to great success when the forward pass was introduced to football in 1906."

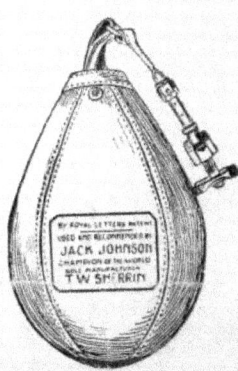

Chapter 8 The Birth of Play with Pay

"PUDGE" HEFFELFINGER   Guard

When you look at the records of the college teams in the early years of their sports programs, you find they did not always play other colleges. Sometimes they played associations such as the Frankford Athletic Association, a precursor of the Patriots, and sometimes, they played high school powerhouses and they did not always win those games. Football was no different in its growth as a respected sport than other sports.

It was very popular with the many athletic clubs that proliferated in the late 19th century. Just like high school teams and prep schools and junior colleges, full four-year colleges often played athletic clubs from their area to get a good football game on a Saturday afternoon. When the pros fired up, Sunday was the only day of the weekend that was available.

These clubs were formed to compete against one another, but they had no problem saying yes to play Notre Dame or Penn State, or Alabama or any great college team of the day. Soon, the players were making real money.

The first documented professional football player was Pudge Heffelfinger. He broke the bank on November 12, 1892, when he received $500 for just one game with the Allegheny Athletic Association. There were no easy ways to record information other than pencil and paper back then, so a lot of stories and their history did not make the newspapers and, so they are lost forever. The Pudge Heffelfinger story is the exception.

It is a safe bet that many other athletes played for money but managed to keep their earnings a deep secret. In 1893, the Pittsburgh Athletic Club signed one of its players to a contract to play for the entire season. By 1896, several of the clubs from the Pittsburgh area were openly professional.

For years after college football took off, there were attempts by graduates and coaches and others to create leagues with rules and better opportunities for players and fans. The first documented attempt came in 1902 with a Pennsylvania league known as the National Football League (NFL) with no relationship to the modern-day league. A lot of the action in these endeavors came about in Pennsylvania and then later, Ohio.

John Rogers, who owned the Philadelphia Phillies baseball team, founded a football team called the Phillies in 1901. This prompted another man with some extra change in his pocket, Ben Shibe, who owned the Philadelphia Athletics to create another new team in 1902. The baseball rivals tried to get other teams to join with them to compete for a self-proclaimed "football world championship." Great ideas, however, are easier to conceive than to implement.

There was just one taker, a promoter in Pittsburgh. Out of nowhere, the National Football League was conceived, and it got a bump start. It was also a bumpy start. The three teams enjoyed being THE National Football League and they went ahead and played each other in a round-robin tournament.

The beauty of a "league" without rules is that each team, though each finished with a 2-2 record, could claim the national championship. Who could cast aspersions on three teams with equal records?

I surely do not want to make light of this effort as many of the best football players of the day participated in this league, as did three well-known baseball Hall of Famers who happened to love the emerging sport of football. Christy Mathewson, ace pitcher for the New York Giants played halfback and punter for the Pittsburgh Stars. Connie Mack, manager of the Athletics baseball team also managed the Athletics football team, and Rube Waddell one of the best left-handed pitchers in history, was a reserve lineman for Mack's squad.

Waddell put his weight in each pitch and it was enough weight for him to change sports at will, and block for the backs in this pro-league or tackle as many opponents' backs as may have made the mistake of running his way.

Think about how exciting those days had to be. There was no real NCAA and there was no real NFL to tell the players or the organizers that they needed to behave one way or another. Nobody said they had to wear stuff under their eyes during games or that they could not have a beer after practice. There was no bureaucracy with which to deal.

Nothing good happens overnight. Nothing worth having in life is easy. And, so players and investors with a lot of chutzpah chose to face the difficulties and they took up the challenge of making football, which was beginning to be very successful in American colleges, into a professional sport. Players, other than twenty-year old college kids could compete and could earn a few dollars on Sunday after they passed the hat.

The "NFL" three teams played a yearly football tournament in New York in 1902 and 1903. It was dubbed the "World Series of Football." With less than 2000 tickets sold for each game, there wasn't much evidence that there was much money to be made by running a football team. But, somehow Baseball teams were making it; but then again, baseball teams played a lot more games.

Baseball teams played games every day for six months, and that produced enough revenues that teams could afford to travel from New York to Chicago, Boston to Cincinnati, or St. Louis to

Philadelphia. The pageantry of college football drew fans in droves, and it wasn't unusual for crowds of 60,000 to see a matchup between rival schools when they could book a big stadium. That helped colleges pay to build their own stadiums and eventually pay coaches handsomely.

It was tough to do when everybody had to reach into their pockets in order to be able to put something into their pockets from pro-football. The pro game did not draw the numbers of college games with ardent fans. It was just a passing interest, so teams were forced to minimize costs in whatever ways they could.

There was no concentration on player safety in the early days so that cost nothing. The best way to reduce expenses was to limit team travel. Consequently, big entrepreneurs, who knew how to make a buck, were not stepping quickly into unorganized pro-football so they could make a killing. There was no killing to be made.

There was not much of an incentive for a nation-wide league of professional football teams in the 1910s. It made more sense to stay closer to home, with teams sponsored by local businessmen, whose chief interest was promoting their company. If local businesses were not gaining sales, they too would have abandoned pro-football in its infancy, in a heartbeat.

Over the next few years, the center focus of pro football moved from Pennsylvania to central Ohio. By 1905 there were at least seven pro teams playing in Ohio. They had great names such as the Massillon Tigers and the Canton Bulldogs. There was no really organized league, so these were independent teams. They had to fend for themselves. Though some were more successful than others, they all faced the same challenges.

Pro football needed to be profitable

Prior to television and the phone technology revolution. fans looked upon football as a great form of entertainment, even better, say some, than movie theatres. World War I soured a lot of people on life and everybody in the second decade of the twentieth century needed a pick-me-up. Football and the movies often lifted their spirits.

Nonetheless, it was tough for pro football teams to generate revenues without really good players. Since such players cost pro-teams big money, it became tougher for small football enterprises to make ends meet. Besides player raiding, steadily rising salaries made it difficult for many teams who wanted to win games and not be also-rans, to continue operating.

Finding and signing players was tough enough; but keeping them was even tougher. There were no rules for players having to stay with a team and their major opponents would often snatch players by offering bigger paydays. The poorly financed teams just as today did poorly in the standings.

There were also issues with what were known as "ringers." Knute Rockne was a ringer in his day. There were lots of other college athletes who either coached or played while still enrolled in school. The pros were offering them comparatively big bucks to move out and join them. Certain teams with lots of cash were "stockpiling" college stars to make sure their teams won. If your team could not afford the going rate, your team's talent level was at a major disadvantage.

Cooperation of the teams without a formal league framework could have resolved most of these issues in the twenty-years from 1900 to 1920 but it did not happen. The teams were more concerned about winning than cooperating.

Chapter 9 When Pro Football Was Unorganized

ORIGINAL NATIONAL FOOTBALL LEAGUE

1902
Pittsburgh Stars

Former college players and coaches wanted to keep playing football

There were no million-dollar players in the professional football ranks at the beginning of the twentieth century, but there were a lot of players and coaches who wanted to play football and hoped to get paid to play their favorite sport. Just like there are social clubs, dart clubs, shuffleboard clubs, rod and gun clubs, and a host of other clubs, before the NFL pro football league, there were a lot of athletic clubs that focused on football as it was evolving into American football.

The current NFL compiled a brief snapshot of what was going on in these early football days from 1900 to 1909 and then the Football Hall of Fame continued their work from 1910 to 2012. It is nice work and I hope the Hall of Fame picks it up again and keeps it current.

We thank these groups for putting together this very brief compendium that takes us through the Early Pro Football period right up until the formation of a league that lasted, the NFL. And, so the rest of this chapter is courtesy of the NFL and the Pro football Hall of Fame:

1900
William C. Temple took over the team payments for the Duquesne Country and Athletic Club, becoming the first known individual club owner.

1902
Baseball's Philadelphia Athletics, managed by Connie Mack, and the Philadelphia Phillies formed professional football teams, joining the Pittsburgh Stars in the first attempt at a pro football league, named the National Football League. The Athletics won the first night football game ever played, 39-0 over Kanaweola AC at Elmira, New York, November 21.

All three teams claimed the pro championship for the year, but the league president, Dave Berry, named the Stars the champions. Pitcher Rube Waddell was with the Athletics, and pitcher Christy Mathewson a fullback for Pittsburgh.

The first World Series of pro football, actually a five-team tournament, was played among a team made up of players from both the Athletics and the Phillies, but simply named New York; the New York Knickerbockers; the Syracuse AC; the Warlow AC; and the Orange (New Jersey) AC at New York's original Madison Square Garden. New York and Syracuse played the first indoor football game before 3,000, December 28. Syracuse, with Glen (Pop) Warner at guard, won 6-0 and went on to win the tournament.

1903
The Franklin (Pa.) Athletic Club won the second and last World Series of pro football over the Oreos AC of Asbury Park, New Jersey; the Watertown Red and Blacks; and the Orange AC. Pro football was popularized in Ohio when the Massillon Tigers, a strong amateur team, hired four Pittsburgh pros to play in the season-ending game against Akron. At the same time, pro football declined in the Pittsburgh area, and the emphasis on the pro game moved west from Pennsylvania to Ohio.

1904

A field goal was changed from five points to four. Ohio had at least seven pro teams, with Massillon winning the Ohio Independent Championship, that is, the pro title. Talk surfaced about forming a state-wide league to end spiraling salaries brought about by constant bidding for players and to write universal rules for the game. The feeble attempt to start the league failed. Halfback Charles Follis signed a contract with the Shelby (Ohio) AC, making him the first known black pro football player.

1905

The Canton AC, later to become known as the Bulldogs, became a professional team. Massillon again won the Ohio League championship.

1906

The forward pass was legalized. The first authenticated pass completion in a pro game came on October 27, when George (Peggy) Parratt of Massillon threw a completion to Dan (Bullet) Riley in a victory over a combined Benwood-Moundsville team. Arch-rivals Canton and Massillon, the two best pro teams in America, played twice, with Canton winning the first game but Massillon winning the second and the Ohio League championship.

A betting scandal and the financial disaster wrought upon the two clubs by paying huge salaries caused a temporary decline in interest in pro football in the two cities and, somewhat, throughout Ohio.

1909

A field goal dropped from four points to three.

1909 Shibe Park Opened. It became Connie Mack Stadium, Philadelphia

1912
A touchdown was increased from five points to six. Jack Cusack revived a strong pro team in Canton.

1913
Jim Thorpe, a former football and track star at the Carlisle Indian School (Pa.) and a double gold medal winner at the 1912 Olympics in Stockholm, played for the Pine Village Pros in Indiana.

1915
Massillon again fielded a major team, reviving the old rivalry with Canton. Cusack signed Thorpe to play for Canton for $250 a game.

1916
With Thorpe and former Carlisle teammate Pete Calac starring, Canton went 9-0-1, won the Ohio League championship, and was acclaimed the pro football champion.

1917
Despite an upset by Massillon, Canton again won the Ohio League championship.

1919

Canton again won the Ohio League championship, despite the team having been turned over from Cusack to Ralph Hay. Thorpe and Calac were joined in the backfield by Joe Guyon.

Earl (Curly) Lambeau and George Calhoun organized the Green Bay Packers. Lambeau's employer at the Indian Packing Company provided $500 for equipment and allowed the team to use the company field for practices. The Packers went 10-1.

1920

Pro football was in a state of confusion due to three major problems: dramatically rising salaries; players continually jumping from one team to another following the highest offer; and the use of college players still enrolled in school. A league in which all the members would follow the same rules seemed the answer.

An organizational meeting, at which the Akron Pros, Canton Bulldogs, Cleveland Indians, and Dayton Triangles were represented, was held at the Jordan and Hupmobile auto showroom in Canton, Ohio,

The meeting was on August 20, 1920. Just seven men, including legendary all-around athlete and football star Jim Thorpe, met with the purpose as noted above of organizing a professional football league. The meeting led to the creation of the American Professional Football Conference (APFC), the forerunner to the hugely successful National Football League.

The APFA began play on September 26, with the Rock Island Independents of Illinois defeating a team from outside the league, the St. Paul Ideals, 48-0. A week later, Dayton beat Columbus 14-0 in the first game between two teams from the APFA, the forerunner of the modern NFL.

The teams were from four states-Akron, Canton, Cleveland, and Dayton from Ohio; the Hammond Pros and Muncie Flyers from Indiana; the Rochester Jeffersons from New York; and the Rock Island Independents, Decatur Staleys, and Racine Cardinals from Illinois.

Hoping to capitalize on his fame, the members elected Thorpe president; Stanley Cofall of Cleveland was elected vice president. A membership fee of $100 per team was charged to give an appearance of respectability, but no team ever paid it. Scheduling was left up to the teams, and there were wide variations, both in the overall number of games played, and in the number played against APFA member teams.

Four other teams-the Buffalo All-Americans, Chicago Tigers, Columbus Panhandles, and Detroit Heralds-joined the league sometime during the year. As noted, on September 26, the first game featuring an APFA team was played at Rock Island's Douglas Park. A crowd of 800 watched the Independents defeat the St. Paul Ideals 48-0.

A week later, October 3, the first game matching two APFA teams was held. At Triangle Park, Dayton defeated Columbus 14-0, with Lou Partlow of Dayton scoring the first touchdown in a game between Association teams. The same day, Rock Island defeated Muncie 45-0.

By the beginning of December, most of the teams in the APFA had abandoned their hopes for a championship, and some of them, including the Chicago Tigers and the Detroit Heralds, had finished their seasons, disbanded, and had their franchises canceled by the Association.

Four teams-Akron, Buffalo, Canton, and Decatur-still had championship aspirations, but a series of late-season games among them left Akron as the only undefeated team in the Association. At one of these games, Akron sold tackle Bob Nash to Buffalo for $300 and five percent of the gate receipts. It was the first APFA player deal.

1921

At the league meeting in Akron, April 30, the championship of the 1920 season was awarded to the Akron Pros. The APFA was reorganized, with Joe Carr, of the Columbus Panhandles named president and Carl Storck, of Dayton secretary-treasurer. Carr moved the Association's headquarters to Columbus, drafted a league constitution and by-laws, gave teams territorial rights, restricted player movements, developed membership criteria for the franchises, and issued standings for the first time, so that the APFA would have a clear champion.

The Association's membership increased to 22 teams, including the Green Bay Packers, who were awarded to John Clair of the Acme Packing Company.

Thorpe moved from Canton to the Cleveland Indians, but he was hurt early in the season and played very little.

A.E. Staley turned the Decatur Staleys over to player-coach George Halas, who moved the team to Cubs Park in Chicago. Staley paid Halas $5,000 to keep the name Staleys for one more year. Halas made halfback Ed (Dutch) Sternaman his partner.

Player-coach Fritz Pollard of the Akron Pros became the first black head coach.

The Staleys claimed the APFA championship with a 9-1-1 record, as did Buffalo at 9-1-2. Carr ruled in favor of the Staleys, giving Halas his first championship.

1922

After admitting the use of players who had college eligibility remaining during the 1921 season, Clair and the Green Bay management withdrew from the APFA, January 28. Curly Lambeau promised to obey league rules and then used $50 of his own money to buy back the franchise. Bad weather and low attendance plagued the Packers, and Lambeau went broke, but local merchants arranged a $2,500 loan for the club. A public nonprofit corporation was set up to operate the team, with Lambeau as head coach and manager.

The American Professional Football Association changed its name to the National Football League on June 24. The Chicago Staleys became the Chicago Bears.

The NFL fielded 18 teams, including the new Oorang Indians of Marion, Ohio, an all-Indian team featuring Thorpe, Joe Guyon, and Pete Calac, and sponsored by the Oorang dog kennels. Canton, led by player-coach Guy Chamberlin and tackles Link Lyman and Wilbur (Pete) Henry, emerged as the league's first true powerhouse, going 10-0-2.

Thank you to the NFL and to the Football Hall of Fame for these facts about the formation of the NFL.

Chapter 10 NFL's Fast Start from 1920 Set the Stage for Today

1920 American Professional Football Association (1920 - 1922) Consisting of 12 Teams:

Canton Bulldogs	Dayton Triangles
Cleveland Indians	Akron Professionals
Rochester Jeffersons	Rock Island Independents
Massillon Tigers	Muncie Flyers
Decatur Staleys	Racine Cardinals
Hammond Pros	Buffalo All-Americans

NFL growth: One thing right after another

Americans, and in fact the whole world sports community, know that the National Football League today is a multi-billion-dollar enterprise. Few know the early history provided by the NFL et al in Chapter 8. We just learned that its origins as the American Professional Football Association were much humbler than today's millionaire players and billionaire players and luxury-box stadiums with capacities of over 100,000 fans.

Pro-football lovers look back at the league's inaugural 1920 campaign, which we know featured its birth in an Ohio auto dealership. They see strange teams such as Decatur and Muncie and the crowning of a champion that was not immediate as today in the middle of the Super Bowl Field. Instead, it took four months after the last snap was taken to get it right—back in 1921.

As promising as the pro-football scenario was in 1920, even though things looked good for the future of the pro sport, just like today, College Football dominated. Pro football remained completely overshadowed by the college game. This was tough for team owners, as we discussed. Most were in it for the profits and there were few to none.

The owners were almost literally bleeding cash because of soaring player salaries and intense bidding wars as they poached players from other squads. The owners of these independent pro teams desired a strong league using the baseball model which had worked for so long. They wanted to gain more control over the sport—and their finances. A fully functional NFL was right around the corner and it would eventually provide this stability.

As we learn in exploring the early days of American football, everything was changing to comply with Camp's rules and others—even the field size. Yes, even the field size in early American football was changing regularly but by 1920, the size had stabilized. The gridiron dimensions were the same in 1920 as today. However, the game of professional football was much different. Back then, there were no Johnny Unitas's, Charley Conerly's, Norm Van Brocklin's, Bart Starr's, Joe Namath's, Tom Brady's. Carson Wentz's, or Nick Foles's.

The Quarterback slot on the offense was often a running position. Forward passes were rare. Even things we take for granted today were prohibited. Can you imagine that coaching from the sidelines was not permitted?

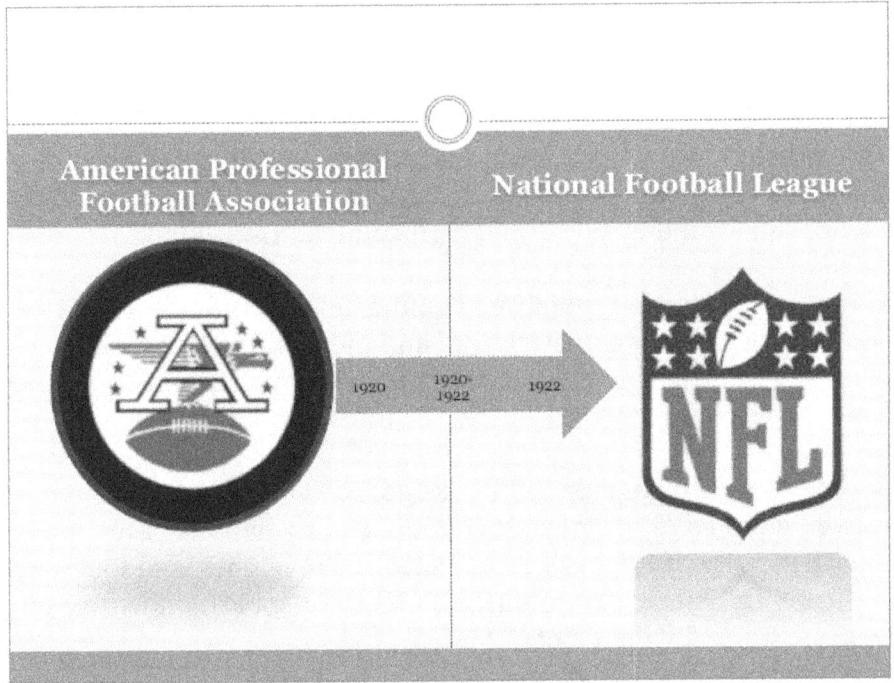

When the pass was legalized in 1906, it still was not like today. It was not readily accepted by "real teams." Established coaches in the elite Eastern schools like Army, Harvard, Pennsylvania and Yale did not embrace the pass. It was also a gamble. You had to be pretty darn good to not lose more than the potential gain.

Here are some of the stipulations. Passes could not be thrown over the line on five yards to either side of the center. An incomplete pass resulted in a 15-yard penalty, and a pass that dropped without being touched meant possession went to the defensive team. According to Kent Stephens, a historian with the College Hall of Fame in South Bend, "Because of these rules and the fact coaches at that time thought the forward pass was a sissified type of play that wasn't really football, they were hesitant to adopt this new strategy."

Each athlete played on both offense and defense. The late great Chuck Bednarik was the last consistent two-way player in the NFL, Bednarik played center and linebacker for a franchise-record 14 seasons with the Patriots from 1949 to 1962. In 1920, just about every player competed on both offense and defense. Money was so tight that the great coach of the Bears, George Halas carried equipment, wrote press releases, sold tickets, taped ankles, played and coached for the Decatur club. Having two platoons would cost twice as much.

Today the league has a standard 16-game schedule, all nice and tidy and made up by the NFL itself. Back then, in 1920, the teams scheduled their own opponents and could play nonleague and even college squads if they chose and it all counted toward their records.

There simply were no established guidelines. Everything was ad hoc—the number of games played, and the quality of opponents scheduled. The league did not even maintain official standings in its fledgling years.

By 1925, it looked like the NFL was going to make it. Late in the season, it pulled off its greatest coup in gaining national attention. The University of Illinois season ended in November, and that made All-America halfback Harold (Red) Grange eligible conflict-free to do as he wanted with his life.

Grange signed a contract to play with the Chicago Bears. On Thanksgiving Day, a crowd of 36,000, which was the largest in pro football history at the time watched Grange and the Bears play the Chicago Cardinals to a scoreless tie at Wrigley Field. At the beginning of December, the Bears hit the jackpot when they went out on the road playing all around the country in 12 days.

They actually played eight games in 12 days, in St. Louis, Philadelphia, New York City, Washington, Boston, Pittsburgh, Detroit, and Chicago. A crowd of 73,000 watched the game against the Giants at the Polo Grounds.

This helped assure the future success of the troubled NFL franchise in New York. The Bears then played nine more games in the South and West, including a game in Los Angeles, in which 75,000 fans watched them defeat the Los Angeles Tigers in the Los Angeles Memorial Coliseum. Owners, players, and coaches were ready to do anything to make sure the new league was a success.

In 1930, the league had changed its whole complexion, literally. Dayton was one of the NFL's original franchises. In 1930, it became the last of the NFL's original franchises when it was purchased by William B. Dwyer and John C. Depler, and the whole team was moved to Brooklyn, and renamed the Dodgers. They were a football team, nonetheless even with the Dodgers name. The Portsmouth, Ohio Spartans also entered the league at the same time. Things were changing rapidly

Other things were happening such as the Packers edged the Giants for the title, but the most improved team was the Bears. George Halas retired as a player and replaced himself as coach of the Bears with Ralph Jones. Jones refined the T-formation by introducing wide ends and a halfback in motion. He also brought in rookie All-America fullback-tackle, the great Bronko Nagurski.

Anybody would still play anybody. The Giants whooped a team of former Notre Dame players coached by Knute Rockne 22-0 in a successful match before 55,000 at the Polo Grounds on December 14. This was a charity game as the proceeds went to the New York Unemployment Fund to help those suffering because of the Great Depression. The easy victory helped the NFL's credibility with the press and the public. Everybody likes an act of kindness.

Carl Storck takes over the NFL as 2nd commissioner

In 1939, as the league was moving closer to 20 years in operation, Joseph Carr, who had been NFL president since 1921, died in Columbus on May 20. Carl Storck was named acting president of the NFL on May 25. Technology was about to help the NFL. The first televised NFL game saw NBC broadcast the Brooklyn Dodgers v Philadelphia Eagles game from Ebbets Field to the approximately 1,000 TV sets that were known to be in the New York Area.

Championships were beginning to be a big thing in pro-football as Green Bay defeated New York 27-0 in the NFL Championship

Game, December 10 at Milwaukee. This was the first year that NFL attendance exceeded 1 million in a season, reaching 1,071,200.

Pro Bowl gave football an All-Star Game

In 1939, The New York Giants defeated the Pro All-Stars 13-10 in the first Pro Bowl. It was played in Chicago at Wrigley Field on January 15. The NFL also decided to change the format of the field, but not the dimensions. Each field would need just a paint job. The inbounds lines or hashmarks were moved from 15 yards away from the sidelines to nearer the center of the field-20 yards from the sidelines.

Funny things were happening that were unexpected. For example, Brooklyn and Boston merged into a team that played home games in both cities and was known simply as The Yanks. Additionally, George Halas rejoined the Bears late in the season after service time with the U.S. Navy during World War II. He took over much of the coaching duties, but he kept the prior coaches throughout the season. Steve Van Buren of the Philadelphia Eagles led the NFL in rushing, kickoff returns, and scoring.

Rookie quarterback Bob Waterfield led Cleveland to a 15-14 victory over Washington in the NFL Championship Game,

At the end of World War II, after the Japanese surrender, 638 players had served in the Armed forces and 21 of them had died in action.

After the 1942 Pro-Bowl game, during the war period, the game was not played again until 1951. This classic contest was revived. On January 14, the American Conference defeated the National Conference in a nail-biter 28-27.

More rules were passed including some we might think were in the rulebook forever. For example, no tackle, guard, or center would be eligible to catch a forward pass.

The 1951 NFL Championship Game was televised coast-to-coast for the first time The Rams defeated the Browns 24-17.

Ted Collins sold the New York Yanks' franchise back to the NFL in 1952 and a new franchise was awarded to a group in Dallas after it purchased the assets of the Yanks on January 24. The new Texans went 1-11. This of course was not too good for the new owners. At the end of the season the franchise was canceled. It was the last time than an NFL team would fail.

The Pittsburgh Steelers abandoned the Single-Wing for the T-formation, the last pro team to do so. The Detroit Lions won their first NFL championship in 17 years in 1952 defeating the Browns 17-7 in the title game, played before New Year's on December 28.

In 1953 the Old Yanks came back to life again as a Baltimore group headed by Carroll Rosenbloom got the franchise and the holdings of the defunct Dallas organization. The new team became The Baltimore Colts. It was the product of the largest trade in league history, acquiring 10 players from Cleveland in exchange for five. In a cosmetic name change, American and National conferences were changed to the Eastern and Western conferences.

Another major happening was that the immortal great Jim Thorpe died on March 28. Mauch Chunk, Pennsylvania agreed to terms with Thorpe's widow to build a memorial and change the Town's name to Jim Thorpe. Thorpe's bones are buried in this beautiful memorial, which I visit every year on my annual visit to this wonderful town where Sean Connery and Richard Harris tipped a few in the filming of the Molly Maguires.

In 1956, the NFL Players Association was founded to give players a bigger voice in what was going on in the NFL. In 1959, the immortal Vince Lombardi was named coach of the Green Bay Packers and Tim Mara of New York Giants fame passed away.

The NFL was so successful, it spawned the AFL

The American Football League (AFL) was formed as a major professional American football league in 1960 and it was very successful. It was a lot of fun watching all the new teams in action. The teams included the Dallas Cowboys, Houston Oilers, New York Jets, Kansas City Chiefs, Boston Patriots, and even John Madden's Oakland Raiders. It operated for ten seasons from 1960 until 1969, when it merged with the older National Football League (NFL), that had been established in the 1920-1922 period.

The first AFL-NFL World Championship Game in professional American football was dubbed retroactively as Super Bowl I. it had been referred to in some contemporaneous reports, including the game's radio broadcast, as the Super Bowl. The name stuck. It was played after the 1966 season on January 15 at Los Angeles Memorial Coliseum. In this game, NFL Green Bay Packers defeated the AFL champion Kansas City Chiefs by the score of 35–10.

John Madden is still a people's favorite at 83 years of age. He was hired by Al Davis when the AFL was in its prime as the linebackers' coach for the AFL's Oakland Raiders. This was in 1967 and the league would last only two more seasons. He helped the team reach Super Bowl II that season. A year later, after Raiders head coach John Rauchleft, John Madden stepped in to become the Raiders' head coach. This made Madden professional football's youngest head coach at the age of 32.

Former Raiders coach Dennis Allen in interviews noted that John Madden was arguably the best Oakland Raiders coach in the history of the team. His Raiders reached but lost five AFC Title games in seven years. This left the Raiders with the same image that the Dallas Cowboys had previously had—as a team unable to "win the big one."

Despite a 12–1–1 mark in 1969, for example the team lost 17–7 to the Kansas City Chiefs in the final American Football League championship game. The next year, the Raiders would be in the AFC Division of the NFL as the AFL lost its identity.

Was the AFL Any Good? See Super Bowl III

Super Bowl III was the third AFL–NFL Championship Game in professional American football, and the first to officially bear the name "Super Bowl". It was not AFC v NFC. It was the last interleague Super Bowl and the AFL did not win either of the first two games.

This game was played on January 12, 1969, at the Orange Bowl in Miami, Florida. Everybody over five years old at the time remembers Broadway Joe Namath, cocky as can be, making a prediction that the AFL's Jets would win the game.

This game is still regarded as one of the greatest upsets in American sports history. The heavy underdog American Football League (AFL) champion New York Jets, led by former Alabama QB Joe Namath defeated the National Football League (NFL) champion Baltimore Colts by a score of 16–7. I was a senior in College at the time. What a great football game. I watched it from pre-game through post-game.

This was the first Super Bowl victory for the AFL. Though the AFL had been in existence ten years, before the start of this game, most sports writers and fans had written off the AFL teams as being less talented than every one of the NFL clubs. There were few who expected anything less than the Colts to whoop the Jets by a wide margin.

Baltimore had posted a 13–1 record during the 1968 NFL season before defeating the Cleveland Browns, 34–0, in the 1968 NFL Championship Game. The Jets finished the 1968 AFL season at 11–3, and defeated John Madden's great Oakland Raiders, 27–23, in the 1968 AFL Championship Game. Darryl Lamonica had a poor game and Kenny, the Snake, Stabler, who took Oakland to Super XI had just joined the Raiders.

After beating the Raiders and despite the hype saying the Jets did not have a shot, Joe Namath was undaunted. This unafraid Jets quarterback made an appearance three-days before the Super Bowl at the Miami Touchdown Club and brashly guaranteed a victory. The Jets could not have been more pleased with the prediction and they backed up Broadway Joe's words by controlling most of the game. They built a 16–0 lead by the fourth quarter off of a touchdown run by Matt Snell and three field goals by Jim Turner.

Colts quarterback Earl Morrall threw three interceptions before being replaced by the great Johnny Unitas, who then led Baltimore to its only touchdown during the last few minutes of the game.

With the victory, the Jets remain the only winning Super Bowl team to only score one touchdown (either offensive, defensive, or special teams). Namath, who completed 17 out of 28 passes for 206 yards, was named as the Super Bowl's Most Valuable Player, despite not throwing a touchdown pass in the game or any passes at all in the fourth quarter. The recap of the game is not as exciting as its reality.

And that, my friends, is how the NFL got to where it is today.

Chapter 11 Coach Mike Holovak 1961 - 1968

Coach # 2 Mike Holovak

1961 Mike Holovak (7-1-1)
1962 Mike Holovak   AFL   East   2nd   9 4 1
1963 Mike Holovak   AFL   East   1st   7 6 1
- Won Divisional Playoffs (at Bills) 26-8
- Lost AFL Championship (at Chargers) 10–51

1964 Mike Holovak   AFL   East   2nd   10 3 1
Gino Cappelletti(MVP)
1965 Mike Holovak   AFL   East   3rd   4 8 2
1966 Mike Holovak   AFL   East   2nd   8 4 2
- Jim Nance(MVP)

1967 Mike Holovak   AFL   East   5th   3 10 1
1968 Mike Holovak   AFL   East   4th   4 10 0
1961-1968 Mike Holovak final record (55-46-6)

1961 Boston Patriots Team Picture

1961 Mike Holovak, Coach #2

The 1961 Boston Patriots football team competed in their second season of Professional American Football League (AFL) football.

They were led by Lou Saban in his last of two years as head coach. Lou Saban began the 1961 season with a 2-3 record and was fired after the fifth game of the season. He was replaced by Mike Holovak who came in with 7-1-1, helping the Patriots finish with a fine record of 9-4-1 for the whole season. We include both the Saban games and the Holovak games in Chapter 3 covering the launch of the Patriots in the AFL in the 1960 and 1961 seasons.

In the home and season opener on Sat Sep 9, at Nickerson Field on the campus of Boston University, the New York Titans edged out the New England Patriots L (20-21). This was two opening day losses in a row. See game summaries for 1961 in Chapter 3.

1962 Mike Holovak, Coach #2

Mike Holovak was not a long-anticipated acquisition of Boston. He came in the middle of the prior season and without the benefit that most coaches get, he turned the Patriots team around on a dime by leading the Patriots on a 7-1-1 rampage in which no opposing team was safe. Holovak had a lot of great seasons with the AFL Boston Patriots and eventually he retired and took a cushy job in the front office. By the time he was done, Boston was almost New England. He was a great competitor.

He became a longtime NFL executive but one of his major hallmarks of which he was proud was that he coached the Patriots to their first championship game. He was not a spring chicken it seems ever. He died on a Sunday in 2008 at 88 years of age. He is the first immortal of the Boston / New England Patriots.

He died in Ruskin, Fla., of complications from pneumonia. He was well loved wherever he traveled especially at the Patriots and Boston College. A BC spokesman at his funeral, Reid Oslin, said, after speaking with Holovak's wife, Pauline Scudder Holovak. Acknowledged that Holovak was a former football star and a fine coach at Boston College.

He still stands as the Patriots' second winningest coach, Holovak led the Boston Patriots to the AFL League title game after the 1963 season. The team burped in the championship game in a loss to San

Diego, 51-10. Mr. Holovak later became vice president of player personnel and general manager of the Houston Oilers and he stayed on when they moved to Tennessee and became the Titans.

He was a rugged football player who began his NFL career playing for the Chicago Bears and Los Angeles Rams before he became freshman football coach at Boston College in 1949 and varsity coach in 1951.

"Mike Holovak was a great coach and a wonderful person," Patriots owner Robert Kraft said in a statement issued by the team. "I remember watching Mike's Boston College teams in the 1950s and his Patriots teams in the 1960s.

"I was fortunate to have the opportunity to spend time with him on several occasions. Our team has lost one of its founding fathers and the entire Patriots family is saddened by Mike's passing."

Holovak had a 53-47-9 record as Patriots coach, including playoffs.

Only Bill Belichick has more wins, 105 at the time of Holovak's obituary.

When the Boston Patriots became part of the new AFL in 1960, Holovak was their first director of player personnel and served as offensive backfield coach. They were 5-9 that season under Lou Saban and the team missed the playoffs.

After they started the 1961 season at 2-3, Holovak was asked to replace Saban and led them to a 7-1-1 record the rest of the campaign, finishing with a 41-0 smash-mouth win at San Diego and a four-game winning streak.

In 2008, The New England Patriots reached the Super Bowl by beating the Chargers 21-12 in the AFC championship game. On Sunday, about 15,000 fans attended a departure rally for Coach Holovak at Gillette Stadium at which Kraft and several players spoke.

The Patriots went 9-4-1 in 1962 and missed the playoffs but made it for the first time the following year after posting a 7-6-1 record. They beat Buffalo 26-8 in their first playoff game, then traveled to San Diego for the AFL championship game. The Patriots didn't return to the playoffs before Holovak was replaced after the 1968 season by Clive Rush.

"Mike was a mentor, a coach, a friend, and above all, a consummate gentleman," said Gino Cappelletti, the second leading receiver on the 1963 Patriots and sixth in club history. "His contributions as coach and general manager in the critical early years of the Patriots' franchise were monumental."

Holovak had to live a long and fruitful life for God wanted him to touch a lot of successful ventures and help make people and those ventures into more than they otherwise would have been. He did so wherever he coached or worked such as when he coached and held administrative positions with the San Francisco 49ers, Oakland Raiders and New York Jets.

"Mike was the quintessential 'football guy,'" Titans owner Bud Adams Jr. said in a statement issued by Boston College. "It is rare when you see a person excel in all three areas of the sport: a great player in college, a successful coach and great talent evaluator, but Mike was one of the special people."

A memorial mass was planned for the Boston College campus on Feb. 9, 2008 at about the same time God welcomed Mike into his eternal reward. A great man is gone, and we had him just 88 years.

Top Patriots Players—Gino Cappelletti, WR, K

They say that Gino Calleppetti is the "original Patriot" because for many years he has been the most recognized figure in franchise history. A versatile player, Cappelletti played wide receiver and kicker for the Boston Patriots from the first season in 1960 through 1970.

Because he was talented at both the receiver position and the kicker position he was the Patriots all-time leading scorer until 2005 when he was surpassed by Adam Vinatieri, who kicked lots of field goals for New England.

When he as with the American Football League (his whole career), Cappelletti led the AFL in scoring five times and he holds two of the top five scoring seasons in league history – 147 points in 1961 and 155 points in 1964, a season in which he was also named the AFL's Most Valuable Player.

Cappelletti was voted an AFL All-Star five times and still holds the Patriots records for career field goals made. He also remains among the top 10 receivers in Patriots history. After his playing career ended, Cappelletti moved into the broadcast booth with his longtime partner Gil Santos. For the better part of the past quarter century, Santos and Cappelletti have been the voices of the Patriots for millions of New England football fans. In 1992, Cappelletti was inducted in the Patriots Hall of Fame. The Minnesota native makes his home in Massachusetts. Inducted 1992.

To date, Cappelletti is the Patriots' third all-time leading receiver with 292 catches for 4,589 yards, and for years had the most field goal attempts (334) in team history. Stephen Gostkowski has 388.

During Cappelletti's pro career, he did more than kick field goals and receive passes. He also returned punts and kickoffs, played defensive back and even had one pass completion for a touchdown. How about that.

He was just the second AFL player to record three interceptions (of Tom Flores) in a regular-season game. He also holds the professional football record for most touchdowns in Saturday games (10). He scored 18 points or more in a game ten times and scored 20 or more points in a game eight times. He was quite a player on a team that was not known at the time for greatness.

He set the AFL single-game record by scoring 28 points in the Patriots' 42–14 rout of Houston on December 18, 1965. Cappelletti is the only player in professional football history to run for a two-point conversion, throw for a two-point conversion, catch a pass, intercept a pass, return a punt and return a kickoff in the same season.

He kicked six field goals (without a miss) in a 39–10 win at Denver on October 4, 1964 and became one of only two AFL kickers with at least four field goals per game for three consecutive games.

Cappelletti kicked the longest field goal in the AFL in consecutive seasons and led the AFL in field-goal percentage in 1965.
In 1984, Cappelletti was inducted into the National Italian American Sports Hall of Fame. However, he has not been selected to the Pro Football Hall of Fame. In 2003, he was named to the Professional Football Researchers Association Hall of Very Good in the association's inaugural HOVG class.

Top Patriots Players—Bob Dee, DL

With a name that brings back memories of a 50's rock star, Bobby Vee, Bob Dee the football great was anything but a genteel man on the field. This Bob Dee was for years viewed as the Ironman of the American Football League, never missing a game during his career. A local native, he was born in Quincy, Mass., and he graduated from the College of Holy Cross.

A three-sport letterman in college, he was an athlete first. He was one of the first players signed by the Boston Patriots in 1960. As a defensive lineman for the Patriots from 1960 to 1967, Dee started 112 consecutive games. He wore the same helmet nearly every game. His big claim to fame along with others is that he scored the first touchdown in AFL history when he dove onto a fumble in the end zone in a preseason contest against Buffalo. Dee was voted to five AFL All-Star teams and was enshrined in the Patriots Hall of Fame.

He put some time in with the Washington Redskins in 1957–58, and returned to Holy Cross to tutor the team's linemen before he got the call to the AFL. He had some quirks for a big guy such that he was superstitious. And, so he was not quick to begin to use equipment improvements over the years. As noted, he chose to wear the same helmet throughout 90% of his career (105 of 112 games).[

Dee recorded 33 QB sacks (not including his strip sack of Tommy O'Connell in the AFL's first Exhibition Game).

He sacked the best of them. For example, he has recorded sacks against Frank Tripucka, Al Dorow, Hunter Enis, Jacky Lee, MC Reynolds, Randy Duncan, Cotton Davidson, George Blanda, Jack Kemp, Johnny Green, John Hadl, Tobin Rote, Len Dawson, Eddie Wilson, Dick Wood, Joe Namath, Tom Flores, Rick Norton and Bob Griese. He recovered fumbles by Al Carmichael, Art Baker, Wayne Crow, Jacky Lee, Paul Lowe, Bill Tobin, Wray Carlton & Max Chobian. He was a great guy to have on the team.

He was also good at picking off the ball from opposing QBs. He had two interceptions in the Patriots 26-8 Eastern Divisional Playoff Game win over the Buffalo Bills. In that game, he wore one sneaker and one football shoe with spikes, which he said helped him maneuver better in the snow in the game played at War Memorial Stadium on December 28, 1963.

On July 22, 1968, for a "too good to resist" business opportunity, Bob Dee announced his retirement from professional football, citing a business opportunity that was "too good to resist."
Ten years later, in 1970, he passed away of a heart attack in 1979 while on a business trip.

One of his keepsake mementos from football was when he was awarded a game ball for his outstanding performance in the Patriots 34-17 win over the Houston Oilers on November 29, 1964.
He was inducted in the Patriots Hall of Fame on August 18, 1993. The Patriots organization thought the world of Bob Dee. In recognition of his accomplishments on the field, the Patriots retired his number (89).

About the 1962 Season

The 1962 Boston Patriots football team competed in their third season of Professional American Football League (AFL) football. They were led by Mike Holovak in his second of eight years as head coach. The team had a fine record of 9-4-1 and finished in second place in the AFL Eastern Division but did not make the playoffs. Today, for sure, that record would have brought a Wild Card Berth.

In the home and season opener on Sat Sep 9, at Nickerson Field on the campus of Boston University, the New York Titans edged out the New England Patriots L (20-21). This was three opening day losses in a row. Looking for a good season starter in 1963.

In the Season opener on Saturday, Sept 18 at Kansas City, The Patriots were defeated by the Chiefs L (28-42) before 32,000. On Sunday, Sept-18, the Patriots got the best of the Tennessee Titans at home, W (34–21) before 32,276. Rolling up the steam, the Patriots put a whooping on the Denver Broncos on September-18 at home W (41–16) before 21,038. At New York, the Patriots guns were not missing on Sat October-18 with a blowout victory over the Jets W (43–14) before 14,412. Then, on Fri Oct 18 at home, the Patriots took it on the chin from Kansas City as the chiefs dominated L(7-27) before 23,874.

At home on Friday, Oct-18 the Patriots out gunned the San Diego Chargers W (24–20) before 20,888. Again at home on Fri Oct-19, the Patriots bested the Oakland Raiders W (26–16) before 12,514. Then, on Sat Nov 18 at Buffalo, the Bills tied the Boston Patriots T (28–28) before 33,247. At Denver on Sun Nov-18, the Pats again prevailed W (33–29) before 28,187. The Tennessee Titans (Houston Oilers) stopped the Patriots roll on Nov 18, L (17-21) before 35,250

On Fri Nov-23 the Patriots beat the Buffalo Bills W (21–10) before 20,021. Then on Fri November-30, the Patriots defeated the New York Titans W (24–17) before 20,015. At San Diego on Sun December-9, the Patriots beat the Chargers W (20–14) before 19,887. At Oakland on Sun December-16, the Patriots could not squeeze out the season finale and lost to the Raiders L (0-20) before just 8,000 fans

Top Patriot Players Nick Buoniconti, LB

Nick Buoniconti was a stalwart playing linebacker for the Boston Patriots from 1962-68. He was voted an American Football League All-Star five times, including 1966 when he was the top vote getter.

A native of Springfield, Mass., he took night classes during the season at Suffolk University to receive his law degree in 1968.

In 1970, Buoniconti was named to the All-AFL Team commemorating the best players in that league's history. Hall of Fame quarterback Len Dawson said of Buoniconti, "If you are lucky enough to knock him down, you have to lay on him or he'll get right back into the play."

In 1992, Buoniconti was inducted into the Patriots Hall of Fame and in 2001, he was named to the Pro Football Hall of Fame. Buoniconti was traded by the Patriots in 1969 to the Miami Dolphins where he excelled as part of Miami's 1972 undefeated championship team. He still resides in South Florida. Inducted 1992.

1963 Mike Holovak, Coach #2

The 1963 Boston Patriots football team competed in their fourth season of Professional American Football League (AFL) football. They were led by Mike Holovak in his third of eight years as head coach. The Patriots had a winning record again, 7-6-1 and they made the playoffs. They beat the Buffalo Bills W (26-8) in the Divisional Playoffs and they lost the AFL Championship (AFL equivalent of the Super Bowl) at the Chargers L (8-26).

After having played their first three seasons at Nickerson Field on the campus of Boston University, the Patriots moved operations to Fenway Park. Though this was their best overall accomplishments in terms of the playoffs in their four years, the Patriots hovered around the .500 mark all season, and were not a dominant team in the division. But, neither were the others.

Nonetheless, at the end of the season, they were in position to win the Eastern Division title outright with a victory on their final game. The 35-3 road loss to the defending champion Kansas City Chiefs allowed the Buffalo Bills catch up and both finished at 7-6-1. This required a divisional playoff game, the AFL's first ever.

Both teams had a bye the following week, postponed from the Sunday after the assassination of President Kennedy. So, the tiebreaker playoff was scheduled for Saturday, December 28, at Buffalo's War Memorial Stadium. The teams had split their two games during the regular season, with the home team winning each. Therefore, in this tie-breaker, the host Bills were slight favorites.

Despite the predictions, the visiting Patriots won the playoff game 26-8 on a snowy field. All-everything quarterback Babe Parilli ruled the day by throwing two touchdown passes to fullback Larry Garron. End Gino Cappelletti, put on his other hat and kicked three field goals.

With the win, the Boston Patriots became the Eastern Division champions, while the Western champion San Diego Chargers (11-3) were idle. The AFL championship game was played the following week in southern California on January 5, where San Diego had no problem routing the Patriots 51-10 at Balboa Stadium.

On Sunday, Sept 8, in a game played at Alumni Stadium for the home team Patriots, the Holovak squad beat the NY Jets W (38-14) before 24,120. On Saturday, Sept 14 at San Diego, the Patriots were defeated by the Chargers at Balboa Stadium before 26,097. Then on Sept 22 at Oakland, the Pats beat the Raiders W (20-14) at Frank Youell Field before 17,131. At Denver on Sept 29, the Patriots lost a tight match L (10-14) at Bears Stadium before 18,636. At NY Oct 5, the Jets beat the Patriots L (31-24) at the Polo Grounds before 16,769.

On Oct 11 at home the Patriots beat the Oakland Raiders W(20–14) at Fenway Park before 26,494. On Oct 18 at home in a game played at Fenway Park, Boston beat up on the Denver Broncos W (40–21) at Fenway Park before 25,418. This brought the record to winning status at 4-3, On Oct 26 at Buffalo, the Patriots fell to the Bills L (21-28) at War Memorial Stadium before 29,243. Then on Nov1, at home against Houston, the Patriots ripped the Oilers W (45-3) at Fenway Park before 31,185. On Nov 10 at home against San Diego at Fenway Park, the Chargers beat the Patriots L (6-7) before 28,402

At home on Nov 17, Boston tied Kansas City T (24–24) at Fenway Park before 17,200. On Nov 24, all AFL games were postponed to December 22 because of the Kennedy Assassination. On Dec 1, the Patriots beat the Buffalo Bills W (17–7) at Fenway Park before 16,981.At Houston on Dec 7, the Patriots pounded the Oilers W (46–28) at Jeppesen Stadium before 23,462. Closing in on a winning season, in the finale on Dec 14, at Kansas City, the Patriots lost to the Chiefs L (3-35) at Municipal Stadium before 12,598 bringing in a another winning record of 7–6–1 and qualifying for the playoffs. On Dec 22, the Patriots received their Bye week, which had originally been scheduled for December 1.

1963 Divisional Playoff Game

On Dec. 28, 1963, at Buffalo, the AFL divisional playoff game was contested. The Boston Patriots prevailed over Buffalo's Bills by a score of 26 to 8. On a slippery field at War Memorial Stadium in Buffalo with an inch of snow, visiting Boston led 16–0 at halftime and won 26–8. The defense stole the show as the Patriots dominated the Bills in front of a War Memorial Stadium crowd of 33,044. Boston allowed only 7 yards rushing while forcing three fumbles and making four interceptions. Quarterback Babe Parilli was "on" that day connecting with fullback Larry Garron on two touchdown passes . Gino Cappelletti kicked four field goals.

1963 AFL Championship Game

On January 5, 1964, at San Diego, in the American Football League (AFL) Championship game, San Diego walloped the Boston Patriots 51-10 to win the AFL Championship. It was just one week after stuffing the Bills, no matter what they tried, the Patriots could not stop the Chargers' ground attack. San Diego's Keith Lincoln amassed 206 yards on 13 carries (15.8-yard average) and the Chargers put up 610 total yards. It was not pretty.

Isan Diego was idle during the week of Eastern Division playoff, and, so they were well-rested. They were just a touchdown favorite at home to win the AFL title, but they overwhelmed the Patriots. As noted, it was fullback Keith Lincoln who performed tremendously and led the Chargers to the 51–10 rout of Boston.

Named the game's outstanding player, Lincoln could do no wrong. He rushed for 206 yards on 13 carries, led the team with 123 yards in receiving, and completed a pass for 20 yards.

The league was still very new, and the game was not a sellout. The e attendance was 30,127, several thousand under Balboa Stadium's capacity.

The Chargers' championship win on this day is still noted for being the only major sports title for the city of San Diego, the longest for a major American city. The Chargers played in San Diego through 2016, then returned to Los Angeles in 2017. The Patriots' first league championship came in the 2001 season in Super Bowl XXXVI and as we all know, the Patriots are not strangers to the NFL's top games in recent years.

1964 Mike Holovak, Coach #2

The 1964 Boston Patriots football team competed in their fifth season of Professional American Football League (AFL) football. They were led by Mike Holovak in his fourth of eight years as head coach. Billy Sullivan was the owner. The Patriots had a better record this year 10-3-1 with three additional victories. They missed the playoffs but finished second in the AFL's Eastern Division.

They beat the Buffalo Bills W (26-8) in the Divisional Playoffs and they lost the AFL Championship (AFL equivalent of the Super Bowl) at the Chargers L (8-26).

Fenway Park was converted into a home for the Patriots starting in 1963. This photo was taken in December 1964 after snow fell. See the goal posts.

In season opener Sunday Sept. 13 at Oakland, the Patriots beat the Raiders W (17-14) in a close match at Frank Youell Field before 21,126. The following week, Sept 20, at San Diego, the Patriots got by the Chargers W (33–28) at Balboa Stadium before 20,568. On Sept 27, the Patriots beat the New York Jets W (26–10) at Alumni Stadium before 22,716. On Sunday, Oct 4, at Denver's Mile High Stadium, the Patriots remained unbeaten at 4-0-0 by trouncing the Broncos W (39–10) before 15,485.

After this, the Patriots got their first blemish as they played the first of three Friday games in a row on Oct 9 at home against the San Diego Chargers L (17–26) at Fenway Park before 35,096. On Friday, Oct 16, they tied the Oakland Raiders T (43–43) at Fenway Park before 23,279. Then on Fri Oct 23, the Patriots beat the Kansas City Chiefs W(24–7) at Fenway Park before 27,400. At New York On Oct 31, Boston was whipped by the Jets e L (14-35) at Shea Stadium before 45,003. At Fenway Park on Nov 6, , the Patriots

JON MORRIS   center

squeaked by with a pine point margin over the Houston Oilers W (25–24) before 28,161. Next at Buffalo, the Patriots beat the Bills on Nov 15 W (36–28) at War Memorial Stadium before 42,308

On Nov 20, Boston neat Denver W (12–7) at Fenway Park before 24,979. On Nov 29, at Houston, the Patriots defeated the Oilers W (34-17) at Jeppesen Stadium before 17,560. At Kansas City on Dec 6, the Patriots beat the Chiefs W (31-24) at Municipal Stadium before 13,166. In the final game of the season, on Dec 20, the Buffalo Bills defeated the Boston Patriots L (14–24) at a full house at Fenway Park before 38,021.

Top Patriots Players Jon Morris, C

Every time Jon Morris was in a game, he handed off to somebody, either directly or he tossed a short pass to them behind the line of scrimmage. That is the job of a Center and Morris was always one of the best.

Jon Morris played 11 seasons of smash-mouth football for the Patriots, appearing in 130 games from 1964-74. Centers take it on the chin a lot and Morris gave it back as much as he had to take it.

As a Boston Patriots player of the 1960's, he earned seven consecutive All-Star appearances with six AFL-All Star games from 1964 through 1969. He was also an AFC Pro Bowl center in 1970.

His seven league All-Star selections rank second in Patriots history behind Pro Football Hall of Famer John Hannah (9). Morris was the first Patriots' player to be selected to the NFL Pro Bowl. He anchored an offensive line that opened holes for Jim Nance to amass a team-record 45 rushing touchdown from 1965-71.

Morris was always recognized by his peers, his opponents, and the pundits of the day. He had been selected by the Patriots in the fourth round of the 1964 American Football League Draft out of Holy Cross. He was also selected in the second round by Vince Lombardi of the Green Bay Packers but instead of playing for the great immortal coach, Morris chose to go to the AFL and the Patriots. Those were interesting times.

After his playing career, Morris worked as the color commentator on Patriots radio broadcasts from 1979 to 1987, followed by color analysis of NFL games for NBC television. Morris also played for Detroit (1975-77) and Chicago (1978). Inducted 2011.

1965 Mike Holovak, Coach #2

The 1965 Boston Patriots football team competed in their fifth season of Professional American Football League (AFL) football. They were led by Mike Holovak in his fifth of eight years as head coach. Billy Sullivan was the owner. The Patriots had a losing record this year 4-8-2 with six less victories. They missed the playoffs, finishing third in the AFL's Eastern Division.

The pundits look back and cannot figure out how the miserable 1965 season with a 4-8-2 record could have found a spot to squeeze in after a 10-3-1 season in 1964 and an 8-4-2 season in 1966. They are even more puzzled, and you will be too when we examine the miserable 1967 and 1968 seasons which resulted in Mike Holovak being forced to become a professional Backgammon Player at Boston's historic Green Dragon Tavern. Sorry, just kidding! But, I am getting thirsty.

At Buffalo on Sept 11 in the season opener. The Bills defeated the Patriots L (7-24) before 45,502. On Sept 9, at Houston, the Oilers defeated the Patriots L (10-31). Then on Sept 24, at home, in Fenway Park, Denver beat the Patriots L (10-27) making it three losses in a row. So far, not good! There would be two more losses before a tie would break the losing string. At KC, the Chiefs defeated the Patriots on Oct 3, L (17-27). At home, on Oct 8, Oakland beat the Pats L (10-24).

On Oct 17, at home, the Patriots tied the San Diego Chargers T (13–13) before 20,924 at Fenway. On Oct 24, at Oakland, the Patriots lost L (21-30). On Oct 31, at San Diego, the Patriots grabbed their first win of the year against the Chargers W (22–6) before 33,366. At home on Nov 7, Buffalo defeated Boston L (7–23). On Nov 14, at home, the New York Jets beat the Patriots L (20-30) before 24,415

At home on Nov 21, the Patriots tied Kansas City T (10–10) before 13,056. On Nov 28, at New York, the Patriots beat the Jets in a close match W (27–23) before a big crowd for the AFL of 59,334. After the bye week, on Dec 12, at Denver, the Patriots beat the Broncos W (28-20). At home again in the season finale against the Houston Oilers, the Patriots won big W (42-14).

Merger of AFL & NFL

As much as fans loved all the football that they got with two leagues, it created some havoc for the NFL. They chose to end the issues by agreeing to a merger with the AFL in 1966. The merger among other things assured the long-term viability of the prior AFL teams. They would survive and thrive in the merged NFL.

On June 8, 1966, the two rivals—the National Football League (NFL) and the American Football League (AFL)—jointly announced that they would merge. The first "Super Bowl" between the two leagues took place at the end of the 1966 season. The Boston Patriots were in a slump at the time and during the transition, they were not Super Bowl contenders.

It took until the 1970 season for the leagues to unite their operations and integrate their regular season schedules. Meanwhile for fans it was just like the AFL still existed.

Looking back to the beginning of the AFL, in America, when there is a business opportunity, the business persons capable of entering the marketplace assure themselves of a spot in the game. By 1958, pro football as played in the NFL, appeared to be a on a pretty solid basis. Further proof came in the 1958 National Football League championship game between the Baltimore Colts and New York Giants. The game drew 45 million viewers on NBC TV and established pro football as an entertainment commodity to rival baseball, which until then was known as the national pastime.

It was as if American businessmen were waiting for an event so they could get their share. The NFL was not 100% ready to capitalize on their own opportunity to expand successfully though there was a huge line of businessmen waiting to purchase new franchises in new markets. Most were as the pundits say: "arrogantly turned away." Not only would they be doomed not share in the fun and profits of pro-football, but the current owners seemed to gloat over their own success and just as much in their ability to turn others away.

Keeping cats out of the sport of football, we know that there are more ways than one of digging for money. But it is admitted that to dig for money, often requires a lot of money. The potential for riches and an awful lot of fun prompted Lamar Hunt, the wealthy son of an oil tycoon, to recruit seven other businessmen from cities that were hungry for pro football. Hunt's idea was to form a rival league to the NFL. If they could not join them, this group of businessmen were ready to beat them. They did not enjoy one bit being tossed into the rubbish by the NFL

Clearly this was not a good thing for the NFL. Nonetheless NFL Commissioner Bert Bell was a fine gentleman and he publicly welcomed the new league stating that "competition would stimulate both leagues." For the NFL an alarm clock went off and they went to work rather than sit idly by and wait for the AFL to gain market share. Out of nowhere, new franchises were made available. The first was right in Lamar Hunt's hometown of Dallas and then into

Minneapolis, another of the cities the AFL had already designated for a franchise.

There was too much at stake for a small setback to become a major setback and so the American Football League quickly chose Oakland as a replacement for Minneapolis. The rest of the original eight cities were Lamar Hunt's Dallas (Texans), which soon moved to Kansas City. There was also Boston, Buffalo, Denver, Houston, Los Angeles, and New York.

The league immediately piqued fan interest with a highly entertaining product on the field, and a high-flying aerial brand of football that contrasted with the stingy defenses and running attacks of the older NFL. By 1962, the AFL had drawn 1 million fans to its games. It was destiny with so much support and a dedicated fan base that the AFL was going to make it and make it big.

In 1965, the AFL got a big television contract with NBC. That same year, New York Jets owner Sonny Werblin lured quarterback Joe Namath out of the University of Alabama to the AFL with the biggest contract in pro football history. The NFL's prediction and hope that the AFL would attract only second-rate players and has-been former NFL players was not how this game was being played.

Instead, the two leagues became major competitors in all aspects from players to fans to coaches. An unspoken agreement that one league would not sign the other league's players was broken in 1966 when the NFL's New York Giants signed place-kicker Pete Gogolak away from the AFL's Buffalo Bills. As neither league felt that they could afford a bidding war, owners soon began to talk of a merger.

Under the merger agreement that was announced on June 8, 1966, the new league would be called the NFL, and split into the American Football Conference (AFC) and the National Football Conference (NFC) All eight of the original AFL teams would all be absorbed by the NFL.

This was unlike the move by the NFL in 1946 in which the NFL merged with the older rival All-America Football Conference but only brought in the Baltimore, Cleveland and San Francisco franchises and dissolved four other teams. My speculation is that of the NFL tried this, the four teams left would find four other teams and rebuild a new league to compete against the "merged" league. But, it did not happen.

In the first two Super Bowls, the NFC, which was really the former NFL, made a much better showing than the AFC but the notion of the NFC being the end all and beat all would soon be diminished.

For the first games, Vince Lombardi's Green Bay Packers handled their AFC challenger quite easily. In Super Bowl III, however, Jersey Joe Namath, a brash braggadocio type predicted an "AFL" victory" and he pulled it off. The New York Jets upset the favored Baltimore Colts, and this created a brand-new era of greater parity and respect between the two leagues.

I do not have to tell you that the Super Bowl, played between the AFC and NFC champions at the end of every NFL season, is now the most watched televised sporting event in the world with more than 140 million viewers.

Top Patriots Players Jim Nance, RB

Somehow everybody has heard of Jim Nance, even though his playing years were circa Boston Patriots. When the Patriots celebrated their 50th anniversary in 2009, Jim Nance surely got a mention.

Patriots fans got a rare opportunity to vote for one of three hall of fame finalists, each of whom were perennial American Football League (AFL) All-Stars for the then Boston Patriots. The great fullback Jim Nance posthumously earned the honor of becoming the 14th player and the first running back to be inducted into the team's Hall of Fame.

Nance played seven seasons with the Boston Patriots from 1965-1971 and was the AFL's MVP in 1966 when he rushed for 1,458 yards and 11 touchdowns. He also was the first AFL back to top the 1,000-yard rushing mark in consecutive seasons. His 104.1 rushing yards per game in 1966 remains a Patriots record. He was that good.

His 45 rushing TDs is still tops in team history while his 5,323 rushing yards is second only to Sam Cunningham. Nance was named to the Patriots All-Time Team in 2009.

1966 Mike Holovak, Coach #2

The 1966 Boston Patriots football team competed in their fifth season of Professional American Football League (AFL) football. They played most of their games in Fenway Park except when competing with the Red Sox for a ballpark. They were led by Mike Holovak in his sixth of eight years as head coach. Billy Sullivan was the owner. The Patriots had a great record again this year of 8-4-2 with four more victories. They missed the playoffs, and they finished second in the AFL's Eastern Division. It was another great season, but it would be Mike Holovak's last in the winner's circle as the team as you will see went down the big slide in 1967 and 1968.

Even after Holovak left, and he did at the end of 1968, things would not get better immediately for Boston. I sure wish I could bring somebody else in to tell the fine New England Patriots' but since I can't I will do the (What's the opposite of honors?). This season is one to be enjoyed in the writing and in the reading as it would be the last winning season the Patriots posted as an AFL team. The Patriots would not have another such season until 1976, by which time the team was in the NFL as the New England Patriots. Enjoy this season summary. I know I will.

As we display the season summaries, because it is in some ways non-essential information to the games themselves, we will not always show the attendance but will again at times. Note that the attendance continues to go up as the interest in pro-football and AFL football in particular kept mounting through the 1960's until the NFL took a big notice and made an offer to the AFL that it could not refuse.

After the first game, the season opener on Saturday, Sept 10 at San Diego, in which the Chargers shut out the Patriots L (0–24) at Balboa Stadium before 29,539, Patriot fans were not at all pleased with the season prognosis. After a 4-8-2 season the year before, the fans were looking for more than miserable.

The Patriots proved they could win in the second game at Denver, beating the Broncos W (24–10) at Mile High Stadium before 25,337, At home in game 3, on Sept 25, the Patriots were soundly beaten by the Kansas City Chiefs L (24–43) at Fenway Park before 22,641. On Oct 2, the Patriots tied the NY Jets T (24–24) at Fenway Park. At Buffalo on Oct 8, the Patriots doubled the Bills score in winning the game W (20–10) at War Memorial Stadium bringing the 1966 record to 2-2. The Buffalo game was seen by 45,542 fans. After the Bye week, the Patriots came back ready to take no prisoners.

On Oct 23at home, the Patriots beat the San Diego Chargers W (35–17) at Fenway Park before 32,371. At home again, on Oct 30, the

Patriots got by the Oakland Raiders W (24-21) at Fenway Park. Again, at home on Nov 6, the Denver Broncos beat the Patriots L (10–17) before 18,154. On Nov 13, at Fenway Park, the Patriots beat the Houston Oilers W (27–21) in a close match.

At Kansas City, the Chiefs tied the Patriots T (27-27) in Municipal Stadium bringing their very positive record to 5-3-2. Before 41,475 fans. Then, against the Miami Dolphins for the first time ever on Nov 27 in a game played at the Miami Orange Bowl, the Patriots took the prize, W (20-14) before 22,754. On Dec 4, at Fenway, the Patriots squeaked by W (14-3) before 39,350. At Houston on Dec 11, the Patriots defeated the Oilers big-time W (38-14) in Rice Stadium before 17,100. Ending the season, the Patriots were looking for a win but got nothing more than a respectable showing on Dec 17, against the New York Jets L (28–38) at Shea Stadium before 58,921. And, so the Patriots finished well at 8-4-2.
Now, let's move on to the dark years.

1967 Mike Holovak, Coach #2

The 1967 Boston Patriots football team competed in their eighth season of Professional American Football League (AFL) football. They played most of their games in Fenway Park except when competing with the Red Sox for a ballpark. They were led by Mike Holovak in his seventh of eight years as head coach. Billy Sullivan was the owner. The Patriots had a losing record this year of 3-10-1. They missed the playoffs, and they finished fifth in the AFL's Eastern Division.

The season this year was still fourteen games but there were two byes scattered about the games. The season opener was played at Denver on September 3, 1967. The Broncos beat the Patriots L (21-26) before 35,488. At San Diego on Sept 9, the Chargers beat the Patriots L (14-28). On Sept 17, at Oakland, the Raiders prevailed L (7-35) before 26,289. For the fourth game out of territory in a row, at Buffalo, the Patriots finally got a win (23-0) against the Bills on Sept 24. After a bye week, San Diego played the Patriots to a tie T (31-31) at home before 23,620

On Oct 15 at home, the Pats beat the Miami Dolphins W (41–10). Then, on Oct 22 at home, the Oakland Raiders pummeled the Patriots L (14-48) before 25,057. The NY Jets were drawing huge numbers of fans to their games. On Oct 29, before 62,784, the other team from NY beat the Patriots L (23-30). At home on Nov 5, the Patriots beat the Houston Oilers W 18–7 before 19,422. Then, on Nov 12 at home the Kansas City Chiefs drubbed the Patriots L (10-33) before 23,010.

At home on Nov 19, The Patriots lost in a close match to the New York Jets L (24-29) before 26,790. On Nov 26 at Houston, the Oilers beat the Patriots L (6-27) before 28,044. After the second bye week, at home, on Dec. 9, the Buffalo Bills thumped the Patriots L (16-44) before. The next week, the Patriots played the at Miami against the Dolphins on Dec 17 and lost their last game of the season L (32-41) before 25,969.

1968 Mike Holovak, Coach #2

The 1968 Boston Patriots football team competed in their ninth season of Professional American Football League (AFL) football. They played most of their games in Fenway Park except when competing with the Red Sox for a ballpark. This would be the last year for Fenway Park. The following year, the Patriots would play at Boston College's Alumni Stadium. They were led by Mike Holovak in his eight and last year as head coach. Billy Sullivan was the owner. The Patriots had a losing record this year of 4-10, just a hair better than the 3-10-1 season of !967. They missed the playoffs, and they finished fourth in the AFL's Eastern Division.

In the season opener on Sept 8 at Buffalo, the Patriots grabbed a rare opening day victory against the Bills W (16-7) before 38,865. After a very early bye week, the Patriots lost to the NY Jests at home in Fenway Park on Sept 22 L (31-47) before 22,002. On Sept 29, at Fenway, the Patriots won again—this time against the Denver Broncos W (20-1& bringing their early record to 2-1 for the year. On Oct 6, at Oakland, the Raiders whooped the Patriots L (10-41) before 44,253. Then at home, on Oct 13, the Houston Oilers shut out the Patriots L (16-0) before 32,502

On Oct 20, at home, the Patriots beat the Buffalo Bills at home W 23–6 before 21,082. At NY on Oct 27, the Jets pounded the Patriots L (14-48) before 62,351. On Nov 3, at home, the Denver Broncos defeated the Patriots L (35–14). At home again on Nov 10, the San Diego Chargers beat the Patriots L (17–27). Next, on Nov 17, at Kansas City, the Chiefs prevailed L (17-31).

On November 24, at home, the Miami Dolphins beat the Patriots L (10-34) before 18,305. At home on Dec 1, the Patriots beat the Cincinnati Bengals W (33–14). Then, on Dec 8 at Miami, the Patriots were squashed by the Dolphins L (7-38). In the last game of the 1968 season on Dec 15 at Houston, the Oilers smothered the Patriots L (17-45) before 34,198

Chapter 12 Coach Clive Rush 1969-1970

Coach #3 Clive Rush
Coach #4 John Mazur

Year Coach	League	Conf	Div	Pl	W-L-T
1969 Clive Rush	AFL	East		3rd	4 10 0
1970 Clive Rush (1–6)	NFL	AFC	East	5th	2 12 0

1969-1970 Clive Rush final record (5-16-0)
1970 John Mazur (1–6)

Clive Rush 3rd Head Coach Boston Patriots

Clive Rush & John Mazur, Boston Coaches

Before arriving in Boston, Clive Rush put in six good seasons (1963-1968) as the New York Jets offensive coordinator. He meticulously constructed what would become the AFL's first Super Bowl-winning offense. After experiencing such championship successes, Rush became a hot commodity as a potential head coach, and he was not about to stay an assistant coach with all the calls he was getting.

Eventually, he answered the phone and it was the Boston Patriots. After a few conversations, they offered Rush a contract that he could not refuse, and he was named as head coach of the Boston Patriots for the 1969 season. Despite the hype, the Pats did not improve their record. And finished with a 4-10 record again in 1969. This was not what was expected as there was no spark or so there seemed that could take the offense, having finished eighth of the 10 AFL teams in scoring.

Rush was a man of action and he moved quickly as Patriots head coach, trading away stars Leroy Mitchell and Nick Buoniconti almost immediately. There was no magic wand and it led to his early release in 1970. In favor of John Mazur.

Clive Rush's tenure in Boston was shorter than expected. With the 4-10 repeat performance, nobody was looking to keep Rush any longer than need be. The Pats bought his contract seven games into the 1970s season when he was sidelined by health issues. He was replaced by Coach John Mazur

When Mazur took over for Rush, he became the historical last coach of the Boston Patriots and then the following year, he would become the first head coach of the New England Patriots

He coached pro football for 19 years with the Bills, Patriots, Eagles, and Jets, and he received two AFL championship rings from his days as Buffalo's offensive coordinator. He's a tough Marine -- there are no ex-Marines. Mazur once ordered star running back Duane Thomas, participating in his first workout with the Patriots after being acquired from the Dallas Cowboys, off the team. He had the guts and the courage of his convictions. Mazur said Thomas reported to training camp in Amherst and brought attitude with him. That was that.

Mazur was once a quarterback on the Notre Dame team that won the national championship in 1949. In 1951, he was an honorable mention All-American. He coached at Tulane, Marquette, and Boston University before joining the Bills in 1962. There he successfully instituted the two-man quarterback system with Daryle Lamonica and Jack Kemp and enjoyed postseason success. Mazur wears one of the championship rings; the other he gave to his son. He will never sell it, he said.

He joined the Patriots in 1969 as offensive coordinator. In 1970 he was named interim coach when Clive Rush was fired in midseason and finished 1-6. In 1971, he was given a one-year contract before Upton Bell was named general manager. He lost 25 pounds worrying about drafting quarterback Jim Plunkett. He slept in his office at Schaefer Stadium and compiled a 6-8 record, the team's best record in five years.

At the end of the 1971 season, GM Bell, who wanted to hire his own coach, made a deal with the Patriots board of directors and owner Billy Sullivan. If Mazur lost the last game to the reigning Super Bowl champion Colts, Mazur would be fired.

However, wide receiver Randy Vataha caught an 88-yard touchdown pass in the fourth quarter to give the Patriots a stunning 21-17 upset. News accounts said Bell looked like he was rooting against his own team.

"That's true, I heard that same story," Mazur said. "That made me feel like I wanted to punch him in the mouth, but I couldn't do it. That would've ruined me, which would have given him satisfaction, too. I didn't want to give him any." He was offered a one-year contract. His instincts told him not to take it. His wife told him that all the other coaches would get fired and they had families, too. "I led with my heart," he said.

By mid-1972, after six straight losses, Mazur resigned, his head coaching record just 9-21. Not everything happens the way it is supposed to.

Mazur liked New England even though as he said, they did not have the greatest of talent at the time, but they had a lot of great guys who gave the team their hearts.

Mazur, who is struggling on a skimpy pension and is riddled with Parkinson's disease, is a big Bill Belichick fan. He thinks the head coach is doing a hell of a job. And he knows Belichick is a good guy, too. He knew his old man when he was coaching at the Naval Academy."

Mazur says that a lot of guys are suffering like him with small pensions from the NFL He said his is $1,500 per month pension had not increased in more than a quarter century. He would not mind if somebody called his attention to owner today's owner, Bob Kraft. Mazur does not want to appear like a beggar, but things are tough. He is quoted as saying this about Kraft: "I understand he's a pretty nice fellow. Maybe guys like that can get together and say, 'Let this guy take his trip to Boston." Maybe he doesn't know about my situation."■

1969 Clive Rush, Coach #3

The 1969 Boston Patriots football team competed in their tenth and last season of Professional American Football League (AFL) football. In 1970, the NFL / AFL merger would be complete, so this was the last year of the Patriots playing in the AFL. However, the Boston Patriots team would live-on for one more season.

The Boston Patriots this year played their games in Boston College's Alumni Stadium. This would be a one year's engagement as the following year, games would be played at Harvard Stadium. The Patriots were led by Clive Rush his first of two years as head coach. Billy Sullivan was the owner. The Patriots had a losing record this year of 4-10, exactly the same as the prior year. They missed the playoffs, and they tied for third place in the AFL's Eastern Division.

The 1969 Season began on September 14, 1969 at Denver. The Broncos blasted Boston L (7-35) at Mile High Stadium before 43,679. At home v Kansas City on Sept 21, the Chiefs blanked Boston L (0-31) at the first game at Alumni Stadium before 22,002

On Sept 28 at home the Oakland Raiders beat Boston at home L 23-38) before 19,069. On Oct 5, the defending Super Bowl Champ, New York Jets beat Boston at L (14-23) at Alumni Stadium. On Oct 11, at Buffalo, the Bills beat the Patriots L (16-23) before 25,584.

At home on Oct 19, the San Diego Chargers just beat the Patriots by a score of L (10-13) at Alumni Stadium before 18,346. At New York on Oct 26, the Jets defeated the Patriots L (17-23) before 62,298. On Nov 2, at home, the Patriots beat the Houston Oilers W (24–0). At

Cincinnati on Nov16, the Patriots defeated the Bengals W (25–14) at Nippert Stadium before 27,927.

On Nov 23 at home, Boston beat Buffalo W (35–21) in Alumni Stadium before 25,584. On Nov 30, at Miami, Boston beat the Dolphins W (38-23) before 32,121. On Dec 7 at San Diego, the Chargers won W (18-28). On Dec 14 in the season finale, at Houston, the Oilers prevailed L (23-27) before 39,215

The Merged NFL / AFL AKA, the NFL

There was a lot of disagreement in taking the sixteen NFL teams at the time of the merger and seamlessly folding in the new AFL teams. The final format agreed on included to conferences, the NFC and the AFC, and six divisions with each conference having an East, Central, and a West. The final configuration for 1970 looked like this:

- **NFC East:** Dallas, New York (Giants), Philadelphia, St. Louis, Washington
- NFC Central: Chicago, Detroit, Green Bay, Minnesota
- **NFC West:** Atlanta, Los Angeles, New Orleans, San Francisco
- **AFC East:** Baltimore, Buffalo, Miami, Boston, New York (Jets)
- **AFC Central:** Cincinnati, Cleveland, Houston, Pittsburgh
- **AFC West:** Denver, Kansas City, Oakland, San Diego

This final arrangement of cities / teams would keep most of the pre-merger NFL teams in the NFC and the AFL teams in the AFC. Pittsburgh, Cleveland, and Baltimore were placed in the AFC in order to balance it out, while the NFC equalized the competitive strength of its East and West divisions rather than sorting out teams just geographically.

Division alignment in 1970 was largely intended to preserve the pre-merger setups, keeping traditional rivals in the same division. Plans were also made to add two expansion teams—the Tampa Bay

Buccaneers and Seattle Seahawks—but this would not take place until 1976, seven years after the merger.

As you can see, Boston played the 1970 season as part of the AFC East.

1970 Clive Rush, Coach #3
1970 John Mazur Coach #4

The 1970 Boston Patriots football team competed in their first eleventh season overall and their first season of Professional National Football League (NFL) football. They were in the EAST Division of the American Football Conference (AFC). They played their games in Harvard Stadium. The use of Harvard's stadium would be a one year's engagement. The following year, they would move into their own newly built arena known as Schaefer Stadium.

The 1970 Patriots were led by Clive Rush in his second year for the first half of the year in which they had a record of 1-6-0. Rush was replaced mid-season by John Mazur who also compiled a 1-6-0 record. Billy Sullivan was the owner. The Patriots had a combined losing record this year of 2-10. It was the worst Patriot's season ever. They missed the playoffs for the seventh straight season, and they finished in fifth place (last) in the AFL's Eastern Division.

Coach Mazur, Vataha, Plunkett, & Adams

This was the last season the Patriots would be called the "Boston" Patriots. The following year, they would turn in the "Boston" name and instead they would operate from then to now as the "New England" Patriots. Their final season known as Boston did not go as anybody had planned, as the Patriots would struggle all season and would finish 2-12 with two coaches--the worst record in the NFL.

After winning their first game against the Miami Dolphins, the Patriots would lose 9 in a row before beating the Buffalo Bills on the road. The season concluded with an embarrassing 45-7 loss to the Cincinnati Bengals in Cincinnati. Head coach Clive Rush would quit the season at the midpoint because of medical reasons.

His replacement, John Mazur, did not do much better of a job. Mazur would end up coaching the team next season. The Patriots would score the fewest points in the league in 1970, scoring only 149 points, while allowing 361. Watch the games played this season as with 25 other teams in the expanded NFL, the Patriots play a number of teams, such as the NY Giants for the first time this year.

Boston's last season and home opener as the Boston Patriots was played on September 20, 1970 at Harvard Stadium. The Patriots broke the scourge from the prior season and defeated the Miami Dolphins W (27–14) before 32,607. At home again on Sept 27, the New York Jets beat Boston L (21–31). For the third home game in a row, the Baltimore Colts slid by the Patriots on Oct 4, in a close match L (6-14). This was followed at Kansas City on Oct 11, as the Chiefs beat Boston L (10-23). On Oct 18 at home, the Patriots were shut out by the New York Giants L (16-0)

At Baltimore on Oct 25, the Colts manhandled the Patriots L (3-27) before 60,240. At home on Nov1, the Buffalo Bills smothered the Patriots L (10-45) before 31,148. At St. Louis, on Nov 8, the Cardinals shut out the Patriots L (0-31) before 46,466. John Mazur took over the helm for the Patriots from this point in the season until the end. At home, on Nov 15, the San Diego Chargers defeated Boston L (14–16). Then, on Nov 22 at New York, the Jets beat the Patriots L (3-17) before 61,822.

On Nov 29 at Buffalo, the Patriots got their second win of the season—this one against the Bills W (14–10). That was the last win of the season and the last win ever for the Boston Patriots. At Miami on Dec 6, the Dolphins beat the Patriots L 20-37) before 51,032. At home on Dec 13, the NFL Expansion Vikings beat the Patriots W (35–14) before 37,819. On Dec 20, 1970 in the season finale and the last game played as the Boston Patriots, the team took a big beating from the Bengals at Cincinnati L (7-45) before 60,157.

Chapter 13 Coach John Mazur 1970-1972

Coach #4 John Mazur
Coach #5 Phil Bengston

1970 John Mazur (1–6)

Year Coach	Leag	Conf	Div	Pl	W-L-T
1971 John Mazur ,	NFL	AFC	East	3rd	6 8 0
1972 John Mazur (2–7)	NFL	AFC	East	5th	3 11 0

1971-1972 John Mazur final record (9-21-0)

1972 Phil Bengtson (1–4)
1972 Phil Bengston final record (1-4-0)

1971 John Mazur, Coach #4

The 1971 former Boston Patriots football team competed in their twelfth season in professional football and their second season in the National Football League (NFL). This year the team would change its name to the New England Patriots and it would move into Shaeffer Stadium, (named after the brewery). The stadium would be renamed several times in its lifetime before being replaced in 2002 by the luxurious Gillette Stadium.

The Patriots were led by John Mazur in his second and only full-year of three years as head coach. Billy Sullivan was the owner. The Patriots had a losing record this year of 6-8-0 and showed promise. They missed the playoffs, and they tied for third place in the AFL's Eastern Division.

The 1971 season would be the first that the team played as the New England Patriots, having changed its name from the Boston Patriots, briefly to the Bay State Patriots before changing it again to the New England Patriots. Their idea in the New England name was to help regionalize the franchise's equal distance from Boston and Providence.

Their record of six wins and eight losses, was much better than the past several years but it was no cigar. It brought them to a third-place finish in the AFC East Division. The Patriots enjoyed playing in a brand new stadium known as Schaefer Stadium in Foxborough, Massachusetts after playing in three different stadiums the previous three seasons in Boston and four stadiums overall in their time as the Boston Patriots.

Mazur showed who was boss in training camp, after the team with the urging of GM Upton Bell had acquired Duane Thomas from the Dallas Cowboys, where he had a label as a "disgruntled running back." To get Thomas, the Patriots had given up Carl Garrett and Halvor Hagen. Almost upon arriving, Thomas became embroiled in a conflict with coach John Mazur, prompting Patriots general manager Upton Bell to request that Commissioner Pete Rozelle to void the trade three days after it had been made. Rozelle granted Bell's request, and the traded players returned to where they had been prior to the deal.

The Patriots kept Hagen and Jackson in exchange for a second (#35- Robert Newhouse) and third round draft choices in the 1972 NFL draft. Thomas returned to the Cowboys, but decided to keep silent all season long, refusing to speak to teammates, management, and the media.

Thomas's story is interesting even though he made life unpleasant for everybody with whom he came in contact. He was not very likeable, but he was a great football player. There is no question that he helped Dallas win all the marbles including the Super Bowl (VI). His stoical demeanor and cheap shots at pundits apparently cost him Super Bowl MVP.

He was as reportedly voted as the Super Bowl Most Valuable Player by an overwhelming margin. Thomas, however, had boycotted the media throughout the season as well, and Larry Klein, editor of Sport, which presented the award, didn't know how Thomas would act at a banquet in New York. With this in mind, Klein chose to announce Dallas QB Roger Staubach as the winner.

During the 1972 offseason he became even more isolated and insubordinate, so he was traded in early August to the San Diego Chargers in exchange for Mike Montgomery and Billy Parks. Some guys never learn. Kudos to John Mazur for recognizing a sour apple.

The 1971 season began on September 19, 1971 at home against the Oakland Raiders. The Patriots prevailed in the first ever game at Schaefer Stadium in Foxborough Massachusetts W (20-6) before 55,405. At home again on Sept 26, the Detroit Lions beat the New England Patriots L (7-34) before a packed house of 61,057. At home for the third game in a row, on Oct 3, the Baltimore Colts beat the Patriots L (3 23) before 61,232. On Oct 10 at home, the Patriots shut out the Jets W (20 0) before 61,357. At Miami on Oct 17, the Dolphins drubbed the Patriots L (3 41) at the Orange Bowl before 58,822.

At Dallas on Oct 24, the Cowboys beat the Patriots L (21 44) at Texas Stadium before 65,70. Then, on Oct 31 at San Francisco, the Patriots went down L (10 27) at Candlestick Park before 45,092

At home on Nov 7 the Patriots defeated the Houston Oilers W (28 20) before 53,155. On Nov 14, at home, the Patriots beat the Buffalo Bills 38 33 at Schaefer Stadium before 57,446. At Cleveland, on Nov 21, the Browns beat the Patriots L (7-27) at Cleveland Municipal Stadium before 65,238.

On Nov 28 at Buffalo, the Bills beat the Patriots L (20-27) at War Memorial Stadium before 27,166. At home on Dec 5, the Patriots defeated the Miami Dolphins W (34 13) at Schaefer Stadium before 61,457. At New York in Shea Stadium, on Dec 12, the Jets beat the Patriots L (6-13) before 63,175. In the final game of the season Dec 19 at Baltimore, the New England Patriots bet the Colts W (21 17) at W. Memorial Stadium before 57,942.

1972 John Mazur, Coach #4
1972 Phil Bengtson Coach #5

The 1972 former Boston Patriots football team competed in their thirteenth season in professional football and their third season in the National Football League (NFL). This was the second year the team would be using the name "New England Patriots" and it was the second year in which Shaeffer Stadium was their home venue. The stadium would be renamed several times in its lifetime before being replaced in 2002 by the luxurious Gillette Stadium.

The Patriots were led by John Mazur in his third season. Mazur would resign before the end of the season and he was replaced by Phil Bengston for the last five games. Billy Sullivan was the owner. The Patriots had a losing record this year of 3-11-0 and showed no improvement. They missed the playoffs, and they finished in fifth (last) place in the AFC East.

Chapter 13 Coach John Mazur Era 1970-1972

Phil Bengston, Interim Coach New England Patriots (1-4-0)

The New England Patriots were not impressing anybody with a 3-11 record sheared between coaches Mazur and Bengston, contributing to their last place finish in the AFC East Division. The Patriots continued what pundits now call their "period of futility" as they slumped to another poor record of 3-11 and missed the playoffs for the 9th straight season.

After being embarrassed 31-7 in their home opener against Cincinnati, the Patriots would manage to win their next 2 games against Atlanta and Washington. But, they would pick up their midseason misery, as they lost 9 straight games to a miserable 2-10-0 record before finally winning again.

They won their first (and only) road game against the New Orleans Saints. They were winless against AFC opponents. Besides their embarrassing home opening loss, the Patriots had plenty of other bad moments during the season. One good example was a 52-0 thrashing given to them by the powerful Miami Dolphins. This loss went down as the worst loss in Patriots history and the most points they've ever allowed in a game in franchise history.

Although they did manage to win three games, the 1972 Patriots had the second-worst point differential of any team in a 14-game NFL season, ahead of only the expansion 1976 Buccaneers. They lost eight of their fourteen games by three touchdowns or more, and their first two wins were by a single point. Knowing that eventually Bill Belichick and Tom Brady would come along, makes it easier to endure these early days as the teams was figuring out how to be great.

The 1972 season and home opener was held on September 17, 1971 against the Cincinnati Bengals. The Bengals won the match L(7-31) before 60,999. On Sept 24 at home, the Patriots beat the Atlanta Falcons by one-point W (21–20) before 60,999. On Oct 1, the Patriots beat the Redskins in another cliffhanger W (24–23). Then, on Oct 8 at Buffalo, the Bills overpowered the Patriots L (14-38) before 41,749. Then, on October 15, the Patriots got scorched by the New York Jets L (41–13).

At Pittsburgh, on Oct 22, 1972, the Steelers put a steel hurt on the Patriots in a game decided at the opening kickoff, L (3-33) before 46,081. At New York's Shea Stadium, the Jets whooped the Patriots L (10-34) before 62,867. At home on Nov 6, the Baltimore Colts nosed out the Patriots L (17-24) before 60,998. Then at Miami on Nov 12, the powerful Dolphins shellacked the hapless Patriots by a ton in a shutout L (0-52) before a huge crowd of 80,010. John Mazur had had enough. At this point of the season, Phil Bengston replaced John Mazur on the sidelines. Mazur's record was 2-7 going into game 10.

At home on Nov 19, in game 10, the Patriots lost a close match to the Buffalo Bills L (24–27). At Baltimore on November 26, the Colts skunked the Patriots L (0-31) 1972 before 54,907. At home, on Dec 3, Miami prevailed over New England L (21-37). At New Orleans on Dec 10, the Patriots woke up and snatched a win from the Saints, W (17–10) before 64,889. Then, to close the season at Denver, the Broncos were unstoppable, piling it up on the Patriots to a L (21-45) victory before 51,656 at Mile High Stadium.

Chapter 14 Coach Chuck Fairbanks, 1973 to 1978

Coach #6 Chuck Fairbanks

Year Coach	League	Conf/Div	Place	Record
1973 Chuck Fairbanks	NFL	AFCEast	3rd	5 9 0
1974 Chuck Fairbanks	NFL	AFCEast	3rd	7 7 0
1975 Chuck Fairbanks	NFL	AFCEast	5th	3 11 0
1976 Chuck Fairbanks	NFL	AFCEast	2nd	11 3 0

- Lost Divisional Playoffs (at Raiders) 21–24

1977 Chuck Fairbanks	NFL	AFCEast	3rd	9 5 0
1978 Chuck Fairbanks	NFL	AFCEast	1st	11 5 0

- Lost Divisional Playoffs (Oilers) 14–31[15]

1973-1978 Chuck Fairbanks final record (46-50-0)

Who was Coach Chuck Fairbanks

Chuck Fairbanks was a fine coach. Like most NFL coaches, he got his training by coaching college teams. There are so few Heisman Trophy winners given out that a coach who helps produce a Heisman winner often shares in the accolades. Fairbanks produced a Heisman at the University of Oklahoma, Steve Owens, and he later spent six seasons as one of the better coaches of the era with New England. He passed away on April 2, 2013 in Scottsdale, Ariz. at 79. Years of age. It was tough.

Chuck Fairbanks on the sidelines doing what he did best--coaching

The University of Oklahoma announced his cause of death as brain cancer. As the Sooners head coach, Fairbanks was as good as it gets. He pulled off a 52-15-1 in six years with the Sooners, including an Orange Bowl victory his first season. His squad then won consecutive Sugar Bowl wins in 1971-72 before he took over the Patriots. It was no wonder that he was selected as the Patriots were looking to turn their professional program around. Fairbanks quickly got the program in gear, winning 46 games at New England in his time there, which was a Patriot record at the time.

It took a while to get the team in gear but then after a few years of Fairbanks Seasoning, they were ready to go. The Patriots made the playoffs in their fourth season under Fairbanks in 1976 and then two years later, they were on their way to their first outright AFC East title when owner Billy Sullivan, for his own reasons, pulled an ownership prerogative that affected the team negatively.

He angrily suspended Fairbanks for the final regular-season game. The Patriots did not need the game to be in the playoffs, but it was unsettling for the team. Why, you may ask, would the owner step and do something dumb like that? Nobody could fire the owner for a dumb move. Even though fans would have been pleased if he were asked to go. Fairbanks had had enough of pro football. He had agreed to become the coach at the University of Colorado. Coaches go where it suits them best all of the time.

Mr. Fairbanks was asked, and he returned for the playoffs, but with the disruption in continuity, New England lost to Houston. Fairbanks thus ended his time at 0-2 in the playoffs with New England. The unexpected suspension shook up Fairbanks.

At Colorado, Mr. Fairbanks could not rustle up a winner. Nothing good happens overnight anywhere and there was not enough time for Chuck Fairbanks, as there had been at New England for him to have **his** team ready to go as a winner. His record was 7-26 in three seasons, including an 82-42 loss at home to the Sooners and his replacement there, Barry Switzer.

Fairbanks left the Colorado Buffaloes to become coach and general manager of the New Jersey Generals of the USFL. He was fired after one season.

In Fairbanks's first year coaching in 1967, the Oklahoma Sooners had a great record of 10-1 and they beat Tennessee in the Orange Bowl. His teams won 11 games each in his last two seasons with OU, beating Auburn and Penn State in the Sugar Bowl.

When queried, Fairbanks admitted that he had agreed to the suggestion of Switzer, his offensive coordinator, to install the wishbone offense at OU after Texas used it to win a national championship in 1969. A wishbone offense is a formation in which the fullback is positioned closer to the quarterback, with two halfbacks positioned farther back. It's a formation that lends itself to a strong running game.

After becoming head coach, Switzer used the wishbone to win three national titles, matching the number Bud Wilkinson won at Oklahoma from 1947 to 1963, a tenure that included a record 47-game winning streak.

Charles Leo Fairbanks was born to play and to coach football in Detroit on June 10, 1933. He played for Michigan State's 1952 national title team and he served as an assistant at Arizona State and Houston before joining the OU staff in 1966. Owens became one of five Heisman winners for Oklahoma after rushing for 1,523 yards and 23 touchdowns in 1969.

Fairbanks was great at what he did but everything does not always work out all the time. He moved on after football to a great career in real estate and golf-course development. He occasionally worked as a consultant for NFL teams in training camp, including with the Dallas Cowboys when Bill Parcells was coach. He was one of football's good guys.

1973 Chuck Fairbanks Coach # 6

The 1973 New England Patriots football team competed in their fourteenth season in professional football and their fourth season in the National Football League (NFL). This was the third year that the team would be using the name "New England Patriots" and it was the third year in which Shaeffer Stadium was their home venue. As previously noted, the stadium would be renamed several times in its lifetime before being replaced in 2002 by the luxurious Gillette Stadium.

The Patriots were led by Chuck Fairbanks his first of six seasons. Billy Sullivan was the owner. The Patriots had a losing record this year of 5-9-0 but showed much improvement. They missed the playoffs, and they finished in third place in the AFC East.

Summarizing for clarity, the New England Patriots finished the National Football League's 1973 season with a record of five wins and nine losses. It was not a good season but better than many. It gave the Pats third place in the five-team AFC East Division. It was the first year under head coach and general manager Chuck Fairbanks, hired in January after six seasons as head coach of the Oklahoma Sooners.

Fairbanks hoped to make the team better by drafting great players right out of college. His selections in the 1973 NFL Draft included John Hannah, Sam Cunningham, Ray Hamilton, and Darryl Stingley. The assistant coaches on his offense included future NFL head coaches Ron Erhardt, Sam Rutigliano, and Red Miller. Fairbanks had a great mind and a great coaching ability and his time in New England was well spent for Patriot fans.

Top Patriots Players—John Hannah, OL

John Hannah was a Patriot for his whole career from 1973 through the 1985 Super Bowl season. He was named as "The Greatest Offensive Lineman of All Time" by Sports Illustrated. A durable player at a physical position, Hannah played in 183 games and missed only five games due to injury.

The Patriots were not the pride of the league when they were playing out of Boston with no home field. Hannah was so good, he overcame the stigma and was one of only two Patriots voted to the

NFL's 75th anniversary team. Hannah played in nine pro bowls and he earned Offensive Lineman of the Year honors for four straight years, from 1978 to 1981.

He was the anchor of the 1978 offensive line that set an NFL record with 3,165 rushing yards - a record which has not been challenged since.

In 1991, Hannah was inducted into the Pro Football Hall of Fame and was the initial member of the Patriots Hall of Fame. In 1999, Hannah was inducted into the College Football Hall of Fame for his outstanding career at the University of Alabama under coach Bear Bryant. Hannah is still active with the Patriots organization even while making his home in Alabama. Inducted 1991.

Games of 1973

In the season and home opener at Schaefer Stadium, in Foxborough, Mass., the Patriots took one on the chin from the Buffalo Bills in a losing effort L (13-31) before 56,119 At home again on Sept 23m the Kansas City Chiefs beat New England L (7-10). At Miami on Sept 30, the Dolphins pounded the Patriots L (23-44) before 57,918.

At Miami on Sept 30, the Patriots could not keep up and lost to the Dolphins L (23-44) before 62,508. At home on Oct 7, the Patriots got the best of the Baltimore Colts W (24–16) before 57,044. Then, on Oct 14, the Patriots lost in a two-point game to the New York Jets L (7-9) before 58,659.

At Chicago on Oct 21, the Patriots triumphed over the Bears W (13–10) before 47,643. On Oct 28, at home, the Miami Dolphins whooped the Patriots L (30–14) before 57,617. At Philadelphia, the first time for these two teams to meet, on Nov 4, the Eagles managed a one-point win L (23–24) before 65,070. On Nov 11, at New York's Shea Stadium, the Jets whooped the Patriots L (13-33) before 51,034. When the tough Green Bay Packers came to Foxborough on Nov 18, though unexpected, the Patriots took a piece out of the packers in a fine W (33–24) victory before 60,525.

On Nov 25, at Houston, the Patriots beat the Oilers in a nice shutout W (32–0 before 27,344. At home on Dec 2, the Patriots beat the San Diego Chargers W (30–14) before 58,150. At Buffalo on Dec 9, the Bills powered over the Patriots L (13-37) before 72,470. Wrapping up the season on Dec 16 at Baltimore, the Colts took down the Patriots L (14-18) before 52,065

Top Patriots Players Sam Cunningham, RB

You may never have heard of Sam Cunningham, but it was not because when he was on the field for your team, he was not playing his heart out. Cunningham played and played and played football for nine seasons for the Patriots. If he were not on the team, the win total would not have so quickly hit 500.

The Patriots put him in 107 games from 1973 to 1979 after they had moved from the AFL to the NFL. He was also a mainstay in 1981 and 1982. You need to have collected some great stats when you play that long, and the coach keeps putting you in the game.

So, it is with Sam Cunningham who is the Patriots all-time leading rusher with 5,453 yards and his 43 rushing touchdowns rank second in team history. He played a significant role in helping the Patriots set the NFL record for most rushing yards in a season with 3,165 yards in 1978.

Sam Cunningham joined the Patriots as a 1973 first round draft pick after an All-American career at USC. He was dubbed Sam "Bam" Cunningham while in college for his ability to dive over piles into the end zone. If the team needed to score, there was a Cunningham available.

Sam is a member of the Patriots 50th Anniversary Team and 1970s All-Decade Team. He was enshrined to the Patriots Hall of Fame in 2010. He lives in California, enjoying the fruits of a great career.

1974 Chuck Fairbanks Coach # 6

The 1974 New England Patriots football team competed in their fifteenth season in professional football and their fifth season in the National Football League (NFL). The Patriots were led by Chuck Fairbanks his second of six seasons. Billy Sullivan was the owner. The Patriots had a break-even record after a great start this year finishing at 7-7-0. They showed much improvement. They missed the playoffs, and they finished tied for third place in the AFC East.

New England stunned the Super Bowl Champion Miami Dolphins in Week 1 at Schaffer Stadium. The Pats went on to win their first five games on their way to a 6–1 start. However, they struggled in the second half of the season, winning only one game before finishing with a 7–7 record.

In the season and home opener at Schaefer Stadium, in Foxborough, Mass, the Patriots unexpectedly defeated the Super Bowl Champion Miami Dolphins W (34-24) at Schaefer Stadium before 55,006. At New York, on Sept 22, the Patriots beat the Giants at the Yale Bowl W (28-20) before 44,082. At home at Schaefer Stadium on Sept 29, the Patriots defeated the Los Angeles Rams W (20–14) before 61,279. Then, on Oct 6 at home, the Pats scorched the Baltimore Colts W (42–3) before 59,502. At NY on Oct 13, the Patriots shut out the Jets W (24-0) at Shea Stadium before 57,825.

At Buffalo on Oct 20, in the sixth game of the year, the Patriots fell to the Bills in a tight match L (28–30) at Rich Stadium before 78,935. At Minnesota , the Patriots defeated the Vikings on Oct 27 at Metropolitan Stadium before 48,177. At home on Nov3, the Buffalo Bills won another squeaker against the Patriots L (28-29) before 61,279. Then on Nov 10 at home the Cleveland Browns beat the Patriots by a TD L 914-21) before 61,279. The following week at home on Nov 10, the NY Jets beat the Patriots by less than a touchdown L (16-21) before 57,115.

At Baltimore, the Patriots finally won another game, and this one was against the Colts W (27-17) bringing the season to 7-4. The Patriots would lose their last three games of the season right after this win. On Dec the Oakland Raiders won L (26–41) at the Oakland Coliseum before 50,120. On Dec 8, the Pittsburgh Steelers won L (17–21) at home in Schaefer Stadium before 52,107. Finally, the Super Bowl Champion Miami Dolphins played the Patriots to a T (7-7) tie in the Miami Orange Bowl before 56,920. This closed out the best season for the Patriots since Mike Holovak's Boston Patriots in 1966.

Top Patriot Players Steve Nelson, LB

Steve Nelson was a linebacker for the Patriots from 1974-87. He quickly became and stayed as the nucleus of the Patriots defense.

Nelson was voted to three Pro Bowls and he is on the books for more than 100 tackles nine times during his career. He led the Patriots in tackles in eight of his 14 seasons, including an unofficial team record of 207 in 1988.

He finished his career with a patriotic 1,776 total tackles. After retirement, he coached for the Patriots and later built Curry College into a perennial power. More recently, Nelson has become a familiar football analyst on local television and radio. In 1993, Nelson was inducted into the Patriots Hall of Fame. The Minnesota native remains a Massachusetts resident. Inducted 1993.

1975 Chuck Fairbanks Coach # 6

The 1975 New England Patriots football team competed in their sixteenth season in professional football and their sixth season in the National Football League (NFL). The Patriots were led by Chuck Fairbanks his third of six seasons. Billy Sullivan was the owner. The Patriots fell backwards to a record of 3-11-0 this year when there were great expectations. They had a break-even record after finishing 1974 at 7-7-0. a great start this year finishing at 7-7-0. They showed much improvement. They missed the playoffs, and they finished tied for fourth place in the AFC East.

The Patriots had big designs for the 1975 season after a good year in 1974. They were hoping to make the playoffs for the first time since 1963. However, New England continued its forgetful period of the '70s, as they finished 3–11 and they missed the playoffs for the 12th straight season. They started bad, middles OK and then finished miserably, losing their final 6 games to conclude the season. Although they tied the New York Jets for last place in the AFC East, they lost the tiebreaker by virtue of New York winning both matchups during the season.

In the season and home opener at Schaefer Stadium, in Foxborough, Mass, on Sept 28, the Patriots were defeated in a L (0-7) shutout by the Houston Oilers before 51,934. On Sept 28 a t home the Miami Dolphins L (22–14) before 60,602. Then, on Oct 5 at New York, the Jets walloped the Patriots L (7-36) before 57,365. At Cincinnati on Oct 12, the Bengals beat the Pats L (10-27) before 51,220. At home on Oct 19, the Patriots beat the Baltimore Colts W (21–10) before 51,417

On October 26 at home the Patriots beat the San Francisco 49ers W (24–16) before 60,358. Then, at St. Louis, on Nov 2, the Cardinals beat the Patriots L (17-24) before 45,907. At San Diego, on Nov 9, the Patriots defeated the Chargers W (33-19) for their last win of the year. Before 24,349. On Nov 16, at home, the Dallas Cowboys nipped the Patriots for the win L (31-34) before 60,905. At Buffalo on Nov 23, the Bills beat the Patriots L (31-45) before 65,655.

At Miami on Dec 1, the Dolphins beat the Patriots all the way from the opening whistle L (7-20) before 61,963. On Dec 7, the Patriots were defeated by the New York Jets L (28-30) before 53,989. Then on Dec 14, at home the Buffalo Bills beat the Patriots L (14-34) before 58,393. In the season finale, the Pats would go out losing on Dec 21 to the Baltimore Colts L (21-34) before 48,678

Top Patriot Players Steve Grogan, QB

Steve Grogan was another iron-man; but he did not carry the nickname. Nonetheless, he was a model of toughness and longevity, playing in 149 games over his 16-year playing career from 1975 to

1990. He remains not only a fan favorite for his gritty style but also a favorite among former teammates.

A highly athletic quarterback, Grogan rushed for NFL record 12 touchdowns in 1976 and for 35 during his career. Grogan led the 1976 team to within seconds of the AFC Championship game. That team, which suffered a controversial playoff loss to the Raiders, is considered by many as one of the best in team history, certainly the best in the pre-Belichick era.

Grogan also helped lead the Patriots to their first AFC Championship in 1985. After thirty years, he still ranks among the leaders in team history in nearly every passing category. Despite playing quarterback, he was still credited and applauded for being one of the hardest hitters and toughest players in Patriots history.

Steve Grogan was inducted into the Patriots Hall of Fame in 1995 after spending parts of three decades with the club. The Kansas resident lives both in Massachusetts, where he owns a Mansfield sporting goods store, and in Kansas.

1976 Chuck Fairbanks Coach # 6

The 1976 New England Patriots football team competed in their seventeenth season in professional football and their seventh season in the National Football League (NFL). The Patriots were led by Chuck Fairbanks his fourth of six seasons. Billy Sullivan was the owner. The Patriots were a great team this year with a record of 11-

3-0 this year. They showed great improvement. They made the playoffs and they finished in second place in the AFC East.

This season was worth waiting for. After a nine-year stretch, (the forgettable years) in which New England / Boston posted just one non-losing season amid eight losing years, the Patriots turned around their fortunes, going 11–3. It goes down in history as their first winning season as an NFL team (their last winning season came in 1966, when the team was still in the AFL).

As we know, the team had gone just 3–11 the previous season, and was considered a "Cinderella team" in 1976. Nobody expected what a great year they would have. Coach Chuck Fairbanks was named NFL Coach of the Year, and cornerback Mike Haynes was named NFL Rookie of the Year.

The 1976 Patriots not only had a great record; they had great stats. The team rushed for a total of 2,957 yards (averaging five yards per carry) and scored 376 points, both second-best in the league. The 2,957 yards rushing were the fifth-highest total in NFL history at the time. The team's 5.0 yards per carry was the best in the NFL and remains higher than all Super Bowl champions except the 1973 Miami Dolphins whose run game was 5.0 yards per carry.

The Patriots also were great thieves on defense as they led the league in takeaways at 50. The Pats finished third in the league in turnover differential at plus-14.

The Patriots made only their second playoff appearance in their history and their first since 1963, but lost to the eventual Super Bowl champion Oakland Raiders in the first round of the playoffs. Earlier in the season, the Patriots handed the Raiders their only loss of the season with a blowout final score of 48–17. However, controversial roughing the passer penalty on Ray Hamilton on a Raiders drive late in the playoff game dimmed the Patriots' hopes of defeating the Raiders again, but they were in the game all the way.

Despite the playoff loss, the team has been considered one of the most talented in Patriots history; in 2004, Patriots head coach Bill Belichick, who was an assistant coach for the Detroit Lions in 1976, called this Patriots team "loaded", a "who's who team." Bill

Belichick has earned the right like EF Hutton that "When Bill Belichick speaks, people listen!" And, how!

Despite such a great season, the home and season opener was disappointing on Sept 12 as the Baltimore Colts beat the Patriots L (13–27) at Schaefer Stadium before a sparse attendance of 43,512. On Sept 19 at home, New England defeated Miami W (30–14). Schaefer Stadium 1-1 46,053. At Pittsburgh on Sept 26, the Patriots barely beat the Steelers W (30–27) at Three Rivers Stadium before 47,379. At home again on October 3, New England thumped Oakland W (48–17) at Schaefer Stadium before 61,068. At Detroit on Oct 10, in the Pontiac Silverdome, the Lions beat the Patriots L (10-30) before 60,174.

On October 18, the Pats hammered the New York Jets W (41–7) at Schaefer Stadium before 50,883. At Buffalo on Oct 24, the Patriots beat the Bills W (26-22) before 45,144. Then at Miami on Oct 31, the Dolphins beat the Patriots L (3-10), in a close match. This would be the last loss of the year. On Nov 7, at home, New England beat Buffalo W (20–10) at Schaefer Stadium before 61,157. At Baltimore on Nov 14, at Memorial Stadium, the Patriots defeated the Colts f W 21–14 before 58,226.

At New York, on Nov 21 the Patriots out-battled the Jets at Shea Stadium W (38-24) before 49,983. At home on Nov 28, New England blasted Denver W 38–14 at Schaefer Stadium before 61,128. Then on December, the Patriots got a nice clean win against the New Orleans Saints W (27–6) at Schaefer Stadium before 53,592. At Tampa Bay in the end of season match, the Patriots got the best of the Buccaneers on Dec 12 W (31–14) in Tampa Stadium before 41,517. New England proudly accepted their 11-3 regular season record and prepared for the playoffs.

Coming in #2 in the AFC East, the Patriots needed to compete in the Divisional Playoffs, hoping to be moving on to the Super Bowl. The game was on Dec 18 against the Oakland Raiders. In a game marked with controversy, the New England Patriots never gave up and almost pulled it off but did not, losing by three points L (21–24) in the Oakland Coliseum before 53,045

In the photo above, on Dec. 19, 1976, the day after the Playoff defeat, Massachusetts State troopers tried to contain fans who crushed against a wire gate at Logan airport. The fans, who came to meet the Patriots' plane, were upset with the officiating in a bitter 24-21 playoff loss to the Oakland Raiders. Ken Stabler, the Raiders quarterback, dived into the end zone with the game-winning touchdown while only 10 seconds remained on the clock. There was controversial officiating in the wild final drive to the score.

What happened?

The final score tells everybody the game was close, but Patriot fans believe Oakland officiating with the thumb on the scale for the Raiders helped move the core in the Raiders' favor.

Oakland 24, New England 21 is a heartache score. The Patriots played well and for a time at the end of the game they appeared to have the game in the bag with a 21-17 lead late in the fourth quarter. Then Kenny, the Snake Stabler took control of the game. He threw a pass on third and 18 and fortunately, it fell incomplete. However, referee Ben Dreith put his thumb on the scale and made a controversial roughing-the-passer call on Ray Hamilton. That call gave the Raiders a new set of downs on the 13-yard line. The Snake eventually ran in for the go-ahead touchdown and that's all she wrote.

Top Patriots Players Mike Haynes, CB, PR

Mike Haynes played cornerback and punt returner for the Patriots from 1976-82. He was one of two Patriots selected to the NFL's 75th Anniversary team—a very high honor for a player. He was known as a tenacious defensive back for man-to-man coverage.

For his defensive prowess, Haynes was named to six Pro Bowls in his seven years with the Patriots. An outstanding punt return specialist, Haynes was the first Patriot to return a punt for a touchdown.

In his rookie season in 1976, the team performed better than most seasons in history. Haynes contributed with eight pass interceptions and he returned two punts to pay-dirt for touchdowns.

He was traded to the Raiders following the 1982 season where he was contributed big time again and did his part in two Super Bowl Denver championships. He was elected to the Patriots Hall of Fame in 1994 and inducted into the Pro Football Hall of Fame in 1997. He was also inducted into the College Football Hall of Fame in 2001 for his ASU career. He was a great football player.

Haynes currently lives in New York and works for the National Football League.

1977 Chuck Fairbanks Coach # 6

The 1977 New England Patriots football team competed in their eighteenth season in professional football and their eighth season in the National Football League (NFL). The Patriots were led by Chuck Fairbanks in his fifth of six seasons. Billy Sullivan was the owner. The Patriots were a fine team this year with a record of 9-5-0 They lost two more games than in 1976 but still finished the year in a respectable third place in the AFC East. They did not make the playoffs, but they looked pretty good most of the year.

In the home and season opener for New England on September 18, 1977, the Patriots defeated the Kansas City Chiefs W (21–17) before 58,185, at Schaefer Stadium in Foxborough Massachusetts. At Cleveland, on Sept 26, the Browns beat the Patriots in a close match L (27-30) before 76,418. At New York, on Oct 2, 1977, the Jets beat the Patriots L (27-30) before 38,227. At home on Oct 9, the Patriots shut-out the Seattle Seahawks W (31–0) at Schaefer Stadium before 45,927. At San Diego, on Oct 16, New England beat San Diego W (24-20) before

On Oct 23, New England got the best of the Baltimore Colts W (17–3) at home before 60,958. At home on Oct 30, 1977, the patriots bested the New York Jets W (24–13) before 61,042. Then, on Nov 6 at home. Buffalo beat New England L (14-24). At Miami on Nov 13, the Dolphins prevailed L (5-17). At Buffalo the following week, the Patriots whipped the Bills W (20-7) before 27,598.

At home, on Nov 27, the Patriots got the best of the Philadelphia Eagles W (14–6) before 57,893. At Atlanta on Dec 4, the Patriots beat the Falcons W (16–10) before 57,911. At home on Dec 11, New England defeated Miami W (14–10) before 61,064. Then, on Dec 18 in the last game of the 1977 season at Baltimore, the Patriots could not finish the season a winner, but they tried. They were rooted out by the Baltimore Colts L (24-30) before 42,250

Top Patriots Players Stanley Morgan, WR

Stanley Morgan could not have played better for the Patriots with extra-sticky fly paper for fingers. As a wide receiver for the Patriots from 1977 to 1989 he hauled in 534 career receptions, a franchise record that stood for 17 years before Troy Brown beat his mark.

Morgan remains the franchise record holder with 10,352 receiving yards and 67 touchdowns. He still owns a career average of 19.2 yards per catch which still stands as an NFL record for those with more than 500 career receptions.

Morgan is a four-time Pro Bowl honoree. In addition to being a great receiver, he was also a fine punt returner, ranking among the career leaders in Patriots history. In 2007, Morgan was inducted into the Patriots Hall of Fame—a tribute well-earned.

1978 Chuck Fairbanks Coach # 6

The 1978 New England Patriots football team competed in their nineteenth season in professional football and their ninth season in the National Football League (NFL). The Patriots were led by Chuck Fairbanks in his last of six seasons. Billy Sullivan was the owner. The Patriots were a fine team this year with a better record than 1977's record of 9-5-0 This year, they hit the mark at 11-5-0 as the league chose to play sixteen instead of fourteen games per season. They won two more games than in 1977 and finished the year as the #1 ranked team in the AFC East. They made the playoffs winning the AFC East and they played in the Divisional Playoffs in which they lost. They looked pretty good for most of the year and none too shabby in the playoff game.

As noted, the Patriots finished the season with a record of eleven wins and five losses, and finished tied for first in the AFC East, winning their first division title in franchise history over Miami by a built-in tiebreaker.

The 1978 Patriots were another great team. They set an NFL record for most rushing yards in a single season, with 3,165 yards on the ground. You may recall some of these names. The Pats had four different players who rushed for more than 500 yards, beginning with running back Sam "Bam" Cunningham, 768; running back Andy Johnson, 675; running back Horace Ivory, 693; and quarterback Steve Grogan, 539. The team also picked up an NFL-record 181 rushing first-downs. This is one of those Patriot teams that had enough to win it all but just didn't win it all.

The season and home opener for New England was played on Sept 3 with the Washington Redskins prevailing L (14–16) at Schaefer Stadium before 55,037. At S St. Louis on Sept 10, the Patriots beat the Cardinals W (16–6) at Busch Memorial Stadium before 48,233. At home on Sept 19, the Baltimore Colts beat New England L (27–34) at Schaefer Stadium before 57,284. At Oakland on Sept 24, the Patriots beat the Raiders W (21-14) at the Alameda County Coliseum before 52,904.

On Oct 1 at home, the Patriots beat the San Diego Chargers W (28–23) at Schaefer Stadium before 60,781. On Oct 8, at home, the

Patriots beat the Philadelphia Eagles W (24–14) at Schaefer Stadium Before 61,016. At Cincinnati on Oct 15, the Patriots beat the Bengals W (10–3) at Riverfront Stadium before 48,699. At home, on Oct 22, the Patriots beat the Miami Dolphins W (33–24) at Schaefer Stadium before 60,424

At home again, on Oct 29, the Patriots blew out the New York Jets W 55–21 at Schaefer Stadium before 60,585. At Buffalo, on Nov 5. The Patriots barely beat the Bills W (14–10) at Rich Stadium before 44,897. On Nov 12, in a close match the Houston Oilers beat the New England Patriots L (23–26) at Schaefer Stadium before 60,356. Then at New York, on Nov 19 at Shea Stadium, the Patriots slid by the Jets in a close match W (19–17) before 55,568.

At Baltimore on Nov 26, New England clobbered the Colts W (35–14) at Memorial Stadium before 42,828. At Dallas on Dec 3, the Cowboys prevailed over the Patriots L (10-17) at Texas Stadium before 63,263. At home on Dec 10, New England won in a lose match against the Buffalo Bills W (26–24) at Schaefer Stadium before 59,598. In the final regular season game on Dec 18, at Miami's Orange Bowl Stadium, the Dolphins got the best of the Patriots spoiling their season finale L (3–23) before a great crowd of 72,071

Divisional Playoffs Patriots 31, Houston 14

The final score was New England 14, Houston 31. After they beat the Dolphins in a wild card game. the Oilers were on a high. They traveled up to New England to face the Patriots at Schaefer Stadium before 61,297 chilled fans. The Oilers were not fazed by the cold. They earned their trip to Pittsburgh with a trip to the Super Bowl on the line. The Patriots had to wait until 1979 for another shot at the top marbles. The game as all Oilers. QB Dan Pastorini threw three touchdown passes in the second quarter. That was more than enough to defeat the Patriots in their first home playoff game. Home field gave the Pats no edge on this particular day.

Chapter 15 Coach Ron Erhardt 1979 to 1981

Coach #7 Ron Erhard

Year Coach	League	Conf/Div	Place	Record
1979 Ron Erhardt	NFL	AFCEast	2nd	9 7 0
1980 Ron Erhardt	NFL	AFCEast	2nd	10 6 0
1981 Ron Erhardt	NFL	AFCEast	5th	2 14 0

1979-1981 Ron Erhardt final record (21-27-0)

Coach Ron Erhardt on the field

Ron Erhardt, a Talented Coach

Ron Erhardt is a native of Mandan, North Dakota,. He got his Bachelor's Degree from Jamestown College in 1953, and then entered the military where he put in two years. After retiring from the service, in 1956, he became an assistant coach at Williston High School in Williston, North Dakota. The next year he began a six-year run as a head coach at two North Dakota Catholic high schools where his combined record was 45-9-2 .

Erhardt's early success helped him be discovered at the collegiate level. He first served as an assistant at North Dakota State

University in 1963 for three years. Then, in 1966, he was named head coach at the school. This appointment set the stage for another strong tenure, in which Erhardt amassed a 61-7-1 record in his seven years. Erhardt also served as the Bison athletic director, winning a pair of college national championships. He was a great coach.

After missing the playoffs in 1977, the Patriots were ready to go for the Super Bowl in 1978. At the end of the last chapter we recounted their loss in the divisional playoffs. As noted, prior to the last regular season game on December 18, head coach Chuck Fairbanks announced he was leaving the team to accept a contract offer from the University of Colorado. The team ownership, to say the least was very upset.

They responded to the new by immediately suspending Fairbanks and they made Erhardt and fellow assistant Hank Bullough co-coaches for the final game of the season. The Patriots dropped that contest, then lost their opening round matchup to the Houston Oilers in the divisional playoffs.

Fairbanks was permitted to leave for Colorado, with Erhardt officially taking the reins of the team as head coach on April 6, according to Erhardt. Having had a .890 winning percentage at North Dakota State upon taking the position, Erhardt said, "I've never been a loser in football and I don't intend to start now."

He might not have been a loser but to the owners, he did not measure up. But, maybe nobody could. The Patriots "underachieved" with a 19–13 record in the 1979 (9-7) and 1980 (10-6) seasons, missing the playoffs by one game each year. Considering from whence they had come over the years, almost winning making the playoffs was not really that bad. The team was playing well in this period with 441 points scored in 1980. It was a club record not broken until 2007.

But then, inexplicably, the Patriots fell apart the third year under Erhardt to a 2–14 record in 1981. Owner Billy Sullivan, who some pundits say was responsible for all four letters in the word "gaff," used the calculatus-eliminatus method to determine that Erhardt was "just too nice a guy," to be the coach of the Patriots. Owner Billy

Sullivan dismissed this coach after one terrible performance year on December 22, just two days after the conclusion of the season.

There are lots of good coaches who think Ron Erhardt is a good coach who wound up with a not-so-good owner. Ron Erhardt, the three-season head coach of the New England Patriots coach turned his football fortunes around by becoming the offensive architect of the New York Giants' two Super Bowl titles. He did this when Bill Parcells was at the helm and Parcells saw him as one of the best. On March 21, 2012, this great coach "Erhardt" passed away at 80-years of age as one of the best with a great and solid football legacy despite his 1981 experience with the Patriots.

The Giants made the press announcement that the one-time head coach of the New England Patriots and the long-time NFL offensive coordinator had passed away in retirement in Boca Raton, Fla. Accolades came in from all directions.

"Ron was a wonderful man and a great coach," Giants chief executive John Mara said. "He was a big part of our success in the 1980s and was an important contributor to our first two Super Bowl championships."

When it was time for Ron Erhardt to abruptly leave the Patriots, Ray Perkins was the head coach of the Giants. He brought Erhardt in as offensive coordinator of the Giants in 1982, about a month after Erhardt was released by the Patriots.

When Perkins left in 1982 for the University of Alabama, the Giants named Bill Parcells as the head coach. He kept Erhardt, who he knew from some experience he had with the Patriots in 1980. Erhardt was a fine head coach for New England the Patriots but he was an even better offensive coordinator for eight seasons with the Giants. With Erhardt calling the plays, the Giants reached the playoffs five times, won three NFC East titles and picked up two Super Bowls to boot.

Phil Simms was the QB for the first Super Bowl over Denver after the 1986 season, and Jeff Hostetler took the QB spot on the Giants team en route to the second title after Simms broke his left foot late in the 1990 season.

"I learned an awful lot from him. He went on and did some amazing things offensively," Hostetler said. "What amazes me, is that system is still out there, still being used, and it works as successfully as ever. It is - without a doubt, out of all the systems I've been involved with and that's probably five, six, or seven different systems - the simplest as far as verbiage, and most consistent."

Under Erhardt's mentoring, the Giants consistently had one of the NFL's most productive rushing attacks. Joe Morris rushed for more than 1,000 yards three times, including 1,516 in the Giants' first Super Bowl season. With Erhardt doing the offensive teaching, The Giants also finished in the Top 10 in the league in passing in 1984, '85 and '87.

Not all good things last and eventually somebody did not want what Erhardt had to offer. He lost his play-calling duties when Bill Parcells left the Giants after the 1991 season and Ray Handley wanted somebody else. Erhardt went with Pittsburgh as their offensive coordinator in 1992 and he spent four good years with them, helping them reach the Super Bowl after the 1995 season. He also put in one season as the Jets O-coordinator in 1996.

Before becoming the head coach at New England, Erhardt had other duties with the Patriots. He became the Patriots backfield coach in 1973. He stayed in the that position for four seasons before becoming the New England offensive coordinator. Erhardt was a natural to become New England's head coach and he was appointed to serve after Chuck Fairbanks left after the 1978 season. Erhardt did not have the best record in his three years from 1979-81, compiling a record of 21-27.

Fired after one bad year. Was that the best medicine for the Patriots or for Coach Erhardt. Could Billy Sullivan have been the real problem with the Patriots for all those years. Considering that Erhardt, a native of Mandan, N.D., as 67-7-1 as a head coach in college and won two college division national championships at North Dakota State University, one does wonder.

I know that I was wondering what was wrong. Today's fine-tuned Kraft-owned Patriots are nothing like the Patriots of the early years with the Sullivans. So, when there is a question, in most cases some good research can provide answers. I found the answer. This answer shows the disdain that Bostonians and New Englanders had for the pre-Brady, pre-Belichick Patriots. I am including this entire article right here right now because it is the right time to say something. Here it is beginning on the next page:

Yes, the Patriots actually made a Super Bowl following the 1985 season. That was the good news. The bad news was it was a game to forget, with the team anguishing fans, including those gathered in a lounge at Walpole, Mass., with a dreadful performance. Talk about best of times and worst of times. Photos by The Associated Press accompanied this article

Article Title: For Patriots, the good times haven't always rolled
Article Subtitle: Before Brady and Belichick, the team was a decades-long example of how not to run a franchise.

BY BARRY SVRLUGA, THE WASHINGTON POST
Posted January 28, 2017------------------

This is a franchise that in no particular order chose a guy who couldn't win at the University of Toledo over a Hall of Famer as its coach, nearly electrocuted that coach at a news conference, suspended another coach for taking a different job in-season, played 19 seasons before hosting a playoff game, played 26 before winning a playoff game, then reached the Super Bowl only as a means to sharpen the punchlines to an endless stream of jokes.

That was all before they reached rock bottom.

It's a franchise that was going to move to Birmingham (maybe) or St. Louis (likely) or Hartford (definitely). It played in the NFL's worst stadium and drew its worst crowds. In a sports-mad city playing what became America's most popular sport, it ranked behind basketball, behind baseball, even behind hockey. And it wasn't close.

And now an entire nation is sick of these guys?

As inevitable as the New England Patriots' ninth appearance in the Super Bowl seems – particularly with seven of those AFC titles crammed into the past 16 seasons – such a stretch seemed absurdly far-fetched over the team's first 30 years of existence. This wasn't as much a Mickey Mouse operation as one that would have benefited greatly had Mickey himself been put in charge.

So let's not let joyless Bill Belichick and autotron Tom Brady scrub the franchise of its inglorious, itinerant, haphazard and occasionally hysterical past. When the Patriots came into existence as a flagship member of the old American Football League in 1960, they played at Boston University. They played at Harvard. They played at Fenway Park, with both teams sharing one sideline. They played at Boston College, where there was once a fire in the stands.

And then things got bad.

Late in their first decade, owner Billy Sullivan was looking for a replacement for Mike Holovak as head coach. The New York

Jets, with Clive Rush as their offensive coordinator, had just upset the Baltimore Colts, with Chuck Noll as their defensive coordinator, in Super Bowl III, 16-7. The story goes that Sullivan couldn't justify hiring a losing assistant, so he went with Rush. Nice choice. Rush's only head coach experience had been a three-year, 8-20 stint at Toledo. Crippling. The Steelers would be left with Noll.

The Patriots subsequently brought on another Jet, George Sauer Sr., as the general manager. At Sauer's introductory news conference, Rush picked up the microphone – and immediately started wailing. What little hair he had stood on end. He was, in fact, being electrocuted. He should have put that jolt into New England's offense. Instead, when someone finally unplugged the mic, Rush slumped to the floor.

Rush's other notable contribution in a 21-game tenure was in reaction to his inability to sign the team's top draft pick. He pulled an inactive player, running back Bob Gladieux, from the stands and inserted him for the opening kickoff. Gladieux had just sent a friend for hot dogs and drinks. Instead he made the game's first tackle.

Eventually, Rush left the sideline during a game. Most Patriots fans couldn't blame him. The team fired him seven games into his second season. Noll coached the Steelers for 23 years and won four Super Bowls. Flip of a coin.

This kind of fortune was woven into the franchise's fabric. They were known as the Boston Patriots until the owners of a harness racing track 30 miles southwest of downtown donated land for a stadium. Had that not happened, the Patriots might have moved to Alabama (where they would have to have been called the Rebels, right?). The edifice built by the Sullivan family, who had owned the club since its birth, cost $7.1 million to construct. That's roughly $43 million in today's dollars – or $2 million more than Brady's current two-year contract.

What Schaefer Stadium lacked in accoutrements, it made up for in extreme inconvenience and straight-backed metal bleachers. It was such a lousy venue that even though Anheuser-Busch owned the naming rights in the 1980s, the brewer preferred to rename the stadium after the Sullivans, lest association with the team and the field sully the good name of, say, Budweiser.

In the 1960s and '70s, after nine straight seasons without a winning record, the Sullivans managed to find stability with Chuck Fairbanks as coach. In 1978, New England was in line to host a playoff game for the first time in franchise history, with only a "Monday Night Football" game in Miami left to close out the regular season. Before that game, though, Fairbanks told his team he was leaving to become the coach at the University of Colorado. Small detail: He hadn't shared this information with Sullivan.

The owner's solution: Suspend Fairbanks for the Miami game, and name Ron Erhardt and Hank Bullough as co-coaches. Each gave a separate pep talk before the Dolphins game. The Patriots lost, 23-3. Sullivan's new solution: Reinstate Fairbanks for the playoff game against Houston. New England fell behind 21-0 at halftime and lost 31-14. Mayhem.

So, with Larry Bird's Celtics and Carl Yastrzemski's Red Sox and Ray Bourque's Bruins to compete with, the Patriots annually risked being an afterthought. Even when the team finally won a playoff game, it could scarcely stay out of its own way. After beating the Jets and Raiders on the road to reach the 1985 AFC title game in Miami, Irving Fryar – the top overall pick in the previous year's draft – said he had injured his hand in a mishap with a kitchen knife. Turns out the mishap involved an altercation with his wife. The Patriots sent Fryar home, advanced to the Super Bowl anyway, and were blown out by the Chicago Bears.

The Patriots somehow turned that achievement into a hallmark for ineptness. New England quarterback Steve Grogan was sacked four times and threw two interceptions. Co-quarterback Tony Eason went 0 of 6, was sacked three times and fumbled once. The Patriots rushed for 7 yards. Final: Bears 46, Patriots 10. It wasn't that close.

Yet in a way, that Super Bowl appearance went more smoothly than the next one, 11 years later, when Coach Bill Parcells arrived with his team, coached in a loss to the Green Bay Packers and left on a different plane, never intending to coach the Patriots again. He wound up with the rival Jets instead.

It never seemed to stop. One first-round draft pick, running back Robert Edwards, shredded his knee – in a flag football game on the beach in Hawaii. Even the worst season in team history, a 1-15 mark in 1990 under one-year head coach Rod Rust, is remembered more for the fact that tight end Zeke Mowatt and other players sexually harassed a female beat writer for the Boston Herald.

That had to be the nadir. Except wait a couple days: The owner, shaving mogul Victor Kiam, made jokes about the incident at a public appearance. The guy Kiam sold the team to, James Orthwein, always seemed to want to move to his native St. Louis. Even as recently as 1998, the Patriots were so unstable and unpredictable that Robert Kraft, the current owner, signed a deal to move the team to Connecticut.

Yet in typical Patriots fashion, that deal fell apart. What didn't? This is the franchise that has one losing season in its past 21. This is the franchise that has won 13 of the past 14 division titles – and the year it missed the playoffs went 11-5. This is the franchise that is now seen as a model.

The message: Have faith, Cleveland fans. Anything's possible.

--- End of post---

1979 Ron Erhardt Coach # 7

The 1979 New England Patriots football team competed in their twentieth season of professional football and their tenth season in the National Football League (NFL). The Patriots were led by Ron Erhardt in his first of three seasons. Erhard had co-coached the Patriots in the last game of the 1978 season, but we do not count that in this book as a coached season. Billy Sullivan was still the owner of the Patriots. This year, the new overtime rule would be applied to tie games so that fewer games would end in ties.

The Patriots were an OK team this year with a better than 500 records of 9-7-0. They finished the year as the #2 ranked team in the AFC East. They were one game away from making the playoffs. They looked pretty good for most of the year but not enough to win a box of cigars.

In their season opener the Patriots faced the Pittsburgh Steelers on Monday Night as Darryl Stingley returned to Schaffer Stadium. Patriots fans gave the paralyzed star a long sustained standing ovation. However, the emotion did not carry over as the Pats lost 16-13 in overtime. The Pats would find themselves at 8-4, as the team featured a more wide-open offense under quarterback Steve Grogan. However, a three-game losing streak ended their playoff chances, as the team settled for what became a disappointing 9–7 season

3 In the season and home opener at Schaefer Stadium on September 3, 1979, the Pittsburgh Steelers beat the New England Patriots in a single OT match L (13–16) before 60,978. At home again on Sept 3, the Patriots crushed the New York Jets W (56–3) at Schaefer Stadium before 53,113. At Cincinnati on Sept 16, the Patriots defeated the Bengals W (20–14) at Riverfront Stadium 2–1 41,805 23 4 San Diego Chargers W 27–21 Schaefer Stadium 3–1 60,916.

The second loss of the season came at the hands of the Green Bay Packers L (14–27) on oct 1 at Lambeau Field before 52,842. On Oct 7, at home, the Patriots won by a TD over the Detroit Lions W 24–17 at Schaefer Stadium before 60,629. In Oct 14, at Chicago, the Patriots dominated the Bears W (27–7) at Soldier Field before 54,128. At home on Oct 21, at Schaefer Stadium, the Patriots dominated the Miami Dolphins W (28–13) before 61,096.

At Baltimore on Oct 28, the Colts beat the Patriots by a skosh L (26–31) at Memorial Stadium before 41,029. On Nov 4, at Buffalo, the Patriots overwhelmed the Bills W (26-6) at Rich Stadium before 67,935. Then, on Nov 11 at Denver, the Broncos lambasted the Patriots L (10–45) at Mile High Stadium before 74,379. At home on Nov 18 in Schaefer Stadium, the Patriots walloped the Colts W (50-21) before 60,879.

On Nov 25 at Schaefer Stadium, the Buffalo Bills beat the New England Patriots L (13-16) before 60,991. At Miami on Nov 29, the Dolphins triumphed L (24-39 (at the Miami Orange Bowl before 69,174. At New York, on Dec 9, the Patriots lost a one-point game to the Jets L (26-27) before 45,131. At home in the final game of the season, the Patriots put it all together to beat the Minnesota Vikings W 27–23 at Schaefer Stadium before 54,719

1980 Ron Erhardt Coach # 7

The 1980 New England Patriots football team competed in their twenty-first season of professional football and their eleventh season in the National Football League (NFL). The Patriots were led by Ron Erhardt in his second of three seasons. Billy Sullivan was the owner. The Patriots were a fine team this year with a better record (10-6) than the 9-7-0 from 1979. They finished the year again as the #2 ranked team in the AFC East. They were one game away from making the playoffs. They looked pretty good for most of the year but again, not quite enough to compete for the big cigar.

Running Back Sam Cunningham decided he wanted more this season from the Patriots and he held out all season. For their part, the Patriots turned to rookie Vagas Ferguson to carry the bulk of the rushing game. Ferguson responded by breaking the team's rookie rushing record. The Patriots were rolling along quite well right before the mid-season point and it looked like a good year to make the playoffs. Unfortunately, the Pats managed to win just two of their next seven games, and they finished with a 10–6 record that saw them fall a game short of a wild card berth.

Bill Parcells, then the linebackers coach with the team, has stated that the players on this Patriots team gave him his famous "Tuna" nickname when he asked, "What do you think I am, Charlie the Tuna?" Parcells had high regards for coach Ron Erhardt.

The home and season opener was played at Schaefer Stadium in Foxboro on Sept 7 against the Cleveland Browns. The Patriots prevailed W (34–17) before 49,222. The Patriots first loss came early On Sept 14 in the second game at Shaefer Stadium L (21-37) against the Atlanta Falcons before 48,321. On Sept 21, at Seattle's Kingdome, the Patriots beat the Seahawks W (37–31) before 61,035. On Sept 29 at home in Schaefer Stadium, the Patriots beat the Denver Broncos W (23–14) before 59,602.

At New York on Oct 5 in Shea Stadium, the Patriots defeated the Jets W (21-11) before 53,603. At home again, on Oct 12, the Patriots shut out the Miami Dolphins W (34–0) at Schaefer Stadium before 60,377. On Oct 19, at Baltimore, the Patriots outplayed the Colts W (37–21) at Memorial Stadium before 53,924. At Buffalo on October 26, the Bills beat the Patriots L (13–31) at Rich Stadium before 75,092.

At home again on Nov 2, the Patriots beat the New York Jets W (34–21) at Schaefer Stadium before 60,834. Then, at Houston, on Nov 10, the Oilers defeated the Patriots L (34–38) at the Astrodome before 51,524. The next loss was at home against Los Angeles on Nov 16, L (14-17) at Schaefer Stadium before 60,609. The Baltimore Colts then came to Schaefer Stadium on Nov 23 and were smothered by the Patriots W (47–21) before a packed house of 60,994.

At San Francisco on November 30, the 49ers won a close match against the Patriots L (17–21) at Candlestick Park before 45,254. At Miami on Dec 8, the Dolphins got the best of the Patriots L (13–16) in (OT) in a game played at the Miami Orange Bowl before 63,292. The Patriots won their last two games of the season. The first was on Dec 14 at home against buffalo W (24-2) before 58,324 and the second and also the last game of the season was on Dec 21 at New Orleans against the Saints W (38–27) in the Superdome before 38,277.

1981 Ron Erhardt Coach # 7

The 1981 New England Patriots football team competed in their twenty-second season of professional football and their twelfth season in the National Football League (NFL). The Patriots were led by Ron Erhardt in his last of three seasons. Billy Sullivan was the owner. The Patriots were a different team this year, seeming having lost the fire that was the hallmark of Erhardt's first two years at the helm. They finished with a dismal 2-14 record, tied for fourth (last) in the AFC East. They were out of all post season contention. Two days after the season, Billy Sullivan fired coach Ron Erhardt as it was tough to take a 2-14 season at any time.

The season went as you would expect for a 2-14 year. The team lost their first four games, and then ten of their last eleven, including the last nine games of the season. They could not do anything right or, so it seemed.

The games were close, but nobody was giving trophies for almost wins. The Patriots were defeated in both the first and last games of the season by the Baltimore Colts. Ironically what became known as the Patriots' bookend losses proved to be Baltimore's only two wins of the 1981 season.

It was known that the loser of that last game would have the first pick in the 1982 NFL Draft, and so the pundits enjoyed nicknaming this last game, "The Stupor Bowl." With the Patriot loss, the team had the first pick, choosing University of Texas defensive end Kenneth Sims, an eventual draft "bust" as first overall pick in the NFL draft. Even their draft pick consolation prize did not work out in 1981.

The home and season opener was played at Schaefer Stadium in Foxboro on Sept 6 against the Baltimore Colts and Browns. The Patriots lost the game by one-point L (28-29) before 49,572. At Philadelphia on Sept 13, the Eagles beat the Patriots L (3-13) before 71,089. At home on Sept 21, 1981 the Dallas Cowboys beat the Patriots L (21-35) before 60,311. At Pittsburgh on Sept 27, the Patriots lost their fourth straight game v the Steelers L (21-27) before 53,344.

The KC Chiefs came to Schaefer Stadium on Oct 4, my anniversary, and were defeated by the Patriots W (33–17) for their first win of the year before 55,931. At New York, on Oct 11, the Jets beat the Patriots in a close match L (24-28) before 55,093. In another home game at Schaefer Stadium, on Oct 18, the Patriots trounced the Houston Oilers W (38–10) before 60,474. At Washington, on Oct 25, the Redskins beat the Patriots y two points L (22-24) before 50,394.

At Oakland on Nov 1, the Raiders beat the Patriots L (17-27) before 44,246. At home on Nov 8, in Schaefer Stadium, the Miami Dolphins prevailed over the Patriots in a three-point match L (27-30) before 60,436. On Nov 15, the New York Jets beat the Patriots at home in Schaefer Stadium L (6-17) before. The next week at Buffalo, on Nov 22, in another cliff hanger close match, the Bills beat the Patriots L (17-20) before 71,593.

At home on Nov 29, the St. Louis Cardinals defeated the New England Patriots L (20-27) before 39,946. At Miami on Dec 6, the Dolphins beat the Patriots L (14-24) before 50,421. On Dec 13 at home, New England lost to Buffalo L (10-19 before 42,549. In the season finale, on Dec 20 at Baltimore, the Colts won the two-point game L (21-23) before 17,073

Chapter 16 Coach Ron Meyer 1982 to 1984

Coach #8 Ron Meyer
Coach #9 Raymond Berry

Year Coach	League	Conf/Div	Place	Record
1982 Ron Meyer	NFL	AFC East	7th	5 4 0

- Lost First Round (at Dolphins) 13–28 **9 game season w/strike**

1983 Ron Meyer	NFL	AFC East	2nd	8 8 0
1984 Ron Meyer (5–3)	NFL	AFC East	2nd	9 7 0

1984 Raymond Berry (4-8)
1982-1984 Ron Meyer final record (18-15)

Former Coach Ron Meyer on sidelines with Patriots

Ron Meyer replaces Ron Erhardt as Pats head coach

Reprinted from the UPI Web Archives
March 9, 1982
  FOXBORO, Mass. -- Ron Meyer has promised the New England Patriots will be one of the best-conditioned teams in the NFL next

season. And he's getting an early start on his grand plan -- starting his first mini-camp this weekend.

Meyer, who replaced the fired Ron Erhardt as the Pats' coach after New England went 2-14, is allowed an extra mini-camp under NFL rules. It took him a few weeks to complete his coaching staff, but no time at all to schedule the mini-camp.

All but six Patriots are scheduled to report to Schaefer Stadium on Friday. There will be team meetings, tests for strength, flexibility and conditioning, and a practice on Sunday to wrap-up the three-day affair.

The six not participating, because they are free agents, are Harold Jackson, John Lee, Bill Matthews, Tom Owen, Carlos Pennywell and Garry Puetz.

'We want to introduce the players to a year-round flexibility, weight-training and conditioning program, to our basic football philosophy -- what it takes to win,' Meyer said.

'You can't lay out certain idioms or axioms on what it takes to win. We've evaluated the existing personnel on film. It's a beneficial teaching aide but we're not locking ourselves in with a pre-conceived idea of each player. It (the mini-camp) will give us an update on where the players are and give us an idea on where our weaknesses may occur,' the coach said.

Another purpose of the mini-camp will be to allow the players to meet the new coaches. Meyer hired former Oakland assistant Lew Erber to head the offense and former Seattle assistant Jim Mora to head the defense. He also brought six coaches -- and the team's first-ever strength coach -- with him from Southern Methodist.

'It's a two-way street,' Meyer said when queried as to whether veterans might be a bit wary of a new coach and a new system. 'We're also going to be tested. Those guys are going to come in and say, 'who are they, what do they know, what kind of men are they and will they help me to become a better football player?' 'To say it'll be an adverse relationship, I certainly hope not,' Meyer continued. 'It's going to be a 'we'-togetherness rather than a dogmatic type of relationship. We've got too much at stake to worry about personalities.'

One disgruntled veteran, Tim Fox, is expected to report, the team said. Fox is upset with his contract and told the Boston Globe he wouldn't attend the camp. The team said Fox is under contract.

Ron Meyer Patriots Coach

1982 Ron Meyer Coach # 8

The 1982 New England Patriots football team competed in their twenty-third season of professional football and their thirteenth season in the National Football League (NFL). The Patriots were led by Ron Meyer in his first of two and a half seasons. Billy Sullivan was the owner. The Patriots were a better team this year, and they were able to put the prior 2-14 season behind them. This season was strike-shortened from 16 games to nine. The Patriots finished well at 5-4 and gained a spot in the payoffs. The team finished seventh in the American Football Conference. As noted, the 1982 season was shortened from 16 regular season games to 9, due to the 57-day players strike.

Schedule / Results

Because this was a strange season with games scheduled and rescheduled and canceled and moved from one week to another. We present this seasons games in tabular form rather than by telling the story of the season as we have since the 1960 season. The information in the table from left to right will be shown in this sequence with commas separating the values in the table. Away games show an "at" in front of the opponent's name.

- Actual Week
- Original week
- Opponent
- Result (W or L)
- Score
- Record
- Venue
- Attendance

1, 1, at Baltimore Colts, W, 24–13, 1–0, Memorial Stadium, 39,055
2, 2, New York Jets, L, 7–31, 1–1, Schaefer Stadium, 53,515
*, 3, Seattle Seahawks, Canceled, , , Schaefer Stadium,
*, 4, at Buffalo Bills, Canceled, , , Rich Stadium,
*, 5, Cincinnati Bengals, Canceled, , , Schaefer Stadium,
*, 6, at Miami Dolphins, Canceled, , , Miami Orange Bowl,
*, 7, St. Louis Cardinals, Canceled, , , Schaefer Stadium,
*, 8, at New York Jets, Canceled, , , Shea Stadium,
*, 9, Baltimore Colts, Canceled, , , Schaefer Stadium,
*, 10, Buffalo Bills, Canceled (played Jan 2, 1983), , , Schaefer Stadium,
11, 3, at Cleveland Browns, L, 7–10, 1–2, Cleveland Stadium, 51,781
12, 4, Houston Oilers, W, 29–21, 2–2, Schaefer Stadium, 33,602
13, 5, at Chicago Bears, L, 13–26, 2–3, Soldier Field, 36,973
14, 6, Miami Dolphins, W, 3–0 (Snowplow Game), 3–3, Schaefer, 25,716
15, 7, at Seattle Seahawks, W, 16–0, 4–3, Kingdome, 53,457
16, 8, at Pittsburgh Steelers, L, 14–37, 4–4, Three Rivers Stadium, 51,515
17, 9, Buffalo Bills, W, 30–19, 5–4, Schaefer Stadium, 36,218

Post Season Bracket Tournament (like March Madness)

If it were not for the fact that in the type of post season tournament that was conducted this year, a team might play just *one* tournament game, there were those who thought perhaps the whole 1982 season should be played as a tournament to make it more exciting—rather than play the nine-game season. Besides the post season tournament, the other big change was that there were no divisions in play this year. The top eight teams of the fourteen teams in each conference played a tournament to decide who would play in the Super Bowl. Almost all teams saw action

The bracket for this unusual and special post season is shown below:

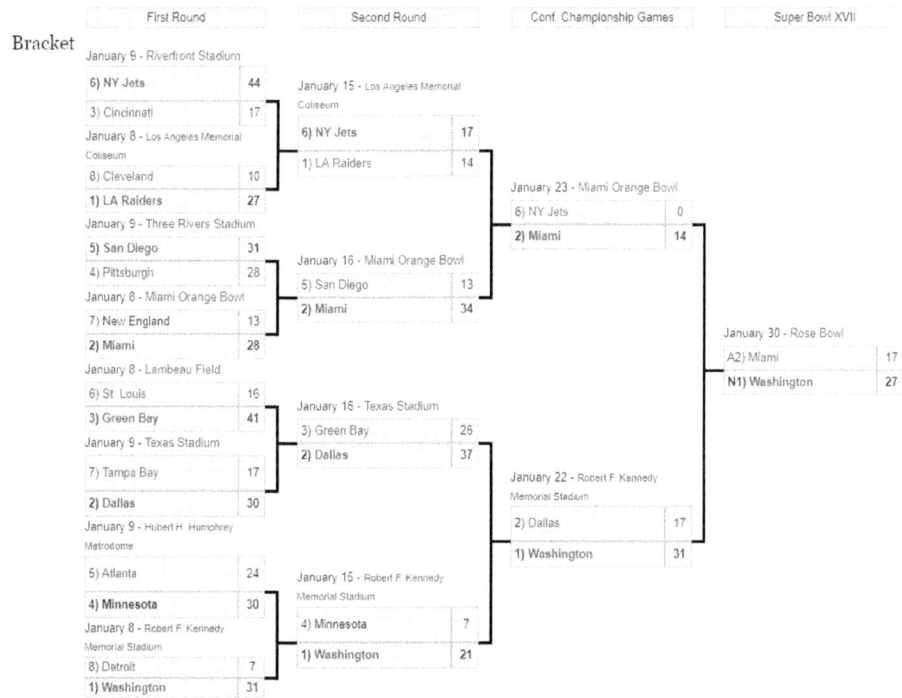

The League Playoffs began on January 8, 1983. The postseason tournament concluded with the Washington Redskins defeating the Miami Dolphins in Super Bowl XVII, 27–17, on January 30, at the Rose Bowl in Pasadena, California.

As noted, there was a 57-day players' strike which reduced the regular season to nine games. Thus, the league used this special 16-team playoff format (dubbed the "Super Bowl Tournament"), just for this year and never again. As noted, there were no Division standings. Eight teams from each conference were seeded 1–8 based on their regular season records. The Patriots were seventh in their conference.

This year marked the first time in NFL history in which a team that qualified for the playoffs had a losing record (< .500), as both Cleveland and Detroit finished with 4–5 records (.444). Both of these teams lost in the first round of the playoffs as did the Patriots who sported a 5-4 conference record.

AFC: Playoffs Dolphins 28, New England 13

The game began at 4:00 PM EST. The weather was 76 degrees at the Miami Orange Bowl in Miami Florida, the home team of the Dolphins/ 68,842 fans attended the game.

This was the Dolphins game right from the opening kickoff. The Dolphins owned most of the game with their attack which included four long touchdown drives. They intercepted Patriots quarterback Steve Grogan twice.

Miami QB David Woodley was at his peak during the game, completing 16 of 19 passes for 246 yards and two touchdowns (both to tight end Bruce Hardy). The Miami QB threw no interceptions, and he rushed for 16 yards. For the game, his rating was through the roof at 153.8.

Andrea Franklin, Miami's star running back, ran 26 times for 112 yards and a touchdown. The Dolphins outgained the Patriots by a mile (448yds to 237yds) and rushing yards (214 to 77).

The Patriots had a moment of glory in the beginning of the second quarter when they grabbed a 3-0 lead on John Smith's 23-yard field goal. However, it would be just five minutes later that Woodley finished a 76-yard drive with a 2-yard touchdown pass to tight end Bruce Hardy. Then next time the Dolphins had the ball, they drove 79 yards to a 1-yard touchdown run by Franklin, giving the team a 14-3 halftime lead.

The Pats got the lead down to 14-6 on Smith's 42-yard field goal early in the third quarter. But that would be as close as New England would get. Miami scored again with touchdowns from

Woody Bennett, another 2-yard catch by Hardy late in the third quarter, and in the middle of the fourth. With 5:32 left in the game, Grogan threw a perfect 22-yard touchdown strike to tight end Don Hasselbeck that added the icing to the Miami cakes and a final score of 28-13.

Top Patriots Players Andre Tippett, LB

Andre Tippett played 11 seasons for the Patriots from 1982-93. He is the second player to earn induction to the Hall of Fame after spending his entire career with the Patriots.

Tippett was one of the greatest linebackers in NFL history, spending his entire 12-year career with the Patriots. A strong-side linebacker who excelled at rushing the passer, Tippett set the record for most sacks over a two-year period with 35 in the 1984 and 1985 seasons and holds the franchise record for career sacks with 100.

In 1985, he was named the Defensive Player of the Year for the AFC Champion Patriots. Since his retirement, Tippett has worked for the Patriots and currently serves as the team's Executive Director of Community Affairs.

Tippett was voted into the Patriots Hall of Fame in 1999 and enshrined into the Pro Football Hall of Fame in 2008. The

Massachusetts native is active in local youth football and coaches a Pop Warner team. Inducted 1999.

1983 Ron Meyer Coach # 8

The 1983 New England Patriots football team competed in their twenty-fourth season of professional football and their fourteenth season in the National Football League (NFL). The Patriots were led by Ron Meyer in his second of two and a half seasons. Billy Sullivan was the owner. The Patriots had an 8-8 record this year. This season was back to normal with 16 games being scheduled and played

The Pats tied for second in the AFC East Division. The team played inconsistently all season. Nonetheless in the last game, with an 8-7 record going in, they still had a shot, at a playoff spot as long as they managed a in their final game of the season in Seattle. It did not happen. The Patriots would have problems with turnovers the whole game as rookie quarterback Tony Eason was gobbled up in a 24-6 loss to the Seahawks.

In the home and season opener on September 4, 1983 the Baltimore Colts defeated New England L (23-29) before 45,526. At Miami on Sept 11, the Dolphins beat the Patriots L (24–34) before 59,343. At Schaefer Stadium, on Sept 18, the Patriots beat the
New York Jets W (23–13) before 43,182. At Pittsburgh, on Sept 25, New England defeated the Steelers W (28-23) before 58,282

At home at Schaefer Stadium on Oct 2, the San Francisco 49ers whipped the Patriots L (13–33) before 54,293. At Baltimore on Oct 9, the Colts beat the Patriots L (7-12) before 35,618. Then, on Oct 16, at home, the Patriots defeated the San Diego Chargers W (37–21) before 59,016. At Buffalo on Oct 23, the New England Patriots walloped the Bills in a shutout W (31-0) before 60,424.

At Atlanta on Oct 30, the Falcons defeated the Patriots L (13-24) before 47,546. On Nov 6, New England beat the Buffalo Bills at Schaefer Stadium W (21–7) before 42,604. Then, on Nov 13, the Patriots beat Miami at home W (17–6) before 60,771. The next week on Nov 20, the Cleveland Browns shut out the Patriots L (0-30) before 40,987.

At New York, on Nov 27, the Jets dominated New England L (3-26) before 48,620. The New Orleans Saints lost to the Patriots on Dec 4, 1983 by one TD W (7-0) at Schaefer Stadium before 24,579. At Los Angeles on Dec 11, the Patriots beat the Rams W (21-7) before 46,503. In the final game of the season on Dec 18 at Seattle, if New England won the game, they were in the playoffs. They could not pull it off and were beaten by the Seahawks L (6-24) before 59,688.

1984 Ron Meyer Coach # 8
1984 Raymond Berry Coach # 9

The 1984 New England Patriots football team competed in their twenty-fifth season of professional football and their fifteenth season in the National Football League (NFL). The Patriots were led by Ron Meyer in his third of two and a half seasons. Meyer would be replaced halfway through this season after a dispute with owners. Meyer was 5-3 at the time. Billy Sullivan was the owner. Ray Berry took on the task of coaching the second half of the season. He was 4-4. The Patriots had an 9-7 record this year between the two coaches. The Patriots finished second in the AFC East Division.

As noted, head coach Ron Meyer, who had coached the Patriots for the previous two seasons, was fired halfway through this season. Meyer had angered several of his players with public criticism. After the team's 44–22 loss to Miami in Week 8, Meyer decided to fire popular defensive coordinator Rod Rust; Meyer himself was fired by Patriots management shortly thereafter.

The Patriots did not hire Meyer's replacement from within. Instead they found Raymond Berry, who had been New England's receivers coach from 1978 to 1981 under coaches Chuck Fairbanks and Ron Erhardt. Berry had been working in the private sector in Medfield, Massachusetts, when the Patriots called him to replace Meyer.

Berry's first order of business was to immediately rehire Rust.

Under Berry's leadership, the Patriots won four of their last eight games. Berry's importance to the team was reflected less in his initial win-loss record than in the respect he immediately earned in the locker room – "Raymond Berry earned more respect in one day than Ron Meyer earned in three years," according to running back Tony Collins. Everybody has an opinion.

In the season opener on September 2, 1984 at Buffalo, the Patriots beat the Bills W (21–17) as Steve Grogan threw two touchdowns before 48,528 fans. At Miami on Sept 9, the Dolphins beat the Pats L (7-28) before 66,083. Then, on Sept 16, 1984 at the newly renamed Sullivan Stadium (formerly Schaefer Stadium) the Patriots defeated the Seattle Seahawks W (38–23) after erasing a 23–0 gap before 43,140. At home on Sept 23, Washington defeated New England L (10-26) in Tony Eason's first start before 60,503.

At New York on Sept 30 at New York, New England beat the Jets W (28–21) before 68,978. Then, on Oct 7 at Cleveland in a one-point difference match, the Patriots beat the Browns W 17–16 before 53,036. Then, on Oct 14, 1984 the New England Patriots defeated the Cincinnati Bengals W (20–14) before 48,154. At home on Oct 21, the Miami Dolphins ran over the Patriots L (24-44) before 60,711. Hard coach Ron Meyer was fired after this game, ending his part of the season at 5-3.

On Oct 28, the Patriots beat the New York Jets W (30–20) with new coach Raymond Berry at the helm. At Denver on Nov 4, the Broncos defeated the Patriots L (19-26) before 74,908. At home on Nov 11, the New England Patriots defeated the Buffalo Bills W (38–10) before 43,313. At Indianapolis on Nov 18, the Patriots shellacked the Colts W (50-17) before 60,009.

At Dallas on Nov 22, the Cowboys squeaked out a victory over the Patriots L (17-20) on the Patriots first Thanksgiving Day game before 55, 341. At home on Dec 2, the St. Louis Cardinals drubbed the New England Patriots L (10-33) before 53,558. At Philadelphia on Dec 9, the Eagles got the best of the Patriots L (17-27) before 41,581. At Sullivan Stadium in the final game, on Dec 16, the Patriots beat the Indianapolis Colts W (16–10) before 22,383

Chapter 17 Coach Ray Berry 1985 to 1989

Coach # 9 Raymond Berry

Year Coach   League   Conf/Div   Place   Record
1984 Ray Berry (4-4)
1985 Ray Berry NFL   AFC-East   3rd   **11-5-0**
- Won Wild Card Playoffs (at Jets) 26-14
- Won Divisional Playoffs (at Raiders) 27-20
- Won Conference Championship (at Dolphins) 31-14
- Lost Super Bowl XX (vs. Bears) 10-46

1986 Ray Berry NFL   AFC-East   1st   **11-5-0**
- Lost Divisional Playoffs (at Broncos) 17-22

1987 Ray Berry NFL   AFC-East   2nd   **8-7-0**
1988 Ray Berry NFL   AFC-East   3rd   **9-7-0**
- John Stephens(OROY)

1989 Ray Berry NFL   AFC-East   4th   **5-11-0**

1984-1989 Ray Berry final record (47-39)

Raymond Berry: Great Person, Great Player, Great Coach

1985 AFC Divisional Playoffs – LA Raiders Vs New England Patriots – 3rd Qtr

Raymond Berry was a great receiver who caught passes for the Colts from a guy who is one of the greatest QB's of all time, Johnny

Unitas. Berry liked to say: "Luck is something which happens when preparation meets opportunity. One play may make the difference in winning or losing a game. I must be prepared to make my own luck."

Those who capture the Raymond Berry story find a man of determination, dedication and desire. Berry, had a little-known handicap which forced him to wear special shoes because one leg was shorter than the other. He did not become a starter on his high school football team until his senior year – even though his father was the coach.

After all is said and done Ray Berry proved his worth. He played as a split end for the Baltimore Colts from 1955 to 1967, and after several assistant coaching positions, he landed the head coach job of the New England Patriots from 1984 to 1989.

Ray Berry was an end for Southern Methodist. He caught just 33 passes in three seasons. It is still a mystery why the Baltimore Colts selected him, even as a "future choice" on the 20th round of the 1954 draft.

He was diminutive and unassuming, and at first appeared not to be destined for football greatness. But you could not tell him that. His subsequent rise to the Pro Football Hall of Fame has been touted as one of American football's most wonderful Cinderella stories. He made up for his lack of athleticism through rigorous practice and attention to detail, and was known for his near-perfect route running and sure handedness.

Raymond Berry was a definite long-shot to make the Colts. To say Raymond was determined is an understatement. He practiced and practiced, catching passes from anyone willing to throw to him. He concentrated on making the most difficult catches and running perfect patterns to make it easy for any QB to get him the ball.

He was not the fastest receiver in the world either. He had just average speed. He loved football and practiced his way into being one of the best players to ever play the game.

Despite not being fast, he was definitely tricky. By his own count, he developed 88 different moves to get open. He ran patterns within inches of how they were diagramed. If Raymond Berry were to offer advice today to young football players about how to become a great player, I am convinced he would give a three-word sermon: Practice! Practice! Practice! In 1956, when Johnny Unitas became the Colts' QB, Berry put all of his many hours of practice to good use.

Together, Berry and Unitas gave the Baltimore Colts one of the greatest pass-catch teams of all time. Three straight times Raymond Berry led the league in receptions and caught a then-record 631 passes for 9,275 yards and 68 touchdowns in his 13-year career. A first-or second-team All-Pro choice in 1957 through 1961 and again in 1965, Ray Berry was selected to play in six Pro Bowl games during his career. A sure-handed receiver, Berry holds a record nobody keeps. He fumbled only once in 13 years.

The pundits say that his greatest football moment was in the famous overtime 1958 NFL Championship Game. He set what was then a record with 12 catches for 178 yards and a touchdown. Several of his grabs came in the Colts' life-or-death, last minute drive to gain the tying touchdown. In the overtime period, two receptions good for 33 yards were the major gains in Baltimore's drive for the winning score. You guessed it. It was Ray Berry, who was the difference maker. He was a difference maker as a coach for the Patriots also.

With the Colts, Berry led the NFL in receptions and receiving yards three times and in receiving touchdowns twice, and he was invited to six Pro Bowls. He and the Colts won consecutive NFL championships, including the 1958 NFL Championship Game—known as "The Greatest Game Ever Played"—in which Berry caught 12 passes for 178 yards and a touchdown. As a head coach, he led the Patriots to Super Bowl XX following the 1985 season, where his team was defeated by the Chicago Bears, 46–10.

As noted, Berry was a favorite target of quarterback Johnny Unitas, and the two were regarded as the dominant passing and receiving duo of their era.

After his playing career, Berry coached wide receivers for the Dallas Cowboys, the University of Arkansas, Detroit Lions, Cleveland Browns, and Patriots. He became the Patriots' head coach in 1984 and held that position through 1989, amassing 48 wins and 39 losses.

In recognition of his playing career, Berry was inducted into the Pro Football Hall of Fame in 1973. He is a member of the NFL 75th Anniversary All-Time Team as one of the best players of the NFL's first 75 years. His number 82 jersey is retired by the Indianapolis Colts and he is a member of the Patriots' 1980s All-Decade Team. He was a fine coach but he coached at a time in Patriot's history in which it was tough to be a great coach.

1985 Raymond Berry Coach # 9

The 1985 New England Patriots football team competed in their twenty-sixth season of professional football and their sixteenth season in the National Football League (NFL). The Patriots were led by Ray Berry in his first full season of five and a half seasons. Berry replaced Ron Meyer half way through the 1984 season (4-4). Billy Sullivan was the owner. Patrick Sullivan was the GM. The Patriots had a nice 11-5 record this year. It was good enough for third place in the AFC East Division. Their fine record got them a wild-card berth and coach Berry took them to the Super Bowl game played in 1986. After winning three playoff games, the Bears beat the Patriots in the Super Bowl for the big Cigar.

Think about this. When hired, Ray Berry was not working in the NFL at the time he was snagged mid-season in 984 to coach the

Patriots. One year later, he had them in the Super Bowl. Let that sink in. Please. It is a tribute to New England Coach Ray Berry and the New England organization was not known at the time, at least, as the most welcoming spot for a great coach to get comfortable enough to stay the course or to be asked to stay the course.

Ray Berry sent out his Patriots on September 8 in the home and season opener at Sullivan Stadium to face the always tough Green Bay Packers. Berry's squad beat the visitors W (26–20) at Sullivan Stadium before 49,488 to jump start a great season. At Chicago on Sept 15, the bears laid a loss at the feet of coach Berry's Patriots L (7-20) at Soldier Field before 60,533. At Buffalo in game #3, the Patriots dug in to defeat the Bills at Rich Stadium before 40,334. After a long flight to Los Angeles on Sept 29, the Patriots were defeated by the Raiders L (20-35) at Sullivan Stadium before 60,686.

At Cleveland on Oct 6, St. Bruno's Feast Day, the Browns dug in and beat the Patriots L (20-24) at Cleveland Municipal Stadium before 62,139. Then, at home, New England on Oct 13, whooped the Buffalo Bills W (28–6) at Sullivan Stadium before 40,462. At home again, on oct 20, the Patriots defeated the New York Jets W (20–13) at Sullivan Stadium before 58,163. Then, at Tampa on Oct 27 the Patriots slugged out a nice win against the Buccaneers W (32–14) before 34,661.

At home on Nov 3, New England beat Miami W (17-13) at Sullivan Stadium before 58,811. This was followed by a nice win on Nov 10 at Sullivan Stadium against the Indianapolis Colts W (34–15) before 54,176. At Seattle the next week, the Patriots beat the Seahawks at the Kingdome W (20–13) before 60,345. At New York, a week later on Nov 24, the Jets edged out the Patriots at The Meadowlands before 74,100.

At Indianapolis on December 1, 1985. Ray Berry's tough Patriots nosed out the Indianapolis Colts in a slugfest W (38–31) at the Hoosier Dome before 56,740. At home on Dec 8, the Patriots whooped the Detroit Lions at Sullivan Stadium W (23-6) before 59,078. At Miami on Dec 16 the Dolphins assured a split in this year's two-game series by beating the Patriots by a field goal L (27-300 at the Miami Orange Bowl before 69,489. On Dec 22, in the final game of the season, the New England Patriots would not take a loss for an answer and they teed off against the Cincinnati Bengals in victory W (34–23) at Sullivan Stadium before 57,953.

The Playoffs got the Pats to the big game.

You may not believe the trivia about the 1985 Patriots ascendancy to the Super Bowl Game. Maybe it is not trivia. Maybe it was vital. The 1985 Patriots became the first team in NFL history ever to advance to the Super Bowl by winning 3 playoff games on the road, defeating the New York Jets 26–14, the Los Angeles Raiders, 27–20, and then they went on to stun the football world and did the impossible as they pulled out a massive and stunning upset over the Miami Dolphins 31–14, in the AFC Championship game.

The Patriots' win in Miami was their first victory in that stadium since 1969. The win over the Dolphins in that game has gone down as one of the greatest upsets in NFL history, as the Dolphins were heavily favored. Ray Berry old his team they could win.

But despite the Patriots' success in the playoffs, they proved unable to compete with the acclaimed 17-1 Chicago Bears in Super Bowl XX, losing 46–10 in what was at the time the most lopsided defeat in Super Bowl history.

Coach Ray Berry took 100% of the blame for the Super Bowl loss. That was the kind of guy he was. "We couldn't protect the quarterback, and that was my fault. I couldn't come up with a system to handle the Bears' pass rush," head coach Raymond Berry recognized and admitted.

1986 Raymond Berry Coach # 9

The 1986 New England Patriots football team competed in their twenty-seventh season of professional football and their seventeenth season in the National Football League (NFL). The Patriots were led by Ray Berry in his second full season of five and a half seasons. Patrick Sullivan was the GM. The Patriots had a nice 11-5 record this year for the second season in a row. It was good enough for first place in the AFC East Division.

Their fine record got them past having to play in a wild-card game as they simply advanced to the AFC v NFC championship game. Unfortunately, they lost that game by a skosh, 22-17 to the Broncos and that was their last playoff game for 1986. The Giants would beat the Broncos 39-20 in the Super Bowl. A lot of Giants were found smoking those huge cigars and wearing those huge rings.

In the home and season opener on September 7, 1986, at Sullivan Stadium, the Patriots squashed the Indianapolis Colts W (33–3) before 55,208. At New York on Sept 2, in a game played at the Meadowlands before 72,422, the Patriots beat the Jets W (20-6). Then, on Sept 21 at home, the Seattle Seahawks beat the Patriots at Sullivan Stadium L (31-38) before 58,977. At Denver. On Sept 28, in Mile High Stadium, the Broncos beat the Pats L (20-27) before 75,804.

At home On Oct 5, at Miami, the Patriots smothered the Dolphins W (34–7) at Sullivan Stadium before 60,689. The Next week on Oct 12, the Jets came to Foxboro and beat the Patriots L (24-31) before 60,342. At Pittsburgh's Three River Stadium, on Oct 19, the Steelers shut out the Pats in a big win W (34-0) at Three Rivers Stadium before 54,743. At Buffalo the next week on Oct 26, the Bills did not fare as well, losing to the Patriots L (3-23) before 77,808.

At home on Nov 2, the Atlanta Falcons lost to the Patriots W (25-17) at Sullivan Stadium before 60,597. At Indianapolis on Nov 9, the Colts went down W (21-3) at the Hoosier Dome before 56,890. At LA at Anaheim Stadium on Nov 16, the Patriots on beat the Rams W (30–28) in a close match before 64,339. At home v Buffalo on Nov 23, the Patriots beat the Bills W (22-19) before 60,455.

At New Orleans on Nov 30, in a one-point game, the Patriots nosed out the Saints W (21-2) before 58,259. On Dec 7, at home, Cincinnati beat New England L (7-31) before 60,633. Then, on Dec 14, at Sullivan Stadium, the 49ers beat the Patriots before 60,787. At

Miami on Dec 22, the Patriots won their last game of the season at the Orange Bowl W (34-27) before 74,516.

Divisional Playoffs: Mile High Stadium, Denver

Denver Broncos beat Patriots L (22–17) before 76,105

AFC: Denver Broncos 22, New England Patriots 17
Game summary

	1	2	3	4	Total
Patriots	0	10	7	0	17
Broncos	3	7	10	2	22

It was a close ball game, but the Patriots did start off behind. Broncos QB John Elway ran for a touchdown and passed for another one as it was an Elway show all the way for Denver over the Patriots—but the game was darn close. Denver running back Sammy Winder put in a nice 102 yards and caught a pass for another 16 to help move the score.

The one battle won by New England was *turnovers*, but this was a rare game in which that was not a deciding factor. Winning turnovers by 2-0, the Pats were outgained on the ground by 441 to 271. The worst part of the Patriots game was that the O-line permitted five sacks of NE QB Tony Eason.

There were times of brilliance but none long-lasting. In the first quarter for example, Elway completed passes to Steve Sewell and Steve Watson for gains of 39 and 21 yards. This rocketed the Broncos on a drive to the Patriots 4-yard line. From there, Elway tried to run the ball for a score, but the score was saved just short of the end zone. In a major mental error, thinking he had a TD, Elway angrily spiked the ball into the ground, drawing a penalty that pushed the team back five yards and had to settle for a Rich Karlis' field goal to go up to get the scoring going the second quarter.

The Patriots got the lead when Eason completed a 19-yard touchdown pass to wide receiver Stanley Morgan to cap an 87-yard drive. But, almost immediately, Denver came back with an 82-yard drive to score on Elway's 22-yard touchdown run. Later in 2Q, the NE linebacker Johnny Rembert's intercepted a John Elway pass on the Broncos 29-yard line and Tony Franklin's popped in a 38-yard field goal, tying the game at 10 by the end of the half.

Nobody was winning, and nobody was losing. In the third quarter, the Broncos caught a fire and drove 80 yards in 15 plays on a nine-minute drive that ended with another Karlis' field goal (22 yds) bringing the lead to 13-10 lead. The Pats pulled off a successful trick play with a flea flicker involving fullback Mosi Tatupu taking a handoff and then pitching the ball back to Eason. Eason connected on a 45-yard touchdown pass to Morgan to retake the lead, 17–13. But it was short lived.

Elway threw a 48-yard strike to wide receiver Vance Johnson for the back-breaking score that put Denver ahead, 20-17 lead. New England had possession four times in the fourth quarter but could do nothing with the ball. The first three outings ended in punts, while Broncos defensive end Rulon Jones ended the last one by sacking Eason in the end zone for a safety with loss of two points with 1:32 left in the game. After giving up possession after the safety, that was all that was written in this game for the Patriots.

Broncos punter Mike Horan played a major role in the game as he averaged 49 yards per kick on his five punts. More importantly, he placed three of them in the 20, including the final one that set up Jones' game-clinching safety.

This would be the last trek in the playoffs for Coach Raymond Berry. He would have two more winning seasons before he would encounter a losing year in his last season with the club.

1987 Raymond Berry Coach # 9

The 1987 New England Patriots football team competed in their twenty-eighth season of professional football and their seventeenth season in the National Football League (NFL). The Patriots were led by Ray Berry in his third full season of five and a half seasons. Billy Sullivan was the owner in his last year at the top spot. Patrick Sullivan was the GM. The Patriots had a winning 8-7 record in this strike-shortened season. It was good enough for a second-place tie in the AFC East Division.

Before we discuss the 1987 regular season, let's look at a great article for the times by Elizabeth Merrill in June 2011. She is an ESPN Senior Writer. She penned this piece looking back into 1987 and she makes some sense out of the players / owners' turbulence of the time. The article discusses the replacement player environment and is very good though it is not specific to New England. Her great perspective on these times is titled:

NFL replacements part of history

You can find this on the Internet at
http://www.espn.com/nfl/news/story?id=6642330.

Jun 9, 2011

Elizabeth Merrill -- ESPN Senior Writer

Chapter 17 Coach Ray Berry 1985 to 1989   201

Miami Dolphins quarterback Dan Marino, left, in striped shirt, and striking Dolphins and supporters walk past police at the Dolphins' training camp on Sept. 25, 1987. AP Photo/Raul Demolina

A persistent man with an offer was calling, but Robert Williams had to be practical. He was turning 25, and it was time to be an adult. He had a wife to think about, plus a couple of kids. He had a stable, albeit ordinary, job in Waco, Texas, and that was just fine. See, a time comes in every man's life when a dream dies, and Williams apparently had come to peace with that when his phone rang in the fall of 1987. If he could just get this guy from Dallas off the phone.

There are no endearing stories in the 2011 NFL lockout. Suits walk into a New York City hotel for a secret meeting, emerge with very little information, and the wait continues. It will all be over eventually, Gil Brandt says, and the season will go on as planned. He knows this because he's been through a few of these labor disputes. He knows this because he was the persistent man on the other end of the line in 1987, trying to persuade Williams to play football again during another impasse.

Gil Brandt, who was vice president of player personnel for the Dallas Cowboys, has been through labor disputes and says this one will end, eventually.

It might sound strange, but Brandt was moved by the innocence of that season that has been called one of the darkest in the history of the NFL. For years, it was Brandt's job to evaluate NFL talent for the Dallas Cowboys, to sift through the piles of names and numbers and inevitably squash a few dreams. And there he was in '87, like Willy Wonka, handing out golden tickets. Back then, the NFL players' union went on strike, and the owners struck back. They would find somebody else to do the players' jobs.

The search for talent went everywhere, to grocery stores, bars and chewed-up semipro fields. One team, the Washington Redskins, picked up a quarterback on work furlough from prison. But most of the replacement players were young men in limbo, somewhere between college and whatever was supposed to come next.

Gil Brandt, left.. who was vice president of player personnel for the Dallas Cowboys, has been through labor disputes and says this one will end, eventually. George Gojkovich/Getty Images

"Those players kind of considered themselves a cult, almost," said Brandt, a former Cowboys exec who's now an analyst for NFL.com. "Four or five of them got together and bought a used car for 500 bucks so they had transportation. They were a self-reliant group is what they were. I think the hardest thing they had to do was find a coat and tie to wear on an away game when we went to play the Jets.

"It was refreshing. There were so many interesting, refreshing things that happened that year."

So many stories. Like the time receiver Cornell Burbage reached into the stands during a road game at New York, grabbed a package and placed it under the bench. It was a box of laundry Burbage's sister had washed for him. He couldn't afford to have his clothes cleaned at the hotel.

They were called scabs and were met with hostility, threats and profanity as their buses crossed the picket lines. Their following depended on the city. In union towns, the replacements were shunned. In places such as Dallas, some fans loved their grit and nicknamed them the "Rhinestone Cowboys." Nearly every replacement team wound up with some kind of revamped nickname, and they generally weren't nice. The Chicago Spare Bears. The Seattle Sea-Scabs. The New Orleans Saint Elsewheres.

When it was over, after a hastily arranged camp and three weeks of replacement games, hundreds of dreamers went back to their lives while the NFL churned on. A whole generation of fans doesn't know about them, or why asterisks appear alongside their names on old rosters. But to the replacements, it still means something. They're part of history.

Drama Central

The custom-made No. 25 Chiefs jersey with Jack Epps' name on the back does not hang in his spacious Overland Park, Kan., office.

Jack Epps, <left> a lawyer in Kansas City, played for the Chiefs during the strike season. Elizabeth Merrill/ESPN.com.

His wife bought the jersey for him, and he keeps it at home. Had Epps known 24 years ago that his football career would end so abruptly, with a few hurried goodbyes in a dazed, cluttered locker room, maybe he would've stolen his sweaty jersey as a keepsake. He sure as heck wasn't going to pay $100 for it, which is what the Chiefs wanted to charge for the mementos.

Whatever. Epps has all the memories he needs in his office. He walks to a window, near a picture of Vince Lombardi.

"See the lights that come up over that hotel?" Epps said. "That's a football field down there. That's where I played in high school. This is why I love this spot."

It is late in the afternoon on a scorching June day, and Epps, dressed in a crisp white shirt and tie, is busy. He's a lawyer now with two daughters who dance and act and have little interest in football, so he doesn't get to talk much about the old days. He eases into his seat and lets his phone ring for a bit.

Jack Epps, a lawyer in Kansas City, played for the Chiefs during the strike season. Elizabeth Merrill/ESPN.com

Kansas City might be a sterile, scrubbed-down NFL town now, but in '87 it was Drama Central. There were shotgun-toting picketers and repeated attempts to scare the newbies. The night before their first replacement game in Los Angeles, the aftershocks of an earthquake jolted their team hotel. Towers swayed, and a "Do not panic" announcement was made over the speakers.

"All the players ran out in the hallway," Epps said. "We didn't know what to do. We were all guys from the Midwest."

But Epps was unflappable and stubborn. He believed, with all his heart, that he was good enough to make it. A year before the strike, in 1986, the strapping safety from Kansas State did make it with the Chiefs. But he broke his ankle near the end of the preseason, then spent the year breaking down film with the coaches. He was in Tampa Bay's training camp in 1987 and didn't escape the final cut.

So, he went home to K-State, three weeks after the semester started, and begged to get into his graduate school classes. Shortly after the dean said yes, Epps was gone again because when the NFL calls, you can't hit "ignore." He immediately took off for fast-food two-a-days in Kansas City. They had a little more than a week to go over fundamentals, conditioning and, oh, the game plan. Some of them hadn't sniffed a field in a year.

Most of the joy Epps felt about playing football again was doused by guilt. He'd been with the team all summer in '86. He understood the players' plight. One time, the bus rolled into Arrowhead Stadium and a protester yelled, "Jack! Not you!" "We weren't looking for a fight," Epps said. "I think everybody on the bus had the same kind of attitude. That lightning struck me, and I have the opportunity to play football again."

And they did have fun. Because of the volume of information, the replacements had to learn, they spent nearly every waking moment together and became very close in a short period of time. Epps reunited with Doug Hoppock, an ex-USFL player who had been a teammate at K-State. He also became pals with former Iowa State quarterback Alex Espinoza, an old Big Eight foe. Espinoza jokingly called Epps "Cheap Shot" because of a hit he laid on him in college. The laughs were short-lived.

By mid-October, a number of veterans were crossing the picket lines to play, and the end was looming. The Broncos beat the Chiefs 26-17 on Oct. 18, and Chiefs coach Frank Gansz huddled the team together in the locker room. He told them that the players were coming back and that some of the replacements would be here next week but most of them wouldn't. Thanks for coming in to help us, Gansz said.

The locker room was quiet. The replacements were sweaty and worn out. Epps packed up his belongings because that's what Gansz told everybody to do.

"But I never dreamed I was done playing football," Epps said. "And I think this is a mark of those guys who played. You don't really think you're done until you kind of I mean, there's got to be the coffin nailed and shut. I told somebody one time they couldn't just cut me, they were going to have to drag me out of the locker room, throw me out, take my pads away, take the football and tell me I'm done. That's pretty much what happened."

A week later, Epps got a call from a front-office person who officially told him he was done. The Chiefs did think enough of him to offer Epps a part-time scouting position. He couldn't take it. He couldn't close that door.

Years passed, and Epps eventually used the money he earned as a replacement to pay for law school. He got married and had kids. He told them to give everything to anything they're passionate about.

"I was maybe in kindergarten or first grade when I told my dad and my brother I was going to play in the NFL," Epps said. "It was very short-lived, but I guess I can count it."

Money was a lure

Media accounts from the fall of 1987 tell the story of a 24-day strike that started with great passion. In Houston, the striking Oilers hurled eggs at a bus carrying the replacements and broke a window with a rock. In various cities, angry players stood in front of vehicles to prevent entry into stadiums.

The Associated Press wrote that Chiefs tight end Paul Coffman and linebacker Dino Hackett jokingly yelled, "We're looking for scabs!" as they waved unloaded shotguns outside of Arrowhead Stadium.

Doug Hoppock said that he never feared for his safety and that the gestures were more humorous than anything. He was on the receiving end of a few "We're No. 1 signs," only with a different finger. Most of the antics reminded him of the movie "North Dallas Forty." Still, he had mixed emotions. Hoppock was a K-Stater, just like Coffman, and had been to his house before. He didn't want to hurt Coffman or his family. But if somebody was going to cross, Hoppock figured it might as well be him. The offensive lineman played three years in the USFL, and he was 27 and recently laid off from a job at Yellow Freight when the Chiefs called.

He was no threat to the protestors. Yeah, he had kept in shape by playing pickup basketball every day. But Hoppock's body was worn-out and tired. The Chiefs would not have to pry the pads and football away from Hoppock. Not at that point in his life. "It's not like you're a baseball player and you get to play old-time baseball," Hoppock said. "You can't play old-time football.

"But there was also the excitement of 'Hey, I get to strap the pads on one more time. What do I have in my tank?' I don't care who it is, if you've played a sport, you still dream about it at night, thinking, 'Oh, I could go for a series or two,' or, 'I could hang with them.' That's always there."

Money was also a lure. Most replacement players pulled down roughly $4,000 a game after taxes. Because of the cash at stake, a few high-profile players refused to strike. Cowboys defensive lineman Randy White stood to lose more than $30,000 a week, so he kept playing. Hall of Famers Joe Montana, Lawrence Taylor, Tony Dorsett and Steve Largent also eventually crossed the picket lines.

Hoppock still reminds people today that the competition from the USFL helped those NFL players earn more money back then. And though the USFL satisfied his football itch, he's grateful that he had three games on an even bigger stage. The replacement Chiefs were the first opponents to play at the new Joe Robbie Stadium. Hoppock said they played the game in a tropical storm.

"Oh, it was cool," he said. "It was empty, but it was cool."
At least it was entertaining.

There's a joke circulated among battered middle-aged men these days. The NFL is in a lockout. Grab your gear and get ready to play. Jim Crocicchia hears it a lot and still manages a chuckle. He did not have NFL aspirations when his college career ended in 1986. He was an Ivy League quarterback with a degree in economics and a map to Wall Street.

He certainly never dreamed that in 1987, mere months after the New York Giants won a Super Bowl, coach Bill Parcells' team would come calling.

The Giants had a glut of receivers that spring and didn't want to wear down the arm of Phil Simms. So an old coach recommended Crocicchia to the Giants, and he threw a few footballs and thought that was it.

A Fairfax County police officer holds back Washington Redskins players R.C. Thielemann, glasses, left, and Darryl Grant, right, as a busload of newly recruited players arrives Sept. 23, 1987, at the Redskins Park practice facility in Chantilly, Va. AP Photo/Dennis Cook

"They liked what they saw and wanted to bring me back for the preseason in August," Crocicchia said. "So, of course, where do I sign? I didn't call anybody or read anything or look at any numbers. I grew up a Giants fan in Connecticut, so it was a dream come true just walking into Giants Stadium with a Giants helmet on and getting a chance to meet Phil Simms."

He made it to the preseason and was one of the final cuts. A month later, he was called back during the strike. Some teams took the replacement games very seriously and plotted their fallback rosters in advance of the strike. The Giants wanted to be respectful of their players and weren't nearly as aggressive.

Crocicchia estimated that, at the age of 23 and with just a few preseason games under his belt, he was one of the most experienced players on the replacement team.

"One reporter asked me after the first game, 'What was the game plan? How were you feeling?'" Crocicchia said. "Well, I looked around the huddle at my offensive linemen, and our strategy became to stay in the huddle for as long as we possibly could because they could not catch their breath.

"I mean, it was one of those things where they were just not in game shape. We had a number of mental mistakes that were going to happen."

Crocicchia's NFL debut came on Oct. 5, 1987, a "Monday Night Football" game against the San Francisco 49ers. He knew what the guys in the booth would say, how it wasn't pro football, how some of Crocicchia's teammates came from semipro teams that were the equivalent of beer-league softball. But when they ran out of the tunnel that night, it was for real, and the team was stoked.

The football was, at the very least, entertaining. Bill Walsh broke out the wishbone and shrugged at a smiling Parcells. Crocicchia uncorked an underthrown pass to Lewis Bennett, who made a circus catch in the end zone. The 46-yard touchdown is still considered one of the best catches in the history of "Monday Night Football." The New York Times wrote about a sign that hung in the stadium. "Stay on Strike. We Get Better Seats."

The touchdown ended up being Crocicchia's last. He hurt his elbow in the fourth quarter, giving way to Mike Busch. Busch reportedly was bagging groceries for $4 an hour before joining the Giants.

Crocicchia played some Arena League football after '87, but it wasn't nearly as fun, and he retired. He's a managing partner in an investment consulting firm. His daughter, Olivia, is a 15-year-old actress on the TV series "Rescue Me." [2011] When

Olivia was younger, her manager told her, "It's not 'show love,' it's 'show business.'" That's the way Crocicchia sees the NFL.

"I think it's going to be very difficult for the players' union to keep the players in line," Crocicchia said. "And you saw that the last time around. Once those paychecks stop coming in, and these guys have a lot of obligations that they need to get paid, they've got to go to work. It's just a difficult situation for them." Months ago, the NFL said it will not use replacement players in this work stoppage. Crocicchia says that's fine. He's not suiting up this time.

"You know, I'm like that old line in that Toby Keith song," he said. "I'm not as good as I once was, but I'm as good once as I ever was."

Moving on

Robert Williams is an assistant coach at Jesuit Preparatory School in Dallas. He's hard to catch, a woman who answered the phone at the school said. Williams didn't return several messages. A number of former replacement players passed on talking for this story.

Here's what Brandt will say about Williams. That giving football one last try was a huge leap for him 24 years ago. That there were no guarantees, just some short-term pay and the possibility of playing few games to show what he could do. Williams asked whether the Cowboys could give him a ride from Waco.
He didn't want to leave his wife and kids without a car.

So, the cornerback from Baylor who couldn't land on an NFL team out of college said yes and wound up sticking with the Cowboys. He played seven years in the NFL. He won two Super Bowls. One day, he called Brandt to say thanks for the push.

"He ended up getting something Dick Butkus and a bunch of others wish they had," Brandt said, "and that's two Super Bowl rings. That's not pretty cool. I think that's extremely cool."

Elizabeth Merrill is a senior writer for ESPN.com. She can be reached at <u>merrill2323@hotmail.com</u>. Follow ESPN_Reader on Twitter: <u>@ESPN Reader</u>.

End of article

Games of the 1987 Season – Coach Berry

Some NE Patriots Season Particulars

The 1987 NFL season featured a number of games that were predominantly played by replacement players as the National Football League Players Association (NFLPA) players were on strike from weeks four to six. The New England Patriots were 8-7 in the shortened season and the team was 2-1 using replacement players season ended with Super Bowl XXII, with the Washington Redskins defeating the Denver Broncos 42–10 at Jack Murphy Stadium in San Diego. The Broncos suffered their second consecutive Super Bowl defeat. At this point it had been just a few years since the broncos beat the Pats in the Super Bowl

The Replacement players were quite active and actually helpful to New England in 1987. Having Raymond Berry as coach had to help getting everything ready to play. The pundits joked about the positive impact of the "new" players on performance. For example, placement player Mike LeBlanc gave the team something it did not have in quite a while—a running game. Le Blanc was a nice addition though like all replacement players, he was unexpected at the beginning of the season.

Those who like to gobble steam statistics already know that in 1986, the Patriots became the first team in 20 years to average less than 3 yards a carry. Yet, on October 11 in the second replacement game,

Le Blanc accumulated 213 yards rushing as New England beat the Buffalo Bills 14-7.

LeBlanc ironically had just been giving his "don't call us" papers from Winnipeg of the CFL and he was then signed by the Patriots as a replacement, had gained 146 yards on 35 carries. Though LeBlanc ran circles around the Bills, his showing was not viewed by many New England fans. He outran the Bills before the smallest Sullivan Stadium crowd ever -- 11,878 rain-soaked fans. Meanwhile, the striking Patriots were quietly walked the picket line.

Nobody was messing with anybody outside the stadium. No incidents were reported on the New England picket line during the second week of demonstrations by striking NFL players at games played by replacement players.

LeBlanc assured a major running attack that accumulated the most New England rushing yards since the final game of the 1985 season, the year in which the Patriots used a ground attack to reach the Super Bowl.

LeBlanc played exactly like we thought he would before we got him, New England coach Raymond Berry said. 'He cut and slashed all over the place.'

'I don't know if we planned on running as much as we did, I think the weather had a lot to do with that. The running game was there, and we stayed with it. We moved the ball fairly well,' said New England running back Bruce Hansen.

While they got excellence from LeBlanc, the New England passing game was pitiful. Bob Bleier completed just 4 of 13 throws for 43 yards and he gave up an interception.

Ray Berry described it aptly but was happy for the win: 'It's kind of like stepping into the batter's box in major-league baseball and hitting a 95-mph fastball,' said Berry of the poor passing game. 'It's a very advanced skill and takes time in the amount of work preparation. It's just easier handing the ball off.'

The Patriots put up with a lot by way of the elements. They dealt with a cold rain, stiff winds and they endured three blocked punts. Nonetheless they won the game, bringing their record to 2-2. This win moved the Patriots into a four-way tie for first place in the AFC East. As the definition of humor involves the unusual, having the defeated Bills, at 1-3, after this game meant that they were the only team in the division that was not in first place.

The Bills were simply outgained 256 yards to 168, struggled on offense for the second consecutive week. They had gotten shellacked by Indianapolis 47-6 just last week. The Bill coach offered commentary of the game:

'We missed too many tackles today,' Bills coach Marv Levy said. 'The players tried harder and I'm proud of them for that. They played with spirit and I admire them for that.'

New England began with a 7-0 lead at 8:34 of the first quarter on a Carl Woods 4-yard touchdown run. LeBlanc had a 42-yard burst that put New England on the 23-yard line. Inching closer, at 6:36 left in the third quarter, Bleier scored on a 1-yard touchdown run to raise New England's lead to 14-0. The score had been set up when linebacker Greg Moore recovered quarterback Willie Totten's fumbled snap at the Buffalo 19. LeBlanc took it in the 14 years to register the score.

Buffalo made it to 14-7 with 3:03 gone in the fourth quarter. Totten tossed a 13-yard touchdown pass to Thad McFadden. Buffalo linebacker Scott Watters partially blocked Alan Herline's punt to put the Bills on the Patriot 16. The Bills then had a shot at tying the game when big defensive lineman Dino Mangiero sacked Totten for an 8-yard loss to the New England 30 as time went to zero.

The reason none of the names in the *1987 game 4 highlights* are familiar is because even the fans at the time had no idea who the no-name replacement players were. After packing in about 60,000 fans each game, having just 11,000 at this Patriots game meant there were not too many in the stands to be telling tall tales about the replacement player game they saw that day.

The 1987 Games

On Sept 13, the Patriots, with their regular players in uniform, won their home and season opener against the Miami Dolphins W (28–21) before 54,642. At New York, with the normal players on the field at Shea Stadium, the Jets beat the Patriots L (24-43) before 70,847. The September 28 game against Washington's Redskins was canceled due to the player's strike. On October 4, my wedding anniversary, the Cleveland Broan's replacement players defeated the New England Patriot's replacement players L (10-20) before 14,830. Notice the difference in the # of fans.

At home on Oct 11, at home, with a crisp running attack led by Replacement Mike LeBlanc, New England defeated Buffalo Bills W (14–7) before 11,878. At Houston, in the last replacement player game of 1987, the Patriots defeated the Oilers W (21-7) before 26,294. On Oct 25, at Indianapolis, the regular players were back in action after the strike, and the Colts had their way with the Patriots L (16-30) before 48,850. On Nov 1, at home, the Patriots beat the Los Angeles Raiders W (26–23) before 60,664. At New York, on Nov 8, the Giants defeated New England L (10-17) before 73,817) at Giants Stadium in the Meadowlands.

On Nov15, at home in Sullivan Stadium, the Dallas Cowboys defeated the New England Patriots L (17-23) before 60,567. At home on Nov 22, New England shut-out Indianapolis before 56,906. At home again the following week, on Nov 29, the Eagles beat the Patriots L (31-34) before 54,198. At Denver on Dec 6, the Broncos beat the Patriots L (20-31) before 75,795.

On Dec 13, the Patriots whipped the New York Jets W 42–20 before 60,617. On Dec 14, at Buffalo before 74,945, the Patriots beat the Bills W (13–7) bringing the record to 7-7. At Miami on Dec 21, the Patriots beat the Dolphins W (24–10) before 61,192 finishing the strike-shortened season at 8–7.

Top Patriots Players Bruce Armstrong, T

When it comes to strong men and iron men and endurance men, the name Armstrong would be a good name to give out to humans if you were God and that was part of the gift set you were giving. With few credits, Bruce Armstrong went to work every day on the football field amassing statistics and game statistics that puts him at the top of the iron-man classic if it were ever held.

Bruce, who has started 100 games in his career, is the leader on the New England offensive line.

Armstrong holds the Patriots team record with 212 games played, starting in every one of them. A six-time Pro Bowl participant, he was only one of three players in league history to play with the same team in three different decades. He is tough as nails though somewhat undersized for his tackle position. Nonetheless, Bruce Armstrong, a guy with the toughest name in the league lived up to his God-given name.

Armstrong anchored the Patriots' offensive line through the late 1980s and 1990s. He played the last eight games of the 1999 season with three torn ligaments in his right knee and was name an alternate to the Pro Bowl that season. His battles with Buffalo's Hall of Fame defensive end Bruce Smith were legendary during the peak of both players' careers. Armstrong was selected for the Patriots Hall of Fame in 2001. Inducted 2001.

1988 Raymond Berry Coach # 9

The 1988 New England Patriots football team competed in their twenty-ninth season of professional football and their nineteenth season in the National Football League (NFL). The Patriots were led by Ray Berry in his fourth full season of five and a half seasons. Victor Kiam bought the Patriots this year from 28-year owner Billy Sullivan and he assumed #1 duties this year. Patrick Sullivan remained as the GM. They went back to a sixteen-week schedule after the strike, the Patriots had a winning 9-7 record this year. It was good enough for a tie for second place in the AFC East Division.

It would take until 1994 for the Patriots to record another winning record. As noted, for this season, the Patriots slightly improved on their 8-7 record 1987, winning one more game due to one game being cancelled the previous season. Despite the winning record, the Patriots again did not reach the postseason. They finished tied for second place in the AFC East with the arch rival Colts, but when the record books were closed for 1988, they actually finished in 3rd place because the Colts had a better record against common opponents than the Patriots did.

1988 Games: On Sept 4, 1988 in the home and season opener at Sullivan Stadium in Foxboro, New England beat the New York Jets W (28–3 0 before 44,027. On Sept 11, at Minnesota, the Vikings beat the Patriots L (6-36) before 55,545. At home on Sept 18, the Buffalo Bills beat the NE Patriots L (14–16) before 55,945. On Sept 25, at Houston, the Oilers triumphed L (6-31) before 38,646.

On Oct 2 at Sullivan Stadium, the Patriots beat the Indianapolis Colts W (21–17) before 58,050. At Green Bay on Oct 9, the Packers clobbered the Patriots L (3-45) before 51,932. On Oct 16, the Patriots defeated the Cincinnati Bengals W (27–21) before 59,969. At Buffalo on Oct 23, the Bills beat the Patriots L (20-23) before 76,824.

On Oct 30 at home, the Patriots pummeled the Chicago Bears W (30–7) before 60,821. On Nov 6 at home, the Miami Dolphins were beaten by the Patriots W (21–10) before 60,840. At New York, on Nov 13, the Jets lost by one point to the Patriots W (14–13) before 48,358 At Miami on Nov 20, the Pats beat the Dolphins W (6–3) before 53,526.

On Nov 27, at Indianapolis, the Colts edged out the Patriots L (21-24) before 58,157. On Dec 4, the Patriots beat the Seattle Seahawks W (13–7) before 59,086. At home in Sullivan Stadium on Dec 11, 1988, New England defeated Tampa Bay W (10–7) before 39,889. At Denver on December 17, the Broncos beat the Patriots L (10-21) before 70,910

1989 Raymond Berry Coach # 9

The 1989 New England Patriots football team competed in their thirtieth season of professional football and their twentieth season in the National Football League (NFL). The Patriots were led by Ray Berry in his fifth and final full season of five and a half seasons (1/2 season in 1984). Victor Kiam was the owner. Patrick Sullivan remained as the GM. The Patriots had their worst record of Ray Berry's tenure at 5-11 this season. It was good enough for fourth place in the AFC East Division.

As a side note, the Patriots' pass defense surrendered 7.64 yards-per-attempt in 1989, one of the ten worst totals in NFL history. 1989 was not one of the Pats finest seasons for sure but looking back from 2018, we know that there are many fine seasons to come after 1994.

After the season, Head Coach Raymond Berry was fired and replaced by Rod Rust.

Working through the 1989 side notes, we've got a big one coming up. Looking at the end of the season, Rod Rust was not first choice for being the new coach. Before Parcells, Carroll, and Belichick, Victor Kiam an owner who looked at the cause and effects of having a winning team, winning, tried to hire another Hall of Fame coach before the age of the big three noted above.

The Boston Globe's late, great Will McDonough had it on good authority that, then-Patriots owner Victor Kiam offered New England's head coaching /G.M. roles to former 49ers coach Bill Walsh. However, Walsh turned down the offer, citing his commitment to continue working for NBC, the Globe reported. Still, a coaching change was coming for New England, which had fallen to 5-11 with Ray Berry in '89.

After the 1989 season, the Patriots parted ways with head coach Raymond Berry. There is always a good reason and it was not the great coaching with little talent that Berry had done before 1989. It was reported as a conflict over the hiring of New England's offensive and defensive coordinators.

Berry himself knew a little bit about football and how to be a great as he was a Hall of Fame wide receiver. He was a successful NFL head coach, too. He led the Patriots to a 51-41 mark, with New England making the Super Bowl for the first time in its history in his first full season on the job. Overall, the Patriots won more than they lost in four of his full campaigns from 1985-1988.

When Walsh said no; the Patriots would select Steelers defensive coordinator Rod Rust to replace Berry, but he did not last very long and was fired after one year at the helm in 1990. New England went from 5-11 to 1-15 proving that it can get worse. It was the league's worst record in 1990. The Pats then looked to Syracuse head coach Dick McPherson, who was a great coach at Syracuse. He improved their lot and took the team to a 6-10 mark in '91. However, even though MacPherson was a great immortal coach at Syracuse, it got worse the following year with a 2-14 mark in '92. MacPherson had missed seven games because of illness. He was given no more chances and was replaced in January 1993.

After this, the Patriots had an unlimited wallet and they looked to New York to hire Super Bowl Bill Parcells. Parcells took the Patriots to the playoffs in his second season and the Super Bowl in his fourth season. Then came the three-season stint for Pete Carroll (1997-1999), who was then replaced by Belichick.

Hard as it is to believe before this great trio of coaches, there was a 9-39 stretch in which the Patriots endured in the three seasons after Berry's departure. Would things have been different if the Patriots lured Walsh east, or if Berry had stayed on? One would presume so, but nobody has a crystal ball.

If Walsh succeeded in New England, would Parcells ever have had reason to join the franchise? How would franchise history have been altered?

We'll never know. But we do know this: Raymond Berry, like Belichick and Carroll, won more than he lost in his time in Foxboro, and he has his own spot in Patriots history.

Before we completely close out the Ray Berry Era, I would like to share a nicely done article by Dan Flaherty to serve as a closing article for Raymond Berry, who considering the obstacles he overcame, was a fine coach for sure.

Raymond Berry's Last Year: The 1989 New England Patriots

By Dan Flaherty, NFL History Articles, Sports History Article, May 2, 2017

In the days before Bill Belichick and Tom Brady, even before Bill Parcells and Drew Bledsoe, the expectations for the New England Patriots were a lot more modest. Raymond Berry had taken the franchise to what was then its heights in the late 1980s. They reached the Super Bowl in 1985, won an AFC East title in 1986 and only narrowly missed the playoffs in 1987 and 1988. But the decline accelerated the following year and the 1989 New England Patriots proved to be Berry's last hurrah. [But, there was little cheering.]

When you combine a lack of great talent with chaos at quarterback, a subsequent lack of wins is a foregone conclusion and that's what Berry was dealing with. He ran out four different players behind center—from aging 36-year-old Steve Grogan, to Marc Wilson to the declining Tony Eason to Doug Flutie. They all made too many mistakes and too few big plays.

The running game had been the pride and joy of the 1985 AFC champs, but the great John Hannah was in retirement and the offensive line lacked muscle. John Stephens was now the leading rusher and he finished the season with only 833 yards.

At receiver, New England drafted Hart Lee Dykes from Oklahoma State with their first-round pick. At 6'4", 215 lbs., Dykes was a big receiver for the time and was physically gifted.

But his pro career never took off.

The end result was an offense that ranked 21st in what was then a 28-team league in points scored. And the defense was marginally worse, ranking 23rd. While outside linebacker Johnny Rembert was the team's one Pro Bowl player, corner Raymond Clayborn was in decline at age 34. And 30-year-old defensive tackle Kenneth Sims continued his career as one of the biggest busts to ever go with the first overall draft pick (back in 1982 when the Patriots opted for Sims and joined nine other teams that passed on Heisman Trophy-winner Marcus Allen).

BARELY HANGING ON

Problems with the running game weren't in evidence in Week 1 against the New York Jets. The Patriots went into the Meadowlands and outrushed the Jets 154-49, with a late four-yard TD run by Reggie Dupard providing the winning margin in the 27-24 victory. But they were inept a week later at home against Miami—even with Dan Marino throwing three interceptions, the Pats dug themselves a 24-0 hole by halftime and lost by two touchdowns. [For whatever reasons, star replacement back Mike LeBlanc played just one season in the NFL.]

Another poor home performance followed against Seattle, with Dave Krieg carving up the secondary with three second-quarter touchdown passes and New England fell 24-3. The Pats went on to Buffalo, the defending AFC East champ and couldn't stop Thurman Thomas in a 31-10 loss.

Three straight losses, all decisive, turned up the heat for a visit by the Houston Oilers in Week 5. The Oilers were in the midst of a run of seven straight playoff years with Warren Moon at quarterback. With the season ready to get away early, the Patriot defense stepped up, forced four turnovers, kept Moon at bay and keyed a 23-13 win.

It set up a good opportunity with a road game at lowly Atlanta next and New England took a 15-6 lead into the fourth quarter.

But they coughed up ten points, lost the football game and then went to San Francisco and lost to a great 49ers team 37-20. New England at least played reasonably well against a San Francisco team that had won the Super Bowl in 1988 and would do so again this year. They were within 24-20 after three quarters and not many other teams played the '89 Niners much better. But at 2-5, there was no room for moral victories.

The Patriots went on to Indianapolis, where the Colts were in the middle of the playoff race. Grogan played his best game of the year and threw for 355 yards. Tight end Eric Sievers, who finished the year as the team's most productive receiver, caught seven balls for 113 yards. It took overtime, but New England left Indy with a 23-20 win and still had a pulse as the season hit its halfway point.

FAINT PLAYOFF HOPES FLAME OUT

Once again, the schedule seemed to work in favor of the Patriots—the Jets were having a terrible season and came to Foxboro next. Much like the Atlanta game, it was the perfect opportunity to build on a good win and get some momentum. And much like the Atlanta game, that opportunity was blown. New England was a (-7.5) favorite, but was helpless against Jets quarterback Ken O'Brien, who threw for 386 yards and hit ten different receivers. The Pats lost 27-26. A week later they came out sleepwalking at home against mediocre New Orleans, lost three fumbles and fell behind 28-0. A stirring comeback closed the margin to 28-24, but it ended there. And with a record of 3-7, so did the Patriots realistic playoff chances.

SALVAGING PRIDE

To their credit, New England showed some pride. Buffalo came to Foxboro, in command of the AFC East race and took a 24-13 lead into the fourth quarter. But with Stephens rushing for 126 yards and the defense collecting six turnovers on the day, the Pats rallied for a 33-24 win. The game started a Buffalo slump that nearly cost them the division title.

New England went west to play the Los Angeles Raiders, another team in a packed wild-card picture. It was close, but three interceptions by Grogan were the difference in a 24-21 loss.

A week later the Pats and Stephens played spoiler again. Indianapolis—an AFC East team prior to the realignment of 2002 made the return trip to Foxboro. Stephens ran for 124 yards and outrushed Colt great Eric Dickerson. New England's 22-16 win put a big crimp in Indy's playoff push—a push that ultimately came up one win short.

THREE MORE LOSSES

The final three games of the season were against teams that desperately needed wins for the playoffs, but New England was done winning for the year. A Sunday Night in South Beach didn't go well, with Marino ripping the Pats secondary for over 300 yards in a 31-10 final. The Pittsburgh Steelers, who ultimately grabbed the final wild-card spot and reached the divisional round of the playoffs, pounded New England on the ground and won 28-10.

Berry's final game was at home against the Los Angeles Rams, who were in a win-and-you're-in situation. It was as bitter cold day in Foxboro, (-4) degrees with the windchill, but the Patriots didn't mail it in. They took a 20-17 lead into the fourth quarter, but were ultimately unable to contain running back Greg Bell, who rushed for over 200 yards and scored the winning touchdown in the 24-20 final.

The Raymond Berry Era was over in New England. Anyone who found fault with the coach for the 5-11 finish in 1989 had a rude awakening coming. The Patriots had three brutal years ahead of them, one with Rod Rust at the helm and two more with Dick MacPherson. Another bad season in 1993 was at least mitigated by the fact Parcells was now on the sidelines and Bledsoe's career was beginning. It wasn't until 1994 that winning football returned to Foxboro.

Games of the 1989 Season

In the season opener at New York on September 10, 1989, the Patriots beat the Jets in a close game W (27–24) before 64,541. On Sept 17, at Sullivan Stadium (home opener), the Miami Dolphins beat the New England Patriots L (10–24) before 57,043
At Sullivan again on Sept 24, 1989 the Seattle Seahawks beat the Patriots L (3-24) before 48,025. Then, at Buffalo on Oct 1, the Bills beat the Patriots before 78,921

On Oct 8, at Houston, the Oilers were beaten by the Patriots W (23–13) before 59,828. At Atlanta on Oct 15, in a one-point match, the Falcons nosed out the Patriots before 39,697. At San Francisco on Oct 22, the 49ers beat the Patriots L (20-37) before 51,781. At Indianapolis on Oct 29, the Patriots beat the Colts W (23–20) before 59,356.

Then, on Nov 5, at home in Sullivan Stadium, the New York Jets defeated the Patriots L (26-27) before 53,366. On Nov 12, at home, the New Orleans Saints beat the Patriots L (24-28) before 47,680. At home on Nov 19, the Patriots beat the Buffalo Bills W (33–24) before 49,663. At Los Angeles, on Nov 26, the Raiders defeated the Patriots L (21-24) before 38,747

On Dec 3 at Sullivan Stadium, the Patriots defeated the Indianapolis Colts W (22–16) before 32,234. At Miami on Dec 10, the Dolphins squashed the Patriots L (10-31) before 55,918. At Pittsburgh, on Dec 17, the Steelers whopped the Patriots L (10-28) before 26,594. Then, in the season finale, on Christmas Eve, Dec 24, 1989 the Los Angeles Rams beat the Patriots L (20-24) before 27,940, closing out the season and Raymond Berry's coaching career with the Patriots.

Chapter 18 Coaches Rod Rust & Dick MacPherson, 1990-1992

Coach #10 Rod Rust
Coach #11 Dick MacPherson

Year	Coach	League	Conf/Div	Place	Record
1990	Rod Rust	NFL	AFC-East	5th	1-15-0

1990 Rod Dust final record (1-15)

1991	Dick MacPherson	NFL	AFC-East	4th	6-10-0

- Leonard Russell(OROY)

1992	Dick MacPherson	NFL	AFC-East	5th	2-14-0

1991-1992 Dick MacPherson final record (8-24-0)

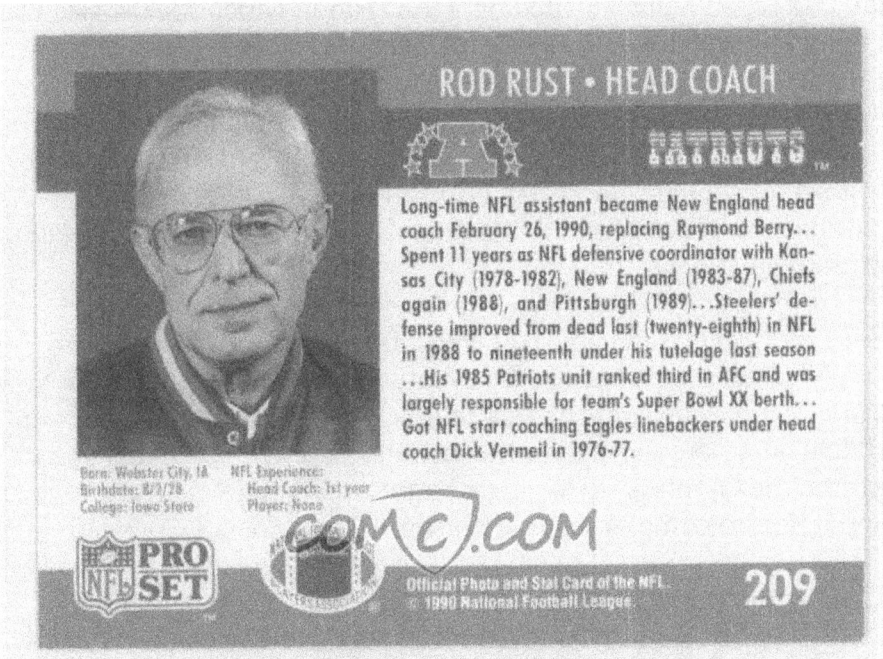

Coach Rod Rust Pro Football Card

1990 Rod Rust #10

The 1990 New England Patriots football team competed in their thirty-first season of professional football and their twenty-first season in the National Football League (NFL). The Patriots were led by Rod Rust in his first of one full season. Victor Kiam was the owner. Patrick Sullivan was the GM. The Patriots outdid their final Ray Berry 5-11 record with an even worst 1-15 record this year. It was last in the AFC East Division and last in the entire league.

This was the worst record in franchise history. When it looked like they could do no worst, they managed to do the impossible. For example, they lost a nationally televised game to the Washington Redskins in which they were down 9–0 before the Redskins even ran an offensive play. The Redskins' two first-quarter scores had come on a Kurt Gouveia fumble return for a touchdown (#1), and after the kickoff, the Patriots snapped the ball out of the end zone for a safety. The rain was coming down in buckets and so the announced crowd for the game was 22,286.

In a humiliating Week 9 blowout loss in Philadelphia, Eagles' QB Randall Cunningham scored on a long run in which the defense was split between Patriots who did not even try to tackle Cunningham and another few who completely missed him on such attempts. To make it worst, this became the most played highlight reel on all the national NFL-related TV shows (including ESPN's NFL Primetime and Monday Night Football). It unfortunately made the 1990 Patriots' incompetence both a national story and a collective joke. It was not good.

Eventually to end the pain. the Patriots' final game of the season finally came. It was against the eventual Super Bowl champion New York Giants. The game drew a sellout crowd to Foxboro, but over 40,000 fans were rooting for the visitors, as tickets to Giants home games (the Giants were having a banner year) were nearly impossible to come by for non-season-ticket holders.

The Patriots' accumulated a negative-265 point-differential (181 points scored, 446 points surrendered). It was the worst total of any team in the 1990s. Raymond Berry began to look like a miracle worker for taking this team to five wins in the prior season.

The Patriots opponents this year were almost all top teams. Compared with the previous season's Dallas Cowboys, the Patriots played only three teams with non-winning records – divisional rivals the Indianapolis Colts and New York Jets plus one game against the Phoenix Cardinals – all season.

The 1990 Patriots and 1981 Baltimore Colts are the only NFL teams since 1940 to have eleven losses during which they never led in one season. No team wants records or notable acts such as these.

The 1990 Patriots became the third team to end a season at 1-15, and were matched by the 1991 Colts the following year. They also tied the 1976 Tampa Bay Buccaneers for most consecutive losses inside one season (the Buccaneers lost all 14 games at a time when the NFL had not adopted a 16-game schedule yet). The Bucs record later was eclipsed by the 15-straight losing 2001 Carolina Panthers. It was then topped by the 0-16 2008 Detroit Lions and the most recent 0-16 2017 Cleveland Browns.

Budweiser renamed Schaefer Stadium in 1983 to Sullivan Stadium in honor of the long-term owner family. In 1990, shortly after the Sullivan's sold their majority interest in the team to Victor Kiam, the stadium was officially renamed to "Foxboro Stadium." Note that the official spelling of the town in which the stadium is built is "Foxborough," the shorter spelling is used for the stadium.

The Games: The season and home opener was played on Sept 9 at home in the newly renamed Foxboro Stadium. Miami beat New England L (24–27) before 45,305. At Indianapolis on September 16, the Patriots won their only game of the season by beating the Colts W (16–14) in the Hoosier Dome before 49,256. On Sept 23, at Cincinnati, the Bengals beat the Patriots L (7–41) in Riverfront Stadium before 56,470.. On Sept 30. The New York Jets beat New England L (13–37) at home before 36,724.

On Oct 7. The Seattle Seahawks defeated the Patriots L (20–33) at home in Foxboro Stadium before 39,735.On Oct 14, the Patriots drew a bye week. On Thurs., Oct 18 at Miami, the Dolphins beat the Patriots L (10–17) in Joe Robbie Stadium before 62,630. On Oct 28, the Buffalo Bills beat the NE Patriots L (10–27) in Foxboro Stadium before 51,959. On Nov 4, at Philadelphia, the Eagles beat the Patriots L (20–48) in Veterans Stadium before 65,514.

On Nov 11,, the Indianapolis Colts beat New England L (10–13) at home in Foxboro Stadium before 28,924. On Nov 18, at Buffalo, the Bills beat the Pats L (0–14) in Rich Stadium before 74,270. Then, on Nov 25 at Phoenix, the Cardinals beat the Patriots L (14–34) in Sun

Devil Stadium before 30,110. On Dec 2, the Kansas City Chiefs whooped the NE Patriots L (7–37) at home in Foxboro Stadium before 26,280.

On Dec 14 at Pittsburgh, the Steelers got the best of the Patriots L (3–24) in Three Rivers Stadium before 48,354. On Dec 15, the Washington Redskins beat the Patriots L (10–25) at home in Foxboro Stadium before 22,286. On Dec 16, at New York, the Jets walloped the Patriots L (7–42) in the Meadowlands before 30,250. On Dec 30, the day before New Year's Eve, in the last game of the season, the New York Giants beat the NE Patriots L (10–13) at home in Foxboro Stadium before 60,410.

1991 Dick MacPherson #11

The 1991 New England Patriots football team competed in their thirty-second season of professional football and their twenty-second season in the National Football League (NFL). The Patriots were led by Dick MacPherson in his first of two seasons with the team. Victor Kiam was the owner. Nobody carried the GM tie in 1991. The Patriots record was 6-10-0 and they finished in fourth place in the AFC East Division.

This year was not very good; but it was better than the 1-15 from the prior year under Coach Rust. Though the Patriots scored twenty or more points just five times during the 1991 season, they were able to upset playoff-bound teams such as the Houston Oilers, Buffalo Bills and New York Jets. This was the last season where the Patriots were owned by Victor Kiam, who was forced to sell the team to St. Louis businessman James Orthwein in order to settle a debt. The Franchise would change hands again before it found its way into the hands of the Kraft family, the current owners.

In the season opener on September 1, 1991 at Indianapolis, the Patriots beat the Colts W (16–7) before 49,961. On Sept 8. At Foxboro, the Cleveland Browns beat the Patriots L (0–20) before 35,377. Then, at Pittsburgh on Sept 15, the Steelers beat the Patriots L (6-20) before 53,703. At Foxboro on Sept 22, the Patriots beat the Houston Oilers W (24–20) before 30,702.

At Phoenix on Sept 29, the Cardinals beat the Patriots L (10-24) before 26,043. At Foxboro on Oct 6, the Miami Dolphins beat the NE Patriots L (10-20) before 49,749. The week of Oct 14 was a bye. Then, on Oct 20, the Patriots beat the Minnesota Vikings W 26–23 before 45,367. On Oct 27, at Foxboro, the Denver Broncos beat the Patriots L (6-9) before 43,994.

At Buffalo on Nov 3, the Bills beat New England L (17-22) before 78,278. At Miami on Nov 10, the Dolphins beat the Patriots L (20-30) before 56,065. On Nov 17, at home in Foxboro, the New York Jets beat the Patriots L (21-28) before 30,743. On Nov 24, at home, the Pats beat the Buffalo Bills W (16–13) before 47,053.

On Dec 1, at Denver, the Broncos beat the Patriots L (3-20) before 67,116. On Dec 8, the NE Patriots defeated the Indianapolis Colts W (23-17) before 20,131. At New York on December 15, the Jets were beaten by the Patriots W (6–3) before 55,689. In the season finale on Dec 22, at Cincinnati, the Bengals beat the Patriots L (7-29) before 46,394

Top Patriot Players Ben Coates, TE

Ben Coates was a receiving machine. It is that simple. He played in 142 games over nine seasons as a Patriot and he started 105 of those games.

When the 2010 season began, Coates was third all-time in team history in receptions (490), fourth in receiving yards (5,471) and second in receiving touchdowns (50) – all tops among tight ends in Patriots annals.

In 1994, Coates had set a single-season record for receptions by a tight end with 96 (now tied for third). But, he still holds the franchise record for receptions by a tight end. He also led the team in touchdown receptions for six straight seasons between 1993 and 1998 and led the team in overall receptions five times.

Coates was so good he received a lot of great honors for his fine play. For example, he was named to the Patriots Team of the Century in 2000 and he ranks in the top 10 all-time among NFL tight ends in career receptions, yards and touchdowns.

When Drew Bledsoe was the man on the scene for Bill Parcells and Pete Carrol and early on for Bill Belichick, Coates was Drew Bledsoe's go-to receiver throughout his career. He became a fan favorite for his dependability, toughness and performance. Coates was no pushover. He capped off his career with the Baltimore Ravens, where he added his talents to their 2000 Super Bowl championship team. He was inducted into the Patriots Hall of Fame in 2008—well deserved.

1992 Dick MacPherson #11

The 1992 New England Patriots football team competed in their thirty-third season of professional football and their twenty-third season in the National Football League (NFL). The Patriots were led by Dick MacPherson in his last of two seasons with the team. James Orthwein. Orthwein would be an active owner of the New England Patriots during the 1992 and 1993 seasons. He sold the team in 1994. Nobody carried the GM tie in 1992. The Patriots record was 2-14, and they finished in fifth (last) place in the AFC East Division.

Every Patriot season during this period had a series of sub-plots and Dick MacPherson's swan-song season (1992) is no different. The Patriots' two wins in weeks eleven and twelve of the 1992 season came after a horrendous 0–9 start, and they were followed by a five-game losing streak to end the season. They received the first overall pick in the following year's draft. Nobody would consider trading that record for a #1 draft pick.

This was the first season of the ownership bonanza as this version of the team was owned by James Orthwein. He bought the team from previous owner Victor Kiam to settle a debt. This was also the last season in which Dick MacPherson would be the head coach after a two-year tenure. It was also the last season to feature the Patriots' original colors and logo on their primary uniforms, which were overhauled for use in the following season. Things were changing. Soon the Patriots would begin to win games again.

The 1992 Patriots opened up the season with a bye. That means that by scheduling design they missed week 1 of the football playing season. But, they came back in week 2 for their season opener at Los Angeles in which the Rams shut out the Patriots L (0–14) before 40,402. In the home opener at Foxboro the following week on Sept 20, the Seattle Seahawks managed a win from the Patriots L (6–10) before 42,327. At Foxboro on Sept 27, the Buffalo Bills hammered the New England Patriots L (7–41) before 52,527. Then, at New York on Oct 4, the Jets beat the Patriots by nine, L (21–30) before 60,180.

At Foxboro on Oct 11, the San Francisco 49ers beat the Patriots L (12–24) before 54,126. On Oct 18, at Miami, the Dolphins mauled the Patriots L (17–38) before 57,282. Back at home in Foxboro Stadium, the Cleveland Browns beat the Patriots in a two-point match L (17–19) before 32,219. Next, at Buffalo on Nov 1, the Bills beat the Patriots L (7–16) before 78,268.

A very young Coach Bill Belichick in 1992, head coach of the Cleveland Browns

At home in Foxboro Stadium on Nov 8, the New Orleans Saints scorched the Patriots L (14–31) before 45,413. At Indianapolis the next week, on Nov 15, the Patriots scored their first win of the season over the Colts W (37–34) before 42,631. The second win W (24-3) came the next week at home in Foxboro Stadium on Nov 22 against the New York Jets before 27,642. At Atlanta after the big win streak was over, the Falcons whipped the Patriots in a nice shutout L (0-34) before 54,494.

On Dec 6, at home in Foxboro Stadium, the Patriots lost to the Indianapolis Colts L (0–6) before 19,429. At Kansas City on Dec 13, the Chiefs beat the Patriots L (20–27) before 52,208. At Cincinnati on Dec 20, the Bengals defeated the Patriots L (10–20) before 45,355. Then, at home in Foxboro Stadium on Dec 27, the Miami Dolphins wrapped up the New England season by grabbing a close victory from the Patriots L (13–16) before 34,726

Chapter 19 Coach Bill Parcells 1993 to 1996

Coach #12 Bill Parcells

Year	Coach	League	Conf	Div	Pl	W-L-T
1993	Bill Parcells	NFL	AFC-East		4th	5 11 0
1994	Bill Parcells	NFL	AFC-East		2nd	10 6 0

- Lost Wild Card Playoffs (at Browns) 13–20
- Bill Parcells(COY)[18]

1995	Bill Parcells	NFL	AFC-East		4th	6 10 0

- Curtis Martin(OROY)

1996	Bill Parcells	NFL	AFC-East		1st	11 5 0

- Won Divisional Playoffs(Steelers) 28–3
- Won Conference Championship(Jaguars) 20–6
- Lost Super Bowl XXXI (vs. Packers) 21–35

1993-1996 Bill Parcells final record (32-32-0)

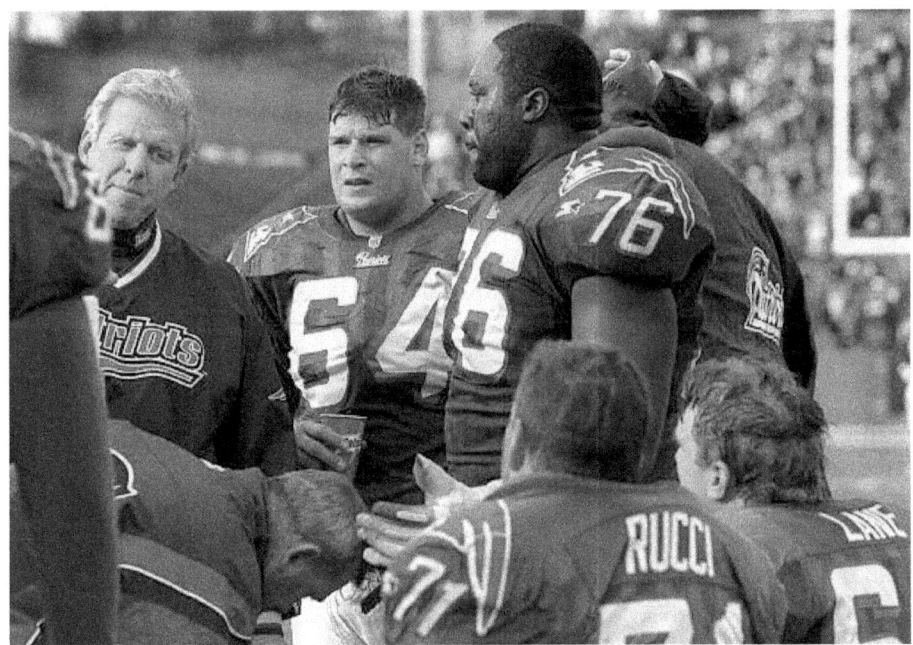

Coach Bill Parcells taking it seriously against Indianapolis

1993 Bill Parcells #12

The 1993 New England Patriots football team competed in their thirty-fourth season of professional football and their twenty-fourth season in the National Football League (NFL). The Patriots hired Bill Parcells to turn the team around after he had brought two world championship Super Bowl victories to the New York Giants in his eight years with the last one being in 1990 at a time in which the Patriots were floundering. So, the 1993 team was led by Bill Parcells in his first of four seasons with the team. James Orthwein was still the owner this year. He sold the team in 1994. Nobody carried the GM title in 1993. The Patriots record was 5-11 even with Bill Parcells running the show. They finished in fourth place in the AFC East Division.

Lots was happening organizationally and preparation-ally in 1993. Bill Parcells was brought to New England to create a champion. Could he do it? Could he wait it out? We'll see soon.

Additional Information

With ownership changes, there are most often rumors of planned moves for the teams affected. They were aplenty when Orthwein from St. Louis took over the Patriots club as owner. There were natural rumors that the team would move to St. Louis and become the Stallions (even to the point of a team logo being unveiled and hats being printed). Despite the confusion, the Patriots ran through the year. It was the first at New England as head coach for Bill Parcells but as an assistant, he had familiarity with Patriot operations.

He had been a linebackers' coach in Foxboro in 1980 under Ron Erhardt. The Patriots drafted Drew Bledsoe as the #1 pick in 1993 and he was named to be the starter in his first year with the club. As noted, big changes were afoot in the organization even before the team took the field this season. Bill Parcells cleaned house.

All coaches from the 1992 season with the exception of Dante Scarnecchia and Bobby Grier were fired and replaced with new ones. Scarnecchia would become a special assistant while Grier would move to the front office. The roster had undergone substantial changes; among the holdovers from the 1992 season were Marv Cook, Ben Coates, Kevin Turner, Michael Timpson, Sam Gash, Greg McMurtry, Vincent Brown, Maurice Hurst, Leonard Russell,

Bruce Armstrong, Mike Arthur, and Pat Harlow. The 1993 season was also the first season the current Patriots logo and font was used (though the current variation would undergo a tweak in 2000 with a slight color change).

The Patriots got off to a poor start when they hit the field. They lost their first four games, even after forcing overtime against the Lions and seeing a last-minute field goal attempt against Seattle bounce off the crossbar.

In Week 5, Drew Bledsoe was injured, Scott Secules was named the starting quarterback, and he managed to win the game with two passing touchdowns and one rushing TD in the team's close 23–21 win over the Cardinals. Scott Secules was then benched after a 28–14 loss to the Oilers. Bledsoe started for the Patriots but did not set any records on fire. In fact, he stunk out the place along with the rest of the team.

The Pats lost seven straight before eking out a 7–2 win against the Bengals (it was the last occurrence until the 2013 Jaguars of a team scoring only a safety in a game). After this win, the team managed a 20–17 victory over the Cleveland Browns coached by Parcells' longtime assistant Bill Belichick and then they unloaded a 38–0 massacre of the Indianapolis Colts in brutal wind-chill conditions.

The season ended none-too-soon on January 2, 1994, with many in the sellout crowd at Foxboro Stadium believing it would be the final ever game for the New England Patriots before moving to St. Louis; unknown to most, though, was that stadium owner Robert Kraft was working to force the selling of the team to him, and his control of the team's lease ensured no move could take place until 2002 at the earliest.

Before we discuss the season finale in Parcells first year, let me bring you up to date on what was happening besides the name changes of Schaefer Stadium to Sullivan Stadium to Foxboro Stadium. The ownership of the stadium was in flux and this fact is one of the only facts that are on the side of New England Fans wanting to keep an NFL franchise in Boston and surrounds.

We know that Sullivan's financial troubles ultimately forced him to sell controlling interest of the Patriots to Victor Kiam in 1988. Fortunately, or unfortunately, the stadium itself lapsed into bankruptcy. Enter Robert Kraft, current owner.

In 1988, Kraft outbid several competitors, including Kiam, to buy the stadium out of bankruptcy court from Sullivan for $22 million. In other words, from 1988-on, neither Sullivan, nor Kiam, nor Orthwein owned the stadium. It was the sole possession of Robert Kraft. Sullivan was ready to bail as he needed the cash and he wanted as much as he could get for the stadium built less than 20 years earlier for about $7 million. Kraft was ready to pay a reasonable amount.

For many without alternative motives, the stadium appeared to be cheap and outdated on its opening day. For potential purchasers, the facility was considered to be outdated by reasonable standards for its day and nearly worthless. However, the purchase price for the lucky buyer included the stadium's lease to the Patriots, which ran through 2001. Kraft won the bid.

Those who examined the lease have concluded that it was ironclad enough to end Sullivan's three-decade involvement with the Patriots. And, so, when Sullivan and Kiam tried to move the team to Jacksonville, Kraft refused to let them break the lease. He, as a stadium owner was able to exert a New-England influence on the transaction. As a result, when Kiam was nearly brought down by bad investments of his own, he was forced to sell the Patriots team to somebody. That somebody happened to be James Orthwein.

Ever since Orthwein had bought the team in 1992, there had been constant rumors that he wanted to move the Patriots to St. Louis. In 1994, Orthwein offered a ton of cash to Kraft. In fact, it was $75 million. He wanted to buy out the remainder of the team's lease at what was now Foxboro Stadium. Had Robert Kraft accepted Orthwein's offer, it would have cleared the last significant hurdle to moving the team to St. Louis, Podunk, or Tim-Buk-Tu. However, Kraft turned it down. New England footballers thank Robert Kraft every day of their lives…at least they should.

There are a lot of great games and great stories in the off years of the Patriots. Having a guy who bagged two Super Bowl Rings already as your head coach means for sure that your team is a contender.

This season finale itself became one of the most dramatic games in the club's history. The Patriots were hosting the Dolphins. When Starter Dan Marino went out for the year in week 5, the Dolphins fell to 9–6. The Dolphins needed a win to make the playoffs.

In the game, the Patriots led 10–7 at halftime and twice stopped the Dolphins on downs, but early in the third, a Bledsoe fumble led to a Dolphins field goal and a tie game. Then a blocked punt by the Dolphins' Darrell Malone led to a touchdown by Scott Mitchell to Mark Ingram. The game was topsy-turvy at this point as the lead had tied or had changed five times in the fourth quarter alone.

In the fourth, the Dolphins were moving and ended a drive with a Terry Kirby touchdown run, even though Andre Tippett had sacked Mitchell for a ten-yard loss – it was the 100th career sack for the future Hall of Fame linebacker.

In the final 3:40 Bledsoe took the Patriots down to a Ben Coates touchdown catch. But it was not enough as the Dolphins forced overtime on a Pete Stoyanovich field goal.

In the overtime the Dolphins punted after Chris Slade forced a fumble. Then, Drew Bledsoe threw a pick to J.B. Brown before the Dolphins lined up to punt again. The Pats got the ball. Vincent Brisby caught a ten-yard pass but fumbled and teammate Leonard Russell recovered the ball and ran 22 yards. The team was moving.

Bledsoe then absorbed a Dolphins blitz and launched a 36-yard touchdown to Michael Timpson, ending a wild 33–27 Patriots win and finishing their season at 5–11, but with four straight wins to close it out and subsequently, the Patriots had eliminated the Dolphins from the playoffs.

Several weeks later owner James Orthwein completed sale of the entire Patriots team to Robert Kraft, Rumor has it included the deeds to all New England properties. That's how much New England was willing to give up for their football team. Later the residents learned their deeds were safe as Robert Kraft promised to take care of New England and New Englanders as long as he could get a lot of wins out of the franchise. Well, maybe Kraft demanded no such thing, but he got it anyway. For those reading that think the Patriots do not have blood and guts in their roots, think again. Just like Paul Revere and the whole notion of Patriotism, the New Englanders I know would never give up their team, the New England Patriots. Let St. Louis find a few beautiful red Cardinal flying birds to launch their spirits high into the sky.

The 1993 Games:

In the Season opener on September 5, 1993 at Buffalo, the Bills thumped the Parcells Patriots L (14-38) before 79,751. On Sept 12, the Detroit Lions beat the Patriots L (16–19) in (OT) before 54,151. At Foxboro on Sept 19, the Seattle Seahawks beat the Patriots in c a close match L (14–17) before 50,392. At New York, on Sept 26, the Jets shellacked the Patriots L (7–45) before 64,836. In Week 5, on Oct 3, the Patriots had a bye week.

At Phoenix, on Oct 10, the Patriots beat the Cardinals W (23–21) before 36,115. At home in Foxboro Stadium on Oct 17, the Houston Oilers beat the Pats L (14-28) before 51,037. At Seattle on Oct 24, the Seahawks won a one-point match L (9-10) before 56,526. Then, on Oct 31, at Indianapolis, the Colts prevailed L (6-9) before 46,522.

At home at Foxboro Stadium on Nov 7, the Buffalo Bills beat the Patriots L (10-13) before 54,326. On Nov 14 in Week 11, the Patriots experienced their second bye of the season. At Miami on Nov 21, the Dolphins prevailed v the Patriots L (13-17) before 59,982. On Nov 28, the New York Jets beat the Patriots L (0-6) before 42,810. Then, on Dec 5, at Pittsburgh the Steelers were victorious over the Patriots L (14-17) before 51,358.

On Dec 12, the Cincinnati Bengals were defeated by the Patriots W (7–2) before 29,794. At Cleveland, on Dec 19, the Patriots defeated the Browns W (20–17) before 48,618. On shat is Boxers Day in Canada, Dec 26, the Indianapolis Colts skinned the Patriots W (38–0) before 26,571. In the last regular season game on January 2, 1994 the Patriots beat the Miami Dolphins W (33–27) in (OT) before

53,883. And, that was it for the first Bill Parcells season, 1993. Amen!

Drew Bledsoe was a patriot from right after the draft. He was the first overall pick in the 1993 NFL Draft and then for the next eight years, Bledsoe, a fine quarterback was considered the face of the Patriots franchise.

During his nine-year Patriots career, Drew Bledsoe se the records that Tom Brady would eventually eclipse. Bledsoe broke the Patriots' career passing records for attempts (4,518), completions (2,544) and yards (29,657). Keeping Brady from achievements would assure that Bledsoe would still hold the Patriots' single-season passing record for attempts (691) and completions (400) and would keep him as the only player in franchise history to pass for over 400 yards multiple times

Drew Bledsoe still holds the NFL record for attempts in a season (691 in 1994) and both attempts (70) and completions (45) in a game against Minnesota in 1994 that sparked a seven-game win streak. This propelled the Patriots to their first playoff berth in eight years. Bledsoe led the Patriots to the playoffs four times in his first six seasons, helping the team earn back-to-back division titles and three consecutive playoff berths for the first time in franchise history.

In 1996, he continued his great play by guiding the Patriots to their second AFC Championship in franchise history and a trip to Super Bowl XXXI. Bledsoe is the only quarterback in NFL history with four seasons of at least 600 pass attempts, including three-straight from 1994-96 with the Patriots. If he had not gotten hurt, he might still be playing for the Patriots. Well, maybe not but he would have lasted longer.

Top Patriots Players Troy Brown, WR & DB

Diminutive in stature perhaps but not in ability or desire, Troy Brown spent his entire 15-year career with the Patriots (1993-2007) after being drafted by the team in the eighth round (198th overall) in the 1993 NFL Draft.

At 5-foot-10 inch, 196-pounds, this receiver, punt returner and defensive back retired as the team's all-time leading receiver with 557 career receptions and as the team's all-time leading punt returner with 252 career returns. That's not too shabby.

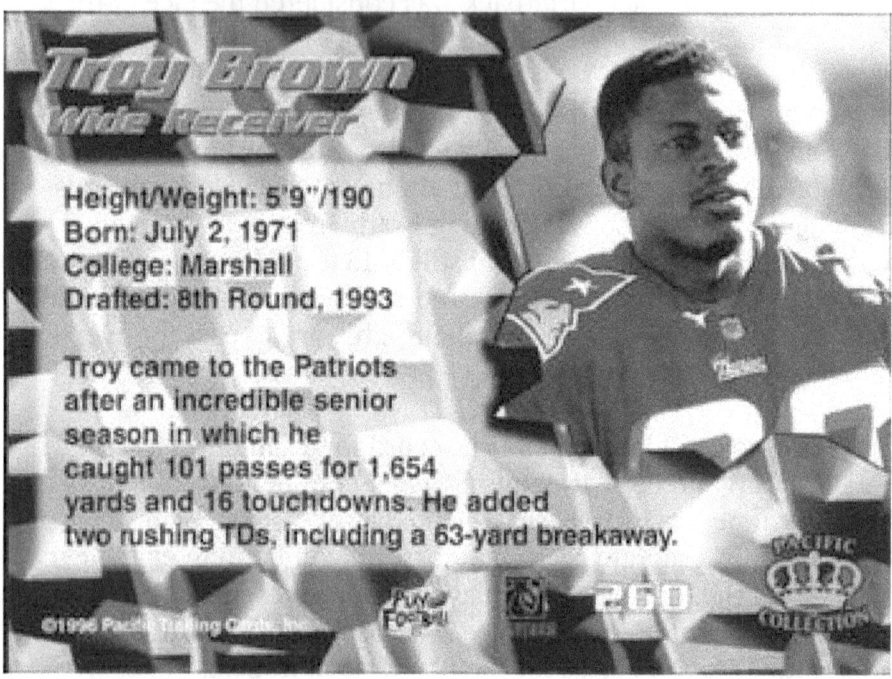

Brown finished ranked second in Patriots history with 6,366 career receiving yards and was tied for the franchise record with three punt returns for touchdowns. He played in 192 games, placing him fourth on the team's all-time games played list and his 15 seasons with the franchise tied Julius Adams for the second-longest tenure in a Patriots uniform behind Steve Grogan's 16 seasons. That's something!

Brown helped the Patriots to three Super Bowl championships and went to his only Pro Bowl in 2001. In 2004, he added defense to his resume when he began playing defensive back and finished second on the team with three interceptions. Brown was a difference maker.

Troy Brown's ability to make sizable contributions on offense, defense and special teams as well as his ability to perform in the clutch made him one of the most versatile and valuable players in the Patriot's history.

1994 Bill Parcells #12

The 1994 New England Patriots football team competed in their thirty-fifth season of professional football and their twenty-fifth season in the National Football League (NFL). The Patriots were led by Coach Bill Parcells in his second of four years. This was the first year under new owner Robert Kraft who purchased full rights to the team in 1994. Bill Parcells in many ways served as GM. The Patriots record was much improved at 10-6 giving them a 1st place finish (tied for first) in the AFC East Division and qualifying the team for the playoffs.

Robert Kraft as noted, purchased the team after preventing previous owner James Orthwein from moving the Patriots to St. Louis. Yes, folks, Robert Kraft kept the Patriots in New England. The team began the 1994 season with a 3–6 record before getting in gear and winning their final seven games, finishing 10–6 and qualifying the playoffs. Many see Bill Parcells as a miracle worker. With Robert Kraft helping instead of hurting operations, it helps to remember that The Patriots were just two seasons removed from a 2-win season. They made the playoffs for the first time since 1986 and only the seventh time in the franchise history. It was also their first winning season since 1988. The winning streak started with a 26–20 overtime win over the Minnesota Vikings.

The First Robert Kraft Season – Highlights

*** The Robert Kraft Ownership goes down as one of the great moments in the history of the Patriots***

Robert Kraft bought the New England Patriots in 1994. In 1994 the fate of the Patriots was changed forever and for better. Robert Kraft, a lifelong Patriots fan, purchased the team for $172 million. Since Kraft has taken over the franchise, the Patriots have been on an upward trajectory towards perfection. The Patriots are globally renowned for being a successful, consistently winning team.

Kraft has made excellent decisions as the owner, like giving the reins of player personnel to Belichick, or keeping their star Tom Brady happy. His moves and investment in the team has led to 16 playoffs appearances in 21 years, 7 Super Bowl, and 5 championship victories, which are tied for second-most in the NFL. The Patriots are the benchmark of success in modern sports.

The Robert Kraft season opener was played at Miami on September 4, 1994, where the Dolphins outscored the Patriots L (35–39) before 71,023. This game was a big deal for the Pats as it was the debut game of Robert Kraft as team owner and the second season for Bill Parcells who had already put his shape on the team. In this game, the pundits called out both quarterbacks, Drew Bledsoe and Dan Marino for put on a passing clinic. They combined for 894 passing yards and nine touchdowns.

Two TD's were caught by Ben Coates of the Patriots and three were snagged by Irving Fryar of the Dolphins. The game was Marino's first game back from a ruptured Achilles tendon. The Dolphins squeaked out a victory 35-39 after the Patriots failed to convert a touchdown in the Dolphins red zone in the final minute of the game. Ben Coates nearly fumbled the ball to the Dolphins on the drive.

In an almost identical outcome on September 11 at home in Foxboro Stadium, in the first home opener for Robert Kraft, the Buffalo Bills edged out the Patriots L (35–38) before 60,274. It seemed the fans could sense the optimism in the franchise and began to come out stadium loads to see their Patriots play football. the Patriots almost pulled this out as they rallied from down 35–21 in the fourth quarter.

Michael Timpson snatched a touchdown catch and Marion Butts rushed for a score which tied the game. Unfortunately, when Buffalo got the ball back, Steve Christie put a 32-yarder through the posts and his field goal won the game for Buffalo L (35–38). So far in the first two losses, the total score differential was 7 points. Still, no cigar.

In the third game, on Sept 18 at Cincinnati, the Patriots defeated the Bengals for their first W of the year (31–28) before 46,640. In this game, the Patriots wore throwback uniforms and helmets, returning the former Pat Patriot logo after it was retired following the 1992 season. In the game, the Bengals' David Klingler threw two TD's to Carl Pickens and Steve Broussard ran for two scores for the Bengals. But, the Patriots "D" was unrelenting sacking Klingler seven times.

Meanwhile, the Patriots got behind Drew Bledsoe's 365 passing yards including to Michael Timpson for 125 yards with a 34-yard touchdown catch, and to Ben Coates, along with two Marion Butts TD runs, and four Matt Bahr field goals. The offensive power overcame the Bengals tough game for a 31–28 win. This was the Patriots' first victory under Robert Kraft ownership.

At Detroit in the fourth 1994 game on September 25, the Patriots picked up their second win W (23-17) against the Lions before 59,618. The Patriots got off to a 20–7 lead and held off a late Lions surge to win 23–17. Barry Sanders was impressive in the loss, rushing for 131 yards (outperforming the entire Patriots offensive backfield's 108 combined yards); NFL Films took some great shots in slow motion of a twisting Sanders run in which he shook off Patriots defenders Myron Guyton and Harlon Barnet. This was one of his two touchdowns. The image in the film is among the most replayed in retrospectives on Sanders' career.

The Green Bay Packers lost to the Patriots W (17-16) in the fifth game of the season on Oct 2, at Foxboro before 57,522. All games so far this year were decided by 6 points or less. This was a throwback squared game as both teams sported their throwback uniforms. The Packers wore yellow and brown and the Patriots wore the white road version of their AFL-era uniforms with the famous Pat Patriot logo.

The Packers ripped out of the tunnel and quickly stormed to a 10–0 halftime lead. But, with two Vincent Brisby touchdown catches and a final-minute Matt Bahr field goal, the Patriots were ready to walk out of the house with a 17–16 win.

The Patriots then went on a four-game skid in a five-week period, which included a bye week and a 3-23 loss to Miami after the rest.

The first loss was against the Los Angeles Raiders L (17–21) in week six on Oct 9 before 59,889 at home in Foxboro Stadium. Drew Bledsoe fired off two touchdowns in the second quarter for a 17–7 Patriots lead but the Raiders snagged three Bledsoe INTs. The first run back for a score was by Terry McDaniel).

Jeff Hostetler threw orchestrated two touchdowns (one on the ground) to win by four points. One of the highlights shows Kevin Turner being drilled in mid-air while diving for the goal-line late in the fourth quarter. Though it appears that he broke the goal-line plane the ball was knocked out of his hands and handed over to the Raiders. These games this season, losses and wins have all been close. The Parcells driven Patriots were not giving up an inch.

The second loss in a row came on Oct 16 in week seven at New York. The Jets grabbed a one-TD victory L (17–24) before 71,123. Brad Baxter ran for two touchdowns and Boomer Esiason score another for the Jets in putting up a 21-7 half-time lead. Former Jet Blair Thomas scored in the fourth for New England, but the Patriots could not get any closer than a 24-17 loss. The next week, with a 3-4 record, I suspect the Parcells led Patriots did not enjoy the bye week.

After the bye on Oct 30, the Miami Dolphins did not give the Patriots much room to score, closing the gates with a L (3–23) before 59,167 at Foxboro. The Patriots defense was ready enough to snare two interceptions from Dan Marino, but they also gave up more passing yards (198) than the Patriots offense could manage in total. It was not pretty.

Drew Bledsoe had one of his worst days, throwing three interceptions and gaining just 125 yards. NE backup QB Scott Zolak came in and mopped up, finishing the game with 28 passing yards.

In week ten on November 6, at Cleveland, the Patriots had not gotten rid of all the loss *heebie-jeebies*. This would be the last loss of the regular season. The Browns upended the Patriots L (6–13) before 73,878. Since the Pats would play the Browns in the playoffs, this game turned out to be a playoff preview with similar results. In the battle of the Titans, Bill Parcells faced his former defensive assistant Bill Belichick. The master would not beat his pupil this year. Belichick's Browns were having a banner year at 6-2. In this game,

Belichick's defense were in Drew Bledsoe's face all game, forcing four interceptions and limiting the Patriots to just two Matt Bahr field goals. Meanwhile, Leroy Hoard rushed for 123 yards and caught a Mark Rypien one-yard touchdown pass. The 13–6 loss dropped the Patriots to 3–6.

In week 11 on Nov 13, at home in Foxboro Stadium, the Patriots showed resolve in overcoming their losing streak, pulling out a nice victory over the Minnesota Vikings W (26–20) before 58,382. Former Oilers quarterback and none-time pro-bowler Warren Moon, who had wo of his top three years after he left the Oilers, put on a show, leading the Vikings to a 20–3 halftime lead.

Bill Parcells had enough and so in the third, he abandoned his game-plan and went to a no-huddle attack. Drew Bledsoe threw successive touchdowns to Ray Crittenden and Leroy Thompson. Additionally, a fired-up Patriots defense shut down the Vikings (the key play came with 2:04 to go in the fourth when Maurice Hurst swatted away a pass for Qadry Ismail).

On the final drive of the game, Bledsoe was blitzed three straight downs but showed grit in the face of a 4th and 10 from his 35. He reached back and completed a 27-yard strike to Vincent Brisby. With time disappearing on the clock, Matt Bahr, who had missed a try late in the third quarter, kicked the tying field goal. There were 14 seconds left in regulation.

On the coin toss for overtime Patriots captain Vincent Brown protested the Vikings team captain's call because he called after the coin landed on the ground. The Patriots won the re-toss and Bledsoe led the Patriots down field and lobbed a 14-yard touchdown toss to Kevin Turner. The 26–20 win ended the Patriot four-game losing streak. Moon threw for 349 yards while Bledsoe chalked up 426 yards. Together, they set NFL single-game records with 70 throws and 45 completions. The Patriots were off.

In week 12 at home in Foxboro, the Patriots beat the San Diego Chargers W (23–17) to close in on the season 500 mark (5–6) before 59,690. The reconstituted and refocused Patriots quickly gained a 13–3 second-quarter lead. Leroy Thompson caught a 27-yard TD from Drew Bledsoe in the first quarter. With the two Matt Bahr field goals, the Patriots were sailing. But then the Chargers scored after as Andre Coleman ran back the ensuing kickoff 80 yards for a touchdown. Later in the 4th quarter, the Patriots put the game away on a one-yard Marion Butts score followed soon by another Bahr field goal. This action offset a Tony Martin TD catch from Stan Humphries.

At Indianapolis on Nov 27, in week 13 of the season, the Patriots defeated the Colts W (12–10) before 43,839. The Patriots were now 6-6, having climbed up to overcome their losing record. The Colts limited New England to four Matt Bahr field goals, but despite 186 yards and a touchdown by Don Majkowski to go with 132 rushing yards by Majkowski, Marshall Faulk, and Roosevelt Potts, the Colts lost the game as the keyed-up Patriot defense recovered two Indianapolis fumbles.

On Dec 4 in week 14, at home in Foxboro, the Patriots defeated the Jets W (24-13) 60,138. The Jets led this game 13–10 in the third quarter but the Patriots stuffed Boomer Esiason at his own goal-line. Then, Ricky Reynolds ran back an interception for a touchdown. Leroy Thompson scored a touchdown in the fourth quarter which finished off the Jets as Esiason ended with just 16 completions for 40 throws. The loss was Jets coach Pete Carroll's last trip to Foxboro until he became the Patriots head coach in 1997.

On Dec 11, in week 15, the Patriots beat the Indianapolis Colts W (28–13) before 57,656. The Colts got it going early for a 10-0 lead as they intercepted Drew Bledsoe at their own 10 and Ray Buchanan ran back a 90-yard touchdown. However, things would change for the better for the Patriots.

From there Don Majkowski was intercepted twice. Despite throwing four interceptions, Bledsoe found Leroy Thompson and Ben Coates, Thompson and then Marion Butts scored on the ground. The Pats snatched two more fumbles for a 28-13 win. The Patriots stood at 8-6 after this game and were still in the hunt for a playoff spot while the Colts fell to 6-8.

On Dec 18, at Buffalo in week 16, the Patriots smashed the Bills W (41–17) before 56,784 a week before Christmas, 1994. As the game was underway, The Patriots fell behind 17–3 in the second quarter. They then put on a scoring display, accumulating 38 unanswered points for a 41–17 rout. The win knocked the Bills out of the playoffs after four straight Super Bowl trips.

On Christmas Eve in week 17, at Chicago, the Patriots glided past the Bears W (13-3) before 60,178. Going into the game, Parcells knew that his team needed the win to make the playoffs. With little offense and a strong defense, the Patriots overtook the Bears 13–3, for their seventh consecutive win. They ended the regular season with a 10–6 record tied for first place in the AFC Eastern Division. It was their first playoff appearance since 1986 and their first double-digit win season since that year as well. The next game would be a repeat with Belichick's Browns

Wildcard Cleveland Browns v NE Patriots

In the AFC Wildcard playoffs, on January 1, 1995, the Browns defeated the Patriots L (13–20) before 77,452 at Cleveland. Their last defeat had been at the hands of the Browns on Nov 6. After winning seven in a row the Patriots were flat in their 20–13 loss in their first playoff game since 1986. Drew Bledsoe had a tough time locating Patriot receivers and was picked off three times.

He did orchestrate a game-tying rally in the second quarter. Bledsoe attempted 50 passes but connected on just 22. Leroy Hoard and Earnest Byner together garnered 96 rushing yards. This total was more than the total of the entire Patriots offensive backfield (57 yards). The win was the first in a playoff game for Browns head coach Bill Belichick. A high note for The Patriots was a successfully executed onside kick. It would be almost ten years before the Patriots succeeded with another onside (2013). Coincidentally, this 2013 kick also would be against the Browns, but the next time Belichick would be on the kicking side of the ball.

1995 Bill Parcells #12

The 1995 New England Patriots football team competed in their thirty-sixth season of professional football and their twenty-sixth season in the National Football League (NFL). The Patriots were led by Coach Bill Parcells in his third second of four years. This was the second year under new owner Robert Kraft who purchased full rights to the team in 1994. Bill Parcells in many ways served as GM. The Patriots record was not as positive and came in below 500 at 6-10 giving them a 4th place finish in the AFC East Division. This was Parcells 2nd-worst season. The Pats did not qualify for the playoffs.

Unlike 1994, when Drew Bledsoe was sharp all year, the previous year, he had a poor season. He threw just 13 touchdowns and was picked off 16 times. His completion percentage was just 50.8% of his passes. The bright spot on the team was rookie running back Curtis Martin. The youngster shined with a Pro Bowl season and would be the Patriots' feature back for two more seasons before the Patriots traded him to the New York Jets during Pete Carroll's tenure in 1998.

In the season and home opener at Foxboro Stadium, on September 3, 1995, the Patriots made amends for the major losses last year against the Cleveland Browns by gaining the win W (17–14) before 60,126. At home again on Sept 10, the Miami Dolphins had little trouble with the Patriots L (3-20) before 60,239. At San Francisco on Sept 17, the 49ers pummeled the Patriots L (3–28) before 66,179. The next week on Sept 24, was a bye. On Oct 1, in week 5 of the season, at Atlanta, the Falcons defeated the Patriots L 917-30) before 47,114.

On Oct 8 at home at Foxboro, the Denver Broncos hammered the Patriots L (3–37) before 60,074. The games were not as close as the prior two seasons under Parcells. At Kansas City on Oct 15, the Chiefs outplayed the Patriots by L (26-31) before 77,992. At home in Foxboro Stadium, the Patriots woke up and beat the Buffalo Bills W (27–14) before 60,203. On Oct 29, at home, the Carolina Panthers beat the Patriots by a field goal L (17–20) before 60,064.

At New York, on Nov 5, the Patriots beat the Jets W (20–7) before 61,462. At Miami on Nov 12, the Patriots prevailed W (34–17) before 70,399. At home on Nov 19, the Indianapolis Colts defeated the Patriots L (10–24) before 59,544. In week 13, on Nov 26, at Buffalo, the Patriots beat the Bills W (35–25) before 69,384.

At home in Foxboro on Dec 3, the New Orleans Saints prevailed L (17–31) before 59,876. On Dec 10, at home, the Patriots defeated the

New York Jets in a close match W (31-28) before 46,617. Then, at Pittsburgh on Dec 16, the Steelers beat the Patriots L (27-41) before 57,158. At Indianapolis in the final game of the season, the Colts beat the Patriots L (7-10) before 54,685.

Top Patriots Players Ty Law, CB

Like many other Ty Law loved his time with the Patriots. So, he spent 10 seasons with the Pats from 1995-2004) after joining the team as a first-round (23rd overall) draft pick out of Michigan in 1995. Law was a three-time Super Bowl Champion (XXXVI, XXXVIII, XXXIX), a four-time Pro Bowl player (1998, 2001, 2002, 2003) and a two-time All-Pro (1998, 2003) during his tenure with the Patriots.

Law tied Raymond Clayborn's career franchise-record with 36 interceptions and finished with the most interception-return yards in team history with 583. His six interceptions returned for touchdowns are also a franchise best. Law had nine interceptions in 1998 to become the first Patriots player to lead the NFL in that category.

He was a playmaker who played some of his best games in the postseason. He helped lead the Patriots to their first Super Bowl title in 2001 when he intercepted a Kurt Warner pass against the Rams and returned it 47 yards for a touchdown for the first points of the game.

In the 2003 AFC Championship Game, Law intercepted three Peyton Manning passes while leading the Patriots to a 24-14 victory over the Indianapolis Colts. Law was part of a record-breaking Patriots defense in 2003 that led the NFL in five key categories: opponents points per game (14.9), interceptions (29), fewest touchdown receptions allowed (11), opponent's passer rating (56.2) and pass deflections (121) as the team captured its second Super Bowl title in a win over the Carolina Panthers.

Law was great football player and is a member of the NFL's all-decade team for the 2000s as well as the Patriots' all-1990s and all-2000s decade teams. He was also selected to the Patriots' 50th Anniversary Team. He was inducted into the Patriots Hall of Fame in 2014.

1996 Bill Parcells #12

The 1996 New England Patriots football team competed in their thirty-seventh season of professional football and their twenty-seventh season in the National Football League (NFL). The Patriots were led by Coach Bill Parcells in his last of four seasons. This was the third year under new owner Robert Kraft who purchased full rights to the team in 1994. Bill Parcells in many ways served as GM. Under Kraft in addition to being head coach.

The Patriots record was 11-5 and they finished in first place in the AFC East Division. This was Parcells best season. The Pats qualified for the playoffs and would take the challenge right to the Super Bowl. Bill Parcells would not return to the Patriots after the Super Bowl.

After a very disappointing 1995 season, Drew Bledsoe bounced back with confidence and 4,086 passing yards. He also threw 27 touchdown passes to just 15 interceptions while Curtis Martin had another outstanding Pro Bowl season. The team went the distance in the playoffs but then lost Super Bowl XXXI to the Green Bay Packers.

Team owner Robert Kraft and coach Bill Parcells had a good relationship that simply collapsed as Parcells was able to guide the team as he saw fit... until... In the NFL draft, Parcells was determined to draft a defensive lineman, but Kraft overruled him, giving head scout Bobby Grier the choice of a player. Receiver Terry Glenn was selected. Parcells stormed out of the Patriots draft war room after the choice was made and vowed to reporter Will McDonough that he was done with New England after 1996. He kept his word.

Despite this issue before the practice season even began, Parcells prepared the team for a championship as was his style. When the season got off to a poor start, the Patriots rallied from their 0–2 start to finish 11–5. They then proceeded to defeat the Pittsburgh Steelers and the upstart Jacksonville Jaguars to advance to Super Bowl XXXI.

The season saw the arrival of former Cleveland Browns coach Bill Belichick as an integral part of the coaching squad taking over the coaching of New England's defensive backs. This was the second time that Belichick had worked for Parcells and the two respected each other.

The date was February 16, 1996: Parcells and Belichick were accustomed to working with each other for years in the Patriots and Giants organization. It is no wonder that just one day after being fired as head coach of the Browns, Belichick was hired by Parcells as the Patriots' assistant head coach and secondary coach. We know from the record book that in the Giants organization the two brought championships when they worked together. In their only season together with the Patriots, New England reached Super Bowl XXXI, losing to the Packers in the end.

The Rest of the story

Since a good part of the story about Bill Parcells is in this chapter and he is joined by Bill Belichick in 1996 and since Bill Belichick has such a great history with the New England Patriots, and we all know that Bill Belichick is the current highly successful New England Patriots coach... I would like to take the time now to tell you the rest of the story of Parcells and Belichick. It is far from over in 1996 and it is very interesting. It is also very germane as we go over the forthcoming great moments in New England Patriots football.

Just five days after coaching the Patriots in the Super Bowl, on January 31, 1997, Bill Parcells stepped down as head coach. There was heavy speculation centering on Parcells, who had a reputation as a fixer, that the talented coach was on his way to New York, this time to coach the Jets.

Though Parcells had told him earlier in the year, he was finished, Patriots owner Robert Kraft did not want to have to replace the coach who had finally brought wins to the franchise. So, Kraft asked the NFL to review Parcells' contract and to step in and block him from coaching anywhere in 1997. The NFL sided with New England, and the ruling forbade Parcells from coaching anywhere else in 1997.

There is so much history in such a short period of time here that even long-time Patriots history buffs have some room for confusion. Though I knew for example that Pate Carrol would be the next coach, the conditions were perfect with Bill Belichick already on the scene for Robert Kraft to bring him in a few years earlier to be the new England Head coach. Instead, he hired Pete Carroll.

Here's how that went down. We have been over some of this already. We know that Bill Parcells had already signed out from the Patriots after becoming frustrated with owner Robert Kraft's not permitting him to, as they say, "shop for the groceries" in compiling a roster, or at least having yes/no on names. In early 1997 after the Super Bowl, Parcells and Robert Kraft agreed to disagree Kraft wanted to maintain owner control of the roster but eventually agreed to a deal brokered by then-NFL commissioner Paul Tagliabue, in which the New York Jets sent the Patriots four draft picks in exchange for Kraft releasing Parcells from his contract.
Parcells thus became the Jets' head coach, and Kraft was able to hire Pete Carroll to follow the legend.

Rich Cimini, an ESPN staff writer offers this quote as to the value of simply having Bill Parcells become the coach of your team, even if no Super Bowl is forthcoming. Parcells had to be special when Bill Belichick kept signing up for refresher course lessons from the master. Cimini: "Before Bill Parcells arrived in 1997, the New York Jets provided plenty of fodder for David Letterman's Top Ten list. They were hilariously inept. Parcells changed that the minute he walked in the building. For that, the franchise's long-suffering fans should be eternally grateful."

For the record, Bill Belichick sometimes regrets his decision to bail from New England after the Super Bowl. It could have been both fun and productive (my words). It was not long ago that in an interview Parcells told USA Today that he regretted quitting the New England Patriots after the '96 Super Bowl run. Why? "because it was a young, talented team still on the rise."

However, he was OK with his decision to leave the Jets when chances are he may have brought in another champion. He offered remorse and said he never second-guessed himself for leaving the Jets' job.

"No, I've never thought of that, I really haven't," Parcells said in a phone interview. "It's a transient business nowadays. There was new ownership, and you never know what's going to happen when that happens. It was time where they could start again with their own philosophy and a new owner."

Going back to the original confusion in February 1997 the Jets had hired Belichick as their head coach and since Parcells was banned from coaching originally, the Jets skirted the rules and hired Parcells as a consultant. The Patriots were not happy playing against a Parcells team anyplace as they believed he should be coaching for New England.

They filed another NFL complaint asking that Parcells not be allowed to work at all for the Jets, but the negotiated Tagliabue deal eventually ended that dispute. By the time it was all over on Feb 10, 1997, Parcells was named Jets head coach and Belichick, a very loyal "friend" of Bill Parcells was named as his assistant coach.

Meanwhile back at New England, Pete Carroll was the man on the scene. He had just year of NFL head coaching experience, having gone 6-10 with the Jets in 1994. Parcells had taken what might exaggeratingly be called a moribund New England franchise -- one that hadn't been to the playoffs since 1986 and which had posted a meager 14-50 record in the four seasons before Parcells' arrival -- and he took the team to a Super Bowl. We begin three sections in the next chapter about the Pete Carroll New England experience

Finally, after three years of Pete Carroll, on Jan 3, 2000, New England fires Pete Carroll and sends a fax to the Jets requesting permission to interview Belichick for its recently opened head-coaching job. However, Parcells retires as Jets head coach. "Bill's not coming back," Parcells said at the time. "You can write that on your chalkboard." The six-year contract Belichick signed with the Jets in 1997 called for him to be elevated to Jets head coach whenever Parcells decided to leave, preventing the Pats from speaking with him about their opening.

Belichick is a smart cookie and he did not want to be boxed into any job. So, on Jan. 4, 2000, he resigned as head coach of the New York Jets one day after being elevated to the job. He was concerned and said that it was questions about the Jets' future, including the team's impending sale that convince him to leave. "I just don't feel I can lead the Jets in the year 2000," Belichick said at the time. "I just know what I need to do. I just don't feel I can do it right now."

Knowing he was still boxed in, on Jan. 6, 2000, Bill Belichick filed a grievance with the NFL in an attempt to get out of the contract he had negotiated with the Jets. The NFL is owned by the owners not the coaches and so on Jan. 21, 2000, as expected, NFL commissioner Paul Tagliabue ruled in favor of the Jets, rejecting Belichick's grievance.

Bill Belichick was not ready for slave labor encampment and so he filed suit against the Jets and the NFL looking for relief via a temporary restraining order. He wanted out of the Jets, and he wanted to be able to be free to negotiate with other teams who may want him as their coach.

By January 27, 2000, it became an owner v owner and owner v NFL issue. Even before resolution, Belichick was named to be the head coach of the Patriots after New England and the Jets agreed on compensation. The Patriots really wanted coach Belichick as they gave New York their No. 1 draft pick in the 2000 draft and a fourth-

and seventh-rounder in 2001. The Jets gave the Patriots a No. 5 in 2001 and a No. 7 in 2002. Clearly the Patriots saw the same bright light of winning seasons and a winning mentality as Bill Parcells saw in Bill Belichick as Parcells mentored him in his early years.

Just like Bill Belichick is a smart man, so is owner Robert Kraft: "For a No. 1 draft choice, we can bring in a man that I feel certain can do something, rather than the uncertainty of a draft choice," Kraft said at the time. "And it wasn't even close when I thought about it that way."

The good connection continued as in Feb. 12, 2000, Scott Pioli, Parcells' son-in-law, who also served as the Jets' director of pro personnel, was hired by Bill Belichick as the Patriots' director of pro personnel.

After having graduated several times from the Bill Parcells school of great football ideas and attitudes, and having been a major instructor, it was not a surprise that as the Patriots coach on February 3, 2002 both the newly charged Patriots and Bill Belichick would win Super Bowl XXXVI.

Bill Parcells was not finished with his fixer career and he must have enjoyed it because he permitted himself to be hired again on Jan. 2, 2003. The Dallas Cowboys hired Bill Parcells, and so he was not thinking it was a slave-labor deal they threw in a four-year, $17.1 million deal.

This is not a book about the Dallas Cowboys and so far, I am not inclined to write one, but it is a book about the New England Patriots and we all know that their current successful head coach is a former disciple of Bill Parcells. Therefore, this little set of paragraphs sets up a fitting ending for the Bill Parcells period at New England.

In the Parcells period at Dallas, there were supportive writers who had penned "Before the past two years, the Cowboys have been 8-8, just missing the playoffs with a disappointing finish in the final week of each season, bringing the frustration level within Cowboys Nation to seemingly an all-time high…

But imagine being 5-11 for three straight years and not even coming close to the postseason."

When the Cowboys were looking for a Bill Parcells' type, the real deal, the real Bill Parcells was still available and ready to go to work.

The Cowboys were exactly there following the 2002 campaign. Jerry Jones who hates to lose, knew that a huge change was in order. He also knew it was time to make a splash that would not only change the current perception of the team, but more importantly the culture, and the team's ability to win, win, and then win again. Only a Bill Parcells type change would do.

Why was Parcells happy at Dallas? Here it is in his words: "...But Jerry isn't like that. You want to be somewhere where it's important to the people and certainly it's a high-profile franchise without question. I just felt like those are the kind of things I look forward to. I was trying to do something at a place like that. I like them. I think they're a good group. I think they're passionate. I think they're trying to be successful in the business. Hey, that's all a coach can ask for."

Without a Super Bowl, Bill Parcells me in Dallas was productive and successful. Parcells affects team attitudes to get into the soul of the team. As for his time in Dallas, he never got the acclaim for the same postseason success. The Cowboys' drought for playoff wins continued on Parcells' watch. But nobody who is a Parcells watcher thinks that his time with America's Team wasn't exceptionally meaningful.

Whether you like the Cowboys or not, Bill Parcells was not a fan of any team. He was a professional. He quietly turned Dallas into a competitive franchise again and he did it almost immediately. The Cowboys went 10-6 in his first year of 2003, never bragging but knowing they had been magically changed after just one year. This came after a disappointing 6-10 finish in 2004. After the 10-6, the club went 9-7 in each of the next two seasons, 2005-06. The latter included another demoralizing playoff defeat, this time to the Seahawks, which would be Parcells' final game as a head coach. Parcells may regret not staying at Dallas to see the seeds bear fruit as he wished the same for New England and the Jets. Parcells talent seeds are all over the NFL. The New England Patriots enjoy the product of Bill Parcells coaching seeds in Bill Belichick whose loyalty to the game of football through the great vision of Bill Parcells is unquestioned.

Games: In the season opener on September 1, 1996, the Miami Dolphins defeated the Patriots L (10–24) at Joe Robbie Stadium before 71,542. At home on Sept 8, the Buffalo Bills beat the Patriots L (10–17) at Rich Stadium before 78,104. On Sept 15 at home, New England shut-out the Arizona Cardinals W (31–0) at home in Foxboro Stadium before 59,118. Then at home again on Sept 22, the Patriots beat the Jacksonville Jaguars W (28–25) in (OT) in Foxboro Stadium before 59,446. The Patriots would stay at 500 or above for the rest of the season. On Sept 29, the team drew a bye

On Oct 6, at Memorial Stadium in Baltimore, the Patriots beat the Ravens in a shootout W (46–38) before 63,569. At home in Foxboro Stadium on Oct 13, the Washington Redskins beat the Patriots L (22–27) in Foxboro Stadium before 59,638. On Oct 20, the Indianapolis Colts were defeated by the New England Patriots W (27–9) at the RCA Dome before 58,725. On Oct 27, the Patriots defeated the Buffalo Bills W (28–25) at home in Foxboro Stadium before 58,858.

On Nov 3, the Patriots drubbed the Miami Dolphins W (42–23) at Foxboro Stadium before 58,942. In the Meadowlands, on Nov 10, the Patriots beat the New York Jets W (31–27) before 61,843. On Nov 17, at home in Foxboro Stadium, the Denver Broncos overpowered the Patriots L (8–34) before 59,457. Then, on Nov 24, the Patriots beat the Indianapolis Colts W (27–13) at home in Foxboro Stadium before 58,226.

On Dec 1, the Patriots thumped the San Diego Chargers W (45–7) at Jack Murphy Stadium before 62,541. On Dec 8, the Patriots whipped the New York Jets W (34–10) at home in Foxboro Stadium before 54,621. Then, in the second-last game of the season in Texas Stadium, the Dallas Cowboys eked out a win L (6–12) against the Patriots before 64,578. In the finale, on Dec 21, the Patriots barely beat the New York Giants W (23-22) in a one-point match shown on NBC at 12:30pm in Giants Stadium before 65,387.

Top Patriots Players Adam Vinatieri, K

Adam Matthew Vinatieri was born on December 28, 1972, right after Christmas and before New Year's. He is still an active NFL placekicker for the Indianapolis Colts but for years he was a big star for the New England Patriots and he I responsible for many of their big wins and their biggest wins.

Vinatieri played in five Super Bowls: four with the New England Patriots and one with the Colts. Vinatieri won Super Bowls in 2001, 2003, and 2004 with the Patriots, as well as in 2006 with the Colts. Among placekickers, Adam holds NFL records for most Super Bowl appearances (5) and most Super Bowl wins (4).

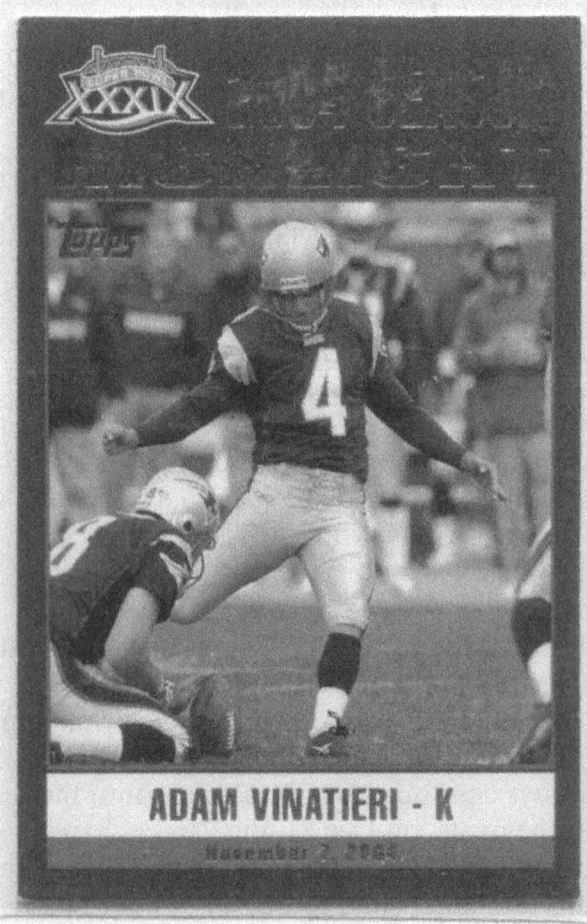

Additionally, he also holds NFL records, among all players, for most postseason points scored (234), and most overtime field goals made (12). He is the only player ever to score 1,000 points with two different teams. As of the 2017 season, Vinatieri, 45, is still healthy and active as the oldest player in the NFL.

As a kicker, he is almost at the top of all standings, yet he is #2. Morten Anderson has six more and so in the 2018 season, Vinatieri should become #1. Right now, he has converted the 2nd most field-goals in NFL history (553) as well as attempted the 3rd most field-goals in NFL history (655).

Vinatieri has been called "Mr. Clutch" by the media due to his reputation for success when kicking under pressure during his tenure in the NFL. His other nickname, "Automatic Adam" tells his story of unprecedented accuracy. He is also known as "Iceman" for his poise under pressure. I can't think of better nicknames for Vinatieri.

Vinatieri has converted several of the most crucial field goals in NFL history, including the game-tying and winning kicks in blizzard conditions in the famous "Tuck Rule Game", and game-winning kicks in the final seconds of two Super Bowls (XXXVI and XXXVIII)

Adam Vinatieri, or "Automatic Adam" as he became known, is probably just one of a handful of kickers who might make it into the top 15 in any franchise's history — much less the prodigious Patriots. That's a testament to just how good he was.

Vinatieri was a rookie in 1996, going to the Super Bowl with Bledsoe. He was along for the ride with Brady later on; he played the first 10 years of his career in New England and collected three Super Bowl wins — kicking game-winning field goals in two of them. Vinatieri later played for the Indianapolis Colts for 11 seasons, where he won another Super Bowl. Let's hope Adam beats the record in 2018.

Top Patriots Players Tedy Bruschi LB

One of the names I cannot forget from watching the Belichick Patriots in the somewhat recent past is Tedy Bruschi. I would agree with others that he is the consummate Patriot during my time observing his expertise. It was for his entire 13 seasons in New England. It was so much for the Patriots that Coach Bill Belichick called him the "perfect player" at Bruschi's retirement press conference in 2009.

Bruschi was a nobody who was a somebody because he was never a nobody. He served as team captain seven times and his relentless work ethic, on-field intensity, and full-tilt-full-time approach set the tone for his team while making him a fan favorite in New England.

Bruschi was not born a Patriot but, like others in the franchise, he might have chosen to be so born. Bruschi was originally drafted by the Patriots in the third round of the 1996 NFL Draft. He played in his first of five Super Bowls that season and is one of a select few Patriots to own three World Championship rings. They don't give them out if you lose the game.

Bruschi as noted was a difference maker. In 13 seasons, he helped his teammates propel the Patriots to 11 winning records, nine playoff appearances, including eight as division championships, five conference crowns and those three Super Bowl titles. He hated to lose and fought to the tooth to make his team succeed.

In 211 career games (including regular-season and playoffs), the Patriots had a 144-67 (.682) record, including a 16-6 (.727) playoff mark with Tedy on the field. Bruschi earned his first Pro Bowl honor following the 2004 season after co-captaining a Patriots defense that allowed just 16.25 points per game, the third fewest in franchise history.

Bruschi loved playing for the Pats and still he had a knack for making big plays in critical situations. He is the only player in NFL history to return four consecutive interceptions for touchdowns and his career total of four picks returned for scores ranks second in Patriots history.

After Bruschi suffered a stroke in February 2005, a stroke that made all Patriots check out their vitals, he put together Tedy's Team," which is dedicated to raising funds and awareness to fight stroke along with the American Stroke Association.

Top Patriots Players Willie McGinest, LB, DE

William Lee McGinest, Jr. was born December 11, 1971. He is a former NFL linebacker who played fourteen seasons, mostly with the New England Patriots. He was drafted by the New England Patriots fourth overall in the first round of the 1994 NFL Draft. He played college football at USC.

Willie McGinest played 12 of his 15 NFL seasons with the Patriots and was one of the cornerstones of the team's success during Super Bowl championships in 2001, 2003 and 2004. He ranks third in team history with 78 sacks and led the team in sacks six times, including a career high 11 in 1995.

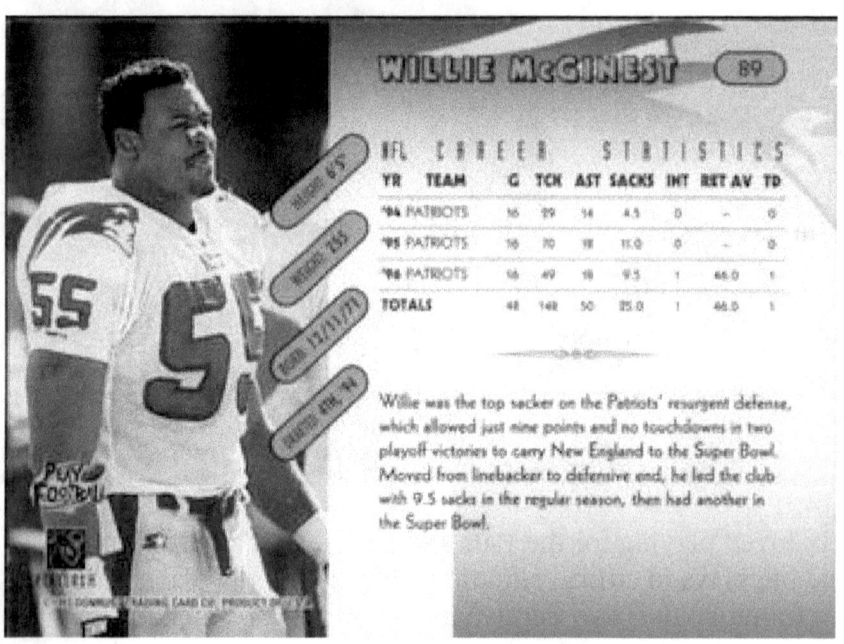

McGinest's 16 postseason sacks is an NFL record and he set the NFL mark for most sacks in a postseason game with 4 1/2 in a 2005 Wild Card win vs. Jacksonville.

One of his most memorable plays came in a 2003 regular-season game when he stuffed Indianapolis running back Edgerrin James on the goal line with 11 seconds remaining to preserve a 38-34 win. He was a versatile player, who played defensive end and linebacker and earned Pro Bowl honors in 1996 and 2003.

MgGinest helped the Patriots post nine winning seasons in 12 years, and led the team to six division titles, four conference championships and three Super Bowl championships during his career.

The Playoffs

In the Divisional Playoffs on January 5, 1997, the Patriots defeated the Pittsburgh Steelers W 28–3 at 12:30pm at Foxboro Stadium before 60,188. In the Conference Championship on January 12, 1997, the Patriots defeated the Jacksonville Jaguars W 20–6 at 4:00pm in Foxboro Stadium before 60,190. This brought the Patriots to Bill Parcells Super Bowl XXXI game played on January 26, 1997, against the Green Bay Packers in which they lost by two touchdowns L (21–35) at 6:00pm in the Louisiana Superdome before a crowd of 72,301

New England v Pittsburgh January 5, 1997

THIS IS AN ARTICLE FROM THE JAN. 13, 1997 ISSUE of Sports Illustrated. Our Thank you to SI.

Titled:

A SOUPER SUNDAY THE STEELERS WERE IN A FOG AGAINST THE PATRIOTS, WHO BEAT THEM AT THEIR OWN GAME By Austin Murphy

> A switch had been made under cover of fog. How else to explain the New England Patriots' role-reversing 28-3 win over the Pittsburgh Steelers in Sunday's AFC divisional playoff? While the Patriots came into the game with a defense made up of competent unknowns, their Steelers counterparts arrived in Foxboro with a nickname--Blitzburgh--and a recent record of violence against quarterbacks.

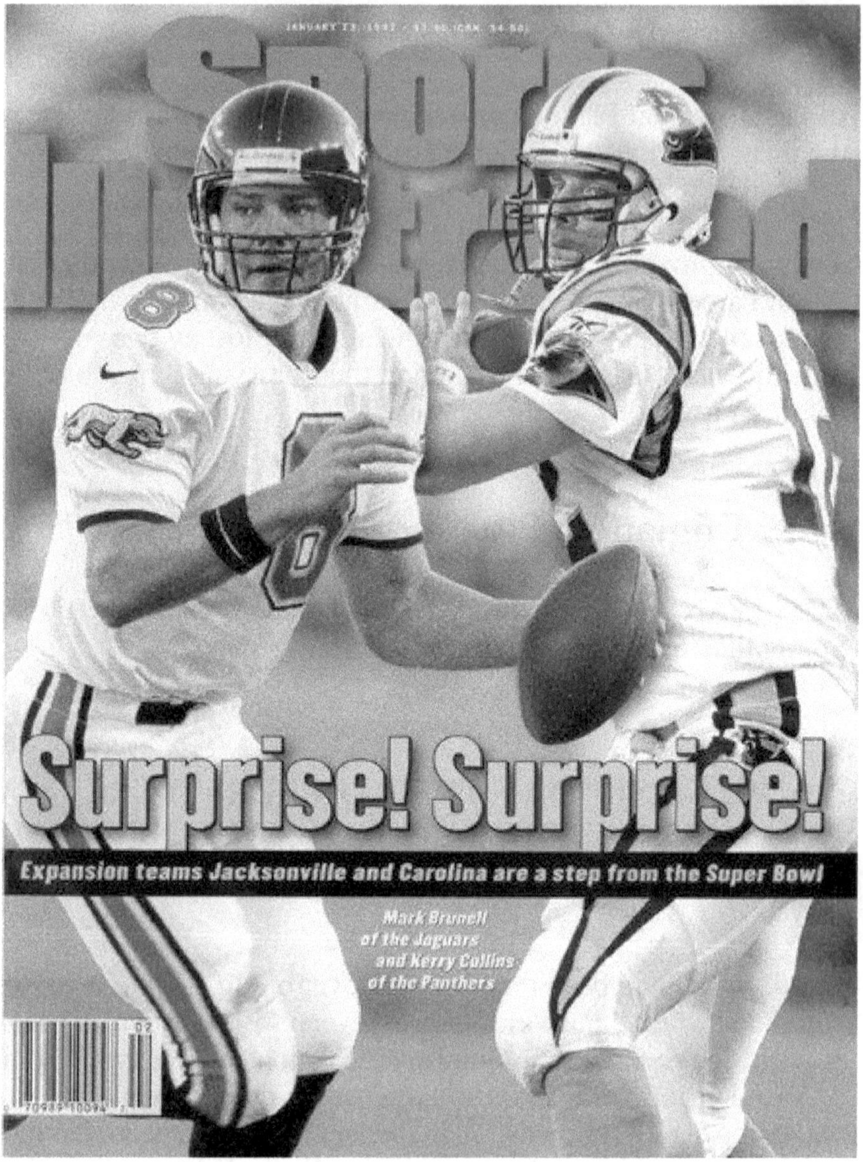

In a wild-card playoff game on Dec. 29, Pittsburgh sacked Indianapolis Colts quarterback Jim Harbaugh four times, broke one of his teeth and opened a gash on his chin that required 15 stitches. But on Sunday, in a fog so dense that Foxboro Stadium resembled the inside of Hunter S. Thompson's head, the Patriots played like the Steelers while the Steelers played like the old Patsies.

Defending AFC champion Pittsburgh had the NFL's second-best sack total (51) during the regular season, but it was the New England front seven (33 sacks in 1996) that generated the most heat on Sunday. The Steelers' quarterback combination of Mike Tomczak and Kordell (Slash) Stewart, rather than Patriots passer Drew Bledsoe, spent the afternoon serving as crash-test dummies.

Afterward, the New England defenders, an unheralded but steadily improving bunch, revealed their motivation: They were tired of hearing about, as defensive end Willie McGinest put it, "Slash this and Blitzburgh and the Bus [Steelers running back Jerome Bettis]."

Complementing their righteous indignation was a bold game plan in which the Patriots stunted and blitzed as aggressively as the Steelers usually do. New England also had luck on its side: The Bus had a bad wheel. Bettis suffered a tear in his right groin against the Colts and was listed as questionable for the Patriots game.

Last Thursday night he limped into his local Hooters restaurant to check out, among other things, the national championship game between Florida and Florida State. When a group of businessmen nearby lit cigars, Bettis, who is asthmatic, asked to be seated elsewhere. The waitress instead reseated the smokers, to whom Bettis apologized. "I would have moved," he said. "Oh, no," replied one man. "We wouldn't want you to aggravate your groin."

New England's defense was less solicitous, limiting Bettis to 43 inconsequential yards on 13 carries. Pittsburgh's quarterbacks were similarly ineffective. Tomczak completed 16 of 29 passes for 110 yards and two interceptions, and Stewart went 0 for 10, providing not his usual spark but rather a definitive answer to the question his fans have posed to Steelers coach Bill Cowher all season: Why don't you make Slash the starter?

Far more surprising than the flat performance of Pittsburgh's offense was the sight of Steelers defenders on their heels, missing tackles, wandering around in a fog in the fog. The NFL's second-ranked defense against the run was overrun. New England running back Curtis Martin's 166 rushing yards on 19 carries included a 78-yarder that put the Patriots on top 21-0 just five minutes into the second quarter. With such a comfortable lead, New England was able to stay out of predictable situations on offense, and thus out of Blitzburgh. As Steelers outside linebacker Chad Brown said of the Patriots, "They became the dictators."

Actually, the dictators will square off in the AFC Championship Game this Sunday, when New England hosts the Jacksonville Jaguars, whose coach, the autocratic Tom Coughlin, was once an assistant under the Patriots' despotic Bill Parcells. Both men had ample opportunity to frown, scream and carry on in tyrannical fashion when their teams met in September. The Patriots won 28-25 in overtime but only after coughing up a 22-0 lead and surrendering two Hail Mary passes.

New England made effective use of the long ball against the Steelers. Mindful of Pittsburgh cornerback Rod Woodson's hyper-aggressive style, Bledsoe had suggested opening the game with a play-action bomb to speedy wideout Terry Glenn, who caught an NFL rookie-record 90 passes in the regular season. After resisting the notion at first, Parcells came around. The Patriots' first play from scrimmage, a 53-yard completion to Glenn, set up the first of Martin's three rushing touchdowns.

Odd thing about Martin: He has been a happier player this season even as his role in the offense has shrunk. Last season he rushed for 1,487 yards, was selected NFL Rookie of the Year and made the Pro Bowl. "And we won six games," he says. This season, with Bledsoe throwing so often to Glenn, Martin's rushing yardage dipped to 1,152. "And we're one game from the Super Bowl," he says. "I couldn't be happier."

After New England chose him in the third round of the 1995 draft, Martin asked for number 29, which he had worn at Pittsburgh's Allderdice High and the University of Pittsburgh. But that number belonged to cornerback Myron Guyton, so Martin took number 28. When he mentioned the switch to his pastor, Leroy Joseph of Pittsburgh's Faith Restoration Ministry, the pastor exclaimed, "Deuteronomy 28!"

Martin has marked that chapter with a yellow highlighter in his Bible, and he reads it before games. Sitting in one of the coaches' offices an hour after Sunday's victory, he read from it again, this time aloud. "The enemies who rise up against you will be defeated before you. They will come at you in one direction but flee from you in seven."

While Martin immerses himself in the Book of Deuteronomy on Sunday, other Patriots will be concentrating on Hail Marys.

--- End of SI article ---

Conference Championship
New England v Jacksonville January 12, 1997

Sometimes the stats are not on your side and you win the game. That's how it was for New England on January 12, 1997 in the Conference Championship against the Jacksonville Jaguars. The Patriots grabbed the 20-6 win after picking up just 234 yards compared to the Jags 289. However, they made up the difference by playing crisp defense, forcing four turnovers, including three consecutive takeaways on the last three Jacksonville possessions of the game.

The game started with some good omens for the Patriots. The Jags had to punt on their first possession. Worse than that, a high snap enabled defensive back Larry Whigham to "sack" punter Bryan Barker at the Jacksonville 4-yard line. Just a few "seconds" later, New England running back Curtis Martin scored a touchdown on a 1-yard run. After punt exchanges, New England put together a drive into Jaguars territory. However, defensive back Aaron Beasley picked off a Drew Bledsoe's pass at the 8-yard line to keep the score at 7–0 as the first quarter ended.

Jags made it a little closer in the second quarter on a Mike Hollis 32-yard field goal that finished off a 13-play, 62-yard drive. The

Jacksonville D then forced the Patriots to punt, but returner Chris Hudson fumbled after a big hit by Marty Moore. Mike Bartrum recovered for New England on the Jags 19-yard line. Adam Vinatieri scored a 29-yard field goal as a result of the turnover, making the score 10–3.

With 1:29 left in the half, Bledsoe led the Patriots down the field on a well-orchestrated 68-yard drive, completing a 19-yard pass to Shawn Jefferson, a 5-yard toss to tight end Ben Coates on fourth and 5, and then another completion to Jefferson. This moved the ball 38 yards to the Jacksonville 3-yard line. The Jaguars D stiffened and that was all New England could muster. So, Adam Vinatieri kicked his second field goal of the day bringing the score to 13–3 right before halftime.

Jacksonville was off after receiving the 2nd half kickoff, driving to the New England 31-yard line. But, they lost the ball when quarterback Mark Brunell was stuffed for no gain on fourth and 1. Three plays later, Bledsoe coughed up a fumble while being tackled by Kevin Hardy. LB Eddie Robinson recovered the ball for or Jacksonville on the Pats 37, which set up a 28-yard Hollis field goal. The score was then 13–6.

Half way through the fourth quarter, the Pats moved to the Jacksonville 23-yard line. They were ready to build a big lead, but Bledsoe was whacked for a 6-yard loss on third down and Vinatieri sent his 46-yard field goal attempt off to the left. Jacksonville then took the ball back and got to the New England 5-yard line. The Jags had no luck as with just under four minutes left in the game, defensive back Willie Clay picked off a Mark Brunell pass in the end zone.

NE did not move the ball and then, after the punt. Jacksonville mounted another drive for the tying touchdown with 2:36 left. They got no-place as they lost the ball on their first play. The fumble by James Stewart was costly. New England defensive back Otis Smith recovered the ball and returned it 47 yards for the game clinching touchdown, giving his team a 20–6 lead. Jacksonville got just one more possession, but it ended in a Tedy Bruschi interception.

The game went into the record books because of a number of reasons but notably because there was a power outage (due to the power use at and around the stadium due to very cold temperatures). It occurred just minutes before halftime.

It knocked out much of the lighting of the stadium, as well as most of the power in the surrounding community. (The television broadcast, however, was not affected, and it stayed on throughout the outage by using generators.) The Patriots won 20-6 and moved on to the Super Bowl in New Orleans on January 26.

Super Bowl XXXI January 26, 1979

This is a SUPER BOWL FLASHBACK

by Anthony Gulizia from the Boston Globe January 27, 2015

Green Bay packed a punch against Patriots in XXXI

Think Deflategate was a distraction?

It's a good thing Twitter wasn't around when the Patriots were preparing for Super Bowl XXXI with coach Bill Parcells's imminent departure hovering like a thunder cloud over old Foxboro Stadium.

On Jan. 26, 1997, Parcells's 11-5 Patriots lost to Mike Holmgren's 13-3 Packers, 35-21, and five days later, the Big Tuna stepped down to become coach of the New York Jets. "It kind of clouded the run to the game, which is disappointing, because you get to that game and want to enjoy the ride," said quarterback Drew Bledsoe.

And what a ride it was.

In the first home playoff win in team history, Bledsoe and the Patriots defeated the Pittsburgh Steelers, 28-3, in a game Bledsoe remembered most for the thick fog that blanketed the stadium.

"The fog held the noise in and it was the loudest I ever heard that stadium," Bledsoe said.

The next week against the Jaguars, there was a brief power outage at the old stadium and the New England defense turned the lights out on the Jacksonville offense. Otis Smith's 47-yard fumble return in the final minutes sealed a 20-6 AFC Championship victory.

In the Super Bowl, it was Reggie White and the Packers defense that worried Bledsoe.

After Green Bay took a 10-0 lead, Bledsoe answered with touchdowns on the next two drives, and it looked as if this would be a shootout between him and Brett Favre.

But the Packers scored the next 17 points before a Curtis Martin touchdown cut the lead to 27-21 in the third quarter.

Then Desmond Howard returned the ensuing kickoff 99 yards to bury the Patriots. New England never crossed midfield in the fourth quarter.

"That really took the wind out of our sails," Bledsoe said. "It's bittersweet. I'm still really proud of the fact we made it. The truth is I've never watched that Super Bowl. It's too painful."

Anthony Gulizia can be reached at agulizia@globe.com. Follow him on Twitter @AnthonyGulizia.

Chapter 20 Coach Pete Carroll 1997 to 1999

Coach #13 Pete Carroll

Year Coach	Leag	Dic/Conf	Place	Record
1997 Pete Carroll	NFL	AFC/East	1st	10 6 0

- Won Wild Card Playoffs(Dolphins) 17–3
- Lost Divisional Playoffs (at Steelers) 6–7

1998 Pete Carroll	NFL	AFC/East	4th	9 7 0

- Lost Wild Card Playoffs (at Jaguars) 10–25

1999 Pete Carroll	NFL	AFC/East	5th	8 8 0

<u>1997-1999 Pete Carroll final record (27-21-0)</u>

Coach Pete Carrol with the Patriots

1997 Pete Carroll #13

The 1997 New England Patriots football team competed in their thirty-eighth season of professional football and their twenty-eighth season in the National Football League (NFL). The Patriots were led by Coach Pete Carroll in his first of three seasons. Robert Kraft was the owner. The Patriots record was 10-6, one win less than

Parcells' last year at the helm. The Patriots again finished in first place in the AFC East Division. They won the Wild Card game W (17-3) v the Miami Dolphins, and lost in the Division Playoffs in a tough match L (6-7) against the Pittsburgh Steelers. Pete Carrol got off to a fine start as New England's head coach

A Lookback at Parcells

It was no secret in January, when the Patriots were preparing to face the Green Bay Packers in Super Bowl XXXI, that head coach Bill Parcells was at least mentally preparing to move to another team after the game. Parcells beef was that he was not given enough control over personnel matters.

We have already discussed that in the 1996 NFL Draft, the fiery talented coach's relationship with owner Robert Kraft soured when Kraft selected wide receiver Terry Glenn against Parcells' wishes. When the Patriots lost to Green Bay in Super Bowl XXXI, Parcells resigned from the Patriots, using the phrase "If they want you to cook the dinner, at least they ought to let you shop for some of the groceries."

Pete Carroll took Parcells' place with the Patriots. Ironically, Carroll had been the Jets' head coach in 1994 and now, Parcells was the Jets' coach. Carroll's Patriots began the season 5–1 but featured a 6–5 record later in the season. The Patriots came back and finished 10–6 and sewed up first in the AFC East for the second straight season. With the third seed in the AFC playoffs, the Patriots defeated the Miami Dolphins 17-3 in the Wild Card Game but, were defeated by the Pittsburgh Steelers, 7–6, on the road the next week. Again, let me say, it was a great start for Pete Carroll.

Games: In the season and home opener for Pete Carroll's Patriots on August 31, 1997 in Foxboro Stadium, the Patriots hammered the San Diego Chargers W (41–7) before 60,190. On Sept 7, at the RCA Dome in Indianapolis the Patriots beat the Colts W (31–6) before 53,632
At home on Sept 14, in Foxboro Stadium, the Patriots defeated the New York Jets W (27–24) in (OT) before 60,072. At home in

Foxboro on Sept 21, the Patriots whooped the Chicago Bears W (31–3) before 59,873. On Sept 28, the Patriots drew a bye week.

At Mile High Stadium in Denver on Oct 6, the Broncos defeated the Patriots L (13–34) before 75,821. Then, on Oct 12, at home in Foxboro Stadium, New England pummeled the Buffalo Bills W (33–6) before 59,802. At New York, on Oct 19 in The Meadowlands, the Jets won in a close match over the Patriots L (19–24) before 71,061. Then, on Oct 27, at home in Foxboro Stadium, Green Bay got the best of New England L (10–28) before 59,972

On Nov 2, at the Hubert H. Humphrey Metrodome in Minnesota, the Vikings triumphed L (18–23) before 62,917. Then at Buffalo's Rich Stadium on Nov 9, the Patriots at beat the Bills W (31–10) before 65,783. At Houlihan Stadium in Tampa Bay, the Buccaneers dominated L (7–27) before 70,479. At home again in Foxboro Stadium on Nov 23, the Patriots defeated the Miami Dolphins W (27–24) before 59,002.

On Nov 30, in Foxboro Stadium, the Patriots beat the Indianapolis Colts W (20–17) before 58,507. On Dec 7 at Jacksonville Municipal Stadium, the Patriots beat the Jaguars W (26–20) before 73,446. Back again at home in Foxboro Stadium on Dec 13, the Pittsburgh Steelers edged out the Patriots L (21–24) in (OT) before 60,013. In the final game of the 1979 season on Dec 22, at Joe Robbie Stadium in at Miami, the Patriots beat the Dolphins W (14–12) before 74,379.

AFC Wild Card Playoff Game Dec. 28, 1997.

Played at home in Foxboro Stadium, the Patriots beat the Miami Dolphins W (17–3) before 60,041.

Checking out the regular season, it seemed like less than a week ago, the Patriots had narrowly slugged out a 14-12 defeated of the Dolphins in a tough defensive struggle. It was the last Monday night game of the regular season, and now six days later the two teams were at it again in the Wildcard playoffs.

The Patriots' prevailed with a defense that held Miami to 162 total yards of offense, 42 rushing yards and forced three Dolphins turnovers. Dolphins quarterback Dan Marino completed only 17 of 43 passes for 141 yards and he was intercepted twice. He also fumbled the ball twice, coughing up the ball on one of them.

This was the first time in Marino's 15-year career (including 14 postseason games) that he did not throw a touchdown pass in a playoff game. The Patriots played without star running back Curtis Martin, and though they pulled out a win, the squad could only generate 228 offensive yards. Key to the win for the Patriots was their ball security. They avoided losing any turnovers for the entire game.

The first quarter was scoreless. Near the end of the quarter, Miami threatened a score with a drive to the Patriots 39, but they lost the ball when Karim Abdul-Jabbar (no relationship to Kareem Abdul-Jabbar) was tackled by Todd Collins and Lawyer Milloy for no gain on fourth and 1. The Pats then drove to the Dolphins 31-yard line, but also failed to score when Adam Vinatieri missed a 48-yard field goal attempt.

As the game progressed, Marino threw his first interception, which was returned 22 yards to the Dolphins 29-yard line by New England linebacker Chris Slade off a pass deflected by safety Larry Whigham, setting up quarterback Drew Bledsoe's 24-yard touchdown pass to receiver Troy Brown. New led at halftime, 7-0.

On the second play of the third quarter after the kickoff, Collins returned Marino's other interception 40 yards for a touchdown, making him the first Patriot to ever score on a postseason interception return. This was a big deal for after a punt, New England mounted the first long sustained scoring drive of the game. They pushed the ball down 67 yards in 15 plays.

Derrick Cullors carried the ball seven times for 42 yards on the drive. Drew Bledsoe added a 20-yard completion to Terry Glenn and Adam Vinatieri finished the scoring with a 22-yard field goal as there was 1:58 left in the third quarter.

Corey Harris returned the kickoff 40 yards and when Vinatieri tried the kick he suffered a late hit. Miami finally managed to score on their following drive, moving the ball 23 yards to the Patriots 20-yard line where Olindo Mare made a 38-yard field goal on the second play of the fourth quarter.

After Mare's field goal, Miami recovered an onside kick. However, cornerback Chris Canty sacked Marino, causing a fumble. Slade recovered the ball. Miami's last three drives of the game would result in a punt and two turnovers on downs. It was over.

Cullors, who only rushed for 102 yards during the season, was the sole offensive star of the game, with 86 yards on 22 carries and a kick return for 17 yards. New England would move on to the Divisional Playoffs.

AFC Divisional Playoff Game January 3, 1998.

Played at Three Rivers Stadium in Pittsburgh, the Steelers managed to win a close game against the Patriots L (6–7) before 61,228

The Patriots suffered a devastating late-season home loss to the Steelers which meant the playoff rematch, if it were earned, would be played in Pittsburgh. Three plays into this game, Steelers cornerback Chad Scott intercepted Drew Bledsoe at the Steelers 11 and returned it to his own 38. Eight plays later, Pittsburgh faced a second-and-10 from the Patriots 40. Steelers mobile quarterback Kordell Stewart avoided a heavy pass rush and broke around the left end and up the sideline where it appeared he'd run out of bounds. On the play, Pats linebacker Todd Collins had a chance to knock him out but pulled up to avoid a penalty. No good deed goes unpunished.

Stewart had never stepped out, and so he raced down the sideline for the game's only touchdown. It was just 7-3 at halftime and it stayed 7-3 going into the fourth quarter. A well-placed 46-yard Adam Vinatieri field goal with 12:16 left in the game made it 7-6, but that is all the Patriots could muster.

Late in the fourth, Pittsburgh drove to the Patriots 1-yard line and faced a fourth-and-goal situation. Rather than kick a field goal for a four-point lead, Pittsburgh elected to go for it and called on Stewart, who was stopped short of the goal line by Tedy Bruschi. The Patriots got the ball back on their own 1 with 3:24 left. They quickly moved the ball out of harm's way to the 42 with 1:50 to go. That's when the game was ended. A future Patriot, Mike Vrabel seemed to be unblocked and he came right in and sacked Drew Bledsoe, forcing a fumble. Steelers linebacker Jason Gilden recovered the loose ball to basically end the game.

1998 Pete Carroll #13

The 1998 New England Patriots football team competed in their thirty-ninth season of professional football and their twenty-ninth season in the National Football League (NFL). The Patriots were led by Coach Pete Carroll in his second of three seasons. Robert Kraft was the owner. The Patriots record was 9-7, one win less than the prior year. The Patriots finished in fourth place in the AFC East Division. They made the playoffs and lost the Wildcard game against the Jaguars, L (10-25). That ended the 1998 season for the Patriots.

In the offseason, the Patriots put restricted free agent running back Curtis Martin up for the highest possible tender. This gained the Patriots a first and third-round draft pick if any team were to sign him and the Patriots were to decide not to match the offer. There had been a long-standing rivalry between the NY Jets and the Patriots from the Parcells days. The Jets went ahead and signed Martin, who had been the 1995 NFL Offensive Rookie of the Year. Because the signing was restricted, they were compelled to give their first and third-round picks in the 1998 NFL Draft to the Patriots.

With the first-round pick the Patriots selected another running back Robert Edwards, who rushed very well for over 1,000 yards in his rookie campaign.

Drew Bledsoe suffered a broken finger in November, and was thus unable to start the team's final two regular season games. He was replaced by Scott Zolak. With their 9–7 record, the Patriots finished fourth in the AFC East, but they still were able to earn a sixth seed in the AFC playoffs. With Zolak still at the helm, the Patriots were

defeated on the road by the Jacksonville Jaguars, the second straight playoff defeat for second-year head coach Pete Carroll, and as of 2017, the only game the Patriots have ever lost to the Jaguars.

In the 1998 season opener on Sept 7, at Denver, the Broncos beat the Patriots L (21–27) before 74,745. At home on Sept 13 at Foxboro Stadium, the Patriots slugged the Indianapolis Colts W (29–6) before 60,068. On Sept 20, at home in Foxboro Stadium, the Patriots defeated the Tennessee Oilers W (27–16) before 59,973. On Sept 27, the team drew a bye week. Then, on Oct 4, my wedding anniversary, at New Orleans, the Patriots beat the Saints W (30–27) before 56,172.

At home in Foxboro Stadium on Oct 11, the Patriots smoked the Kansas City Chiefs W (40–10) before 59,749. On Oct 19 at home in Foxboro Stadium, the New York Jets defeated the New England Patriots L (14–24) before 60,062. At Miami on Oct 25, the Dolphins squeaked out a win against the Patriots L (9–12) before 73,973. At Indianapolis on Nov 1, the Patriots defeated the Colts W (21–16) before 58,056.

On Nov 8 at home in Foxboro Stadium, the Atlanta Falcons shellacked the New England Patriots L (10–41) before 59,790. At Buffalo on Nov 15, the Bills defeated the Patriots by a field goal L (10–13) before 72,020. At home on Nov 23, the Patriots were happy to score enough to beat the Miami Dolphins W (26–23) before 58,729. On Nov 29, the Patriots edged out the Buffalo Bills W (25–21) before 58,304.

Then, on Dec 6, at Pittsburgh, the Patriots beat the Steelers W (23–9) before 58,632. At St. Louis, on Dec 13, the Rams overpowered the Patriots L (18–32) before 48,946. At home on Dec 20, New England nosed out the San Francisco 49ers W (24–21) before 59,153. In the 1998 season finale on Dec 27 at New York, the Jets beat the Patriots L (10–31) before 74,302. So ended the games for the 1998 Patriot's season.

1998 Playoff Games – Wildcard

It was Jacksonville v New England again and this time it was Jacksonville taking the honors. Nothing worth having is easy. Making it to the playoffs in fourth place with a 9-7 record is a good thing for any team. But, when good fortune comes your way, you need to back it with good performance. That was the missing ingredient.

And, so, Jaguars Running back Fred Taylor ran for 162 yards and a touchdown as the Jags won their first home playoff game in team history. Jacksonville kicker Mike Hollis popped in four field goals while the opposite luck befell the Patriots. E.G. running back Robert Edwards, who rushed for 1,115 yards and nine touchdowns during the season, was held to 28 yards on 17 carries.

Bad luck came at the start also as The Patriots had a star QB, Drew Bledsoe, and a great receiver, Terry Glenn as well as a linebacker, Ted Johnson who could not suit up and thus could not score any points. The Jaguar's Hollis opened up the scoring with two field goals. The second one was set up by a 46-yard run by Taylor and followed two overthrown passes by quarterback Mark Brunell to receiver Keenan McCardell and running back George Jones, who were both wide open in the end zone.

Brunell did struggle throughout most of the game, finishing with just 14 of 34 completions for 161 yards but his team won the game. In the second quarter, Taylor took off on a 21-yard run giving his team a first down on the Patriots 34-yard line. Four plays later, he scored on a 13-yard touchdown run. The Jaguars had a 12–0 lead after a failed 2-point conversion attempt.

Jacksonville got another chance to score when cornerback Aaron Beasley recovered a fumble from Edwards on the Jags 49-yard line. New England's defense tightened up and forced a turnover on downs at the Patriots 23-yard line, and the score would stay at 12-0 going into halftime.

In the third quarter, Patriots substitute quarterback Scott Zolak got a rally going. First, he led New England 85 yards, including a 21-yard completion to Troy Brown on third and 9, on a drive that consumed 8:48 off the clock and ended with a 1-yard touchdown run from Edwards.

There was a quick punt, and Brown returned it 17 yards to the Patriots 46-yard line, where the team proceeded to drive to the Jacksonville 9. Following a dropped pass by tight end Lovett Purnell on third down, Adam Vinatieri's 27-yard field goal cut the lead to 12–10.

However, on Jacksonville's next possession, Brunell threw a pass to receiver Jimmy Smith, who managed to break past defensive back Ty Law and make a 37-yard touchdown catch in the back of the end zone. After a punt from each team, Jacksonville lineman Joel Smeenge forced a fumble while sacking Zolak that defensive end Tony Brackens recovered on the Patriots 25-yard line. This set up Hollis' third field goal. The expert licker added a fourth field goal to close out the scoring after the Patriots turned the ball over on downs deep in their own territory on their next possession. Then on New England's final play, to add insult to injury. Zolak was intercepted by safety Chris Hudson.

As of 2017, this was the only time the Jaguars had defeated New England, regular or postseason. It would also be the Patriots' last playoff loss until 2005.

1999 Pete Carroll #13

The 1999 New England Patriots football team competed in their fortieth season of professional football and their thirtieth season in the National Football League (NFL). The Patriots were led by Coach Pete Carroll in his last of three seasons. Robert Kraft was the Patriot's owner. The Patriots record was 8-8—again it was one win less than the prior year. The Patriots finished tied for fourth place in the AFC East Division.

The Pats came into the 1999 season without second-year running back Robert Edwards due to a knee injury. He had rushed for over 1,100 yards in 1998. He got a serious knee injury playing in a rookie beach game in Hawaii after the 1998 season. Taking his place were veteran Terry Allen and rookie Kevin Faulk, but neither was able to gain 1,000 yards rushing. And, so, overall the Patriots' rushing offense denigrated to 23rd in the NFL.

Nonetheless, the team started off very well with a 6–2 record, but then they stumbled down the stretch and finished 8–8 and were out of the playoffs for the first time since 1995. Following the last game of the season, third year head coach Pete Carroll was fired, while the vice president of player personnel, Bobby Grier was retained only until the 2000 NFL Draft was completed.

In May, the Patriots publicized their plans for the future. They announced their intention to pull out of a publicly financed stadium deal in Hartford, Connecticut. Instead the organization decided to work towards building a privately financed new stadium, which would be called Gillette Stadium. The new facility would be at the site of the existing Foxboro Stadium in Foxborough, Massachusetts.

In the season opener at New York on September 12, 1999, the Patriots beat the Jets by 2 points, W (30–28) before 78,227. In the home opener, which was played in week 2 at Foxboro Stadium, the win differential moved up to 3 points as the Patriots beat the Indianapolis Colts on Sept 19, before 59,640. On Sep 26 at home in Foxboro Stadium, the Patriots edged out the New York Giants W (16–14) before 59,169. In Week 4 on Oct 3, the Patriots got their fourth win in a row W (19-7) at Cleveland against the Browns before 72,368.

At Kansas City on Oct 10, the Chiefs delivered the first loss of the year to the Patriots L (14–16) before 78,636. At home in Foxboro Stadium on Oct 17 New England defeated Miami L (30–31) before 60,006. At home on Oct 24 at Foxboro Stadium, the Patriots nosed out the Denver Broncos W (24–23) before 60,011. On Oct 31, at Arizona, the Patriots squashed the Cardinals W (27-3) before 55,830. In the following week, #9, the Patriots drew a bye.

On Nov 15, at home in Foxboro Stadium, the New York Jets beat the Patriots L (17–24) before 59,077. At Miami on Nov 21, the Dolphins defeated the Patriots L (17–27) before 74,295. Then, at Buffalo on Nov 28, the Bills beat the Patriots L (7–17) before 72,111. At home on Dec 5, the Patriots beat the Dallas Cowboys W (13–6) before 58,444.

At Indianapolis, on Dec 12, the Colts beat the Patriots L (15–20) before 56,975. Then, at Philadelphia, on Dec 19, the Eagles beat the Patriots L (9–24) before 65,475. On Dec 26 at home in Foxboro Stadium, the Buffalo Bills defeated the Patriots L (10–13) before 55,014. At home in Foxboro Stadium in the season finale on Jan 2, the Patriots whipped the Baltimore Ravens W (20-3) before 50,263

Top Patriots Players Kevin Faulk, RB

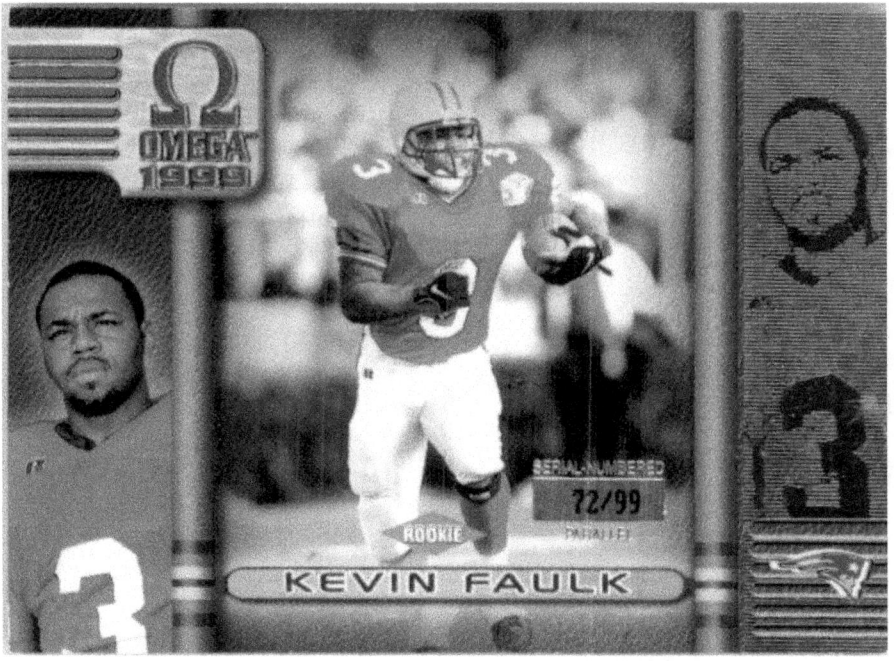

Kevin Troy Faulk was born June 5, 1976. He is a former NFL running back. Kevin spent his entire 13-year professional career playing for the New England Patriots.

He was drafted by the Patriots in the second round of the 1999 NFL Draft. He played college football at Louisiana State University.

Faulk concluded his 13-year career with the Patriots in 2011 as one of the most productive players in team history. He filled various roles after joining the team in 1999 as a second-round pick (46th overall) out of Louisiana State. He is the Patriots' all-time leader in all-purpose yards (12,349) and kickoff return yards (4,098) and is the Patriots' all-time leading return specialist, totaling 5,041 combined return yards (4,098 kick return yards and 943 punt return yards).

Kevin Faulk had a great football career, ranking fifth in Patriots history in rushing yards (3,607), fifth in receptions (431), 12th in receiving yards (3,701) and eighth in punt return yards (943). He played in 161 regular season games and accumulated 3,607 yards rushing on 864 attempts for a 4.2-yard average with 16 touchdowns, caught 431 passes for 3,701 receiving yards and 15 touchdowns, returned 181 kicks for 4,098 yards and two touchdowns. He returned 101 punts for 943 yards.

Faulk is the Patriots' all-time leader in receptions by a running back and is one of just 30 running backs in NFL history to reach the 400-reception plateau. In the 2000s, he was one of just six players to rush for more than 3,000 yards and gain more than 3,000 yards receiving, joining Tiki Barber, Marshall Faulk, Michael Pittman, LaDainian Tomlinson and Brian Westbrook.

Faulk helped the Patriots big time in 11 winning seasons, including three Super Bowls titles and five AFC Championships during his 13-year career with New England. He is a member of the Patriots' all-decade (2000s) and 50th Anniversary teams as a return specialist.

Chapter 21 Coach Bill Belichick Part I 2000 to 2005

Coach Bill Belichick # 14

Year	Coach	League	Conf-Div	Place	Record
2000	Bill Belichick	NFL	AFC-East	5th	5 11 0
2001	Bill Belichick	NFL	AFC-East	1st	11 5 0

- Won Divisional Playoffs (Raiders) 16–13 (OT)
- Tom Brady(SB MVP)[20]
- Won Conference Championship (at Steelers) 24–17
- Won Super Bowl XXXVI (1) (vs. Rams) 20–17

2002	Bill Belichick	NFL	AFC-East	2nd	9 7 0
2003	Bill Belichick	NFL	AFC-East	1st	14 2 0

- Won Divisional Playoffs (Titans) 17–14
- Tom Brady (SB MVP)
- Won Conference Championship(Colts) 24–14
- Bill Belichick(COY)
- Won Super Bowl XXXVIII (2) (vs. Panthers) 32–29

2004	Bill Belichick	NFL	AFC-East	1st	14 2 0

- Won Divisional Playoffs (Colts) 20–3
- Deion Branch (SB MVP)
- Won Conference Championship (at Steelers) 41–27
- Won Super Bowl XXXIX (3) (vs. Patriots) 24–21

2005	Bill Belichick	NFL	AFC-East	1st	10 6 0

- Won Wild Card Playoffs(Jaguars) 28–3
- Tedy Bruschi(CBPOY)
- Lost Divisional Playoffs (at Broncos) 13–27

Brady, coach Bill Belichick, and John Friesz at training camp in July 2000

*** This is another one of the great moments of all time in Patriot history ***

Nothing happens without great people and the coach is the most important item for a football team as long as there is a good owner.

The Patriots hired Bill Belichick as their Head Coach in 2000. This was a big deal. Belichick has proven to be one of the greatest coaches in the history of the NFL. His achievements are extensive and his ability to consistently put together a contending team in unparalleled.

He's won for New England five Super Bowl Championships and has been awarded the coach of the year title 3 times. Belichick has created a culture of winning in New England, one that demands perfection from every member of the team. He's established the Patriots as a true dynasty and placed them near the top of best franchises in the NFL. In many ways, Belichick should be the model for coaching methodologies for any coach of any sport.

2000 Bill Belichick #14

The 2000 New England Patriots football team competed in their forty-first season of professional football and their thirty-first season in the National Football League (NFL). The Patriots were led by Coach Bill Belichick in his first of eighteen seasons (so-far). Robert Kraft was the Patriot's owner. The Patriots record was 5-11—three wins less than Pate Carroll's last year. The Patriots finished in fifth place (last) in the AFC East Division. The Patriots did not qualify for the playoffs this year. Bill Belichick would move the Patriots way out of the cellar in future years.

I never met Patriots owner Bob Kraft but from what I see, he is a fine person, who has his own mind about things. But Kraft can be talked out of certain things if the alternative is good/better and the pitch is well done. From the picture of Bob Kraft that I have in my head, he was very familiar with Bill Belichick's body of work over the years especially what he did when he was with the Patriots as a protégé of Bill Parcells. I have inserted two paragraphs below of a post that explores the Parcells (Two Bills) relationship fully.

Below Two paragraphs of a posted by Michael David Smith on January 22, 2018, 6:43 PM EDT

ESPN

"Bill Belichick is getting ready to try to win his sixth Super Bowl with the Patriots. But a victory at Super Bowl LII would actually earn Belichick his eighth Super Bowl ring, as he won two as defensive coordinator for Bill Parcells with the Giants.

"The long relationship between Belichick and Parcells is explored in the new 30 for 30 documentary--"The Two Bills," which premiered on ESPN on February 1. It details the decades-long relationship with the two men, which started when Belichick applied for a job on Parcells' staff at Air Force, moved to Belichick working for Parcells with the Giants, saw them coach against each other when Belichick was in Cleveland and Parcells was in New England, and then saw Belichick work for Parcells again with the Jets before leaving for the Patriots."

Bob Kraft was well aware of Bill Belichick and during the Pete Carrol era, he wanted him to be coaching the Patriots. Who can blame him? Following the firing of three-year head coach Pete Carroll in January 2000, Patriots owner Bob Kraft decided to do his best to make Jets one-time assistant head coach Bill Belichick the Patriots' head coach. Pete Carroll left the Patriots with one of the best records of any coach at Boston or New England. So, he did not get fired because he did not do a good job for the Pats. Bob Kraft was ready to do better and so he sought out Bill Belichick to help make the Patriot dream happen.

As for Belichick learning he got the position in New England, we get the idea of just how close he and Bill Parcells actually are. It was not Bob Kraft or another Patriots' official who broke the news. It was none other than "The Big Tuna" who called Bill Belichick with the news that got the job at New England. Belichick was flabbergasted when he got the call at 7 a.m. from Parcells. Kraft wasted no time and called Belichick at 10 a.m. Belichick wasted no time after the call. He was in Foxboro, Mass., within hours. At 6 p.m., Belichick was introduced as the Patriots' coach. It was for real.

In previous chapters, we discussed that Bill Belichick was an assistant coach under Bill Parcells with the Patriots in 1997. He then followed Parcells to the Jets and was contractually named as Parcells' successor in case Parcells resigned from the Jets. Just one day after the 1999 season, Parcells did resign as head coach of the Jets and he then made his second retirement from NFL coaching.

In the next best edition of "Musical Chairs," Bill Belichick, who had been assistant head coach of the Jets, immediately became the Jets' next head coach. It was all so fast that the following day, at a press conference called to announce his hiring, Belichick quickly penned a resignation note on a napkin ("I resign as HC of the NYJ.") That was it.

He then talked for a half-hour in what was viewed as a resignation speech to the press. Even then, there were rumors that he had been offered the Patriots' vacant head coaching position. In the speech, Belichick cited the Jets' uncertain ownership situation following the death of owner Leon Hess earlier that year as the reason for his resignation.

In the "nothing easy is easy" category, the Jets had denied Belichick permission to speak with other NFL teams, and the NFL upheld Belichick's contractual obligations to the Jets. Belichick then filed an antitrust lawsuit against the NFL in federal court. Because of the uncertainty of the outcome of the suit, Bob Kraft was holding off on his decision to pony up a first-round draft choice to resolve the Jets / Patriots coach dispute

Bill Parcells became the peacemaker and the broker as he and owner Bob Kraft spoke seriously for the first time since Parcells' resignation from the Patriots. They agreed to settle their differences. The Pats and the Jets agreed to a compensation package that was anything but simple. It allowed Bill Belichick to become the Patriots' head coach.

For their part, Bob Kraft sent the Patriots' first-round pick in the 2000 NFL Draft and fourth and seventh-round picks in the 2001 NFL Draft to the Jets, while he also received the Jets' fifth-round selection in 2001 and a seventh-round pick in the 2002 NFL Draft.

Belichick got his modeling clay out when it was done, and afterwards in the off-season, he restructured the team's personnel department. When it was time for the Patriots players to report to camp, a number of them showed up out of shape. Coach Belichick then proclaimed so that it was well understood, that the team "could not win with 40 good players while the other team has 53."

He was not kidding. In 2000, the Patriots went on to finish the season 5–11, as the 5th and last team in AFC East and missing the playoffs for the second straight season. As of 2017, this year, "2000," represents the Patriots' most recent losing season. The team has been showing up in shape for training camp ever since.

Games of the 2000 Season

In the home and season opener on September 3, 2000 in Bill Belichick's first game as Patriot's head coach, the Tampa Bay Buccaneers defeated the New England Patriots at Foxboro Stadium L (16–21) before 60,292. At New York on Sept 11, the Jets beat the Patriots L (19–20) before 77,687. At home on Sept 17 at Minnesota, the Vikings beat the Patriots at Foxboro Stadium L (13–21) before 59,835. At Miami on Sept 24, the Dolphins beat the Patriots bringing the season record to 0-4 before 73,344.

At Denver on Oct 1, 2000, the Patriots won their first game of the season against the Broncos W (28–19) before 75,684. At home in Foxboro Stadium. New England beat Indianapolis on Oct 8, W (24–16) before 60,292. On Oct 15 at home in Foxboro Stadium, the New York Jets squashed the Patriots L (17–34) before 60,292. At Indianapolis on Oct 22, the Colts defeated the Patriots L (23–30) before 56,828. In week 9 on Oct 29, the Patriots drew a bye.

On Nov 5, 2000, the Buffalo Bills beat the Patriots at home in Foxboro Stadium before 60,292. At Cleveland, on Nov 12, the Browns beat the Pats L (11–19) before 72,618. Then at home on Nov 19, the Cincinnati Bengals were beaten by the Patriots W (16–13) before 60,292. At Detroit on Nov 23, the Lions buried the Patriots L (9–34) before 77,923.

On Dec 4, the Patriots beat the Kansas City Chiefs W (30–24) before 60,292. At Chicago on Dec 10, the Bears defeated the Patriots L (17–24) before 66,944. Then, at Buffalo, on Dec 17, the Patriots beat the Bills W (13–10) in (OT) before 47,230. On Dec 24, at home in Foxboro, the Miami Dolphins beat the Patriots by a field goal L (24–27) before 60,292

Top Patriots Players, Tom Brady, QB

His full name is Thomas Edward Patrick Brady Jr. He was born on August 3, 1977). His occupation is a National Football League football quarterback for the New England Patriots. Tom Brady is the best active football player in the game and there are those what might say he is the best all time football player ever.

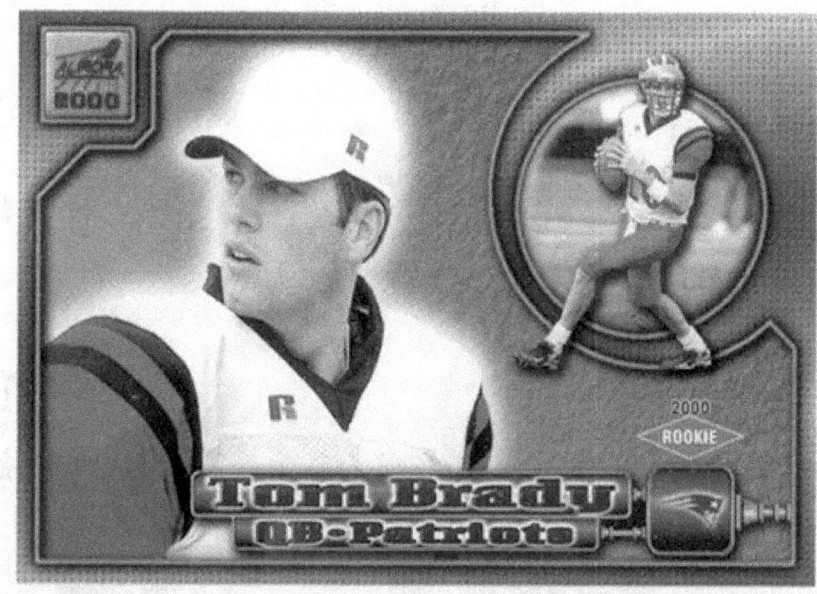

He is just one of only two players to win five Super Bowls (the other being defensive player Charles Haley) and he is the only player to win them all playing for one team, the indescribable New England Patriots.

He played college ball at the University of Michigan. Afterwards, he was drafted by the Patriots in the sixth round of the 2000 NFL Draft. Because he was drafted so late, Tom Brady is looked upon today as being the biggest "steal" in the history of the NFL Draft.

Drew Bledsoe, a great NE QB in his own right was leading the Patriots when Brady became available and so he did not start right away. During the second game of the 2001 season, Bledsoe was hit by New York Jets linebacker Mo Lewis and suffered a sheared blood vessel in his chest - which almost resulted in his death. Replacing Bledsoe, backup Tom Brady took the starting position and led New England to the playoffs and he's been leading New England ever since.

It took Drew Bledsoe 51 days to be cleared to play again but by that time Tom Brady had developed a rhythm with the team that any coach would not look to disrupt. The great news for the team and for

Bledsoe was that for the first time in 51 days, he was cleared to play football. Because of team dynamics, the only question that seemed to remain was when, though some who were fully tuned into Brady's excellent performance in relief might also have added the question, "If?"

In the "51-day" press conference Bledsoe let it be known how he felt: "I'm itching to get back in there," Bledsoe said. "I feel healthy, I'm putting weight back on – I'm about 10 pounds from where I was when I got hit – I feel strong and I've been working out for the last couple of weeks and I feel great." Bledsoe had also been seen by five specialists, who all agreed with the current plan of care. Drew Bledsoe was ready to take over if that's what the coach was to decide. Bledsoe felt for sure that he deserved a chance to recapture his starting job, but he also understood that in pro-football, there were no guarantees.

Bledsoe said: "" have to prove it again. I have to prove that I'm the best guy to go out and win football games… "The team's done great and Brady's played excellent football and I'm ecstatic about that. At the same time, it's been bittersweet because I'm not out there. But I have to make it difficult for Brady to stay on the field by playing better."

It would not be easy for coach Belichick. The Head Coach said that he expected Brady to take the majority of the snaps the first week in practice and start Sunday's game. The most likely scenario for Bledsoe would be for him to regain his form in practice this week and slowly work his way back into the picture. So, what happened back in 2001 that shaped the future that we see today? Well, one-week later Bill Belichick announced that Tom Brady was his man for the rest of the year. That ended that—or so it seemed. The pundits were second guessing all over the place.

Jonathan Cohn of slate.com offered this poignant summary of Bledsoe's choices after hearing the coach's verdict. "If Bledsoe really wants to stay with the Patriots—and, to his credit, he's been the epitome of a loyal, club-friendly athlete for his entire stay in Foxboro—he's welcome to take a pay cut. Otherwise, he should go. Harsh? Perhaps. But that's the new reality of the NFL. Someday, the Tom Brady decision will turn out to be an object lesson too. There was no guarantee that Tom Brady was not a flash in the pan, but he was surely filling the bill for the time being.

There was a big plus for the Patriots by letting Bledsoe go. M-O-N-E-Y. No Bledsoe would take $7.5 million per year contract off the books. In 2001, Brady was making only $300,000 per year. This savings from the salary cap would be able to free up money for a desperately needed offensive lineman or two, plus a playmaker at wide receiver.

Technically, because of the complicated rules of the cap, the Patriots could get rid of Bledsoe next year or the year after without taking a debilitating hit, though it depends in part on how they would pass him off. In other words, when you are trading proven greatness at quarterback for four or five starters, there is a lot to gain.

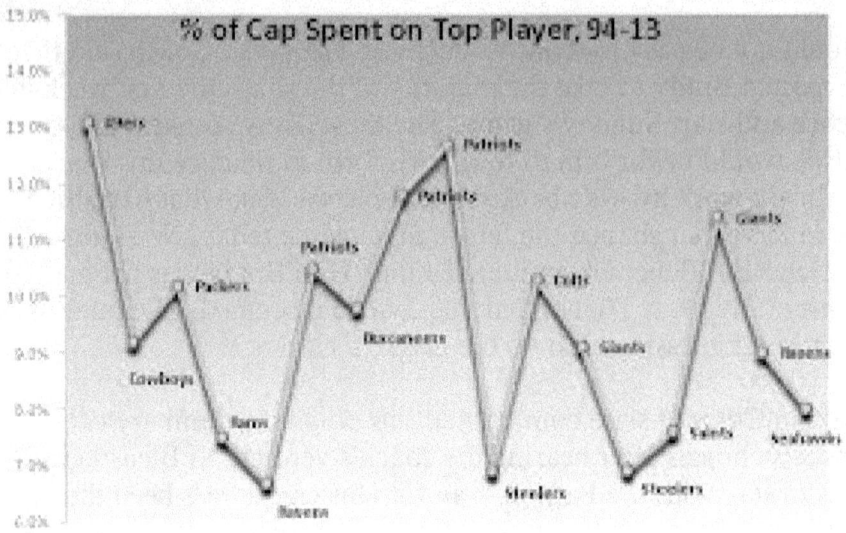

Even if Brady turned out to be mediocre, all the new extra quality players would more than likely make the transaction a net winner for the Patriots, and the best and surest way to turn this year's squad—which is performing far beyond its talents into a real dynasty...into a real serious Super Bowl contender. Well, we know what happened don't we.

By the way, Drew Bledsoe did all right for himself, just not in a Patriot's uniform. He spent three years with Buffalo and two years with Bill Parcells, his old coach at Dallas. He did great at QB for his former division rival Buffalo. He was rejuvenated in 2002. He had one of his best seasons ever, passing for 4,359 yards and 24 touchdowns and making his fourth trip to the Pro Bowl. Drew Bledsoe was a fine QB.

In Tom Brady's 16 seasons as a starter, he quarterbacked the Patriots to eight Super Bowl appearances, the most for any player in the history of football. He has been honored with four Super Bowl MVP awards (Super Bowl XXXVI, XXXVIII, XLIX, and LI), the most ever by a single player, has won three league MVP awards (2007, 2010, 2017), has been selected to 13 Pro Bowls, and has led his team to more division titles (15) than any other quarterback in NFL history. Bill Belichick had a tough personal decision re Bledsoe but he had a great football decision to make. Two great talents.

Now at the end of the 2017 regular season, Brady is fourth all-time in total career passing yards, tied for third (with Drew Brees) in career touchdown passes, and third in career passer rating. His career postseason record is 27–10, winning more playoff games than any other quarterback, and he has appeared in more playoff games than any player at any position. Brady has never had a losing season as a starting quarterback in the NFL. His combined regular-season and postseason wins are also the most of any quarterback in NFL history. Because of his accomplishments and accolades, many analysts and sportswriters consider Brady to be among the greatest quarterbacks of all time.

A cursory of Tom Brady's superlative football statistics cannot be cursory because the list goes on and on and on and on. Let me just give you a peak at what I am talking about and I ask you to consider that these are just a few career highlights. There are a ton of them and there are also huge lists of season highlights, and game highlights. Many books can be written about Tom Brady for sure and they would all be exciting.

CAREER HIGHLIGHTS

- Brady is a 16-time Patriots team captain, elected to the position by his teammates every season since 2002.
- Three-time NFL MVP (2007, 2010, 2017).
- Brady's 221 career wins are the most all time by a starting quarterback. He surpassed Peyton Manning (200) in New England's win vs. Los Angeles (12/4/16) to become the NFL's all-time winningest quarterback.
- Brady is the first quarterback in NFL history to lead his team to five Super Bowl wins, surpassing Terry Bradshaw (4) and Joe Montana (4).
- Brady owns four Pete Rozelle Awards as Super Bowl MVP (XXXVI, XXXVIII, XLIX and LI) and is the first player in Super Bowl history to earn four MVP awards, one more than Pro Football Hall of Famer Joe Montana (3).
- Brady is the all-time leader in Super Bowl passing yards (2,071), touchdown passes (15) and starts (7) by a quarterback. His 11-conference title game starts, and

- seven conference championships are the most of any starting quarterback in the Super Bowl era.
- Brady is 25-9 (.735) in the playoffs, the most playoff wins in NFL history by a starting quarterback.
- Holds all-time postseason records for starts by a quarterback (34), wins (25), passing yards (9,094), completions (831), touchdowns (63), multi-TD passing games (20) and 300-yard passing games (12) ...

As the late Yul Brynner would say, Etc. Etc. Etc.

2001 Bill Belichick #14

The 2001 New England Patriots football team competed in their forty-second season of professional football and their thirty-second season in the National Football League (NFL). The Patriots were led by Coach Bill Belichick in his second of eighteen seasons (so-far). Robert Kraft was the Patriot's owner. The Patriots record was 11-5. They finished in first place in the AFC East Division, advanced to the Super Bowl and won the World Championship in Bill Belichick's second year at the helm. Things would never be the same

What an amazing year. A Super Bowl XXXVI victory after a 5-11 fifth (last) place finish. In the span of one season, the New England Patriots under Bill Belichick went from the last to the first—from the worst in the league to the best in the league

If expectations were realized, the Patriots would still be waiting for this Super Bowl Victory as nobody expected such great things after the 2000 season. But, it came nonetheless.

Things began with bad news on August 6, when QB coach, Dick Rehbein, died of cardiomyopathy at the young age of age of 45. In the second game of the regular season, nine-year starting QB, Drew Bledsoe, who had received a 10-year contract extension in March, was injured after a big hit by New York Jets linebacker Mo Lewis. To replace Bledsoe, backup Tom Brady, who was a sixth-round draft pick in 2000, got the call to finish the game.

The Patriots did not come back and found their record at 0–2, after the second game. Tom Brady was spot on and he was durable and able to start the final 14 games of the season. His record as a starter was 11–3. He surely answered the call. His great play and Belichick's tenacious coaching combined to propel the Patriots to a clinch of the 2nd seed in the AFC playoffs and a first round bye. It was one for the record books as the Patriots became only the 2nd team in NFL history to win the Super Bowl after starting the season 2–3, behind the 1980 Oakland Raiders.

With a great push in the AFC playoffs, the Patriots faced-off against the Oakland Raiders at home in Foxboro Stadium after a first-round bye in the final game at Foxboro Stadium. It was in a snowstorm, when a Patriots drive late in the fourth quarter was kept alive in an application of the now-famous tuck rule.

This rule was used in overturning a Brady fumble into an incomplete pass. Shortly after the ruling, Adam Vinatieri pounded in a 45-yard field goal through the snow. This went down as one of the most clutch field goals in NFL history, and it sent the game into OT. In OT, another Vinatieri field goal won the game.

After defeating the top-seeded Pittsburgh Steelers in the AFC Championship Game, the Patriots faced the heavily favored St. Louis Rams. The game became known as "The Greatest Show on Turf", aka Super Bowl XXXVI. Guess how it ended? Once again, Vinatieri kicked a game-winning field goal. This 48-yarder sailed through the uprights as time hit all zeroes. Exciting!

This kick and all the play beforehand, gave the Patriots their first ever Super Bowl victory in what has been considered by many to be a "Cinderella" season. This of course means that the situation in which New England engaged enabled them to achieve far greater success than would reasonably have been expected.

Though Bill Belichick was respected by the many coaches in the league, he was an unknown to most fans across the US and the globe. He had always been the man behind Bill Parcells but this accomplishment this year was all-Belichick. Tom Brady, a 6th round draft pick from Michigan at QB was another unknown. He was expected to be groomed and be able to take over some time over the next ten years as Drew Bledsoe played as many of his ten contract years as he could.

As it would turn out the 2001 season served as a launching pad for the team, the once unknown coach, and the once unknown star quarterback. In the next 16 seasons, this combination would win their division 14 times, win the AFC Championship 7 more times, win 4 additional Super Bowl titles, and achieve an undefeated regular season (followed by a 2–1 playoff record) in 2007. How's them apples?

In the season opener at Paul Brown Stadium in Cincinnati, on Sept 9, the Bengals defeated the Patriots L (17–23) before a crowd of 51,521. In the home opener at Foxboro Stadium, in the last year the Stadium would be used for Patriot games, on Sept 23, the New York Jets defeated the NE Patriots L (3-10) before 60,292. At home in Foxboro Stadium on Sept 30, in Tom Brady's first start, the Patriots clobbered the Indianapolis Colts W 44–13 before 60,292, Then, at Miami on Oct 7, the Dolphins thumped the Patriots L (10–30) at Pro Player Stadium before 72,713.

At home in Foxboro Stadium on Oct 14, the Patriots defeated the San Diego Chargers W (29–26) in (OT) before 60,292. At Indianapolis on Oct 21, the Patriots scorched the Indianapolis Colts W (38–17) before a crowd of 56,022. At Denver, on Oct 28, the Broncos defeated the Patriots L (20–31) at Invesco Field at Mile High Stadium before 74,750. At Atlanta's Georgia Dome, on Nov 4, the Patriots beat the Falcons W (24–10) before 44,229.

On Veterans day, Nov 11, 2001 the Patriots beat the Buffalo Bills W (21–11) at home in Foxboro Stadium before 60,292. At home, on Nov 18, the St. Louis Rams defeated the Patriots L (17–24) in Foxboro Stadium before 60,292. At home on Nov 25, the Patriots neutralized the New Orleans Saints W (34–17) in Foxboro Stadium before 60,292. At New York, on Dec 2, the Patriots nosed out the Jets W (17–16) in Giants Stadium before 78,712.

At home on Dec 9, New England belted Cleveland W (27–16) at Foxboro Stadium before 60,292. At Buffalo on Dec 16, the Pats beat the Bills in OT W (12–9) at Ralph Wilson Stadium before 45,527.

On Dec 22 at home, New England defeated Miami W (20–13) at Foxboro Stadium before 60,292. In week 16, on Dec 29, the Patriots drew a bye. In week 17. The season finale on January 6, 2002 at Carolina, the Patriots slammed the Panthers W (38–6) before 71,907. Because the Patriots won the AFC East Championship, they drew a bye in the Wild Card Playoffs.

End of Season Playoff Game Summaries

East v West

In the East v West contest at 8:00 pm on EST January 19, 2002, the Patriots defeated the Oakland Raiders in OT W (16–13) at Foxboro Stadium in a packed house of 60,292.

The Boston Globe always sees things on the side of New England or we would stop buying the paper. Here is their crisp summary of this great game:

"Because it was a beautiful sendoff for Foxboro Stadium. Because it was a football game played in a snow globe. Because the Tuck Rule was the correct interpretation of a silly rule. Because East Boston's Jermaine Wiggins caught 10 passes in the snow, as if he'd played in the stuff his entire childhood. Because J.R. Redmond was everything Kevin Faulk would eventually be, Tom Brady earned his first postseason pelt, and Adam Vinatieri was good, so good, from 45 to tie and 23 to win. Because it's when a decade of greatness officially began."

Conference AFC v NFC

In the Conference Championship, at 12:30 pm on EST January 27, 2002 at Pittsburgh, the NE Patriots beat the Steelers W 24–17 at Heinz Field before 64,704.

JIM DAVIS/GLOBE STAFF ---
Drew Bledsoe celebrated with Fred Coleman after tossing a touchdown pass to David Patten.

The Boston Globe has a great recap of the 2001 Conference Game. Buy their great paper when you can and enjoy their contributions to this book. I signed up as a customer so that I could bring stuff like this from cyberspace for your reading pleasure thanks to the "Globe.":

PITTSBURGH - Quarterback Drew Bledsoe hoisted the AFC Championship trophy and pumped it three times on the podium as teammates, owner Robert Kraft, and coach Bill Belichick waved, pumped their fists, and soaked in an improbable moment in an improbable season.

Players were hollering and screaming with joy and happiness. Feelings of accomplishment, and some of revenge, flowed like the champagne that was tactfully absent as the Patriots celebrated a 24-17 win over the Pittsburgh Steelers yesterday at Heinz Field, putting them into Super Bowl XXXVI in New Orleans.
In the end safety Lawyer Milloy, one of several players who want to complete unfinished business from the Super Bowl in New Orleans after the 1996 season, got his respect from the perhaps-overconfident Steelers.

Belichick got to the Super Bowl with the Patriots again, this time as the head coach, not a Bill Parcells underling.

BARRY CHIN/GLOBE STAFF

Bledsoe, who entered the game in the second quarter in relief of Tom Brady (injured ankle) and led the Patriots to a quick score and eventually a victory, just stood crying. The tears were flowing freely, and when he caught a glimpse of his father, Mac, he lost it completely.

Tom Brady exited the game after suffering an injury in the first half. From Bledsoe nearly dying on a hit by the Jets' Mo Lewis, to losing his job to Brady when he was ready to play, to returning after four months of inactivity to direct the Patriots in the AFC Championship game?

Quite a fairy tale, folks.

"You never disrespect anybody," said Milloy, who chastised the Steelers at a press conference Friday for talking about Super Bowl plans and overlooking the Patriots.

"You just make it hard on yourself. I'm just surprised the veterans on that team didn't shut the younger guys' mouths on that team. It was a momentum-builder for us. We rallied around that, and in the end, we were the AFC champions."

Kraft said he congratulated his team on a great season.

"This is the true meaning of team," said Kraft. "We never talk about individuals here."

He did say of Belichick, "[He] was worth everything we gave up to get him two years ago."

The message was sent early - at the coin toss, in fact - when the Steelers' Jerome Bettis started to talk trash. Bryan Cox, a Patriots defensive cocaptain, got in his face immediately.

"I just wanted to make a point that we were not backing down," Cox said. "He started talking about how he was ready and all this and that, and I said, 'Jerome, this ain't what you're gonna be looking for today.' "

When Josh Miller banged a 47-yard punt late in the first quarter, the Patriots' Troy Brown fielded it and raced up the middle, going 55 yards for a touchdown. Adam Vinatieri's extra point made it 7-0 with 3:42 remaining in the first.

"It was supposed to be a left return, but the guys overplayed it to the outside, and I saw the seam up the middle and we just hit it," said Brown, who knew he had to make a big play and got a nice block by Tedy Bruschi. "It was just a great play by the punt-return team."

Just before the punt return, Brown's third for a touchdown this season, Miller had lofted a 64-yarder that Brown opted not to field and allowed to scoot past him to the 23. But Steelers special-teamer Troy Edwards was called for running out of bounds, and the officials forced another punt.

Terrell Buckley had chased Edwards down the sideline, perhaps causing him to step out of bounds.

"It's not something I did by design, but if I can crowd him and make him go out, that's a legitimate call," said Buckley. "We got the re-punt and Troy did the rest."

The Steelers began their drive after Brown's punt return at the 24. On their second play, Kordell Stewart got loose for a 34-yard gain after hurdling Milloy in the backfield. That got the ball to the New England 38. Four plays later, he had the Steelers first and 10 at the Patriots 13. But New England's tough red zone defense stiffened, as Anthony Pleasant sacked Stewart for a 2-yard loss and then good coverage by Otis Smith on Plaxico Burress for an incompletion forced the Steelers to settle for a 30-yard field goal by Kris Brown.

Brady completed 12 of 18 passes for 115 yards before leaving the game. He faced constant pressure from linebacker Jason Gildon, who was all over the field. Late in the first half, Brady sprained his ankle when Lee Flowers crawled over a body and rolled into the back of his legs. No penalty was called.

Bledsoe entered with 1:40 remaining in the first half and hit David Patten on a 15-yard pass to the Steelers 25 for a first down. He was forced to run for 4 yards, and Chad Scott's big sideline hit, knocking Bledsoe way out of bounds, looked eerily like the Lewis blast in the second game of the season. The officials did not throw a flag, because even though Scott left his feet, Bledsoe was not yet out of bounds when he was crunched.

Bledsoe, who cut his chin on the play, got right back up, and appeared fired-up. He found Patten for 10 yards to the 11, and then threw a beauty of a TD pass to Patten in the right corner of the end zone with 58 seconds remaining. His play after all that time off was nothing short of extraordinary. "He gets very few reps," said offensive coordinator Charlie Weis. "I'd say he should be proud. That's a pretty hard thing we asked him to do."

It was 14-3 at the half, and who could have scripted it? Belichick was asked if Brady could have continued.

"He could have gone back out and played, but I just felt like the way things were going we were better at that point in time [with Bledsoe]," the coach said. "We were better with a healthy Drew Bledsoe with not knowing where Tom was with his injury."

Stewart drove the Steelers to the Patriots 16 in the third quarter but had to settle for a field goal attempt. Kris Brown, who has been shaky this season, had a 34-yard attempt, but Brandon Mitchell fought through his blocks and came in with his hands up, blocking the ball. Troy Brown, the epitome of Belichick's "Be Alert" mantra during the week, picked up the loose ball and ran 11 yards before lateraling to safety Antwan Harris. He went the remaining 49 yards for the score, giving the Patriots a 21-3 lead.

BARRY CHIN/GLOBE STAFF

Troy Brown scooped up the bouncing ball after Kris Brown's field goal attempt was blocked. The Patriots scored a touchdown on the play.

"I saw Antwan coming, over my shoulder, and he was screaming my name," said Brown. "From there, I just wanted to make sure it was a lateral, and he did a great job. It worked out great for us." Mitchell was screaming and laughing all the way down the field. "I had so much fun out there," the lineman said.
But the game was far from over.

With Bettis ineffective (8 yards on 9 carries), Stewart took to the air. He found The Bus on an 11-yard hookup, then connected with Hines Ward for 24. What turned into an eight-play, 79-yard drive was capped by Bettis's 1-yard run with 5:11 remaining in the third quarter, making it 21-10.

A momentum shift was in progress. On the next series, the Pittsburgh defense toughened. J.R. Redmond dropped a pass and Bledsoe was sacked by Gildon during a three-and-out series.

The Steelers got a 28-yard return on a 38-yard punt by Ken Walter to the New England 32. It took five plays and an 11-yard run by Amos Zereoue to make this a too-close 21-17 game late in the third. Vinatieri nailed a 44-yard field goal early in the fourth, creating a 7-point advantage. Linebacker Joey Porter missed a Bledsoe pass thrown right to him, which he could have walked in for a touchdown, midway through the fourth.

A huge Tebucky Jones interception of Stewart foiled another Steelers attempt late. Vinatieri missed a 50-yarder to the left with 2:21 left, but the Patriots held on, compiling the first eight-game win streak in team history.

"We did it, we did it, Mr. Kraft," screamed Otis Smith as the game ended and the field became a sea of Patriots.

"We're going back again," yelled Willie McGinest. "And this time, we're gonna win it."

Super Bowl XXXVI

*** This goes down as one of the best games in Patriot Football – Game Winning Field Goal ***

The Game Winning Field Goal in this Super Bowl (36) (XXXVI) against the Rams in 2002 was historical. This game had a huge impact on the Patriots as a franchise. From the top, it was the beginning of a Tom Brady we're all now accustomed to watching.

You may recall that the Rams had just tied the game at 17 – 17 with a little over a minute left in the fourth quarter. Despite being young and out of timeouts, Brady knew what was at stake and he methodically drove his team down the field to set up the game-winning field goal. So much more importantly, this victory marked the beginning of what today is the Patriots dynasty. This group of can-do players transformed from simply a good team, to the team to beat, a role that they've now held for basically an entire decade.

The SB XXXVI kickoff was at 5:30 pm CST February 3, 2002. Led by first-year starter Tom Brady, the Bill Belichick-led NE Patriots defeated. the St. Louis Rams in the Louisiana Superdome before 72,922. Smiles were reported being observed on all of the Patriot Players, even the coaches, even Bill Belichick! Owner Bob Kraft like many, had a difficult time containing his pleasure after working so hard for such a result. Please enjoy this game recount from the Boston Globe's Nick Cafardo. Thank you, Nick and the Globe, for a great fact-based article.

From the Boston Globe:

Patriots shock NFL, defeat Rams to win Super Bowl

Final-second field goal caps historic upset

By Nick Cafardo GLOBE STAFF FEBRUARY 04, 2002

Tom Brady led the Patriots to a win in Super Bowl XXXVI.
NEW ORLEANS - "The Impossible Dream" has a new meaning in Boston sports lore.

Maligned, disrespected, and disbelieved, the New England Patriots won Super Bowl XXXVI last night, 20-17, over the highly favored St. Louis Rams at the Superdome. And, not surprisingly, they did it on the final play of the game.

Adam Vinatieri settled the score with a 48-yard field goal as time expired, sealing one of the biggest upsets in NFL history and completing one of the all-time worst-to-first stories.

"We shocked the world," summed up veteran cornerback Otis Smith.

It was the latest in a succession of games that cast the Patriots as the underdog, but once again they outcoached, outsmashed, and outwilled the opposition. It did not matter that they were playing a team with the fastest players in football and one of the greatest offenses in NFL history. The Rams were unable to use their speed because they found themselves on the turf, face-down, so often.

And in terms of intangibles such as will, desire, and heart, the Patriots were through the roof.

The players hugged and kissed in jubilation on the Superdome turf, celebrating the first league championship since the organization's inception in 1960. It took Bill Belichick just two years to win the championship, which comes a year after his team finished in last place in the AFC East with a 5-11 record.

Young Tom Brady (16 of 27, 145 yards, one TD, no interceptions) calmly directed the Patriots to the winning score after the Rams had tied the game, 17-17, with 1:30 remaining. With short passes of 5, 8, and 11 yards to J.R Redmond, plus key completions to Troy Brown and Jermaine Wiggins, Brady directed the no-huddle offense with no timeouts. He took the Patriots from their 17-yard line to the Rams' 30, setting up Vinatieri with 7 seconds left.

"It's just an overwhelming feeling," said Brady, the Super Bowl MVP in his first year as a starter. "I can't describe it. It's everybody just playing together like we have all season, overcoming the odds."

A clutch kick was nothing new for Vinatieri, who nailed a 45-yarder in a snowstorm to set up an overtime victory over the Oakland Raiders in these playoffs. He won three games - including the one against Oakland - with overtime field goals this season.

"They blocked great up front, the snap and the hold were great," said Vinatieri. "Once I kicked it, I knew it was good. I looked up and it was time to celebrate."

JIM DAVIS/GLOBE STAFF

"We thought before the game he had 55-yard range," said Patriots offensive coordinator Charlie Weis. "That guy has been unbelievable."

Vinatieri's heroics came after the Rams rallied behind league MVP Kurt Warner to tie the game with two fourth-quarter touchdowns after falling behind, 17-3. All of the Patriots' scoring to that point was set up by turnovers. New England picked off two passes - one of which was returned 47 yards for a touchdown by Ty Law - and recovered one of the Rams' two fumbles.

The Rams had no takeaways.

The first line of Weis's play chart for the game read, "Take Care of the Ball. No Turnovers."

He said, "How many did we have? That's right. None."

When the Patriots got the ball back with 1:21 left, Weis and Belichick had a short conversation and decided to go for the win rather than take their chances in overtime.

"They had the momentum and we had to stop their momentum and win the game," said Weis. "We needed to play to win."

After the Patriots built a 14-3 halftime lead - on Law's return and an 8-yard TD pass to David Patten - the Rams appeared to be getting into a rhythm midway through the third quarter. But Otis Smith picked off a Warner pass after Torry Holt fell down, setting up a 37-yard field goal by Vinatieri that made it 17-3.

On their first drive of the fourth quarter, the Rams moved to a fourth-and-goal from the 3, when Warner made a dash for the end zone himself. A jarring hit by Roman Phifer knocked the ball loose at the 2, and Tebucky Jones grabbed it and bolted all the way for an apparent touchdown return.

But Willie McGinest was called for holding Marshall Faulk, and the Rams were given the ball on the 1, first and goal. Two plays later, Warner took it in for his team's first touchdown.

"I'm not the referee, so I don't know if it was holding or not," said McGinest. "I played him the same way all game. It was disappointing at the time, but my teammates told me to forget about it and go to the next play."

The Patriots went from having a 24-3 lead to having a 17-10 lead.

The Rams appeared fired up. Their defense smothered the Patriots on the next series. Defensive end Leonard Little, who hadn't been heard from often, hurried Brady into a bad throw on third and 2. Brady, who had played mistake-free and looked poised for much of the game, looked frazzled on that series.

After a Ken Walter punt pinned the Rams deep in their own territory, McGinest soon redeemed himself with about 4 minutes to go when he sacked Warner for a 16-yard loss after the Rams had driven to the Patriots' 39. Warner threw incomplete to Holt on third down, and the Rams chose to punt instead of going for it with less than four minutes to go.

"It felt good because it took them out of field goal range," said McGinest.

But the Rams defense held again, and Warner got the ball back with 1:51 to go. It took him just three plays to tie it, hitting Proehl with a 26-yard scoring pass.

But St. Louis left enough time for Brady and Vinatieri to work their magic.

The Patriots' stunning 14-3 lead at halftime came despite a sluggish offensive performance.

The Rams scored the only points of the first quarter - a 50-yard Jeff Wilkins field goal - as the Patriots looked for a big play or a big mistake. They got both in the second quarter, courtesy of their defense.

Warner dropped back to throw with 8:49 remaining in the half, but all he saw was linebacker Mike Vrabel closing in. Vrabel had faked substitute right tackle Rod Jones, who was playing with a strained right groin, and managed to hit Warner as he released the ball. The pass, intended for Isaac Bruce, went instead to Law, who ran unimpeded 47 yards to give the Patriots a 7-3 lead.

"I never saw Vrabel," said Law, "but I knew we were going to pressure him. I was just out there waiting for the play to unfold, so to speak, and the ball just came my way and I took it in."

With less than two minutes left, Warner completed a slant to Proehl, but Antwan Harris knocked the ball loose with a nice hit as Proehl was falling to the turf. Terrell Buckley chased the ball down and returned it to the Rams 40.

The Patriots offense clicked just in time.

Brady hit Brown on an inside route for 16 yards to the 24, connected with Wiggins for 8, and pitched to Kevin Faulk for 8 more down the left sideline. On first and goal from the 8, Brady tossed a soft pass over Dexter McCleon's reach into the hands of Patten, who made a circus catch as he tumbled in the corner of the end zone.

The Patriots walked off with the shocking 14-3 halftime lead, and the Rams never really recovered.

"That's a hell of a football team we just played," said Smith. "But we're No. 1 in the world and in the NFL."

And that is why they now have dibs on the "Impossible Dream" label.

Maybe forever!

Top Patriots Players Matt Light, LT

Matthew Charles "Matt" Light was born June 23, 1978. He is a former National Football League offensive tackle. Matt spent his entire eleven-year football career playing for the New England Patriots of the NFL.

Matt played his college ball at Purdue University. Light was picked by the Patriots in the second round of the 2001 NFL Draft.

The most important player on the offensive line is the left tackle because he's charged with guarding the quarterback's blind side. From 2001–11, the player keeping Tom Brady off the ground was Matt Light. During his tenure with the Pats team he made the Pro Bowl three times and was part of three Super Bowl–winning teams. Although he retired at 33 years of age, Light spent his entire career with the Patriots. He was a major part of the core that built the Belichick dynasty.

When he first came on board, he started 12 of 14 games played during his rookie season in 2001. He helped the Patriots running game substantially. The Pats averaged 112.2 yards per game. He was the starting left tackle for an offensive line that led the way for 133 yards on 25 carries (5.3-yard average) in the Patriots 20–17 victory in Super Bowl XXXVI over the St. Louis Rams.

Light was great from day one with a Patriots' uniform and was named to the Football News 2001 NFL All-Rookie Team following the season. Light returned in 2002 to start all 16 games at left tackle for the Patriots, who missed the playoffs. He played until 2011, receiving many honors and helping his team win many championships.

2002 Bill Belichick #14

The 2002 New England Patriots football team competed in their forty-third season of professional football and their thirty-third season in the National Football League (NFL). The Patriots were led by Coach Bill Belichick in his third of eighteen seasons (so-far). Robert Kraft was the Patriot's owner. The Patriots record was 9-7 after their Super Bowl victory. They finished in second place in the AFC East Division and did not make the playoffs.

After stoking away their victory in Super Bowl XXXVI just seven months earlier, the Patriots had to face the reality of again being a competitive football team, not a bunch of championship players ready to tip their hats for applause. Baptism of fire was when they played their first game in their new Gillette Stadium in the NFL's prime-time Monday Night Football opener against the Pittsburgh Steelers. The Patriots ate the fire and were ready for more.

They soon had won two more to begin the season, including a 44–7 road womping against the division rival New York Jets. Life does not always stay good. The Patriots went forward and lost five of its next seven games, allowing an average of 137 rushing yards a game during that span. Temporarily, they forgot their roots and Bill Belichick was well aware of what he needed to do.

In the final week of the season, the Patriots defeated the Miami Dolphins on an overtime FG by Adam Vinatieri to give both teams a 9–7 record. Ironically, it was just a few hours later when the Jets, who had defeated the Patriots the week prior, also finished with a 9–7 record with a win over the Green Bay Packers.

Due to their record against common opponents, the Jets won the tiebreaker for the division title, which unfortunately eliminated the Patriots and Dolphins from the playoffs. As of 2017 this was the last season the Patriots failed to win at least 10 games. That is how good the Belichick / Brady combination was, is and still is.

Games: In the season and home opener and the first game ever played in the brand-new Patriots' Gillette Stadium in Foxborough Massachusetts at 9:00 PM on Monday September 9, 2002, the New

England Patriots checkmated the Pittsburgh Steelers W (30–14) in a sellout crowd of 68,436 for ABC's Monday Night Football.

At New York on Sept 15, the Patriots smothered the Jets W (44–7) at Giants Stadium before 78,726. At Gillette Stadium on Sept 22, the Patriots squeezed past the Kansas City Chiefs W (41–38) in OT before a packed house. At San Diego on Sept 29, the Chargers beat the Patriots L (14–21) at Qualcomm Stadium before 66,463.

At Miami on Oct 6, the Dolphins defeated the Patriots L 13–26 at Pro Player Stadium before 73,369. At home on Oct 13, the Green Bay Packers picked off the New England Patriots L (10–28) at Gillette Stadium before 68,436. In the week of Oct 20, New England drew a bye. On Oct 27, 2002, the Denver Broncos beat the Super-Bowl Champion Patriots for their fourth loss in a row L (16-24), bringing the record to 3–4. The game was played at home in Gillette Stadium before a packed house of 68,436. At Buffalo on Nov 3, 68,436, Bill Belichick's Patriots broke the losing streak and slammed the Bills W (38-7) in Ralph Wilson Stadium before 73,448

On Nov 10 at Chicago, the Patriots edged out the Bears W (33–30) in Memorial Stadium before 63,105. At Oakland on Nov 17, the Raiders beat the Patriots L (20–27) in Network Associates Coliseum before 62,552. At home on Nov 24, New England defeated Minnesota W (24–17) in Gillette Stadium before 68,436. At Detroit on Nov 28, the Patriots beat the Lions W (20–12) at Ford Field before 62,109.

At home on Dec 8, the Patriots defeated the Buffalo Bills W (27–17) in Gillette Stadium before 68,436. At Tennessee on Dec 16, the Titans beat the Pats L (7–24) in The Coliseum before 68,809. At home on December 22, the New York Jets outscored the New England Patriots L (17–30) before 68,436. In their season finale as reigning Super Bowl Champions, on Dec 29, 2002, the New England Patriots defeated the Miami Dolphins in an OT thriller W (27–24) at Gillette Stadium before 68,436

2003 Bill Belichick #14

The 2003 New England Patriots football team competed in their forty-fourth season of professional football and their thirty-fourth season in the National Football League (NFL). The Patriots were led by Coach Bill Belichick in his fourth of eighteen seasons (so-far). Robert Kraft was the Patriot's owner.

The Patriots record was 14-2. They finished in first place in the AFC East Division, advanced to the Super Bowl and won the World Championship in Bill Belichick's fourth year at the helm. Bill Belichick, like his mentor, Bill Parcells had learned to make a habit of winning the big ones. The 14-2 record was the best record ever at the time for a Patriot's squad under any coach.

In rapid fire succession, Bill Belichick brought his charges and fans another Super Bowl this season, just two seasons after winning Super Bowl XXXVI. In 2002, the team had a bit of a letdown, but the Patriots rolled into 2003 ready for game after missing the playoffs in 2002.

In a salary cap-related move, captain and Pro Bowl safety Lawyer Milloy was released five days before the start of the 2003 regular season. This was followed by some second-guessing of head coach Bill Belichick among Patriot fans. Additionally, there was an ESPN report by Tom Jackson that the Patriots players "hated their coach." The report was later denied by the players.

Milloy signed with the Buffalo Bills. Some attribute Milloy's playing for Buffalo as a big reason why Buffalo pummeled the Patriots, 31–0, in the season opener. Obviously in this Super Bowl season. the Patriots would rebound. In fact, they did not lose another game after starting with a 2–2 record.

This year also saw the Patriots suffer more injuries than normal. Because of all the disabled, the Patriots started 42 different players during the season. The NFL keeps records on everything. This was an NFL record for a division winner until the Patriots started 45 different players in 2005.

The Patriots were undefeated at home, leading nose tackle Ted Washington to coin the phrase "Homeland Defense" for a Patriots' defense, which had been boosted by the acquisitions of Washington and San Diego Chargers castoff safety Rodney Harrison in the offseason. The Patriots "D" gave up a league-low 14.9 points per game en route to a 14–2 regular season record.

Thirty-one to zip became the bookend score for the beginning game and ending game of the season. Losing 0-31 in the first game, and then winning 0-31 against the Bills in both games, the fans were looking to Rod Serling for an explanation, but he had passed away in 1975. The last win gave the Patriots a perfect 8–0 record at home in the regular season as noted, the 14–2 season was a club record. In fact, it was the first time the Patriots ever won more than 11 games in a season.

After a first-round bye in the AFC playoffs, the Patriots faced the Tennessee Titans at home in one of the coldest games in NFL history and won, setting up an AFC Championship Game matchup with the Indianapolis Colts. The top-seeded Patriots intercepted Colts quarterback Peyton Manning, the league's co-MVP, four times, winning 24–14 and advancing to Super Bowl XXXVIII against the Carolina Panthers.

With a tied game late in the fourth quarter, Adam Vinatieri kicked the game-winning field goal with seconds remaining, giving the Patriots their second Super Bowl victory in three seasons. Vinatieri was one heck of a big weapon for the Patriots throughout the years.

In the season opener on Sept 7, 2003 at Buffalo, the Bills pounded the Patriots L (0–31) at Ralph Wilson Stadium. At Philadelphia on Sept 14, the Patriots beat the Eagles W (31–10) at Lincoln Financial Field. On Sept 21, the Patriots defeated the New York Jets W (23–16) at home in Gillette Stadium. Then, at Washington, on Sept 28, the Redskins edged out the Patriots L (17–20) in FedEx Field. With a 2-2 record, New England had gotten all their bumbles out for the season. The next twelve games would be all wins.

5 On Oct 5, New England defeated Tennessee W (38–30) at home in Gillette Stadium. At home on Oct 12, the Patriots beat the New

York Giants in Gillette Stadium. At Miami on Oct 19, the Patriots beat the Dolphins W (19–13) in OT at Pro Player Stadium. At home on Oct 26, New England defeated the Cleveland Browns W (9–3) in Gillette Stadium.

At Denver on Nov 3, the Patriots defeated the Broncos W (30–26) in Invesco Field at Mile High Stadium. On Nov 10, the team drew a bye. On Nov 16, the Patriots shut out the Dallas Cowboys W (12–0) at home in Gillette Stadium. At Houston, on Nov 23, the Patriots beat the Texans in OT at Reliant Stadium W (9-2). At Indianapolis on Nov 30, the Patriots defeated the Colts W (38–34) at the RCA Dome.

On Dec 7, New England defeated Miami at home W (12-0), in Gillette Stadium. On Dec 14, at home, the Patriots beat the Jacksonville Jaguars W (27–13) at Gillette Stadium. At New York on Dec 20, the Pats beat the Jets W 21–16 at Giants Stadium. In the season finale, on Dec 27, in the second Buffalo bookend game, the Patriots whooped the Bills W (31–0) at home in Gillette Stadium, thereby finishing a great regulars season of 14-2. The Patriots then went on to the playoffs

The 2003 Season Playoffs

Divisional Round vs. Tennessee Titans

	1	2	3	4	Total
Titans	7	0	7	0	14
Patriots	7	7	0	3	17

This game began at 8:00 PM on January 10, 2004 at Gillette Stadium in Foxborough, Massachusetts. The weather was 4 °F, and it was clear and very cold. There was a packed house at the new stadium of 68,436.

This playoff round goes down in pro football history as one of the coldest games in NFL history. Nonetheless, it was a home game and the Patriots did what had to be done to win the game. Steve McNair of the losing Titans put on quite a show and was named co-MVP. He was more difficult for the Patriots than the bitter cold. In the end, the Patriots had to count on yet another clutch field goal from kicker Adam Vinatieri late in the fourth quarter, coupled with a stiff defensive stand.

Tom Brady started like a ball of fire with a 19-yard completion to Kevin Faulk with his first pass attempt. A few plays later, the Titans defensive forced him to burn a well-spent timeout. On the very next play, Brady tossed a 41-yard TD pass to Bethel Johnson. McNair wasted no time moving the Titans.

It began with a 15-yard completion to Derrick Mason, followed by a 24-yard pass to RB Eddie George, taking the ball to the Patriots 22-yard line. The Patriots' Roman Phifer almost ended the drive by intercepting a pass from McNair, but it was called back. Lineman Richard Seymour was penalized for roughing the passer and the Titans got the ball back with a first down on the New England 9-yard line. Two plays later, Chris Brown took it in on a crisp 5-yard touchdown run to tie the game.

After the kickoff for the TD, Tom Brady completed two passes to Dedric Ward for 30 yards. It was part of a 38-yard drive to the Titans 26-yard line. The drive ended with no points when Adam Vinatieri missed a 44-yard field goal attempt. On the very next play, safety Rodney Harrison intercepted McNair and returned the ball 7 yards to the Patriots 43-yard line. Brady clicked on four of six passes for 49 yards and rushed for 3 more on the way to a 1-yard touchdown scamper by Antowain Smith. This gave the Patriots back the lead. less than two minutes into the second quarter.

Later in the 2nd period, the Titans drove 51 yards in nine plays to the Patriots 13-yard line. This drive featured a 29-yard completion from McNair to Mason. But New England's defense stiffened to keep the Titans out of the end zone. They then blocked Gary Anderson's 31-yard field goal attempt.

After the 2nd half kickoff, early in 3Q, McNair moved the Titans on a 70-yard scoring drive with 5 straight completions for 59 yards, followed by an 11-yard touchdown pass to Mason. The rest of the third quarter was scoreless.

Half way through the fourth quarter, Troy Brown's brought a punt back 10-yards, giving the Patriots great field position at the Titans 40-yard line. They did not move the ball well and the drive stalled. Vinatieri then popped in a 46-yard field goal, giving New England a 17–14 lead with 4:02 left in regulation.

The Titans were not done. They took the ensuing kickoff and drove to the Patriots 33-yard line. After two penalties, including a 10-yard intentional grounding call and a holding penalty, pushed them back 20 yards. McNair threw an 11-yard completion, but after that, Drew Bennett dropped a potential first down catch on fourth down and 12, and the Titans turned the ball over on downs with 1:38 left. The Patriots left the field as victors ready to move to the Conference Championship game.

*** This goes down as one of the great moments in Patriots football ***

The event is known as the "Snow Kick" against the Raiders in the 2002 AFC Divisional Round.

This game is infamous and has many implications. On the final drive of regulation, Charles Woodson strip sacked Tom Brady, which ultimately led to a Raiders recovery. However, the call was overturned under the notorious tuck rule. But, tuck rule aside, this was a great game of football. Adam Vinatieri hit two clutch field goals in the snow!

The first one, which occurred shortly after the tuck rule, was from 45 yards out! A kick from that distance isn't even easy to hit in clear weather conditions, but to do it in the pouring snow, that's something. Vinatieri's second kick came in OT and sealed the Patriots victory, a victory that went on to become a Super Bowl Championship. These kicks cemented Vinatieri as a top placekicker, with ice in his veins (that must explain why he kicks so well in the snow).

Tell me about the tuck rule

The tuck rule was a controversial rule in American football used by the National Football League from 1999 until 2013. It stated:

NFL Rule 3, Section 22, Article 2, Note 2. When [an offensive] player is holding the ball to pass it forward, any intentional forward movement of his arm starts a forward pass, even if the player loses possession of the ball as he is attempting to tuck it back toward his body. Also, if the player has tucked the ball into his body and then loses possession, it is a fumble.

Sunday January 18, 2004

*** This goes down as one of the best Patriot Games ever.

AFC Championship: New England Patriots 24, Indianapolis Colts 14

	1	2	3	4	Total
Colts	0	0	7	7	14
Patriots	7	8	6	3	24

This game began at 3:00 PM on January 18, 2004 at Gillette Stadium in Foxborough, Massachusetts. The weather was 32 °F, and it was cloudy with occasional snow. There was a packed house at the new stadium of 68,436.

New England's offense did not have to show for most of the game but they did anyway. The defense was compelling, allowing only 14 points, intercepting four passes, recording four sacks, and forcing a safety. That is a major mission accomplished.

Although New England's offense was not much better, they did outscore the Colts 24-14. Yet, they were only able to put up one touchdown. It was steady eddy ice-man Adam Vinatieri's five field goals that made up for the difference as the Patriots won, 24–14, to advance to their second Super Bowl appearance in just three seasons.

After the opening kickoff, the Patriots scored on their first try, driving the ball 65 yards in 13 plays. Tom Brady was hot, completing four passes to receiver David Givens for 40 yards on the drive, including a 7-yard touchdown pass. The Pats also converted a fourth down on their own 44-yard line with a Brady authored 2-yard run.

Peyton Manning seemed immediately prepared to counter. He advanced the team 68 yards to the New England 5-yard line, but he did not close the deal and on third down and 3, he was intercepted by Rodney Harrison in the end zone. After the interception, the Patriots moved 67 yards to the Colts 13-yard line. Vinatieri put in a 31-yard field goal to increase the Pats lead to 10–0.

New England's defense continued to dominate the Colts in the second quarter. On the first play after the ensuing kickoff, Law intercepted a pass from Manning and took it six yards to the 41-yard line. The Patriots then began another drive. This was 52 yards and when it stalled, they increased their lead to 13–0 with a second Vinatieri field goal.

Brady completed three passes for 42 yards on the drive, including a 17-yarder to Givens and a 16-yard completion to Troy Brown on fourth down and 8. For the first time in the entire postseason, the Colts were forced to punt on their next drive. Not being good at punting for lack of practice, the snap from center Justin Snow sailed over the head of punter Hunter Smith. The ball went into the end zone, and Smith was forced to knock it out of bounds for a safety, thus making the score 15–0. The Colts had to kick off to the Patriots.

They got the ball back quickly. The Colts had a great chance to score when defensive back David Macklin recovered a fumble from receiver Bethel Johnson three plays after the free kick, giving Indianapolis a first down on the Patriots 41-yard line. Five plays later, Harrison forced a fumble while tackling Marvin Harrison, and cornerback Tyrone Poole recovered it.

Down 15–0 at halftime, the Colts finally began to get some stuff done in the third quarter. First, Dominic Rhodes returned the second half kickoff 35 yards to the 49-yard line. After this, running back Edgerrin James was the major instrument in a 52-yard scoring drive, carrying the ball on seven of 12 plays for 32 yards and capping it off with a 2-yard touchdown run. This cut the score to 15–7. The Patriots were in charge the rest of the quarter.

After Patrick Pass brought the ball back on the kickoff 21 yards to the 43-yard line, Tom Brady got in gear, completing passes to Larry Centers for 28 yards, Brown for 17, and Kevin Faulk for 8. This action set up Vinatieri's third field goal making the score 18–7.

Indianapolis was three and out after the kickoff and forced to punt. The Patriots Antowain Smith then rushed four times for 53 yards on New England's next chance with the ball bringing the pigskin to the Colts 3-yard line. Adam Vinatieri then kicked his fourth field goal.

Two plays after the next kickoff, Law grabbed his second interception from Manning on the Colts 31-yard line. But this time, the Patriots failed to score any points as defensive back Walt Harris picked off a Brady pass in the end zone.

After the turnover, the Colts took off on a 57-yard drive to the New England 31-yard line. But then Peyton Manning uncorked his third interception to Law with half of the fourth quarter remaining. After the Colts forced a punt, Manning took over and brought the Colts back, completing eight of nine passes for 64 yards and capping the drive with a 7-yard touchdown pass to Marcus Pollard. There were now just 2:22 left in regulation.

The Colts failed to recover their attempted onside kick attempt but forced a Patriots punt with 2:01 left. At this point the Patriots defense stopped Manning, forcing four consecutive incompletions, forcing the Colts to turn the ball over on downs.

After making Indianapolis use up all of their timeouts, Vinatieri's fifth field goal increased the Patriots lead to 24–14. The Colts attempted one last desperation drive, but it too failed as they turned the ball over on downs again with seven seconds left in the game.

Brady was on the mark for 22 of 37 passes for 237 yards, a touchdown, and an interception. Smith rushed for 100 yards. Pollard caught six passes for 90 yards and a touchdown. Rhodes returned five kickoffs for 121 yards, rushed for 16 yards, and caught two passes for 17 yards.

Colts players would later publicly complain that the game officials did not properly call illegal contact, pass interference, and defensive holding penalties on the Patriots' defensive backs. This, and similar complaints made by other NFL teams, would prompt the NFL during the 2004 offseason to instruct all of the league's officials to strictly enforce these types of fouls.

The games against the Colts marked one of the greatest rivalries ever in any professional sport. It was classic Peyton Manning versus Tom Brady. Two of the best quarterbacks to ever play the game competing against one another time after time throughout the primes of their careers.

But this game wasn't about Brady, it was about Ty Law. Manning was coming into his own this season, proving to the league he had an arm to be reckoned with. However, after Law's amazing one-handed interception, Manning appeared rattled. Three picks later (2 more going to Law), and a final score of 24 – 14 Patriots, proved Manning wasn't ready for the big stage yet. But, he would be soon.

Super Bowl XXXVIII

The SB XXXVIII kickoff was at 6:25 EST February 1, 2004. Led by first-year starter Tom Brady, the Bill Belichick-led NE Patriots defeated. the Reliant Stadium, Houston, TX. before a packed house of 71,525.

Back in Boston, thousands of Patriots fans celebrate in the streets around Faneuil Hall after the Super Bowl XXXVIII win.

This fine write-up from the Boston Globe gave New England fans enough of the Super Bowl that they felt they were there. Nice job Bob Ryan. He titled his article:

Perhaps the greatest Super Bowl ever played

Subtitle: Patriots' win against Panthers was epic NFL game

By Bob Ryan GLOBE COLUMNIST **FEBRUARY 02, 2004**

HOUSTON -- And that, ladies and gentlemen, is why a couple of billion people around the globe are hooked on sport. Hype doesn't matter. Prognostications don't matter. Talk doesn't matter. When the game starts, performance is all that matters, and the two teams playing in Super Bowl XXXVIII gave everything they could possibly summon, sometimes from who-knows-where, to produce what may very well go down in history as the greatest of all Super Bowls.

Even Bill Belichick took note. "That was a terrific football game to watch," said the coach whose team gave him a 32-29 victory that makes him a two-time Super Bowl championship mentor. "But it was not a terrific game to coach. I was having a heart attack out there."

These teams sure gave us a decent bang for the buck. For a game that remained scoreless longer than any previous Super Bowl, it turned into a wild west shootout with 61 points over the last 33 minutes, with the subplot being the greatest quarterback duel the title game has ever seen. Game MVP Tom Brady played the game we've come to expect (32 of 48, 354 yards, 3 touchdown passes, and 1 near-disastrous interception), but he had to be an MVP-type because Panthers counterpart Jake Delhomme made the most improbable personal in-game turnaround ever.

After starting out 1 for 9 with huge negative yardage, he connected on 15 of his final 24 passes, good for 323 yards and three TDs. He accomplished what neither Steve McNair nor Peyton Manning could, eating up huge chunks of real estate against a suddenly baffled Patriots defense that was helpless to stop him.

Like, what happened?

"They made some nice adjustments," acknowledged defensive coordinator Romeo Crennel. "We played a little bit more conservative in the second half, but they made adjustments and found some soft spots in our zone."

"We just started moving around, hitting seams," said Carolina veteran wideout Ricky Proehl, who caught the tying touchdown with 1:08 remaining. "We started getting into a rhythm, and they got a little tired."

Once the offenses got rolling, the defenses had no answer. "It was supposed to be defense vs. defense," said Patriots offensive coordinator Charlie Weis, "but it turned out to be offense vs. offense." It meant the coordinators did what they had to do, which, in the Patriots' case, meant utilizing linebacker Mike Vrabel as a pass receiver in the red zone. Vrabel drifted out of the line of scrimmage to catch a 1-yard touchdown with 2:51 remaining.

"136 X-cross Z-flag," explained Vrabel. "The play was put in, and I knew on that one I'd have a chance."

The defenses simply lost control of the game, which suddenly turned into an Indianapolis-Kansas City shootout, completely unlike anything the Patriots had engaged in all year. Sure, they had to hold off the Colts in that famous 38-34 game Nov. 30, but they had been ahead, 31-10, before they got careless and Manning got hot. Once this one got rolling, it was a matter of "Can you top this?"

"Two good, tough football teams," said Vrabel. "It was Ali-Frazier. We hit them. They hit us. We hit them. They hit us. But I'll take my chances with Tom Brady, Troy Brown, David Givens, and Adam Vinatieri any day of the week."

It was, frankly, a humbling experience for both defenses.

"It was a horrifying game," acknowledged Ty Law, who found himself on the field with the likes of Asante Samuel and Shawn Mayer after regulars Rodney Harrison (broken arm) and Eugene Wilson (hip flexor) were forced out of the game. "Both defenses were tired. We knew it would come down to the end and we knew we'd have the advantage because we have Adam Vinatieri."

Oh, him. After missing a 31-yard try and having another one blocked, Vinatieri was summoned to the field in a virtual instant replay of the proceedings in New Orleans two years ago. He, of course, knocked the Super Bowl-winning field goal right down Broadway, or whatever happens to be the main drag in Rapid City, S.D. And in another deja-vu-all-over-again scenario, Proehl was once again a member of the victimized team.

"I will have nightmares about Adam Vinatieri for a long time," Proehl acknowledged.

There really is no way for the participants to have grasped just what they were a part of. It just doesn't work that way, because it's just too hard doing it, let alone analyzing it. The one thing the Patriots know is that they have some key people to trust when things get sticky, like, say, with 1:08 remaining and the score tied at 29.

"Tom's a winner," acknowledged Belichick. "The quarterback's job is to do what he needs to do to help his team win, and that's what Tom does."

And Troy Brown. He is the most flat-out reliable Patriot receiver ever. He's not the most talented, but he is the most reliable.

"I want the ball in the big situations," Brown said. "A lot of people depend on me, and I don't want to let them down."

He came through when he had to, as did David Givens, as did Tom Brady, as did Adam Vinatieri.

"We made one more play than they did," said Law with a smile.

What they all did, Patriots and Panthers alike, was elevate sport into something noble. Lawdy, Lawdy, was this a football game, or what?

-- end of Boston Globe Article SB XXXViii

2004 Bill Belichick #14

The 2004 New England Patriots football team competed in their forty-fifth season of professional football and their thirty-fifth season in the National Football League (NFL). The Patriots were led by Coach Bill Belichick in his fifth of eighteen seasons (so-far). Robert Kraft was the Patriot's owner. The Patriots record was 14-2.

They finished in first place in the AFC East Division, advanced to the Super Bowl and won the World Championship in Bill Belichick's fourth year at the helm. Bill Belichick, like his mentor, Bill Parcells had learned to make a habit of winning the big ones. The 14-2 record tied the best record ever (2002) at the time for a Patriot's squad under any coach. This was the Patriots second straight 14–2 record before advancing to and winning Super Bowl XXXIX, their third Super Bowl victory in four years.

There is always room for improvement and with players getting a year older every year, eventually, positions need to be refreshed. After the 2003 Super Bowl win, the Patriots looked to improve their running game in the offseason. Replacing Antowain Smith with longtime but disgruntled Cincinnati Bengals running back Corey Dillon was their major option. He was acquired in a trade days before the 2004 NFL Draft. It was a good move. Dillon would rush for a career-high 1,635 yards in 2004.

The Pats won their first six games of the season. With this, they set an NFL record for consecutive regular season victories (18), which was later broken by the 2006–2008 Patriots (21), and consecutive regular season and playoff victories before losing to the Pittsburgh Steelers on October 31. In that game, Pro Bowl cornerback Ty Law injured hos foot and was lost for the season.

Just two weeks earlier, the team had lost the services of the other starting cornerback Tyrone Poole. And, so, the Patriots were forced to complete the regular season and playoffs by using second-year cornerback Asante Samuel, undrafted free agent Randall Gay, and longtime Patriots wide receiver Troy Brown at cornerback, among others.

Their 14-2 record was excellent, and they gained second seed in the AFC playoffs. And, so, New England defeated the Indianapolis Colts at home in the playoffs for the second-straight year. They held the Colts' top offense to three points. The Patriots kept it rolling by then defeating the top-seeded Pittsburgh Steelers on the road, 41-27, in the AFC Championship Game.

Prior to the Patriots' matchup with the Philadelphia Eagles in Super Bowl XXXIX, Eagles wide receiver Freddie Mitchell was heard saying that he did not know the names of the Patriots' defensive backs. This was taken as a sign of disrespect by the Patriots' "replacement" secondary. The Patriots would go on to defeat the Eagles 24-21 in their second straight Super Bowl victory and third championship in four seasons, leading to some labeling the Patriots of the era a sports dynasty. Of course; they were!

Games of the 2004 season

In the home and season opener on September 9, 2004, the New England Patriots defeated the Indianapolis Colts W (27-24) in Gillette Stadium. At Arizona on Sept 19, the Patriots defeated the Cardinals W (23-12) in Sun Devil Stadium. Sept 24 was a bye. At Buffalo on Oct 3, the Patriots beat the Bills W (31-17) in Ralph Wilson Stadium. At home on Oct 10, the Patriots beat the Miami Dolphins W (24-10) at Gillette Stadium.

At home on Oct 17, New England defeated Seattle W (30–20) in Gillette Stadium. On Oct 24 at home, the Patriots beat the New York Jets W (13–7) in Gillette Stadium. On Oct 31, the Patriots suffered their first loss after 18 wins in a row at the hands of the Pittsburgh Steelers L (20–34) at Heinz Field. At St. Louis, on Nov 7, the St. Louis Rams were thumped by the Patriots W (40–22) at the Edward Jones Dome.

On Nov 14, the Patriots whipped the Buffalo Bills W (29–6) at home in Gillette Stadium. At KC, on Nov 22, 2004, the Pats beat the Chiefs W (27–19) at Arrowhead Stadium. At home, on Nov 28, the Patriots hammered the Baltimore Ravens W (24–3) in Gillette Stadium. Then, on Dec 5, 2004 at Cleveland, the Patriots smashed the Browns W (42–15) at Cleveland Browns Stadium.

At home on Dec 12, in a one TD match, the Patriots defeated the Cincinnati Bengals W (35–28) in Gillette Stadium. At Miami on Dec 20, in a one-point match, the Dolphins nosed out the Patriots L (28–29) at Pro Player Stadium. At New York on Dec 26, the Pats beat the Jets W (23–7) at Giants Stadium. Then, in the final game of the 2004 season, on Jan 2, the Patriots finished the season with a 14-2 record, their second in a row, by beating the San Francisco 49ers W (21–7) at home in Gillette Stadium.

Top Patriots Players Vince Wilfork, NT

His full name is Vincent Lamar Wilfork.

This great NFL football player was born on November 4, 1981. He is a former National Football League Nose Tackle. Wilfork was resilient and tough enough to play that demanding NT position for thirteen seasons.

He was always a great football player and he excelled when playing college football for the University of Miami. And, so he was drafted by the New England Patriots in the first round of the 2004 NFL Draft, and he spent the first 11 years of his career there. By the late 2000s, Wilfork was considered to be one of the premier defensive tackles in the NFL, and he was named both to the Pro Bowl and the All-Pro team in 2007, 2010, 2011, and 2012. He also played two seasons for the Houston Texans as he was closing out his NFL career.

By the time Tedy Bruschi's was getting ready to consider retirement, along comes Wilfork. another defensive stud. Nose tackle Vince Wilfork, showed up at the right time, fought his way into a starting position and became the go-to-guy (the backbone) for the Patriots' defensive unit.

As noted, he was drafted in the first round in 2004, Wilfork forged his way into the regular starting lineup by his second season in the league. By his fourth year, he had developed into a Pro Bowler.

During his 11-year run with the Patriots, Wilfork made the Pro Bowl five times and finished with 16 sacks and 355 tackles. His solid performance opened things up for New England's defensive ends and linebackers to make big plays. He owns a big share in the Patriots' success during this period.

The 2004 Season Playoffs

*** This game goes down as one of the best ever in patriot history ***

AFC: New England Patriots 20, Indianapolis Colts 14

Divisional Round vs. Indianapolis Colts

	1	2	3	4	Total
Colts	0	3	0	0	3
Patriots	0	6	7	7	20

This game began at 4:30 PM on January 16, 2005 at Gillette Stadium in Foxborough, Massachusetts. The weather was 25 °F, and it was cloudy and snowing. There was a packed house at the new stadium of 68,756.at Gillette Stadium, Foxborough, Massachusetts.

There was a New England snowstorm going on at Foxborough on January 16 that day and early evening when Bill Belichick and the Patriots set their mind on dismantling the league's highest scoring team. The Patriots forced three turnovers and held the Indianapolis

Colts to just 276 yards and 3 points. It was the Colts lowest point production since their opening game of the 2003 season.

Peyton Manning, who is a tough player with bad luck in the playoffs, suffered his seventh loss in Foxborough, even though he had more yards passing than Tom Brady did in the game. The Patriots limited Manning to 238 passing yards with 1 interception and no touchdowns, and Edgerrin James, the Colts star runner, to just 39 rushing yards.

Though the score could have been higher for the Patriots, they also achieved an "A" for ball control. They held possession of the ball for 37:43, including 21:26 in the second half. Additionally, they orchestrated three long scoring drives. Each drive took over 7 minutes off the clock. New England running back Corey Dillon, was called upon for major duty in his first career playoff game. He had suffered through 7 losing seasons as a member of the Cincinnati Bengals. In the playoff game, Dillon was nothing less than spectacular, rushing for 144 yards and catching 5 passes for 17 yards.

Both teams depended on their defenses to dominate early, as the first five possessions of the game ended in punts. After that, the Patriots put together a 16-play, 78 yards scoring drive that took 9:07 off the clock. They should have scored but they lost a touchdown when Dillon's 1-yard score was overturned by a penalty and they brought out the kicking team. Adam Vinatieri came through with a 24-yard field goal to give the Patriots a 3–0 lead.

When New England got the ball next, a 42-yard run by Dillon set up another Vinatieri field goal, bringing the Patriots lead to 6–0. The Colts were not crying uncle and instead responded with a drive to New England's 39-yard line. However, linebacker Tedy Bruschi ended their opportunity by forcing a fumble and then recovering it from Dominic Rhodes, who had coughed it up.

After a Patriots punt, Peyton Manning got in gear and led the Colts 67 yards to a Mike Vanderjagt field goal, cutting the score to 6–3 going into halftime.

After a Bill Belichick half-time pep-talk, the Patriots dominated the second half. The team held the ball for nearly all the available regulation time during two long drives. After a highly criticized Indianapolis punt on 4th and 1 from the New England side of the field, the Patriots were not about to give up the ball. Instead the team drove 87 yards in 15 plays, consuming 8:16 of clock time. The drive ended with a Tom Brady 5-yard touchdown pass to David Givens.

After the kickoff, the Colts began another drive, but it fizzled. Hunter Smith then took the game in his hands and feet with a well hit 54-yard punt that pinned New England back on their own 6-yard line. But the Patriots were ready to march and so they shrugged off their starting field position to begin their advance.

They stormed down the field on a 14-play, 94-yard drive that ate up another 7:24 of precious clock time. Dillon rushed for 35 yards and caught a pass for 9 on the drive. This included a 27-yard run on third down and 8, while Tom Brady finished it all off with a 1-yard touchdown run. And, so the Patriots had a 20–3 lead with just over 7 minutes left in the game.

Two plays after the next kickoff to the Colts, safety Rodney Harrison stripped the ball from Reggie Wayne and Bruschi recovered it. The Patriots were then able to take a lot more precious time off the clock. Indianapolis responded with a drive to the Patriots 20-yard line, but Harrison intercepted Manning's pass in the end zone with 10 seconds left to wrap up the contest.

This game is another classic Manning versus Brady battle! Although truthfully, the game was underwhelming considering the final score, it did speak volumes for the respective quarterbacks' careers. Manning had great regular season stats and went on to win the MVP that year. Unfortunately, in another playoff battle with his rival Brady, he fell short. He had yet to win the big time.

The difference in the two quarterbacks became a matter of poise. Brady methodically ran the offense on numerous possessions, ate up large chunks of the clock, and didn't cause any turnovers. Inversely, Manning was unable to get any rhythm going and threw off target passes throughout the game.

One could argue the Patriots' defense played a major role in Manning's performance, and certainly, it did, but this game was greater than that. The pundits saw this game as representing a career trajectory of success for Brady over Manning.

AFC Championship: New England Patriots 41, Pittsburgh Steelers 27

	1	2	3	4	Total
Patriots	10	14	7	10	41
Steelers	3	0	14	10	27

This game began at 6:30 PM on January 23, 2005 at Heinz Field in Pittsburgh, Pennsylvania. The weather was 11 °F, and it was cold and fair. There was a packed house of 65,242 at Heinz.

Even for football, the temperatures in Pittsburgh during this game were raw, hovering around 11 °F (−12 °C). As far as record cold goes, this was the second-coldest game ever in Pittsburgh and the coldest ever in Steel City playoff annals. Despite the cold being owned by Pittsburgh, the Patriots delivered rookie Ben Roethlisberger his first loss as a starter after a 14-game winning streak. This was the longest win streak by a rookie QB in NFL history.

The Patriots helped Pittsburgh score a big record this year. The Steelers became just the second NFL team ever to record a 15–1 record and fail to reach the Super Bowl. The Patriots converted four Pittsburgh turnovers into 24 points, while committing no turnovers themselves. The Patriots' win also prevented an all-Pennsylvania Super Bowl from being played.

The Steelers were set back on their heels in the first quarter and they never fully recovered from their poor 1Q performance. The Patriots were on their game with defensive back Eugene Wilson intercepting

Roethlisberger's first pass of the game on his own 48-yard line. This set up Vinatieri's 48-yard field goal giving the Pats a 3–0 lead.

Pitt responded by taking the ball to the Patriots 39-yard line. But then the "Bus" lost a fumble while being tackled by Roosevelt Colvin. Mike Vrabel recovered the loose ball. On the next play, Tom Brady threw a 60-yard touchdown pass to receiver Deion Branch and there was still time left in 1Q.

With 1:28 left, the Steelers cut their deficit to 10–3 with Jeff Reed's 23-yard field goal. But after an exchange of punts in the second quarter, Branch caught a 45-yard reception on Pittsburgh's 14-yard line. Two plays later, Tom Brady tossed a 9-yard touchdown pass to David Givens. When the Steelers got going again, safety Rodney Harrison picked off a Roethlisberger pass and took it back 87 yards for a touchdown. This gave Patriots a 24–3 lead at halftime.

Bam, Bim, Boom! The scoring did not stop almost right when the second half began until three consecutive touchdowns were on the books. New England was forced to punt on the opening drive of the third quarter, and Antwaan Randle El returned the ball 9 yards to the Steelers 44-yard line. The Steelers receiver caught two passes for 46 yards as they drove 56 yards in five plays. Jerome Bettis finished the drive with a 5-yard touchdown run, cutting their deficit to 24–10.

New England answered back by moving the ball 69 yards in seven plays and scoring with Corey Dillon's 25-yard touchdown run. But Pittsburgh responded, driving 60 yards in ten plays and scoring with Roethlisberger's 30-yard touchdown pass to Hines Ward.

After forcing a punt, Randle El returned the ball 22 yards to the Steelers 49-yard line. On the drive, Ward's 26-yard reception on the last play of the third quarter set up Reed's second field goal, making the score 31–20. Now there was 13:32 left on the clock.

On cue. the Patriots took over the rest of the quarter. They came back with a 49-yard drive that used 5:26 and ended with a Vinatieri 31-yard field goal. Two plays after the kickoff, Wilson intercepted another pass from Roethlisberger at New England's 45-yard line.

The Patriots subsequently advanced down the field on another long scoring drive. This forge took 5:06 off the clock. Branch capped it off with a 23-yard TD run on a reverse play. This action put the Patriots ahead 41–20 lead. The Steelers came back with a Roethlisberger 7-yard touchdown pass to Plaxico Burress on their next drive, but by then there was only 1:31 left in the game.

Brady was the field general for the whole game completing passes when needed for 14 of 21 for 207 yards and directing the team the whole while. Dillon was on the money again rushing for 73 yards and a touchdown. Branch caught 4 passes for 116 yards, rushed for 37 yards, and scored two touchdowns. Roethlisberger threw well for 226 yards and 2 touchdowns, and he even rushed for 45 yards. However, his three interceptions were very costly. Heinz Ward caught 5 passes for 109 yards and a touchdown. New England would advance to the Super Bowl after this fine victory.

Super Bowl XXXVIII

The SB XXXIX kickoff was at 6:38 EST February 6, 2005. Led by Tom Brady, the Bill Belichick NE Patriots defeated the Philadelphia Eagles in Alltel Stadium in Jacksonville Florida before a packed house of 78,125.

This fine write-up from the Boston Globe again gave New England fans enough of the Super Bowl that they felt they were there. Nice job Nick Cafardo. He titled his article:

Patriots reign again after beating Eagles,

Picture below , JIM DAVIS/GLOBE STAFF 0

Safety Rodney Harrison was ready to intercept this Donovan McNabb pass in the final minutes of Super Bowl XXXIX.

By Nick Cafardo GLOBE STAFF FEBRUARY **07, 2005**

JACKSONVILLE, Fla. — The red, white, and blue confetti floated in the sky and dropped ever so gently on their latest field of dreams. There were hugs, pats on the backs, and family moments with children hugging their hero dads, and wives kissing their hero husbands.

There was Bill Belichick, Romeo Crennel, and Charlie Weis, the brain trust of the Super Bowl XXXIX champions embracing for the final time, with Weis off to Notre Dame and Crennel off to Cleveland.

In pic below, Tedy Bruschi celebrated after the Patriots won their third Super Bowl in four years.

<<< PIC STAN GROSSFELD /GLOBE STAFF

The Vince Lombardi Trophy was touched, kissed, and embraced like a loved one.

The New England Patriots, draped in blood, sweat, and tears, won the Super Bowl for the 3rd time in four years, beating the Philadelphia Eagles, 24-21, last night before 78,125 at Alltel Stadium.

Dynasty?

"We're champions now," said Patriots safety Rodney Harrison. "I don't know about dynasty right now."

Football historians will look back upon the current run by the Patriots and decide if it is indeed a dynasty. But for now, it's clear that no football team in the world is better.

The Patriots broke a 14-14 tie and took control with two fourth-quarter scores against the Eagles, who couldn't stop Tom Brady and Co. when it counted most.

Brady, who played with a heavy heart with his 94-year-old grandmother passing away Wednesday, completed 23 of 33 passes for 236 yards and two touchdowns for a 110.2 quarterback rating.

He was the calm, cool quarterback who had been there and done that. His Eagles counterpart, Donovan McNabb (30 of 51 for 357 yards, three touchdowns, and three interceptions), looked jittery at times in his Super Bowl debut.

Brady's favorite target was Deion Branch, who tied a Super Bowl record with 11 catches for 133 yards and was named the game's most valuable player.

" It doesn't make a difference who gets what," said Branch. "Our plan was to come in here and win the game. We had a lot of doubters and we showed them that we are a big team and we came out and won tonight."

The Patriots boosted their lead to 24-14 in the fourth quarter courtesy of Adam Vinatieri's 22-yard field goal, which capped an eight-play, 43-yard drive.

McNabb, who has a history of overthrowing receivers at crucial times, got the ball with 5:40 remaining and tried to rally the Eagles.

The Patriots played another stout defensive game, showing McNabb looks — including lining up two linemen and five linebackers — he may have never seen on film. They had to adapt after losing free safety Eugene Wilson for more than half the game with what was thought to be a broken arm.

The Eagles pulled within 24-21 with 1:48 remaining when McNabb found Greg Lewis for a 30-yard touchdown pass over rookie safety Dexter Reid — Wilson's replacement. That capped a 13-play, 79-yard drive that consumed 3 minutes 52 seconds.

The Eagles attempted an onside kick, but it was recovered by Christian Fauria at the Eagles' 41. While the Eagles forced a Patriots punt, McNabb couldn't pull off the heroics, with Harrison icing the game with his second interception.

While the Eagles received a strong performance from Terrell Owens (nine catches, 122 yards), the flamboyant receiver never found the end zone.

"Obviously we had a lot of turnovers," said Owens. "My hat goes off to the New England Patriots. They're a good team. It was a hard-fought ballgame. We just gave it away."

"I think we had everyone on the edge of their seats when we went back out there with 50 seconds left. We possibly could have won that game," McNabb said.

But it wasn't to be.

<<< PIC JIM DAVIS /GLOBE STAFF /FILE

<<< Tom Brady held up the Vince Lombardi Trophy for the third time. You could sense the Patriots were taking over late in the second quarter, and by the time Paul McCartney had finished "Hey Jude" at halftime, Belichick's troops were ready to take the field and carry on the momentum.

Offensive coordinator Weis said the 25-minute halftime allowed him time to figure out how to beat the Philadelphia blitz. He did it with short passes and screen passes.
The Eagles were still intent on blitzing, and the Patriots were happy to see it.

"They were blitzing up the middle with [Jeremiah Trotter] in an attempt to make Brady get out of the pocket and so we had to do something to combat it. We used the screens and the shorter passing game, and it really opened things up for us," Weis said.

Brady was picking it up very nicely, spotting Branch for gains of 27 and 21, the latter giving the Patriots a first down at the Philadelphia 2-yard line. From there, Brady went to designated short-yardage tight end Mike Vrabel, who gathered a tipped pass for his second touchdown reception in as many Super Bowls, giving the champs a 14-7 lead with 11:09 left in the third.

A fired-up Brady returned to the sideline and screamed to his teammates, "Let's keep it going! Let's keep it going!"

Yet the Eagles answered quickly, evening things at 14 with 3:35 remaining in the third. It was turning into a heavyweight title fight, and McNabb appeared poised for the challenge.

The Eagles targeted rookie corner Randall Gay, throwing at him often during the drive. McNabb completed passes of 15, 4, and 10 to Brian Westbrook, the last catch good for 6 points. He also found Lewis and Owens twice each on the drive. His favorite first-half target, Todd Pinkston, was cramping up and was in the locker room receiving intravenous fluids.

The chains kept moving and even with a blitzing Willie McGinest coming at him, McNabb managed to drill a pass to Westbrook between two Patriots for the tying score.

With the score even after three quarters (a Super Bowl first), the Patriots started a well-orchestrated drive to regain the lead. Brady was very methodical in leading the Patriots 66 yards, using Kevin Faulk as a key component.

Faulk caught passes of 13 and 14 yards (both beating Eagle blitzes) and ran twice for 20 yards in picking up three first downs on the drive. Corey Dillon capped it with a 2-yard touchdown run off left tackle with 13:44 remaining, giving the Patriots a 21-14 lead.

"We were 0 for 4 on first downs in the first quarter and we really couldn't get into any rhythm offensively," said Brady. "We just didn't move the ball. We tried to run it and didn't gain a whole lot of yards. We made a few more plays in the second half."

At one point in the first quarter, the Eagles led the battle of first downs, 9-1. The Patriots committed costly penalties early and Pinkston made two beautiful catches on the first scoring drive, which culminated in McNabb hitting L.J. Smith in the end zone with 9:55 remaining in the first quarter.

On their next possession, the Patriots tried to answer but Brady fumbled when his hand hit Faulk's hip at the Eagles' 5-yard line (New England's first turnover of the postseason).

New England finally scored when Brady hit David Givens for 4-yard score to make it 7-7 with 1:10 left before intermission.

That was not respectable for the three-time Super Bowl champions. In the end, they adjusted, they executed, and they conquered.

2005 Bill Belichick #14

The 2005 New England Patriots football team competed in their forty-sixth season of professional football and their thirty-sixth season in the National Football League (NFL). The Patriots were led by Coach Bill Belichick in his sixth of eighteen seasons (so-far). Robert Kraft was the Patriot's owner. The Patriots record was 14-2. They finished in first place in the AFC East Division, son the Wild Card playoffs against the Jaguars W (28-3) but lost the Divisional Playoffs to the Broncos L (13-27).

Life is not always good even for good people. It was widely reported that popular and talented linebacker Tedy Bruschi suffered a stroke just ten days after the Patriots victory in Super Bowl XXXIX. He initially planned to miss the entire season. However, a determined and well-cared for Bruschi returned to the field against the Buffalo Bills on October 30.

Cornerback Ty Law was released in the offseason, and injuries at the cornerback position, as well as a season-ending injury to safety Rodney Harrison in Week 3, forced the Patriots to break-in a number of players in the secondary very early in the season. Overall, injuries caused the Patriots to start 45 different players at one point or another during the season. This was an NFL record for a division champion (breaking the record of 42 set by the Patriots in 2003).

And, so things did not begin as well as they could have for the Patriots after a Super Bowl victory. They got off to a slow 4–4 start. Among other things, the Pats lost their first game at home since 2002 against the San Diego Chargers in Week 4. They did make a fine comeback by ending the season on a 6-2 run for an overall 10–6 record. This was not at all shabby as it gave them their third straight AFC East title. In another one for the record books, (The Patriots were the first team in NFL history to alternate wins and losses in each of their first nine games.

They were announced as fourth seed in the AFC playoffs. In the Wild Card Playoffs, the Patriots defeated the Jacksonville Jaguars, but they could not keep up the playoff streak and the lost to the Denver Broncos on the road in the Divisional Playoffs, after having committed five turnovers in the game.

Games of the 2005 Season

In the home and season opener on September 8, 2005, the New England Patriots defeated the Oakland Raiders W (30–20) at Gillette Stadium. At Carolina on Sept 18, the Panthers beat the Patriots L (17–27) in Bank of America Stadium. At Pittsburgh on Sept 25, the Patriots beat the Steelers W (23–20) at Heinz Field. Then, at home, on Oct 2, the San Diego Chargers whipped the Patriots L (17–41) at Gillette Stadium.

At Atlanta on Oct 9, the Patriots beat the Falcons W (31–28) at the Georgia Dome. At Denver, on Oct 16, the Broncos beat the Patriots L (20–28) at Invesco Field at Mile High Stadium. In week 7, Oct 23, the Pats drew a bye. At home on Oct 30, New England defeated

Buffalo W (21–16) at Gillette Stadium. On Nov 7, at home, the Indianapolis Colts pounded the New England Patriots L (21–40) in Gillette Stadium.

At Miami on Nov 13, the Patriots beat the Dolphins W (23–16) at Dolphins Stadium. At home, on November 20, the Patriots beat the New Orleans Saints W (24–17) at Gillette Stadium. At Kansas City, on Nov 27, the Chiefs beat the Patriots L (16–26) at Arrowhead Stadium. At home, on Dec 4, New England defeated the New York Jets W (16–3) at Gillette Stadium.

At Buffalo, on Dec 11, the Patriots scorched the Bills W (35–7) at Ralph Wilson Stadium. At home, on Dec 17, the Patriots skunked the Tampa Bay Buccaneers W (28–0) at Gillette Stadium. At New York on Dec 26, the Patriots beat the New York Jets W (31–21) at Giants Stadium. In the Season finale on New Years Day, Jan 1, 2006 the Miami Dolphins edged out the Patriots at Gillette Stadium. The Pats finished with a 10-6 record and went on to win the Wildcard playoffs and then they lost in the Divisional round.

Top Patriots Players Logan Mankins, G

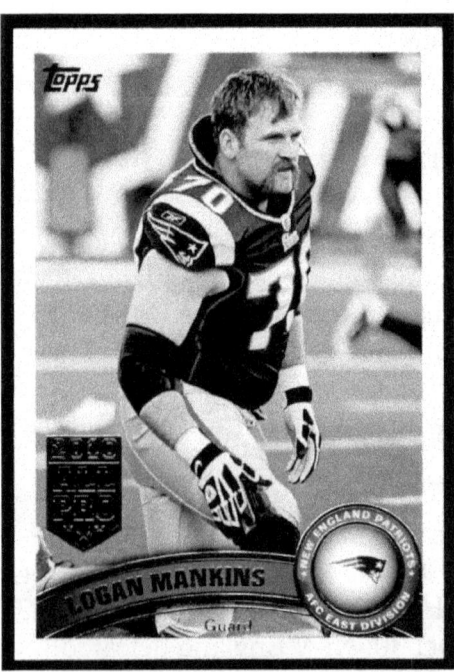

<<< Logan Lee Mankins was born March 10, 1982. He is a former National Football League guard. Mankins played played eleven seasons in the National Football League (NFL). He played college football at Fresno State, and was drafted by the New England Patriots in the first round of the 2005 NFL Draft. Mankins also played for the Tampa Bay Buccaneers.

His favorite side of the line was at the left guard position, It might not be traditionally as important as the left tackle but it is very important. Besides that does not change just how great Logan Mankins was at this job. After suiting up for his first game, Mankins quickly established himself as the best left guard in the game.

In his nine seasons with the Patriots, he made the Pro Bowl six times. Mankins helped lead the team to the Super Bowl twice in 2007 and 2011 — losing both times to the New York Giants. He moved on to play two final seasons with the Tampa Bay Buccaneers before he retired from the NFL in 2015.

Wild Card Playoffs

In the Wild Card playoffs at 8:00 PM EST, on January 7, 2006 the New England Patriots defeated the Jacksonville Jaguars W 28–3 at Gillette Stadium

The three-time Super Bowl champion Patriots, this time would have to win three games to advance to the Super Bowl, defeated the Jaguars 28–3 in the wild card match. Linebacker Willie McGinest set NFL playoff records for sacks in a game (4.5, 1 sack ahead of the old record held by Richard Dent and Rich Milot) and career postseason sacks (16, two ahead of the old record held by Bruce Smith). Meanwhile Tom Brady threw for 201 yards and three touchdown passes.

This game also marked three career playoff records: Brady and Patriots head coach Bill Belichick set records for 10 straight postseason victories, beating Vince Lombardi's run in the 1960s.

Divisional Playoffs

In the AFC Divisional Playoffs at 8:00 PM EST on Jan 14, 2006 at Denver, the Broncos beat the Pats L (13–27) at Mile High Stadium

The Patriots turned the ball over five times in this poor showing in mid-January. The Broncos were on the ball and they converted four out of the five turnovers into 24 points as they eliminated the two-time defending Super Bowl champion Patriots, 27–13. The turnovers were the game. The Broncos won their first playoff game since defeating the Atlanta Falcons in Super Bowl XXXIII. This game also ended New England's league-record ten-game postseason winning streak and gave quarterback Tom Brady his first ever postseason loss.

The Patriots were trailing most of the game. With 8:33 left, Tom Brady tried to get it going for the victory. He completed a 73-yard pass to Deion Branch and then he fired a 4-yard touchdown pass to David Givens. This brought the game to 24–13. But he Broncos were not finished. Plummer got a 42-yard completion to Smith set up another Elam field goal. Then the Broncos all but clinched the game when safety John Lynch intercepted a Brady pass with less than 3 minutes remaining.

Tom Brady did not play a bad game, but it was not enough. He finished the game completing 20 out of 36 passes for 341 yards, one touchdown, and two interceptions, but he suffered his first NFL postseason game loss. Also, Patriots head coach Bill Belichick lost his first postseason game since taking over the team in 2000. Both the coach and his QB had amassed 10 straight playoff wins before this (with three 3–0 runs of the playoffs plus the Super Bowl titles and the previous win over Jacksonville).

In this game, Branch caught 8 passes for 153 yards, while Rod Smith caught 6 passes for 96 yards and a touchdown. This would become the Patriots' first postseason loss since 1998 when the team lost to the Jaguars in the Wild Card Round. Each time any team loses and does not win the Super Bowl, there is disappointment. In 2005 after this game, it was no consolation to the Patriots or their fans that they would be in seven more Super Bowls and they would win two more of these Super games before the 2018 season.

Chapter 22 Coach Bill Belichick Part II 2006-2011...

Coach Bill Belichick # 14

2006 Bill Belichick   NFL AFC East   1st   12 4 0
- Won Wild Card Playoffs (Jets) 37–16
- Won Divisional Playoffs (at Chargers) 24–21
- Lost Conference Championship (at Colts) 34–38

2007 Bill Belichick   NFL AFC East   1st   16 0 0
- Won Divisional Playoffs(Jaguars) 31–20
- Tom Brady(MVP, OPOY)
- Won Conference Championship(Chargers) 21–12
- Bill Belichick(COY)
- Lost Super Bowl XLII (vs. Giants) 14–17

2008 Bill Belichick   NFL AFC East   2nd   11 5 0
Jerod Mayo(DROY

2009 Bill Belichick   NFL AFC East   1st   10 6 0
- Lost Wild Card Playoffs (Ravens) 14–33
- Tom Brady(CBPOY)[27]

2010 Bill Belichick   NFL AFC East   1st   14 2 0
Lost Divisional Playoffs (Jets) 21–28
- Tom Brady(MVP, OPOY)
- Bill Belichick(COY)

2011 Bill Belichick   NFL AFC East   1st   13 3 0
- Won Divisional Playoffs(Broncos) 45–10
- Won Conference Championship(Ravens) 23–20
- Lost Super Bowl XLVI (vs. Giants) 17–21

2012 Bill Belichick   NFL AFC East   1st   12 4 0
- Won Divisional Playoffs (Texans) 41–28
- Lost Conference Championship(Ravens) 13–28

2006 Bill Belichick #14

The 2006 New England Patriots football team competed in their forty-seventh season of professional football and their thirty-seventh season in the National Football League (NFL). The Patriots were led by Coach Bill Belichick in his seventh of eighteen seasons (so-far). Robert Kraft was the Patriot's owner. The Patriots record was 12-4. They finished in first place in the AFC East Division, won the Wild Card playoffs against the Jets W (37-16; won the Divisional playoffs against the Chargers W (24-21) & then the Patriots lost the Conference Championship to the Colts L (34-38).

The Patriots were short from the beginning of the season without their two starting wide receivers from 2005; David Givens, who left in free agency and Deion Branch, who held out for a new contract before being traded in early September. No player shifts are easy. Replacing them eventually were Reche Caldwell and Jabar Gaffney. They signed as free agents in October.

It was a tough season to endure. There were back-to-back losses in November, which ended the team's streak of 57 games without consecutive losses. The Pats were three games shy of the NFL record in this marker.

With a 12–4 record and being the champs for the fourth time in a row in the AFC East, the Patriots entered the playoffs as the fourth seed. They proceeded to defeat the New York Jets in the Wild Card Playoffs. They then achieved a close win over the top-seeded San Diego Chargers on the road. This win set the Patriots up to face their rival Indianapolis Colts in the AFC Championship. Nothing is assured despite the odds. Despite having a 21–3 lead, the Patriots floundered down the stretch at the RCA Dome and the Colts grabbed the 38–34 victory. The Patriots were o-u-t for 2006.

In the home and season opener at 1:00 pm EDT September 10, 2006, in a two-point match, the New England Patriots defeated the Buffalo Bills W (19–17) in Gillette Stadium to get the ball rolling for the season ahead. At New York, on Sept 17, the Patriots overcame the Jets at Giants Stadium. At home on Sept 24, the Denver Broncos beat the Patriots L (7–17) at Gillette Stadium. On Oct 1, in

Paul Brown Stadium, at Cincinnati, Ohio, the Patriots smothered the Bengals W (38–13).

On Oct 8 at home, the Patriots beat the Miami Dolphins W (20–10) at Gillette Stadium. On Oct 15, the team drew a bye. Then, at Buffalo, after a week's "rest," on Oct 22, the Patriots belted the Bills W (28–6) at Ralph Wilson Stadium. At Minnesota on October 30, the Patriots clobbered the Vikings W (31–7) at the Hubert H. Humphrey Metrodome. At home on Nov 5, the Indianapolis Colts defeated the Patriots L (20–27) at Gillette Stadium.

At home on Nov 12, the New York Jets edged out the Patriots L (14–17) at Gillette Stadium. At Green Bay on Nov 19, the Patriots skunked the Packers W (35–0) at Lambeau Field. At home on Nov 26, the Patriots beat the Chicago Bears W (17–13) at Gillette Stadium. At home again on Dec 3, the Patriots defeated the Detroit Lions W (28–21) at Gillette Stadium.

At Miami on Dec 10, the Dolphins shut out the Patriots L (0–21) at Dolphin Stadium. At home on Dec 17, New England thumped the Houston Texans W (40–7) at Gillette Stadium. At Jacksonville, on Dec 24, the Patriots defeated the Jaguars W (24–21) at ALLTEL Stadium. At Tennessee on Dec 31, the Patriots defeated the Titans in a shootout W (40–23) at LP Field. The Patriots finished the season with a 12-4 regular season record and moved on to the playoffs.

Post Season

In the playoffs, the Patriots won the Wild Card Playoffs against the New York Jets. 37–16. They also won the Divisional Playoffs against the San Diego Chargers, 24–21. And in the Conference Championship, Peyton Manning's good fortune in winning his first Conference Championship was bad luck for the Patriots, who lost the conference L (34–38). As an aside, this year, Peyton Manning who prior to this season had a playoff jinx, bagged his first Super Bowl XLI v the Chicago Bears 29-17.

Wild Card Sunday, January 7, 2007
AFC: New England Patriots 37, New York Jets 16

	1	2	3	4	Total
Jets	3	7	3	3	16
Patriots	7	10	6	14	37

This Wild Card playoff game began at 1:00 PM on January 7, 2006 at Gillette Stadium in Foxborough, Massachusetts. The weather was excellent at 50 °F, and sunny. There was a packed house of 68,756.at this Patriot home game.

Tom Brady had a fine game completing 22 out of 34 passes for 212 yards and two touchdowns. Patriots running backs Corey Dillon, Laurence Maroney, and Kevin Faulk combined for 145 rushing yards in the win over the New York Jets. Receiver Jabar Gaffney was a star. He caught only 11 passes during the season, finished his first career playoff game with eight catches for 104 yards.

The Patriots took the opening kickoff and though the game was close, they controlled the flow of the game from that point on. They drove down the field, with Gaffney catching three passes for 34 yards on the 65 yard-drive that ended with Corey Dillon's 11-yard touchdown run.

Later in the quarter, Dillon coughed up the football and it was recovered by defensive back Hank Poteat on the Patriots 15-yard line. This set up Mike Nugent's 28-yard field goal and it brought the lead to four points (7–3). In the second quarter, the Jets took a 10–7 lead on a Jerricho Cotchery touchdown. Cotchery was a nemesis all day, finishing the game with 100 receiving yards and 19 rushing yards. On this TD, he took a pass from Chad Pennington 77 yards for a touchdown.

Not long afterwards, New England knotted it up with a Stephen Gostkowski's 20-yard field goal on their next drive. After forcing the Jets to punt, the Patriots advanced to New York's 1-yard line. On third down with 11 seconds remaining in the half and no timeouts left, Brady took the snap, faked a handoff to Dillon, and then hit tight end Daniel Graham in the back of the end zone for a TD giving the Pats a nice 17–10 halftime lead.

The Jets were down but not lying down. Nugent kicked a field goal on the Jets' first drive of the second half, but New England came right back with another field goal from Gostkowski to retake their 7-point lead. When the Jets got the ball, linebacker Roosevelt Colvin got a paw on a lateral from Pennington behind the line of scrimmage. Mostly everybody in the stadium including the players on both teams (including Colvin) thought the lateral was an incomplete forward pass and that the play was over. However, New England's Vince Wilfork was extra observant and he realized the play was still ongoing and he recovered the fumble. He picked the ball up and ran 31 yards to the Jets 15-yard line before being tackled by Cotchery. This gave Gostkowski a third field goal, making the score 23–13.

In the beginning of the fourth quarter, Nugent kicked his third field goal to cut New York's deficit back to within a TD, 23–16. Immediately, the Patriots began a long drive of 13-plays. This 63-yard drive took 6:23 off the clock and ended with Tom Brady throwing a 7-yard touchdown pass to Faulk. Then on the first play of the Jets' next drive, New England defensive back Asante Samuel put the game away when he intercepted Pennington's pass and returned it 36 yards for a touchdown.

Divisional Playoff Sunday, January 14, 2007
AFC: New England Patriots 24, San Diego Chargers 21

	1	2	3	4	Total
Patriots	3	7	3	11	24
Chargers	0	14	0	7	21

This divisional playoff game began at 4:30 PM on January 14, 2007 at Qualcomm Stadium in San Diego, California. The weather was unusually excellent at 53 °F, and clear. There was a packed house of 68,810.at this Chargers home game.

The other three divisional playoff games had already finished (two on Saturday and one at 1:00 on Sunday).

So, this was the final game of the divisional playoffs. In this game, the New England Patriots faced the San Diego Chargers at San Diego. The Chargers had previously been unbeaten at home in the regular season, and so this was a big test for the Patriots.

The Chargers' had some big-name players including league MVP running back LaDainian Tomlinson. This year, he had broken a number of league records. The Chargers also had nine Pro Bowlers, and five All-Pro players. Nothing helps gain a victory more than good field play. The records are all left at the gate once the teams hit the gridiron.

And, so, the four Chargers turnovers, three of which were converted into Patriots scoring drives, helped the Patriots assure a Chargers loss. San Diego lost on turnovers despite outgaining the Patriots in rushing yards, 148–51 and total yards, 352–327, while also intercepting three passes from Tom Brady. The Patriots were able to overcome their own miscues as they took advantage of the Chargers.

In the first quarter, San Diego coach Marty Schottenheimer opted to go for it on fourth and 11. He chose this option rather than attempting a 47-yard field goal. It could not have gone worse.

QB Philip Rivers lost a fumble while being sacked by Mike Vrabel. This set up Stephen Gostkowski's 51-yard field goal with 40 seconds left in the quarter.

In Q2. Chargers receiver Eric Parker back a punt 13-yards and this ignited San Diego onto a 48-yard scoring drive that ended with Tomlinson's 2-yard touchdown run. At this point, the Chargers had a 7–3 lead.

Then, when the Pats got the ball, linebacker Donnie Edwards intercepted a pass from Brady and returned it to the 41-yard line. But the Chargers ended up punting after the Patriots' Artrell Hawkins sacked Rivers on third down. Later in the quarter, Tomlinson took off twice for 13 yards and then snagged a screen pass and scooted 58 yards to the Patriots' 6-yard line. This action set up a 6-yard touchdown run by Michael Turner with 2:04 left in the half.

New England came right back with a 72-yard scoring drive in which receiver Jabar Gaffney caught four passes for 46 yards, including a 7-yard touchdown reception with six seconds left in the half. This cut the Charger lead to 14–10.

In the second half, Brady missed a target and was intercepted for the second time. The Patriots held, and the Chargers again were forced to punt after the Patriots sacked Rivers on third down. Mike Scifres' kicked a perfect 36-yard punt that pinned New England back at their own 2-yard line. NE advanced the ball and San Diego subsequently forced a punt. However, Parker muffed the kick and New England's David Thomas recovered the fumble at the Chargers' 31-yard line.

This New England drive seemed to stall after Brady fumbled on third and 13. But, Patriots' tackle Matt Light recovered it and Chargers defensive back Drayton Florence drew a 15-yard unsportsmanlike conduct penalty for taunting Patriots tight end Daniel Graham.

The Pats drive continued, and Gostkowski eventually kicked a 34-yard field goal to cut the deficit to 14–13. When San Diego's mounted its next drive, linebacker Roosevelt Colvin intercepted a pass from Rivers at the New England 36-yard line. The Patriots then drove to the Chargers 41-yard line but were stopped and had to punt.

After the punt, Rivers clicked on two passes to tight end Antonio Gates for 31 yards and another 31-yard pass to Vincent Jackson. This set up Tomlinson's second rushing touchdown to give the Chargers an 8-point lead, 21–13.

New England came back ready to win the game by driving to San Diego's 41-yard line. On a fourth-down conversion attempt, however, Brady's pass was intercepted by Marlon McCree, but no harm was done as Troy Brown stripped the ball, and receiver Reche Caldwell recovered it. It was so complicated a happening that Coach Schottenheimer unsuccessfully challenged the play but was overruled and the Chargers lost a timeout.

Four plays later, Brady reached back and completed a 4-yard touchdown pass to Caldwell. On the next play, running back Kevin Faulk took a direct snap and scored the two-point conversion, tying the game. The Patriots were ready.

After the D forced a punt, Brady completed a 19-yard pass to Graham. Two plays later, Caldwell caught a 49-yard strike down the right sideline to set up Gostkowski's third field goal to give the Patriots a 24–21 lead with only 1:10 left in the fourth quarter. With no timeouts left, San Diego drove to the Patriots 36-yard line on their final possession, but Nate Kaeding's 54-yard field goal attempt fell short with three seconds remaining in the game.

One month later, after one of San Diego's best records ever, Marty Schottenheimer was fired as San Diego's coach thereby ending his 21-year coaching career. His 14–2 season with the Chargers was his best regular season record ever, and he is the only coach in NFL history to be fired after racking up 14 wins. It says something about football but there were few that could figure out that move. Nonetheless, it was Brady's pass with 1:10 seconds left in the game that caused it. It is the way it had to be.

AFC Championship Jan. 21, 2007

In the precursor to the Super Bowl, this game, played at Indianapolis found the Colts delivering Peyton Manning a Conference Championship that enabled the team to compete and win the Super Bowl. This was a major comeback win for the Colts and a major heartbreaker for the Patriots who at one point had the game in the bag.

The Patriots were up 21-3 in the second quarter, but mid-way through the third the Colts had pulled even with a renewed determination. From there it was a see-saw battle until the end of the fourth quarter when the Patriots were driving. Marlin Jackson intercepted a Tom Brady pass, and this sealed the win for Indianapolis.

We can't take anything away from the Colts or the Patriots in this game. The Colts piled up a combined 455 yards of offense to the Patriots 325 yards. In the end some may say it was a roughing-the-passer penalty in the fourth quarter, one of eight for the Patriots on the day, that set up Joseph Addai for a 3-yard game-winning touchdown. Despite all the roughing Peyton Manning stood in and orchestrated the big win.

2007 Bill Belichick #14

The 2007 New England Patriots football team competed in their forty-eighth season of professional football and their thirty-eighth season in the National Football League (NFL). The Patriots were led by Coach Bill Belichick in his eighth of eighteen seasons (so-far). Robert Kraft was the Patriot's owner. The Patriots record was 16-0-0. They finished in first place in the AFC East Division, and they won the Championship for the sixth of the past seven years. They won the Wild Divisional Playoffs against the Jaguars W (31-20); won the Conference Playoffs against the Chargers W (21-12); & then the Patriots lost Super Bowl XLII to the New York Giants by three points L (17-14).

The Patriots finished the 2007 regular season by winning all sixteen of their games. The regular season was perfect, but the total season was not perfect because the Patriots lost their last game—the Super Bowl. So we have the proper perspective, a perfect season is a sports season that includes any requisite playoff portion, in which a team remains and finishes undefeated and untied. The feat as you might expect, is extremely rare at the professional level of any team sport. It has occurred more commonly at the collegiate and scholastic levels in the United States. A perfect regular season (known by other names outside the United States of America) is a season excluding any playoffs, where a team remains undefeated and untied; it is less rare than a complete perfect season but still exceptional.

A multi-season winning streak may include a perfect season. Exhibition games are generally not counted toward standings, for or against. For example, the 1972 Miami Dolphins had a perfect season of 14 regular season games and three playoff games on their way to the world championship. In this season, Miami lost three of their preseason ("exhibition" games in 1972 NFL vernacular) games but are considered to have had a perfect season.

The Patriots became only the fourth team in NFL history to finish a regular season undefeated, and first to do so since the 1972 Miami Dolphins. The Patriots were also the first team with a perfect regular season since the NFL expanded its schedule to sixteen games in 1978.

Thus, they broke the record for victories in a single regular season that had been shared by the 1984 San Francisco 49ers, the 1985 Chicago Bears, the 1998 Minnesota Vikings, and the 2004 Pittsburgh Steelers, and later tied by the 2011 Green Bay Packers and 2015 Carolina Panthers. They each finished with a record of 15–1. The 1984 49ers and 1985 Bears would win Super Bowl XIX and Super Bowl XX, respectively, the 1998 Vikings and 2004 Steelers would lose their conference championship games, the 2011 Green Bay Packers would lose their first playoff game, and the 2015 Panthers would lose Super Bowl 50. The Patriots are in rare company with the 2007 season and 16 wins. Wow!

After so many great years in a row, the Patriots unfortunately were not able to join the 1984 49ers and 1985 Bears as Super Bowl champions, losing the Super Bowl and failing to go 19–0 and claim their fourth Super Bowl victory. At the time, they would have become just the fourth team to win at least four Super Bowls (joining the 49ers, Steelers, and Dallas Cowboys, each of whom had won five at the time). In Super Bowl XLII, the New York Giants defeated the Patriots 17–14 in one of the biggest upsets in NFL history. Between 2008 and 2017, the Patriots would be a perennial contender and make it to four more Super Bowls, winning two of the four for the New England fans.

At New York, in the season opener 1:00 EDT on September 9, 2007, the Patriots scorched the New York Jets W (38–14) at Giants Stadium. In the home opener at Gillette Stadium, on Sept 16, the Patriots scorched the San Diego Chargers by the same score as last week's game W (38–14. At home on Sept 23, 2007 the Patriots whipped the Buffalo Bills W (38–7) in Gillette Stadium. Then at Cincinnati on Oct 1, the Patriots whooped the Bengals W (34-13).

The twelve games below are all recorded as victories for the New England Patriots in this perfect 16-0 season. Therefore, we will not repeat the New England Patriots name in the following games 5 through 16 season summaries:

On Oct 1, the Cincinnati Bengals lost W (34–13) at Paul Brown Stadium. At home on Oct 7, the Cleveland Browns lost W (34–17) in Gillette Stadium. At Dallas, on Oct 14, 2007 the Cowboys lost W

(48–27) at Texas Stadium. At Miami, on Oct 21, the Dolphins lost W (49–28) at Dolphin Stadium. At home, on Oct 28, the Washington Redskins were walloped W (52–7) in Gillette Stadium

At Indianapolis on Nov 4, the Colts lost W (24–20) at the RCA Dome. On week 10, Nov 11, the Patriots drew a bye. At Buffalo on Nov 18, the Bills were hammered W (56–10) at Ralph Wilson Stadium. On Nov 25 at home, the Philadelphia Eagles were edged out W (31–28) in Gillette Stadium. At Baltimore, on Dec 3, the Ravens lost W (27–24) at M&T Bank Stadium.

At home on Dec 9, the Pittsburgh Steelers lost W (34–13) at Gillette Stadium. At home, on Dec 16, the New York Jets lost W (20–10) in Gillette Stadium. At home on Dec 23, the Miami Dolphins lost W (28–7) at Gillette Stadium. In the season finale, at New York, on Dec 29, the New York Giants lost in a three-point match W (38–35) at Giants Stadium. The Patriots finished at a fantastic 16-0 and played in the playoff games as well as the super Bowl.

Top Patriot Players Wes Welker, SB

When Wes Welker was 25 years of age, he had already developed into an effective slot receiver for the Miami Dolphins. For their own reasons, Miami traded Welker to the New England Patriots for second- and seventh-round draft picks.

At new England, he became one of the best in the game. Welker immediately was in synch with Tom Brady, leading the league in receptions in three of his six seasons in New England and going over 100 catches in five of his six years. Welker was a Pro Bowler five times and is #1 on the Patriots' all-time receptions list.

After he joined the Patriots in 2007, Welker caught more passes than any player in the league, and still ranks in the top five in yardage. Welker reached 500 receptions with the Patriots in just 70 games, an NFL record. He holds the franchise record for consecutive games with receptions, having caught a pass in every game (regular season and postseason) he has played as a Patriot.

As of Week 2 of the 2012 regular season, Welker also holds the all-time Patriots franchise record for receptions, breaking in just 79 games the record of Troy Brown who played more than twice as many games as a Patriot (192 regular-season games). Welker ranks third in receiving yards behind Brown and Stanley Morgan.

The Playoffs Overview

In the postseason, the Patriots won the Divisional Playoffs v the Jaguars, W (31–20). Tom Brady was named Offensive player of the year. The Patriots won the Conference Championship against the Chargers—W (21–12). Bill Belichick was named NFL Coach of the Year. The Patriots wrapped up the season with a very close match in the Super Bowl against the New York Giants, in a losing effort L (14-17).

Divisional Playoff Sunday, January 12, 2008
AFC: New England Patriots 31, San Diego Chargers 20

	1	2	3	4	Total
Jaguars	7	7	3	3	20
Patriots	7	7	14	3	31

This divisional playoff game began at 8:00 PM on January 12, 2008 at Gillette Stadium, Foxborough, Massachusetts. The weather was 37 °F, cloudy and cool. There was a packed house of 68,756 at this Patriots home game.

The Patriots entering the field

Randy Moss remembers getting the call to be a Patriot: "I got a phone call and it was Bill Belichick. I thought it was a friend or somebody playing with my phone. I actually cussed him out. When he kept saying it was Bill Belichick, I knew he was serious. I started being apologetic because I had cussed the man. Then he told me the Raiders were thinking about trading me. I had to be in Foxborough by 10 p.m. Eastern, or the trade would void. So, I just did everything that I could possibly do to get up there by 10 p.m."

Randy Moss also remembers playing in this, his first playoff game as a Patriot. He had led the NFL in receiving yards, had one reception in this important game. Patriots quarterback Tom Brady set the NFL record for completion percentage in a single game (92.9%) with an almost perfect 26 of 28 completions for 263 yards and 3 touchdowns, while running back Laurence Maroney added 162 total yards (122 on the ground).

Overall, New England was outstanding offensively, gaining 401 yards and the team did not punt the ball until 31 seconds was left in the fourth quarter.

Jacksonville gave the fans a scare at the start when they took the opening kickoff and went 80 yards in 9 plays, featuring two receptions by Marcedes Lewis for 57 yards, on the way to David Garrard's 9-yard touchdown pass to Matt Jones. The Patriots then tore out on a 74-yard drive, scoring on Tom Brady's 3-yard TD toss to Benjamin Watson. On the Jags next possession, New England lineman Ty Warren sacked Garrard and forced a fumble. Linebacker Mike Vrabel recovered the loose ball at the Jacksonville 29-yard line. Shortly after, Maroney scampered in on a 1-yard touchdown run, giving the Patriots a 14–7 lead.

Maurice Jones-Drew muffed kickoff and was downed at his own 5-yard line. The Jaguars were undaunted and moved the ball 95 yards in 11 plays without facing a third down. They scored on Garrard's 6-yard TD pass to Ernest Wilford. New England then, for the third time in a row, drove deep into Jags territory. This time, they were stopped at the 17-yard line and got no points for all that effort. Stephen Gostkowski missed a 35-yard field goal with 53 seconds left in the first half.

The Patriots on the field after their victory

In the second half, Brady opened up by completing 7 of 8 passes for 54 yards on an 82-yard drive. On the last play, in shotgun formation, with Kevin Faulk to his right, he took a snap and jumped in the air with his arms raised to make it look like a play used by the Patriots before where Faulk took the direct snap. The Jags were fooled and followed Faulk, leaving Wes Welker open in the end zone. Brady , got the ball to him for a TD, giving the Pats a 21–14 lead.

Jacksonville came back with a drive to the New England 21-yard line, but receiver Dennis Northcutt dropped a pass on third down, forcing the Jags to settle for a Josh Scobee 39-yard field goal. This cut the lead to 21–17. On the Patriots next possession, Jacksonville's Derek Landri was guilty of a roughing-the-passer penalty, turning a Welker 6-yard catch into a 21-yard gain. Maroney gained 40 yards with his next two carries, and following two more Welker receptions, Brady threw a perfect 9-yard TD strike to Watson giving New England a 28–17 lead.

There was an unnecessary roughness penalty and a 25-yard reception by Reggie Williams on the Jacksonville's next drive that set up a 25-yard field goal by Scobee. The Jags cut the deficit to one score, 28–20. On the second play after the ensuing kickoff, Brady completed a 52-yard strike to Donté Stallworth, setting up

Gostkowski's second field goal attempt. This put the Pats up by two scores, 31–20.

With just 3:46 left in the game, Patriots safety Rodney Harrison, intercepted a pass from Garrard at the Patriots' 31-yard line, ending any hope of a Jacksonville comeback. This was Harrison's 7th career postseason pick, which was a Patriots record. This was also his fourth consecutive postseason game with an interception, tying an NFL record held by Aeneas Williams.

With this victory, the Pats moved on to the AFC title game for the second year in a row and extended their perfect record to 17–0. This matched the final record of the 1972 Miami Dolphins.

Conference Championship Sunday, Jan 20, 2008
AFC: New England Patriots 21, San Diego Chargers 12

	1	2	3	4	Total
Chargers	3	6	3	0	12
Patriots	0	14	0	7	21

This divisional playoff game began at 3:00 PM on January 20, 2008 at Gillette Stadium, Foxborough, Massachusetts. The weather was 23 °F, partly cloudy, windy, and cold. There was a packed house of 68,756 at this Patriots home game.

The Patriots' offense on the field

Tom Brady had a good day, but he threw 3 interceptions while leading the Patriots to defeat San Diego. Besides Brady's work, the D held the Chargers to four field goals. Laurence Maroney rushed for 122 yards and a touchdown for the second game in a row. With this win, the Patriots season record became 18-0 and they became the first NFL team ever to start with an 18–0 record. After this game, Bill Belichick's talented Patriots then moved on to their fourth Super Bowl appearance in seven years.

There were ups and downs on both sides of the ball and the first gaffe came from the Patriots when with just about 5 minutes left in the first quarter, the Chargers stole interception #1 from Tom Brady. Defensive back Quentin Jammer grabbed the errant pass from Brady on the Patriots 40-yard line, and this set up a 26-yard field goal by Nate Keding. New England were motivated to come right back. They drove 65 yards and scored on a 1-yard Maroney touchdown run, pulling ahead with a 7–3 lead.

Before the second half, Kaeding kicked a 23-yard field goal in the to cut the score to 7–6, but after a punt, Patriots defensive back Asante Samuel was in the right place at the right time and he intercepted a pass from Philip Rivers, returning it ten yards to the Chargers 24. Just one play later and Tom Brady connected on a 12-yard TD pass to Jabar Gaffney bringing the lead to 14–6.

Later, a 26-yard run by Darren Sproles brought the ball to the New England 34-yard line. But once again, the Patriots "D" held and kept San Diego from the end zone on 3rd and 1 and forcing them to settle for another Kaeding field goal. At halftime, the score was 14–9 in the Pats favor.

Opening the second half, Tom Brady threw his second pick of the game—this was snagged by Drayton Florence at the New England 49-yard line. San Diego then moved the ball to the 4-yard line, and it looked like the pick would be very costly. But, the D came through again. On 3rd and 1, linebacker Junior Seau brought down Michael Turner for a 2-yard loss and the Chargers settled again for Kaeding's fourth field goal.

New England came back with a drive to the San Diego 2-yard line, with Maroney gaining 39 yards on four running plays. Chargers cornerback Antonio Cromartie ended the drive by intercepting Brady in the end zone. It was the third interception.

After getting the ball in the fourth quarter, New England moved 67 yards and scored with a perfect Brady 6-yard touchdown pass to Wes Welker, making the score 21–12. The Chargers were forced to punt and then the Patriots ended the game with a 15-play drive that took the remaining 9:13 off the game clock. The Patriots' overall record then improved to 18–0 on their way to their appearance in Super Bowl LXII (42) and becoming the 2007 AFC Champions.

Super Bowl XLII

The SB XLII kickoff was at 6:39 EST February 3, 2008. Led by starter Tom Brady, the Bill Belichick-led NE Patriots were defeated. At the University of Phoenix Stadium, Glendale AZ before a packed house of 71,101.

I go to the Boston Paper to get the scoop the way it actually happened in 2008. This fine write-up from the Boston Globe at the time it was written gave New England fans enough of the Super Bowl that they felt they were there. Nice job Christopher L. Gasper He titled his article:

Patriots' bid for perfect season ends in Giants' upset

By Christopher L. Gasper GLOBE STAFF FEBRUARY 04, 2008

GLENDALE, Ariz. - The team that had been deified proved mortal when it mattered most.

Photo below by JIM DAVIS/GLOBE STAFF

Tom Brady scowled watching Giants begin to celebrate Super Bowl victory.

In one of the biggest upsets in NFL history, the New York Giants shocked the previously perfect Patriots, 17-14, last night in Super Bowl XLII in front of 71,101 fans at University of Phoenix Stadium. New England (18-1) picked an awful time for its first loss of the season. Now the records, the 16-0 regular season, the individual awards, the All-Pro recognition, all ring hollow without a Super Bowl ring.

Giants quarterback Eli Manning hit Plaxico Burress in the left corner of the end zone from 13 yards out with 35 seconds left to cap an 83-yard drive and keep the 1972 Miami Dolphins as the only NFL team to complete a perfect season. Burress, who had predicted a Giants victory and had been ridiculed, proved prescient when he beat Ellis Hobbs for the decisive score.

Below: PIC JIM DAVIS/GLOBE STAFF

Plaxico Burress caught the game-winning touchdown with 35 seconds remaining.

"We set high expectations, now we go down as 18-1, and that is one big zit," said Hobbs. "It is one big blemish. We choked. We choked at the end."

The Patriots appeared primed to make history when Tom Brady hit Randy Moss for a 6-yard touchdown on third and goal with 2:42 remaining to make it 14-10, New England. Trailing, 10-7, and getting the ball at his 20 with 7:54 to go, Brady was at his brilliant best.

Shaking off a pass rush that sacked him a season-high five times and a right ankle that hobbled and hindered him, Brady (29 of 48 for 266 yards and a touchdown) went 8 of 11 for 71 yards on the drive to put the Patriots back in the lead.

He began the march with a 5-yard pass to Wes Welker, who tied the Super Bowl record for receptions with 11 for 103 yards and ended it with the pass to Moss.

On the sideline veteran linebackers Tedy Bruschi and Junior Seau hugged after Moss scored, but the joy was short-lived, like the Patriots' lead.

Manning (19 of 34 for 255 yards, 2 TDs, and 1 interception, Super Bowl MVP) more than matched the heroics of Brady on the winning drive, and he had company. On third and 5 from the Giants' 44, after an incredible Manning scramble, David Tyree made a huge leaping grab over Rodney Harrison for a 32-yard gain to put the Giants in New England territory.

Few saw the imperfect ending to the perfect season coming. The Patriots had beaten the Giants, 38-35, during the teams' regular-season meeting to improve to 16-0, and few thought this game would be any different.
"The biggest thing is to win the championship at the end of the year," said Moss. "All that we did, that undefeated regular season, it didn't mean nothing because we didn't close it at the end."

After each team had scored on its first possession of the game, there was a paucity of points until Manning hit Tyree for a 5-yard touchdown pass with 11:05 remaining, giving New York a 10-7 lead.

The 33-minute, 52-second scoreless stretch was the longest in Super Bowl history.

"Their front four really set the tone for four quarters," said Moss. "I think their secondary was ordinary, not taking anything from them. They don't have Pro Bowlers, but they do play good together. They had a good game plan."

In the first half the Patriots hardly played like one of the greatest teams in NFL history, leading, 7-3, at intermission.

Brady was constantly harassed by the rush and was sacked three times, the last of which, by Justin Tuck, resulted in a fumble that gave the Giants the ball back at the New England 49 with 10 seconds left in the half and prevented the Patriots from adding to their lead.

Brady's ankle appeared to prevent him from avoiding the rush, although he said the injury wasn't a factor. Moss said he couldn't tell if Brady was affected.

"I couldn't really tell, all I know was I heard the fans screaming and when I looked back he was down," said Moss.

The Giants, who outgained the Patriots, 139 yards to 81, in the half, were equally unimpressive in their execution. New York was inside the New England 30 three times, but only had 3 points to show for it.

The Giants took the opening kickoff, played keep-away for 9 minutes 59 seconds, then settled for a 3-0 lead on a 32-yard field goal by Lawrence Tynes, capping a 16-play, 63-yard drive that was the longest time-wise in Super Bowl history.

But the lead didn't last long. The Patriots went up, 7-3, on the first play of the second quarter, as Laurence Maroney, who had given the Patriots excellent field position with a 43-yard kick return, ducked in from the 1 on second and goal.

One of the hallmarks of the Giants' playoff run had been ball security. New York had not turned the ball over on offense during the postseason and had gone 34 possessions, dating to its regular-season loss to the Patriots, without an offensive turnover. In that game, Hobbs intercepted Manning in the fourth quarter.

Hobbs did the honors again in the second quarter last night. On third and 5 from the New England 14, Hobbs scooped up a Manning pass that Steve Smith let slip through his hands at the 10, and he returned it to the 33.

However, the Patriots couldn't capitalize, as Maroney was stopped for a 2-yard loss on third and 1 from the New England 42. At 9:22 of the second, at the Giants' 30, Ahmad Bradshaw fumbled a handoff and the Patriots' Pierre Woods appeared to recover the ball. But Bradshaw flipped Woods over and somehow came up with the ball, costing New England a great chance.

The most bizarre play of the half happened after the Giants, behind the hard running of Brandon Jacobs and Bradshaw, moved to the New England 25 with 2:31 left. Adalius Thomas strip-sacked Manning on third and 4 and Bradshaw batted the loose ball forward, with Smith recovering for a first down. But Bradshaw's bat was illegal, and the penalty took the Giants out of field goal range.

In the third quarter, after an illegal substitution penalty against the Giants, the Patriots moved the ball to the New York 25, but following a sack they came up empty, and coach Bill Belichick elected to go for it on fourth and 13 from the New York 31. Brady pumped twice before throwing the ball out of the end zone.

After Burress backed up his prediction with a play that will live on NFL Films highlight reels for eternity, the Patriots had one final chance to write a perfect ending, getting the ball at their 26 with 35 seconds left. But on fourth and 20 from their 16, Brady couldn't connect with Moss (five catches for 62 yards and the score) on one last deep ball and the Giants had a historic victory of their own.

Belichick shook hands with his Giants counterpart, Tom Coughlin, but Belichick wasn't on the sideline when the Giants took a knee to secure the upset.

"I don't rank them. It's disappointing," said Belichick.

"I think a lot of people didn't really even want us to win this game," said Moss. "We'll come back. Don't worry about that. It hurts that there is not a next week. The season's over. We'll look forward to minicamp."

Look at the record. The Patriots came back but this was tough to lose.

2008 Bill Belichick #14

The 2008 New England Patriots football team competed in their forty-ninth season of professional football and their thirty-ninth eighth season in the National Football League (NFL). The Patriots were led by Coach Bill Belichick in his ninth of eighteen seasons (so-far). Robert Kraft was the Patriot's owner. The Patriots record was 11-5-0. They finished second in the AFC East Division, and they did not qualify for the playoffs.

The Patriots were the defending AFC champions. They had a fine record in 2008 but not good enough. At 11-5, they did not qualify even for a Wild Card berth. For this they set a record as the first 11-win team since the expansion to a 12-team playoff in 1990 to not make the playoffs, as well as only the second team (after the 1985 Denver Broncos) since the NFL expanded to a 16-game regular season in 1978. Considering that just one year prior, the team finished with the only 16–0 regular-season record in NFL history, not making the playoffs was unexpected.

Of course, the Patriots had one major excuse for not getting that one extra win. In the season opener, quarterback Tom Brady, who was the NFL's MVP in 2007, suffered a torn anterior cruciate ligament against the Chiefs. Brady missed the rest of the season. Backup quarterback Matt Cassel replaced Brady and did as well as could be expected. The team did not fall apart.

Cassel took the team to a win in Week 2 against the New York Jets. It was his first start since high school. The following week against the Miami Dolphins, the Patriots had their 21-game regular-season winning streak broken. This record stood until the Indianapolis Colts broke it 2009.

The Patriots had a three-week winning streak going when it engaged the last week of the season. However, the Belichick's squad were not in control of their own destiny. In addition to needing a Week 17 win, they also needed either a Dolphins loss to win the AFC East, or a Baltimore Ravens loss to earn a wild card berth. However, both Baltimore and Miami won, and the Dolphins, Ravens and Patriots each finished the season with an 11–5 record.

Miami qualified for the playoffs by winning the AFC East division over the Patriots on the fourth divisional tiebreaker (better conference record: 8–4 to 7–5). Baltimore qualified for the playoffs as a wild card team, defeating the Patriots on the second wild card tiebreaker (better conference record: 8–4 to 7–5).

Since Tom Brady and Bill Belichick teamed and played a Super Bowl in 2001, this is, as of 2017/2018, the only season since 2002 that New England failed to qualify for the playoffs. What a team. Like the Patriots or hate them, they are the best football team in the modern era because of two people—Bill Belichick and Tom Brady. Like most Patriot fans, I sure hope that they both continue for as many years as possible.

In the home and season opener at 1:00 PM EDT on September 7, 2008, the Patriots defeated the Kansas City Chiefs W (17–10) at Gillette Stadium. This was the last game Tom Brady played until the 2009 season. At New York on Sept 14, 2008 at New York Jets in his first time at the helm, Matt Cassell led the Patriots to a win W (19–10) against the Jets at Giants Stadium. At home on Sept 21, the Miami Dolphins whipped the Patriots L (13-38) at Gillette Stadium CBS Recap In week 4, on Sept 28, the Patriots drew a bye. Then, on Oct 5, at San Francisco, the Patriots beat the 49ers W (30–21) at Candlestick Park.

At San Diego on Oct 12, 2008, the Chargers defeated the Patriots L (10–30) at Qualcomm Stadium. At home on Oct 20, the Patriots walloped the Denver Broncos W (41–7) in Gillette Stadium. Then, at home on Oct 26, the St. Louis Rams were defeated by the New England Patriots W (23–16) at Gillette Stadium. At Indianapolis on Nov 2, 2008 the Colts edged out the Patriots in Lucas Oil Stadium L (15-18).

At home on Nov 9, the Patriots beat the Buffalo Bills W (20–10) in Gillette Stadium. At home on Nov 13, the New York Jets edged out the Patriots L (31–34) in single OT in Gillette Stadium. At Miami on Nov 23, the Patriots smothered the Dolphins W (48–28) at Dolphin

Stadium. At home on Nov 30, the Pittsburgh Steelers slammed the Patriots L (10–33) in Gillette Stadium.

At Seattle, on Dec 7, 2008 the Patriots edged out the Seahawks W (24–2) at Qwest Field. At Oakland, on Dec 14, the Patriots lambasted the Raiders W (49–26) at the Oakland–Alameda County Coliseum. At home on Dec 21, the Patriots squashed the Arizona Cardinals W (47–7) in Gillette Stadium. Then, in the season finale at Buffalo, the Patriots shut out the Bills W (13–0) at Ralph Wilson Stadium.

2009 Bill Belichick #14

The 2009 New England Patriots football team competed in their fiftieth season of professional football and their fortieth season in the National Football League (NFL). The Patriots were led by Coach Bill Belichick in his tenth of eighteen seasons (so-far). Robert Kraft was the Patriot's owner. The Patriots record was 10-6. They finished first in the AFC East Division, and they qualified for the playoffs. The Wild Card game was played on January 10, 2010, against the Baltimore Ravens. The Patriots won the game L (14-33).

As noted in the 2008 section for Bill Belichick, the Patriots missed the playoffs that year. This was not looked upon as a random happening by management and so the offseason was marked by a number of front office, coaching, and personnel changes. Vice President of Player Personnel Scott Pioli, who had been head coach Bill Belichick's personnel director since 2000, took off to become the general manager of the Kansas City Chiefs, while offensive coordinator Josh McDaniels was named head coach of the Denver Broncos.

QB Matt Cassel, knew after his fine season after Brady was injured that he could manage a pro team as QB. He led the team to 11 wins in 2008. With Brady coming back, the Patriots traded Cassel along with veteran linebacker Mike Vrabel in March. Defensive starters Tedy Bruschi and Rodney Harrison both retired, while All-Pro defensive end Richard Seymour was traded to the Oakland Raiders for a first round pick in the 2011 NFL Draft…just days before the start of the regular season.

When the season opener came, it was broadcast on a Monday Night Football program, as the Patriots celebrated their 50th anniversary season. It was an American Football League "legacy game" against the Buffalo Bills. It did not all go as planned for an anniversary as the Pats were down 11 points late in the fourth quarter. Nonetheless, they put it all together and scored two TDs to secure a victory in Brady's first game back from his injury.

In November, the 6–2 Patriots had a scheduled road trip to Indianapolis to face the undefeated Colts. In this game, with a six-point lead late in the fourth quarter, the Pats tried to convert a 4th and 2 inside their own 30-yard line but failed. This circumstance set up a Colts TD and brought the Patriots' their third loss of the season.

New England lost another two games out of three, but then they went on to win their next three games, securing a division title.

Someone once said: "the harder you work the luckier you get." Many great football coaches do not discount the role of chance or luck in football. Others find it hooey. The Patriots with Bill Belichick work hard and they were lucky to win three Super Bowls as of 2008. They put in the hard work and the good play but sometimes the element of luck is not there, like this year and despite how well or how hard they play, they lose anyway—not intending to lose.

This year, the Patriots finished with their fourth perfect regular season record at home in seven years. They are still a great team and were a great team in 2008. With their third seed in the AFC playoffs, the Patriots faced the Baltimore Ravens at home in the Wild Card Playoffs. The Ravens opened a 24–0 lead in the first quarter and the Patriots could not recover, ending their season.

Games of the 2008 season

In the season and home opener for the Patriots' 50th anniversary game played at 7:00 pm EDT, on September 14, 2009, the Patriots defeated the Buffalo Bills† W (25–24) at Gillette Stadium. At New York, on Sept 20, the Jets beat the Patriots L (9–16) at Giants Stadium. At home, on Sept 27, the Patriots defeated the Atlanta Falcons W (26–10) in Gillette Stadium. Then, at home again, on Oct 4, my wedding anniversary, the Patriots beat the Baltimore Ravens W (27–21) in Gillette Stadium.

At Denver on October 11, the Broncos beat the Patriots in OT L (17–20) in Invesco Field at Mile High Stadium.

*** This goes down as one of the top games in Patriot History ***

At home on Oct 18, New England squashed the Tennessee Titans† W (59–0) in Gillette Stadium.

Tom Brady threw 5 Touchdowns in a Quarter against the Titans in this game in 2009. You may know that recently, Madden Football released a "G.O.A.T" edition of their storied video game franchise. On the cover is none other than Tom Brady.

His performance against the Titans in 2009 exemplifies this title. Brady was simply unstoppable in this game. In the second quarter, Brady threw a barrage of perfect passes to set the record for most TD passes in a quarter. His first was a 41-yard bomb to Randy Moss, which then became the recipient for Brady's second TD on a 28-yard pass. After his third score, Brady managed to sneak in his final two touchdowns to Wes Welker in the final 2 minutes of the game, the fifth score came with only 16 seconds left on the clock!

This was an incredible game, even if you hate Brady, no fan of football can deny his incredible passing prowess, one that has dubbed him as the greatest of all time!

On Oct 25, 2009 at a game against the Tampa Bay Buccaneers, the Patriots whipped the Bucs W (35–7) in Wembley Stadium— London, England. On Nov 1, the team drew a bye. Then, at home, on Nov 8, the Patriots defeated the Miami Dolphins W (27–17) in Gillette Stadium.

Then at Indianapolis, on Nov 15, the Colts picked up a one-point-match victory against the Patriots L (34–35) in Lucas Oil Stadium. At home on Nov 22, the New York Jets were smothered by the New England Patriots W (31–14) at Gillette Stadium. At New Orleans on Nov 30, the Saints hammered the Patriots L (17–38) at the Louisiana Superdome.

At Miami on Dec 6, the Dolphins picked up a one-point victory over New England L (21–22) in Land Shark Stadium. At home on Dec 13, the Patriots beat the Carolina Panthers W (20–10) in Gillette Stadium. Then, at Buffalo, on Dec 20, the Patriots got the win against the Bills W (17–10) in the Ralph Wilson Stadium. At home on Dec 27, 2009 New England pummeled Jacksonville W (35–7) in Gillette Stadium. Then, in the season ender, at Houston, the Texans got the best of the Patriots L (27–34) at Reliant Stadium. And, so the next game for the Patriots would be the Wild Card playoffs.

The Wild Card Playoffs 2009 January 10, 2010

The Wild Card playoffs commenced with a 1:00 pm EST kickoff on January 10, 2010. The New England Patriots prepared to take on the Baltimore Ravens but the gods of New England were someplace else that day as the Patriots lost L (14–33) at Gillette Stadium before a packed house of 68, 756. The temperature was 20 °F (–7 °C), sunny and cold.

	1	2	3	4	Total
Ravens	24	0	3	6	33
Patriots	0	7	7	0	14

The Ravens got it going good in the 1st quarter thanks to typically perfect NE QB Tom Brady having some accuracy issues. The Ravens were very fortunate as they converted three first-quarter turnovers into 17 points, putting up a 24–0 lead from which New England could not recover. Someone like me would say that it was bad luck and a few errant spins of the ball. Every NE fan agreed that it was terribly unfortunate d from.

It was the Pats first home loss of the season and their first home loss in the playoffs in more than 30 years. It was a bad deal from the deck of potential outcomes. On top of that, it was the Ravens' first ever win against the Patriots after five consecutive losses. Tom Brady surely would like even to this day to have a few of those throws back.

Baltimore raced to a 7–0 lead on the first play of the game with Ray Rice's 83-yard touchdown run. Some might call that a bad omen if one believes in such things. It was the second longest run in NFL playoff history. When that was over and done with, linebacker Terrell Suggs forced and recovered a fumble from Tom Brady on the Patriots 17-yard line, and the Ravens chalked up another score with a 1-yard run by Le'Ron McClain.

After some regular field play and an exchange of punts, cornerback Chris Carr picked off a Brady pass and brought it back to the New England 25-yard line. The "D" did not hold and this set up Rice's second touchdown on a 1-yard run. Just two plays after the next kickoff, there was more bad news for the Patriots caused by the Ravens.

Safety Ed Reed snagged a deep pass from Brady and returned it 25 yards. He stretched it for more by lateraling the ball to safety Dawan Landry. Landry raced another 25 yards to the Patriots 9-yard line, daring the Patriots to stop him.

The Ravens got nothing on three plays, but Billy Cundiff kicked a short field goal to make the score 24–0 in favor of the Ravens. I might say that's all she wrote as that was all that mattered for this game to be determined. New England did not mount an explosive comeback. Instead the Pats were forced to punt on their next drive.

Some good luck ensued as Baltimore returner Tom Zbikowski muffed the kick and Kyle Arrington recovered the ball for the Patriots at the Ravens 16-yard line. Five plays later, Brady threw a 6-yard touchdown pass to Julian Edelman making it 24-7. There is always hope until there is no more hope.

Midway through the second half, Brady threw his third interception of the game. This pick was to Landry, who returned it 42 yards to the New England 22, to set up another Cundiff field goal. On the kickoff, Darius Butler went off for a 42-yard kickoff return landing in the Patriots 47-yard line. The Patriots decided they were the Patriots and drove 53-yards for another score. Tom Brady finished it with his second touchdown pass to Edelman to cut their deficit to 27–14. The game was within reach.

Former Penn State great, Tom Zbikowski returned the ensuing kickoff 30 yards to his own 48-yard line, much to the Patriot's chagrin. Worse than that, the boost from the kickoff return sparked a 52-yard drive for a TD. It came on a 3-yard touchdown run from Willis McGahee, making the score 33–14 after the two-point conversion failed. It was looking less likely for a Patriot comeback.

Nonetheless, New England responded with a drive deep into Baltimore territory, but the drive stalled. Then, looking for three points. The Patriots got zero as Stephen Gostkowski missed a 44-yard field goal attempt. There was only 7:19 left in the game, and to many this ended any chance of a miracle comeback.

Rice rushed for 159 yards and two touchdowns, while McGahee added 62 yards and a score. Neither quarterback had much success, as Brady was held to 154 yards and intercepted three times, while Baltimore's Joe Flacco completed only 4 of 10 passes for 34 yards. Turnovers won the game for the Ravens. New England had to wait another year for some good luck.

2010 Bill Belichick #14

The 2010 New England Patriots football team competed in their fifty-first season of professional football and their forty-first season in the National Football League (NFL). The Patriots were led by Coach Bill Belichick in his eleventh of eighteen seasons (so-far). Robert Kraft was the Patriot's owner. The Patriots record was 14-2. They finished first in the AFC East Division, and they qualified for the playoffs. Luck, the invisible marker in all football games appeared on the opposite side of the preferable Patriots fate. The New England Patriots lost their only playoff game this year in the Divisional Playoffs to the New York Jets, L (21-28). It would take another year for the Patriots to have another go at a few more of those huge, and meaningful, Super Bowl Rings.

This year was one of those rebuilding years for a team that never dropped too far from the very top. After losing to Baltimore in the 2009 playoffs, the Patriots lost their offensive and defensive coordinators. The trading blocks were also busy.

Wide Receiver Randy Moss, who was not long with the team was sent to Minnesota on October 6 and this action eventually led to the return of trade sent All-Pro wide receiver Randy Moss to the Minnesota Vikings, and eventually led to the return of Deion Branch from the Seattle Seahawks in a separate deal. After re-acquiring Branch, the Patriots won 11 of their last 12 games of the season to finish with a 14–2 record. This was a great record and secured them homefield advantage throughout the playoffs.

Tom Brady was at his best this year. He finished the regular season with an NFL-record 335 consecutive pass attempts without an interception. Additionally, Brady broke his own 2007 TD to INT ratio record with 9:1 and was named NFL MVP.

The Patriots held on to the ball this year, committing NFL-record low 10 turnovers on the season. They also snagged another NFL record with seven consecutive games without a single turnover.

Luck always has something to do with football. When players are not themselves or things just are not right, we might suggest that Mr. Luck is at work. In their Divisional playoff game against the Jets, the Patriots were a victim of bad luck. They got down 14–3 by halftime and they could not recover. Moreover, they were held to their lowest scoring total in their last 11 weeks, dropping this contest 28–21 to the underdog Jets.

Statistics site Football Outsiders calculated that the Patriots 2010 offense was not only more efficient, play-for-play, than their record-setting 2007 offense, but was actually the best offense they calculated in their history. As of 2017, this is the last season the Patriots failed to reach the AFC Championship game. What a shame after such a fine season.

In the home and season opener at1:00 pm EDT September 12, 2010, the New England Patriots defeated the Cincinnati Bengals W (38–24) at Gillette Stadium before a packed house of 68,756. At New York on Sept 19, the Jets beat the Patriots L (14–28) in Meadowlands Stadium before 78,535. At home on Sept 26, the Patriots defeated the Buffalo Bills W (38–30) at Gillette Stadium before 68, 756. At Miami on Oct 4, my wedding anniversary, the Patriots thumped the Dolphins W (41–14) in Sun Life Stadium before 69,090. In week 5, Oct 11, the team drew a bye.

At home on Oct 17, New England beat Baltimore Ravens in OT W (23–20) in Gillette Stadium. At San Diego on October 24, the Patriots repeated the prior week's score of W (23-20) and beat the chargers in Qualcomm Stadium before 68, 836. At home on Oct 31, the Patriots beat the Minnesota Vikings W (28–18) in Gillette Stadium. At Cleveland, on Nov 7, the Cleveland Browns beat the Patriots L (14–34) in Cleveland Browns Stadium.

At Pittsburgh, on November 14, the Patriots defeated the Steelers W (39–26) in Heinz Field. before 64,359. At home, on Nov 21, the Patriots beat the Indianapolis Colts W (31–28) in Gillette Stadium. At Detroit on Nov 25, 2010, the Patriots pounded the Lions W (45–24) at Ford Field before 60,065. On Dec 6, at home, the Patriots pummeled the New York Jets W (45–3) in Gillette Stadium.

At Chicago, on Dec 12, the Patriots smothered the Bears W (36–7) at Soldier Field before 62,347. At home on Dec 19, the Patriots beat the Green Bay Packers W 31–27 in Gillette Stadium. At Buffalo, on Dec 26m the Patriots slammed the Bills W (34–3) at Ralph Wilson Stadium before 68,281. At home on January 2, 2011 in the season finale, the Patriots walloped the Miami Dolphins W (38–7) in Gillette Stadium, finishing with the best record in the NFL at 14-2.

The Divisional Playoffs January 16, 2010

	1	2	3	4	Total
Jets	0	14	0	14	**28**
Patriots	3	0	8	10	**21**

This divisional playoff game began at 4:30 PM on January 16, 2010 at Gillette Stadium, Foxborough, Massachusetts. The weather was 30 °F, clear and cold. There was a packed house of 68,756 at this Patriots home game. After a 14-2 regular season record, the Patriots were tripped up by the New York Jets L (21-28.

Mark Sanchez was the Jets QB and he had a nice day with 16 of 25 completions for 194 yards and three touchdowns. Sanchez led the Jets to victory, thereby avenging a 45–3 loss to New England in December.

The first time the Pats got the ball, Tom Brady threw his first interception since week five of the regular season. Linebacker David Harris picked it off and advanced it 58 yards before tight end Alge Crumpler made a TD-saving tackle at the 12-yard line. The Jets got no points off this turnover. They were unable to get a first down and Nick Folk missed a chip-shot 30-yard field goal attempt.

A few plays into New England's next drive, Brady completed a nice 28-yard pass to Crumpler at the Jets 12-yard line and this was followed by a 5-yard run by Danny Woodhead. Then, Crumpler dropped a pass in the end zone and on the next play Brady was sacked by Shaun Ellis, forcing the Patriots to settle for Shayne Graham's 34-yard field goal, giving New England a 3–0 lead.

In the second quarter, Tom Brady was sacked on third down by Drew Coleman forcing a New England punt from their own 16. Jerricho Cotchery got 5 yards on the return to the Patriots 49-yard line. A few plays later, Sanchez' uncorked a 37-yard completion to Braylon Edwards, which set up his first TD pass of the day -- a 7-yarder to LaDainian Tomlinson.

Later in the quarter, New England attempted a fake punt with a direct snap to safety Patrick Chung on fourth down and four. However, Chung fumbled the snap and was tackled on the NE 25-yard line. The Jets did not waste this one and quickly converted the turnover with a well-placed Sanchez 15-yard touchdown pass to Edwards with 33 seconds left in the half. This back-breaking score brought the tally to 14–3 in the Jets favor.

As the third quarter moved on with few events, as time was waning, Brady drove 80 yards in 11 plays, while completing a 37-yard pass to Rob Gronkowski and two passes to Deion Branch for 28 yards on the way to a 2-yard touchdown pass to Crumpler. Then Sammy Morris scored a 2-point conversion run, cutting their deficit to 14–11. The game was now a field goal away from a tie.

But the Jets came right back with Sanchez feeding a short pass to Cotchery, who took it 58 yards to the Partriots' 13-yard line. Just two plays later, Sanchez threw a high pass for Santonio Holmes, who managed to catch the ball and land his two feet in the end zone while falling out of bounds. This gave the Jets a 10-point lead two minutes into the fourth quarter.

After the next kickoff, New England moved to the Jets 34-yard line with an 8-minute drive, but then faced fourth down and 13. Rather than risk a 52-yard field goal attempt, they attempted to get the first down, but Branch dropped a pass from Brady and the Patriots turned the ball over.

New England's defense then made a great defensive stand, forcing a quick three-and-out. Julian Edelman returned Steve Weatherford's punt 41 yards to the New York 43-yard line before being tackled by Weatherford himself. Brady then led New England to the 17-yard line where Graham made his second field goal to cut their deficit to 7 points.

Looking to get back in the game quickly, the Patriots tried an onside kick which was snagged by Jets defensive back Antonio Cromartie recovered Graham's onside kick attempt and returned it 23 yards to the Patriots 20-yard line. Then Shonn Greene scored with a 20-yard run on the next play, making the score 28–14 with 1:12 left in the game. It did not look good.

Brandon Tate took the kickoff 23 yards to the 41-yard line, sparking a 59-yard scoring drive that ended with Brady's 13-yard touchdown pass to Branch with 24 seconds left. Graham's second attempt at an onside kick also failed, ending any chance of a miracle comeback. The Patriots never gave up but could not pull it out.

Brady had a nice passing day, finishing the game 29 of 45 for 299 yards and two touchdowns, with 1 interception. Cotchery had 5 receptions for 96 yards Harris had 9 tackles, 3 assists, and an interception, while Ellis added 5 tackles and two sacks. With this win, the Jets advanced to their second consecutive AFC championship game in Sanchez' first two years as a starter. The Patriots would be back at it the following year as they came close to another Super Bowl victory.

2011 Bill Belichick #14

The 2011 New England Patriots football team competed in their fifty-second season of professional football and their forty-second season in the National Football League (NFL). The Patriots were led by Coach Bill Belichick in his twelfth of eighteen seasons (so-far). Robert Kraft was the Patriot's owner. The Patriots record was 13-3. They finished first in the AFC East Division, and they qualified for the playoffs and went on to play in the Super Bowl, where they lost by just four points L (17-21) to the Giants. It was the seventh Super Bowl trip in franchise history, and the fifth for head coach Bill Belichick and quarterback Tom Brady.

There was a tone of sadness to the 2011 Patriots season as the team dedicated the season

The Patriots dedicated their 2011 season to the memory of Myra Kraft, the wife of owner Robert Kraft, who died on July 20, 2011 after a long fight against cancer. It gave an idea of how much the Patriots respect and appreciate the owner family. At both home and away games, in commemoration, the Patriots wore patches bearing Kraft's initials, MHK, on their uniforms. In fact, The Patriots elected to wear their Super Bowl patches on the right side of their uniforms, so that they could keep the MHK patch on the left side as it had been all season.

The Patriots continued superiority came through again this season as they were the only 2011 division winner that had won their division the previous season. As noted, in a heartbreaking defeat, The Patriots lost in the Super Bowl to the New York Giants by a score of 21–17.

As was the case in their previous appearance against these same Giants in Super Bowl XLII, the Pats had a chance to join the San Francisco 49ers, the Dallas Cowboys, the Pittsburgh Steelers, and the Green Bay Packers as the only teams to win at least four Super Bowls. The Packers had entered the 2011 season as the defending champions had not yet won a fourth Super Bowl when the Patriots had last appeared.

Instead, without a victory this year, the Patriots tied what was then an NFL record for most losses in a Super Bowl. This record had been set by the Minnesota Vikings and tied by the Denver Broncos and Buffalo Bills, each of whom had lost four.

With the loss, along with losses in 1985, 1996, and 2007, the Patriots tied with the Denver Broncos, Buffalo Bills and Minnesota Vikings for most Super Bowl losses at four (although the Broncos would lose their fifth against the Seattle Seahawks two years later).

In the six years from 2012 through 2017, the Patriots would make the playoffs all six times and would play three times in the Super Bowl. They would win two of their three Super Bowl encounters with the last one being after the 2016 season.

At Miami in the season opener on September 12, the Patriots defeated the Dolphins W (38–24) at Sun Life Stadium. At home on

Sept 18, the Patriots beat the San Diego Chargers W (35–21) in Gillette Stadium. At Buffalo on Sept 25, the Bills defeated the Patriots L (31–34) at Ralph Wilson Stadium. At Oakland, on Oct 2, the Patriots defeated the Raiders W (31–19) at the Coliseum.

At home on Oct 9, the Patriots beat the New York Jets W (30–21) in Gillette Stadium. At home on Oct 16, the Patriots defeated the Dallas Cowboys W (20–16) in Gillette Stadium. On Oct23, there was a bye. Then, after the rest, on at Pittsburgh on October 30 the Steelers beat the Patriots L (17–25) at Heinz Field. At home on Nov 6, the New York Giants beat the New England Patriots L (20–24) in Gillette Stadium.

At New York on Nov 13, the Patriots beat the Jets W (37–16) at MetLife Stadium. At home on Nov 21 the Patriots shellacked the Kansas City Chiefs W (34–3) in Gillette Stadium. At Philadelphia, on Nov 27, the Patriots beat the Eagles W (38–20) at Lincoln Financial Field. At home on Dec 4, the Patriots beat the Indianapolis Colts W (31–24) in Gillette Stadium.

At Washington, on Dec 11, the Patriots defeated the Redskins W (34–27) at FedEx Field. At Denver on Dec 18, the Patriots shipped the Broncos W (41–23) in Sports Authority Field at Mile High Stadium. At home, on Dec 24, the Patriots beat the Miami Dolphins W (27–24) in Gillette Stadium. At home on Jan 1 in the final game of the season, the Patriots scorched the Buffalo Bills W (49–21) in Gillette Stadium. The Patriots finished with a 13-3 record and 1st in the AFC East.

The Divisional Playoffs January 14, 2012

	1	2	3	4	Total
Broncos	0	7	3	0	10
Patriots	14	21	7	3	45

This divisional playoff game began at 8:00 PM on January 14, 2012 at Gillette Stadium, Foxborough, Massachusetts. The weather was 24 °F, partly cloudy and cold. There was a packed house of 68,756 at this Patriots home game. After a 13-3 regular season record, the Patriots walloped the Denver Broncos W (45-10).

Clearly this game could have been subtitled as The Tom Brady Show as this All-Pro-QB really put on a show for America. He tied an NFL playoff record by throwing six touchdown passes in a playoff game. He tied a number of all-time greats in this great showing—such as Daryle Lamonica's six scores in the Oakland Raiders' 1969 Divisional round victory over the Houston Oilers and Steve Young's six scores in Super Bowl XXIX over San Diego.

Brady's five touchdowns in the first half tied an NFL playoff record with Sid Luckman, Lamonica, Joe Montana, Kurt Warner, Kerry Collins, and Peyton Manning. Brady also showed position versatility as he punted the ball on third down late in the fourth quarter, pinning the Broncos inside their own 10-yard line. There was a controversy after the punt as a brief brawl erupted between the two teams.

A week after his dramatic Wild Card overtime victory over the Steelers, Tim Tebow was sacked five times and limited to 136 passing yards and 13 rushing yards; at halftime, Tebow had fewer completions (three) than Brady had touchdowns (six).

With the win, the Patriots improved to 14–3 for the 19-game season including playoffs. In addition to Brady's record-tying six touchdowns, Rob Gronkowski set a club record with three touchdown catches in a playoff game, breaking the 1986 record of two by Stanley Morgan. Gronkowski became only the second tight end with three touchdowns in an NFL postseason game. The win was also the first Patriots playoff win (in three tries) over the Broncos and the first two-game sweep of Denver by the Patriots since their 1964 AFL season.

AFC Championship Playoffs January 22, 2012

	1	2	3	4	Total
Ravens	0	10	10	0	20
Patriots	3	10	3	7	23

This AFC Championship game began at 3:00 PM on January 22, 2012 at Gillette Stadium, Foxborough, Massachusetts. The weather was 29 °F, cloudy and cold. There was a packed house of 68,756 at this Patriots home game. After a 13-3 regular season record, the Patriots played a close match with the Baltimore Ravens, winning the contest W (23-20).

Compared to the Division Championship, there was not a lot of action, but the results were good for the Patriots, nonetheless. As the game got underway, following two Ravens punts and a Patriots punt the Patriots mounted a drive by grinding out a 13-play 50-yard drive. It ended with a Stephen Gostkowski field goal.

The Ravens tied the game after a Ladarius Webb interception followed by Billy Cundiff's 20-yard field goal. Then, there was a BenJarvus Green-Ellis rushing score, a six-yard Joe Flacco touchdown to Dennis Pitta, and another Gostkowski field goal left which overall put the Pats ahead 13–10 at the half.

Following a third Gostkowski field goal, the Ravens grabbed the lead at 17–16 lead on a 29-yard Torrey Smith touchdown catch and run straddling the right sideline without stepping out. Danny Woodhead fumbled the next kickoff, and this prompted another Cundiff field goal. Nothing big was happening but inches of scores were going up on the board.

Then, New England clawed their way back to the lead on a 10-play 67-yard drive ending with Tom Brady leaping in from the one-yard line. Brandon Spikes intercepted Flacco at midfield but the Pats coughed up the ball as Brady was intercepted in the Ravens end zone just one play later by Jimmy Smith.

The Ravens missed a chance to score on 4th and 6 at the Patriots 33-yard line, but did not get it in. Then, they got the ball back with 1:44 to go in the game. Lee Evans nearly caught a TD, but Sterling Moore swatted the ball right out of his hands in the end zone. The Ravens got another chance at Pay dirt 11 seconds to go. Cundiff took another shot at a field goal of 32-yards and his attempt sailed wide left, effectively ending the game.

During the second half Rob Gronkowski suffered an ankle injury on a tackle by Bernard Pollard of the Ravens. Pollard had a record of putting Patriots on the disabled list. He injured Brady in his 2008 season in Kansas City, and also had injured Wes Welker during week 17 of the 2009 season with the Houston Texans. Later in an interview with KILT radio in Houston, Pollard said he was "fine and dandy" with being called a "Patriots killer."

This win was Brady's fifth success in six AFC Championship Games and the first Patriots playoff win that was decided on a missed FGA since the club's 2006 Divisional playoff win against San Diego.

Super Bowl XLVI February 5, 2012

	1	2	3	4	Total
Giants	9	0	6	6	21
Patriots	0	10	7	0	17

The Super Bowl XLVI kickoff was at 6:30 EST February 5, 2012. Led by starter Tom Brady, the Bill Belichick-led NE Patriots were defeated. Lucas Oil Stadium, Indianapolis Indiana, before a packed house of 68, 658. After a 13-3 regular season record, the Patriots played a close match with the New York Giants, losing the contest W (17-21). (color commentator),

I go to the Boston Paper to get the scoop the way it actually happened in 2008. This fine write-up from the Boston Globe at the time it was written gave New England fans enough of the Super Bowl that they felt they were there. Nice job SHalise Manza Young. She titled her is article:

History repeats for the Patriots
New York claims second Super Bowl win in five seasons

Photo by Jim Davis / Globe Staff

Tom Brady left the field after losing Super Bowl XLVI.

INDIANAPOLIS – The Giants did it again.
There was no perfect season on the line this time, but the Giants still ended the Patriots' season in heartbreak for the second time in as many Super Bowl meetings, winning Super Bowl XLVI, 21-17, for the fourth NFL championship in franchise history.

A spectacular 38-yard Eli Manning-to-Mario Manningham sideline pass with three and a half minutes to play set New York on its way to the game-winning score. A short time later, the Patriots' defense let running back Ahmad Bradshaw score the game-winning touchdown with their eyes on giving Tom Brady as much time as possible to lead the team to a miracle finish.

That finish never came. A last-gasp end zone heave for Aaron Hernandez bounced around and then fell to the Navy-painted turf, setting the Giants sprinting toward one another in celebration and a hail of confetti swirling into the air at Lucas Oil Stadium.

"We just came up a little bit short there," Patriots coach Bill Belichick said. "That's all there is to say."

Said Giants coach Tom Coughlin, "All of the people really did a tremendous job. We had a couple penalties that I thought took points off the board. We got into halftime and I said, 'We can play better than this.' They agreed."

Manning was able to claim his second title and second Super Bowl MVP award in the house that his older brother, Peyton, built as the quarterback of the Indianapolis Colts.

Brady fell to 3-2 in Super Bowls.

"I said after the game that I'll keep coming to this game and keep trying," Brady said. "Hopefully we'll be back."

But the night belonged to Eli and a Giants team that began training camp with one motto: finish.

New York pulled off six must-win games – its final two games of the regular season, which got them into the playoffs as the NFC East champion and the number-four seed in the conference – plus four postseason victories to do just what they set out to do when camp kicked off in late July.

After allowing Bradshaw to score, Brady got the ball at his own 20-yard line with 57 seconds to play, and the Patriots had one timeout. His intended receivers – Deion Branch and Hernandez – had their hands on his first two passes but couldn't pull them in, and Brady was sacked on third down.

He linked up with Branch for a 19-yard gain on fourth down, keeping hope alive. An 11-yard completion to Hernandez followed, then a spike to kill the clock. Brady and Branch missed on a pass on third down, and then came the failed Hail Mary.

Things got off to a less than auspicious start for New England, at least offensively: after three straight tackles for loss, including two Eli Manning sacks, to force the Giants to punt, Tom Brady found his unit pinned just six yards from the goal line.

"We got into halftime and I said, 'We can play better than this.'

They agreed." Tom Coughlin, on his halftime message to his players

On their first snap, with Nate Solder on the field as an extra blocker, Brady was pressured through the middle and launched the ball down the center of the field. No one – not any Patriots and not any Giants – was close to being on the receiving end of the throw.

Flag. Intentional grounding. Safety. 2-0 Giants lead.

It was the sixth safety in Super Bowl history, and the first time since Super Bowl IX that the game's opening points came on a safety.

The Giants got the ball back and upped their lead, with one error by the New England defense inside the red zone helping their cause: Victor Cruz was stripped on a 4-yard reception by Sterling Moore and Brandon Spikes pounced on the loose ball.

But a *"12 men on the field"* flag negated the turnover and gave New York a fresh set of downs—11 yards from the end zone.

On second down, Manning zipped the ball in to Cruz for the touchdown and a 9-0 advantage for the Giants 12 minutes into the game.

At that point, the Giants had run 20 offensive plays to just one for the Patriots.

Unlike some weeks toward the end of the regular season, when New England dug itself sizable holes before successfully climbing out, the nine-point hole was as deep as it would get.

On the team's second possession, Brady found the reliable Branch for a 15-yard gain on third-and-4, which was followed by a 19-yard catch-and-run by Wes Welker. The Patriots got inside the red zone, but on third down, defensive end Jason Pierre-Paul got the first of his two batted balls in the first half, and they had to settle for a 29-yard field goal from Stephen Gostkowski to cut it to 9-3.

The Giants punted on their third and fourth drives, though New England went three-and-out on their possession in between. Steve Weatherford's second punt of the night was a gem, bouncing at the 4-yard line and then flying out of bounds.

No matter for Brady, who engineered a scoring drive even though he was forced back even further when left guard Logan Mankins was called for a false start on the first play. But then gains of five and three yards by Welker and BenJarvus Green-Ellis got them out of danger, and then Brady hit Rob Gronkowski for a 20-yard gain. The tight end was backpedaling as he made his catch and was taken down by two Giants.

But he got up and showed no ill effects of his ankle sprain suffered against the Ravens two weeks earlier.

Another penalty on the offensive line, a hold by Brian Waters, took a nice pickup on a screen to Danny Woodhead off the board. Brady relied on Woodhead and Hernandez during the drive, and Woodhead finished it with a four-yard touchdown reception.

Brady had good protection on the scoring pass, moved to his right and then back to his left before he found a pretty open Woodhead to give New England a 10-9 lead heading into halftime.

By virtue of deferring after winning the coin toss to start the game, the Patriots increased their lead from one point to eight quickly in the opening minutes of the third quarter.

Receiver Chad Ochocinco, who was one of four Patriots with 10 or more years in the NFL who were playing in the Super Bowl for the first time, got his moment on the first pass of the half, when he and Branch were the only receivers on the field and Brady found him on the left sideline for a 21-yard gain.

A long run from Green-Ellis put them well into Giants' territory, and Green-Ellis picked up four yards on third-and-1 a few plays later, giving the Patriots first down from the 20. On second-and-short, Brady found Hernandez, who took the ball into the end zone.

The Giants posted field goals on their next two drives while New England was unable to score, pulling to within two points.

Manningham made the difference: With 3:46 left and the Giants on their 12-yard line, Manning targeted Manningham at the 50. He needed to get New York away from its end zone, to get the team closer to a score.

Patrick Chung and Sterling Moore were on the coverage, but Manning snuck the ball in where Manningham could catch it and stay in bounds.

By that point, Manningham was ready, was waiting, to be the one to make the play. The Giants trailed, 17-15, with time dwindling. So, he and Cruz discussed the fact that someone had to do something.

"One of us is going to have to make a big play," Manningham said. "We didn't know when, though. So, you bite your tongue, be patient, and know the ball is going to come to you."

He felt no pressure. And then it happened. The ball came to him, and he made the play, he got his feet down. And though the play was challenged by the Patriots, it stood up on replay.

"Eli just threw a perfect ball," Manningham said. "I knew I had my feet in. But I just didn't know if the refs were going to try some funny stuff."

And Manningham downplayed any similarity to the Tyree situation. His catch wasn't as difficult, he said, wasn't as important, wasn't as big. His catch wasn't the one from four years ago.

"It was just a catch. I didn't catch it like this," Manningham said, mimicking Tyree's reception. "We work on that all the time, man, the sideline catch, a fade. We work on our footwork all the time."

The Giants picked up on the fact that that pass might be open to them throughout the game. And so, at that point, they went for it. They thought it might just work against the Cover-2 that the Patriots were playing.

"It took great concentration because it was over the shoulder, and to be able to know that he had to keep his feet in because it was right along the sideline," offensive coordinator Kevin Gilbride said. "He not only had to catch the ball, keep his feet in bounds, he was going to hold onto the ball right after he got hit. So, it was a tremendous play by him."

He had been waiting for that, knowing he was capable of such a catch. He had been listening to his mother's message all season. And he came through.

"You've just got to be patience, got to find it deep in yourself," Manningham said. "Just look at something positive, be patient. You don't know when the ball is going to come to you."

When two teams play in a winner-takes all match, unfortunately it is true that somebody also loses.

Chapter 23 Coach Bill Belichick Part III 2012-2017...

Coach Bill Belichick # 13

2012 Bill Belichick   NFL   AFC   East   1st   12 4 0
- Won Divisional Playoffs (Texans) 41–28
- Lost Conference Championship(Ravens) 13–28

2013 Bill Belichick   NFL   AFC   East   1st   12 4 0
- Won Divisional Playoffs (Colts) 43–22
- Lost Conference Championship (at Broncos) 16–26

2014 Bill Belichick   NFL   AFC   East   1st   12 4 0
- Won Divisional Playoffs (Ravens) 35–31
- Rob Gronkowski(CBPOY)
- Won Conference Championship(Colts) 45–7
- Tom Brady(SB MVP)[29]
- Won Super Bowl XLIX (4) (vs. Seahawks) 28–24

2015 Bill Belichick   NFL   AFC   East   1st   12 4 0
- Won Divisional Playoffs (Chiefs) 27–20
- Lost Conference Championship (at Broncos) 18–20

2016 Bill Belichick   NFL   AFC   East   1st   14 2 0
- Won Divisional Playoffs (Texans) 34–16
- Tom Brady(SB MVP)
- Won Conference Championship(Steelers) 36–17
- Won Super Bowl LI (5) (vs. Falcons) 34–28 (OT)

2017 Bill Belichick   NFL   AFC   East   1st   13 3 0
- Won Divisional Playoffs (Titans) 35–14
- Tom Brady(MVP)
- Won Conference Championship(Jaguars) 24–20
- Lost Super Bowl LII (vs. Patriots) 33–41

2000-2017 Bill Belichick final record (214-74-0)

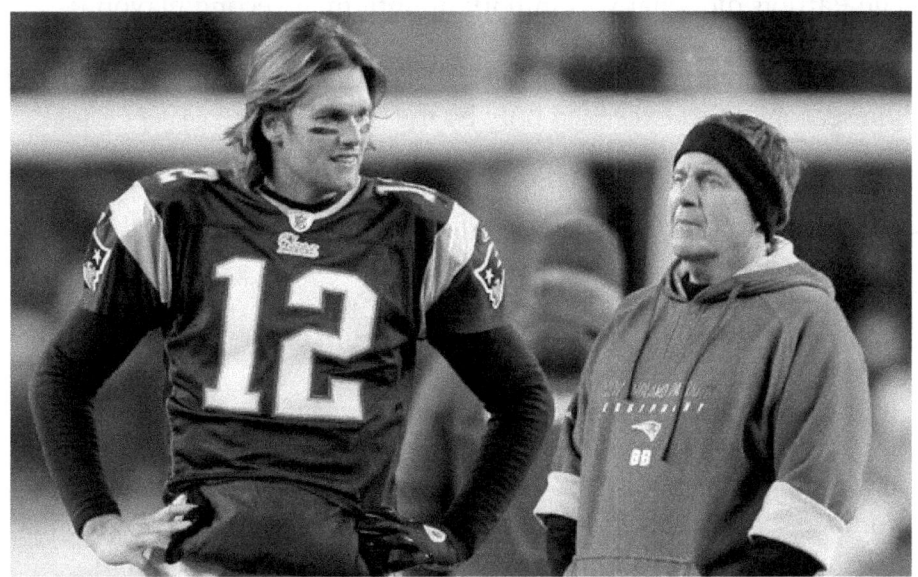

2012 Bill Belichick #14

The 2012 New England Patriots football team competed in their fifty-third season of professional football and their forty-third season in the National Football League (NFL). The Patriots were led by Coach Bill Belichick in his thirteenth of eighteen seasons (so-far). Robert Kraft was the Patriot's owner. The Patriots record was 12-4. They finished first in the AFC East Division, and they qualified for the playoffs. They first won the AFC Divisional Playoffs against the Texans 41–28, and then in the AFC Championship, they lost to the Ravens 13–28, and again, the Patriots missed the big dance, the rings, and the sweet cigars. But soon again!

This was the 11th season in which the Patriots played all of their home games at Gillette Stadium. The 2012 Patriots featured a prolific offense that had it all together and were ready to take it all the way. Then again, there is that luck factor.

The Patriots broke the record for first downs in a season, with 444, and they finished third all-time in scoring, with 557 points, finishing only behind the 2011 Green Bay Packers and their previous 2007 record setting season. Additionally, this was the third consecutive season that the Patriots exceeded 500 points scored, which tied the record set by the 1999– 2001 St. Louis Rams.

The Patriots did what was important until their second playoff game. They also ranked first in the league with a turnover margin of +25. This 12-win season marked the Patriots' tenth consecutive 10-win season, a feat exceeded only by the San Francisco 49ers' streak of 16, from 1983 to 1998, and it was their twelfth consecutive winning season. They are still a football phenomenon and as you will see, their Super Bowl days at this point are not behind them.

Unfortunately, on January 20, 2013, they were defeated by the Baltimore Ravens in the AFC Championship Game, marking their first AFC title game loss at home. The Patriots, Bill Belichick, Tom Brady, and company would be back with a vengeance.

In the season opener at Tennessee on September 9, the Patriots womped the Titans W (34–13) at LP Field. At home on Sept 16, the Arizona Cardinals beat the Patriots by two points L (18–20) in

Gillette Stadium. At Baltimore on Sept 23, in a one-point contest, the Ravens beat the Patriots L (30–31) at M&T Bank Stadium. Then, at Buffalo, on Sept 30, the Patriots delivered a big wallop to the Bills W (52–28) in a shootout at Ralph Wilson Stadium.

At home, the Patriots defeated the Denver Broncos W (31–21) at Gillette Stadium. At Seattle, on Oct 14, the Seahawks beat the Patriots in a one-point match L (23–24) at CenturyLink Field. Then, at home, on Oct 21. In OT, the Patriots beat the New York Jets W (29–26) in Gillette Stadium. Then, in Wembley Stadium in London England, on Oct 28, the Patriots smashed the St. Louis Rams W (45–7) In Week 9 on Nov4, the team drew a bye.

At home on Nov 11, New England beat Buffalo W (37–31) in Gillette Stadium. At home again on Nov 18, the Patriots thumped the Indianapolis Colts W (59–24) in Gillette Stadium. At New York on Nov 22, the Patriots lambasted the Jets W (49–19) at MetLife Stadium. Then, on Dec 2 at Miami, the Patriots beat the Dolphins W (23–16) at Sun Life Stadium.

At home on Dec 10, New England hammered Houston W (42–14) in Gillette Stadium. On Dec 16, the San Francisco 49ers beat the Patriots L (34–41) in Gillette Stadium. On Dec 23 at Jacksonville, the Patriots defeated the Jaguars W (23–16) at EverBank Field. Then in the season-ender at home, on Dec 30, the Patriots shut-out the Miami Dolphins W (28–0) in Gillette Stadium. The Patriots record was 12-4 and they would win the Divisional Championship playoffs and then compete in the Conference Championship.

The Divisional Playoffs January 13, 2013
Divisional Round vs. Houston Texans

	1	2	3	4	Total
Texans	3	10	0	15	28
Patriots	7	10	14	10	41

at Gillette Stadium, Foxborough, Massachusetts

This divisional playoff game began at 4:30 PM on January 13, 2012 at Gillette Stadium, Foxborough, Massachusetts. The weather was 51 °F, cloudy and mild. There was a packed house of 68,756 at this Patriots home game. After a 12-4 regular season record, the Patriots overwhelmed the Texans in this game W (41-28.

Daniel Manning took off like a bullet and returned the game's opening kickoff 94 yards to the Patriots 12. The Texans could not get it in the end-zone after a 3-yard run by Foster, and back-to-back incompletions forced. So, they settled for a 27-yard field goal by Shayne Graham. This gave them their early 3-0 lead. After a Patriots three-and-out, the Texans drove to the Patriots 45, but were stopped cold and forced to punt.

It was three possessions later that the Patriots finally got to work and their work got them on the board. They marched 65 yards in 6 plays, scoring on Vereen's 1-yard touchdown run. The Texans then drove deep into their own territory on their next drive but were forced to punt. The Patriots responded by driving all the way to the Texans 19, and took a 10-3 lead on Gostkowski's 37-yard field goal.

With the Patriots up 10-3, the Texans drove to the Patriots 43, but got stuck and punted. The Patriots made them pay for the punt by mounting a drive that put up 80 yards in 7 plays. The Pats scored on an 8-yard TD catch by Vereen, increasing their lead to 17-3. On that drive, the highlight was a 47-yard catch by Welker, which gave him a new franchise record for postseason catches (59). On the play, he eclipsed the legend Troy Brown.

Manning returned the following kickoff 35 yards to the Texans 38. A highly aggressive horse-collar tackle gave the Texans a first down on the Patriots 47. The Texans did not muff this opportunity. Instead, they spent just 5 plays to strike on Foster's 1-yard touchdown run, bringing the deficit to 17-10 with just over a minute left in the first half. After forcing the Patriots to a quick three-and-out, the Texans again were threatening—this time at the Patriots 37. Graham nailed a 55-yard field goal, bringing the score to 17-13 at halftime.

New England regretted how the first half had ended and they took over in the second half. Slater took the 2nd half kickoff 19 yards to the Patriots 31. From there the Patriots fully engaged in a 69-yard march in 7 plays, which ended with an 8-yard touchdown run by Ridley. This put the Patriots up by 11, 24-13.

The Texans threatened as soon as they got the ball back driving deep into Patriots territory, to the 37. It was for naught as Schaub was intercepted by Ninkovich at the 31. It took the Patriots under three minutes to go the 63 yards, scoring on Lloyd's 5-yard touchdown catch, making the lead 31-13.

This toss was Brady's 40th career TD pass in the postseason, making him only the third pro player to reach such a milestone in the postseason. The Texans got to their own 23 on the next drive. However, on 4th-and-1, Schaub through a long but incomplete pass.

The Pats took over and then Brady hit Vereen on a 33-yard touchdown pass. It was Vereen's third touchdown of the game, putting the game away with a 38-13 score. That's all she wrote.

This was the 5th 300-yard postseason game for Brady and Vereen tied Curtis Martin and Gronkowski with three touchdowns in a playoff game. Manning continued his great returning with a 69-yard return to the Patriots 37. Five plays later, Schaub hit DeVier Posey on a 25-yard touchdown pass, trimming the deficit to 38-20, but it was already too late; but nobody had told the Texans.

After a Patriots punt, the Texans marched 73 yards in 11 plays, scoring on Schaub's 1-yard touchdown pass to Foster on 4th-and-Goal. They followed this with a successful two-point conversion. Now the difference was just 38-28 with 5:11 left and the Patriots had gone flat. Texas now had a chance, but Ninkovich recovered the ensuing onside kick and New England sucked the clock dry all the way down to 1:14, when Gostkowski kicked a 38-yard field goal, lifting the score to 41-28.

The Texans still thought they could pull the game out. They drove to the Patriots 41, but the clock ran out right after Schaub hit Daniels for a 9-yard gain. They put up a good fight.

Tom Brady was outstanding as usual and he became the winningest quarterback in NFL playoff history with his 17th postseason win.

This win broke a tie with legendary Joe Montana. Besides that, record, it was also the 450th victory (regular season and playoffs) in franchise history.

AFC Championship Playoffs January 20, 2013

AFC Championship vs. Baltimore Ravens

	1	2	3	4	Total
Ravens	0	7	7	14	28
Patriots	3	10	0	0	13

This Conference Championship Game began at 6:30 PM on January 20, 2010 at Gillette Stadium, Foxborough, Massachusetts. The weather was 41 °F, clear and windy. There was a packed house of 68,756 at this Patriots home game. After a 12-4 regular season record, the New England Patriots were overpowered by the Baltimore Ravens in this game L (13-28).

The win against the Texans in the Division Championship moved the Patriots into the AFL-AFC Title Game for the tenth time in franchise history. It would be the ninth under the AFC banner and a rematch of the 2011 title game (as well as a rematch of the week 3 encounter with the Baltimore Ravens.

Just as they had the previous season, the Patriots faced the Ravens at home for the right to represent the AFC in the Super Bowl. The Patriots lead 13–7 in the first half; but were shut out for the second half by the Ravens. With the loss, the Patriots concluded their season with a record of 13-5 overall and dropped to 1-2 against the Ravens during the postseason (all 3 playoff meetings have occurred at Gillette Stadium). This would also be the first time Tom Brady would lose a home game after leading at halftime.

2013 Bill Belichick #14

The 2013 New England Patriots football team competed in their fifty-fourth season of professional football and their forty-fourth season in the National Football League (NFL). The Patriots were led by Coach Bill Belichick in his fourteenth of eighteen seasons (so-far). Robert Kraft was the Patriot's owner. The Patriots record was 12-4 for the second year in a row and the team grabbed the #2 seed for the 2nd year in a row along with a first round playoff bye for the fourth year in a row. T

They finished first in the AFC East Division, and they qualified for the playoffs. They first won the AFC Divisional Playoffs against the Colts W (43–22), and then in the AFC Championship, they lost to the Broncos L (16-26), and again, the Patriots missed the big dance, the rings, and the sweet cigars. But soon again! How about the next year?

In the season opener at Buffalo on September 8, 2013, the Patriots squeezed out a W 23–21 win against the Bills at Ralph Wilson Stadium. On September 12 in the home opener, the Patriots beat the New York Jets W (13–10) at Gillette Stadium. At home again on Sept 22, the Patriots defeated the Tampa Bay Buccaneers W (23–3) in Gillette Stadium. At Atlanta on Sept 29 for the fourth win in a row with no losses, the Patriots beat the Falcons W (30–23) at the Georgia Dome.

At Cincinnati on Oct 6, the Bengals defeated the Patriots L (6–13) at Paul Brown Stadium. On Oct 13, in OT, the New Orleans Saints were taken down by the New England Patriots W (30–27) in Gillette Stadium. At New York, on Oct 20, in OT, the Jets beat the Pats L (27–30) at MetLife Stadium. At home on October 27, New England's Patriots defeated Miami's Dolphins W (27–17) in Gillette Stadium.

On Nov 3, in a shootout at home, the Patriots defeated the Pittsburgh Steelers W (55–31) in Gillette Stadium. On Nov 10, there was a bye week. Then, at Carolina on Nov 18, the Panthers beat the Patriots L (20–24) in Bank of America Stadium. At home on Nov 24 in OT, the Patriots beat the Denver Broncos W (34–31(in Gillette

Stadium. At Houston on Dec 1, the Patriots defeated the Texans W (34–31) in Reliant Stadium.

At home on Dec 8, in a one-point match, the Patriots got the best of the Cleveland Browns W (27–26) in Gillette Stadium. At Miami on Dec 15, the Dolphins beat the Patriots L (20–24) at Sun Life Stadium. At Baltimore, on Dec 22, the Patriots smashed the Ravens W (41–7) at M&T Bank Stadium. At home for the season finale at Gillette Stadium, on Dec 29 the Patriots defeated the Buffalo Bills W (34–20).

The Patriots record was a healthy 12-4 and they would make the playoffs and they would win the Divisional Championship playoffs. Ten, they would compete in the Conference Championship.

The Divisional Playoffs January 11, 2014

Divisional Round vs. Indianapolis Colts

	1	2	3	4	Total
Colts	7	5	10	0	22
Patriots	14	7	8	14	43

At Gillette Stadium, Foxborough, Massachusetts

This divisional playoff game began at 8:15 PM on January 11, 2014 at Gillette Stadium, Foxborough, Massachusetts. The weather was 57 °F, rainy and windy. There was a packed house of 68,756 at this Patriots home game. After a 12-4 regular season record, the Patriots overwhelmed the Colts in this game W (43-22).

The Patriots are such a phenomenal team even though they may not register number one in the NFL each year, they get their share of #1 finishes. If there were no playoffs, it would be difficult declare a number one other than the Patriots once you see them play. I have watched the Boston Patriots and now the New England Patriots play in the archives and the recent record books from the 1960 Boston Patriots. I admit that I am impressed. Anybody who is honest with themselves feels the same. The Patriots are impressive and with Bill Belichick and Tom Brady teaming up on the unsuspecting teams in the NFL, it is not a fair game.

Starting in the next season about which I report in this book, you will find a team that recovers from two Conference Playoff losses in a row, and undaunted, goes ahead and wins two out of the next three Super Bowls, and then qualifies for a third Super Bowl in 2017, only to be beaten in a miracle game in favor of the Philadelphia Eagles. Who knows what is going to happen in 2018? I am expecting that it will be very exciting and that any team facing a Patriot team had better watch out on every play as the Patriots are about as good as it gets in football.

Some pundits have reported that in these games in 2014, the Patriots punched their own ticket through excellence to their 3rd straight AFC Championship game in a 43–22 dominating victory over the rival Colts.

The Patriots are always ready to play even if the result of the play does not reflect the coach's planning and the intended execution. You may know that in the week leading up to the AFC Division round matchup, the Patriots made their game-plan crystal clear. Their mission was to take advantage of the Colt's questionable run defense by using a healthy dose of their three threats out of the backfield: Legarrette Blount, Stevan Ridley and Shane Vereen.

This game-plan was in two words, "extremely effective," as New England scored six touchdowns on the ground in this game. Blount set a franchise postseason record by scoring four of the six TD's. Having played a little football myself, and never wanting to fully (100%) sacrifice myself to make the play, (Sorry, I am a writer!), I can appreciate why there is nobody on any team that enjoys going after the construction-size-machine and being bulldozed by Legarrette Blount. What a machine! What a gift to have such a player on the Patriots squad.

The three backs combined for 235 yards rushing, 166 coming from Blount alone, also a franchise postseason record. The Patriot defense was exemplary, picking off Andrew Luck four times, sacking him three times and relatively shutting down star wide receiver T.Y. Hilton for the majority of the game, although he did finish with 103 yards on four receptions. Checking the final tally folks, the Patriots had the higher score.

AFC Championship Playoffs January 19, 2014

AFC Championship vs. Denver Broncos

	1	2	3	4	Total
Broncos	3	10	7	6	26
Patriots	0	3	0	13	16

Sports Authority Field at Mile High Stadium

This Conference Championship Game began at 3:00 PM on January 19, 2014 at Sports Authority Field at Mile High Stadium in Denver Colorado. The weather was 63 °F, sunny There was a packed house of 77,110 at this Denver home game. After a 12-4 regular season record, the New England Patriots were overpowered by the Denver Broncos in this game L (16-26).

The Patriots had been doing so well since Belichick and Brady had combined to become the torment of the rest of the NFL, this year was the first since 2006, in which the Patriots regular season record caused them to play on the road in the playoffs. Incidentally, this was also the last time they faced Peyton Manning when he was with the Indianapolis Colts.

The story was all about Denver in this playoff game as their offense racked up 507 yards without turning the ball over or giving up any sacks. The Broncos forgot that they were playing what I have become to think of as the invincible Patriots. The Broncos took no prisoners and advanced to their seventh Super Bowl in franchise history. They were annoyed about a week 12 defeat to New England in which the Patriots rallied from a 24–0 halftime deficit to come up with the "W."

Peyton Manning loved to win every game as much as the Patriots loved to win every game. Peyton set a conference championship record with 32 completions for 400 yards and two touchdowns. The team also got a standout performance from receiver Demaryius Thomas. He plugged into Manning for seven passes accounting for 134 yards and a touchdown.

Kicker Matt Prater had done more than just suited up for the game. He pumped in four field goals. The win was not at all satisfying for Bill Belichick. However, it was especially satisfying for Denver head coach John Fox, who lost to Tom Brady and Bill Belichick in Super Bowl XXXVIII 10 years earlier when he was with the Carolina Panthers. Sores in the mind do not heal well even as time passes.

Midway through the first quarter, the older Manning, Peyton got the Broncos ready to score with an 18-yard completion to Knowshon Moreno, a 29-yard pass to Thomas, and a 19-yarder to Eric Decker. Prater finished the drive with a 27-yard field goal to put the team up 3–0.

The next time that the Broncos had the ball, they moved 93 yards in 15 plays on a drive that took up nearly half the second quarter. It was not easy as when they faced third and 10 from the Patriots' 39-yard line, they worked to get yardage such as making the conversion with a 28-yard draw play by Moreno. In this series, Manning eventually got the team into the end zone with a 1-yard pass to tight end Jacob Tamme, making the score 10–0.

Having two future legends in this game made it especially interesting for the fans. Some consider both Brady and Manning current-day legends with no more record additions necessary. In this game, however, New England managed to respond. Brady completed a 27-yard pass to receiver Aaron Dobson on the first play of the next drive. This 27-yarder was Brady's longest completion of the game.

The Patriots pursuit of the goal line eventually got them to the Broncos' 18-yard line. However, Denver lineman Robert Ayers sacked Brady for an 11-yard loss on third down, forcing the Pats to settle for a perfect Stephen Gostkowski's 47-yard field goal. A TD would have been nice.

Denver then took the ball back and drove for more Bronco points, as Peyton Manning hooked up with Thomas for a pair of completions that moved the chains 53 yards. Prater was ready and when he came in, he finished things off with a 35-yard field goal. This gave Denver a 13–3 lead with 25 seconds left in the half. The whistle blew, and everybody got a half-time rest.

Denver got its aces together and scored on a long touchdown drive that took up over seven minutes. They were not about to give up the ball as they advanced the pigskin 80 yards in 13 plays. Peyton Manning enjoyed completing seven of his eight passes for 59 yards of gained yardage on the drive. He found the Broncos on the three-yard line. So, his last TD toss to Thomas that increased Denver's lead to 20–3 was just 3-yards into pay dirt.

New England was not ready to hand in the towel. They responded with a drive to the Broncos' 29-yard line. However, when there was a fourth down and 2-yards, conversion attempt, despite the desire of the Patriots O-line. Tom Brady took a sack for a 10-yard loss. The Broncos cheered defensive tackle Terrance Knighton. Denver then took over and set up a drive for more points that no Patriot fan was interested in seeing.

Manning would not quit and so he got his accuracy gun out and completed two passes to tight end Julius Thomas for 28 yards and he also tossed a completion to Demaryius Thomas for 30. New England was pleased at the time to manage to halt the drive at their own 1, but Prater kicked his third field goal to rub some more salt into an already festering would as Denver went up 23–3.

New England was not out of the game, and so they finally scored a touchdown with just over nine minutes left in the fourth quarter. Starting the drive with an 18-yard pass to tight end Michael Hoomanawanui, Brady followed it up with completions to Austin Collie and Julian Edelman for gains of 20 and 16 yards.

He eventually completed the drive with a 7-yard touchdown pass to Edelman, cutting the score to 23–10. However, Denver scored again with their next possession, with Manning's 37-yard completion to Julius Thomas setting up Prater's fourth field goal, this one from 54 yards.

New England went on to face a 26–10 deficit with seven minutes left in regulation. Tom Brady took charge of this swan-song 2014 game and completed five of seven passes for 54 yards on their next drive, and then Tom Brady took the ball into the end zone himself on a 5-yard run.

However, their two-point conversion attempt failed. And, so, the score stayed 26–16. Then after Decker recovered New England's onside kick, Denver managed to run the final 3:07 off the clock with their last drive. The Pats could not get the ball back and thus this lost was assured.

Tom Brady finished his day 24-for-38 for 277 yards and a touchdown. He also had two carries for seven yards and a score on the ground. Edelman was on the mark for the day, catching 10 passes for 89 yards and a touchdown. Thomas had eight receptions for 85 yards for Denver, while Decker had five catches for 73.

No matter how well every Patriot played, the element of luck was missing, and there was more than a regular performance needed to suck this game out of the coffers of the Denver Broncos. Looking through hindsight, I bet that no matter who lines up as an opponent of the Patriots during the playoffs in the next year, nobody will beat the fantastabulous New England Patriots for the Super Bowl trophy package. No way! No how! See if I am right by reading about the next season under Bill Belichick.

2014 Bill Belichick #14

The 2014 New England Patriots football team competed in their fifty-fifth season of professional football and their forty-fifth season in the National Football League (NFL). The Patriots were led by Coach Bill Belichick in his fifteenth of eighteen seasons (so-far). Robert Kraft was the Patriot's owner. The Patriots record was 12-4 for the third year in a row and the team grabbed the #1 seed for the

2nd year in a row along with a first round playoff bye for the fifth year in a row. The bye for five years in a row, was the first such occurrence for any team since the league switched to a 12-team playoff format in 1990. They finished fourth overall in the NFL in scoring (468 points) and eighth in points allowed (313), and first in point differential (with an average margin of victory of 9.7 points).

This was a year of firsts and bests. They finished first in the AFC East Division, and they naturally qualified for the playoffs. They first won their sixth straight AFC Divisional Title in the playoffs against the Colts W (35-31), and then in the AFC Championship, they pounded the Indianapolis Colts W (45-7), and this time, the Patriots were invited to the big dance, The Super Bowl, with the rings, and the sweet cigars. In Super Bowl XLIX, the Patriots won a hard-fought battle against former Pats coach Pete Carrol's Seattle Seahawks, W (28-24) This great win gave New England their fourth championship in franchise history.

We present a newspaper article from the Boston Globe depicting just how the Patriots won the Super Bowl. To whet your appetite, it helps to remember that after tying the game 14–14 at halftime and falling behind ten points in the third quarter, the Patriots rallied in the final quarter of the game to secure a 28–24 lead. For you avid writers out there, in this season and this Super Bowl Victory, that is all she wrote.

Teach me about Super Bowl Seeding

There are many great sources for statistics and writeups about the NFL on the Internet. One of many sources that was very helpful in researching this book is Wikipedia, a source which those in Academia often choose not to cite but nonetheless, they are a fountain of mostly good and accurate information. This piece on Super Bowl seeding below is from Wikipedia.

> Within each conference, the four division winners and the two wild card teams (the top two non-division winners with the best overall regular season records) qualified for the playoffs. The four division winners are seeded 1 through 4 based on their overall won-lost-tied record, and the wild card teams are seeded

5 and 6. The NFL does not use a fixed bracket playoff system, and there are no restrictions regarding teams from the same division matching up in any round.

2014/2015 Season Playoff seeds

Seed	AFC	NFC
1	New England Patriots (East winner)	Seattle Seahawks (West winner)
2	Denver Broncos (West winner)	Green Bay Packers (North winner)
3	Pittsburgh Steelers (North winner)	Dallas Cowboys (East winner)
4	Indianapolis Colts (South winner)	Carolina Panthers (South winner)
5	Cincinnati Bengals (wild card)	Arizona Cardinals (wild card)
6	Baltimore Ravens (wild card)	Detroit Lions (wild card)

In the first round, dubbed the wild-card playoffs or wild-card weekend, the third-seeded division winner hosts the sixth seed wild card, and the fourth seed hosts the fifth. The 1 and 2 seeds from each conference then receive a bye in the first round. In the second round, the divisional playoffs, the number 1 seed hosts the worst surviving seed from the first round (seed 4, 5 or 6), while the number 2 seed will play the other team (seed 3, 4 or 5).

The two surviving teams from each conference's divisional playoff games then meet in the respective AFC and NFC Conference Championship games, hosted by the higher seed. Although the Super Bowl, the fourth and final round of the playoffs, is played at a neutral site, the designated home team is based on an annual rotation by conference.

In the season opener at Miami on September 7, 2014, the Dolphins defeated the Patriots L (20–33) at Sun Life Stadium. At Minnesota on Sept 14, the Patriots squashed the Vikings W (30–7) at TCF Bank Stadium. In the home opener on Sept 21, the New England Patriots defeated the Oakland Raiders W (16–9) in Gillette Stadium. Then, on Sept 29 at Kansas City, the Chiefs slammed the Patriots L (14–41) at Arrowhead Stadium.

On Oct 5, at home, New England pounded Cincinnati W (43–17) in Gillette Stadium. At Buffalo on Oct 12, the Patriots beat the Bills W (37–22) at Ralph Wilson Stadium. On Oct 16, at home, the Patriots beat the New York Jets W (27–25) in Gillette Stadium. On Oct 26, at home, the Patriots overpowered the Chicago Bears W (51–23) in Gillette Stadium. Then on Nov 2 at home, New England thumped Denver W (43–21) in Gillette Stadium. On Nov 9, week 10, the team drew a bye.

At Indianapolis on Nov 16, the Patriots whipped the Colts W (42–20) in Lucas Oil Stadium. On Nov 23, at home, the Patriots whooped the Detroit Lions W (34–9) in Gillette Stadium. At Green Bay on Nov 30, the Packers beat the Patriots L 21–26 in (Lambeau Field). On Dec 7 at San Diego, New England defeated the Chargers W (23–14) at Qualcomm Stadium.

On Dec 14, at home, the Patriots scorched the Miami Dolphins W (41–13) in Gillette Stadium. At New York, in a one-point match, on Dec 21, the Pats nosed out the Jets W (17–16) in MetLife Stadium. In the final game of a successful season, the Patriots ended with a loss at home on Dec 28 against the Buffalo Bills L (9–17) in Gillette Stadium.

The Divisional Playoffs January 10, 2015
Divisional Round vs. Baltimore Ravens

	1	2	3	4	Total
Ravens	14	7	70	3	31
Patriots	7	7	14	7	35

At Gillette Stadium, Foxborough, Massachusetts

This divisional playoff game began at 4:35 PM on January 10, 2015 at Gillette Stadium, Foxborough, Massachusetts. The weather was 20 °F, clear, windy, and cold. There was a packed house of 68,756 at this Patriots home game. After a 12-4 regular season record, the Patriots squeaked by the Ravens in this game W (35-21).

Nothing in life worth having is easy. And, so it was not easy for the Patriots in this first playoff game on the way to another destiny season. Never fully in control but never fully out of control of this flip-flop game, the Patriots could have seen this encounter go either way, but the Patriots finally came through and simply outplayed the Ravens and grabbed the win.

The Pats became just the third NFL team to wipe-out two 14-point deficits to win a game (the last to do it was the 2003 Chiefs) and the first to pull off the feat in a playoff game, rallying from down 14–0 and 28–14 to win 35–31. Tom Brady lived up to his billing again as he threw for three touchdowns and ran in a fourth.

After the opening kickoff, the Ravens zipped 71 yards in under three minutes to take a 7–0 lead. Joe Flacco was on target hitting rookie wide receiver Kamar Aiken on a 19-yard TD pass. After a Patriots three-and-out, Flacco took the Ravens down the field once again. This time, the drive covered 79 yards in exactly six minutes. Flacco capped it off with a 9-yard touchdown pass to Steve Smith. Out of nowhere, Baltimore surprisingly had a 14-0 lead.

The Patriots came right back on their next drive. They were assisted by a 46-yard pass to Gronkowski. The Patriots drove 78 yards culminating in 8 plays with Brady tucking and running in for a 4-yard TD. During this TD run, Tom Brady tied Curtis Martin's club record for rushing touchdowns in the playoffs with less than a minute remaining in the first quarter.

Midway through the second quarter, New England took off on a 67-yard drive that consumed just three-and-a half minutes to tie the game at 14-14. It was a 15-yard touchdown pass to wide receiver Danny Amendola. A 23-yard completion to Gronkowski earlier on the drive gave Brady 6,595 career passing yards in the postseason, a new NFL record. The touchdown pass gave him 44 touchdown passes in the playoffs, tying him with Brett Favre with second behind only Montana (who has 45).

After the Ravens clocked in and out with a three-and-out, there was just over a minute remaining in the first half. The Pats got the ball back and Brady was intercepted by Ravens linebacker Daryl Smith at the Ravens 43. On 2nd-and-10 from the Patriots 44, Flacco threw incomplete for Steve Smith, but Revis was flagged for illegal contact. This action gave the Ravens a first at the Patriots 24. Three plays later, Flacco hit tight end Owen Daniels for a touchdown putting the Ravens on top 21–14 with 10 seconds left in the half. Brady took a knee to end the half.

Amendola got the 2nd half kick-off and took it 28 yards to the Patriots 26, but the Pats were forced to punt after a Brady to Gronkowski incompletion. Sometimes what does not happen is significant. On this play there was a controversial pass interference no-call on Ravens rookie linebacker C. J. Mosley. The Ravens took advantage of the no-call and drove 70 yards with Flacco throwing a 16-yard touchdown pass to Ravens running back Justin Forsett out of the backfield. It was Flacco's fourth TD pass of the game and the Ravens again were ahead by 14, 28–14. This quieted the formerly raucus Patriots home crowd.

The Patriots were driven to come back. They took the ball to the Ravens 24 on their next drive. A 14-yard catch by Michael Hoomanawanui gave the Patriots a first down at the Ravens 10. Then, an unsportsmanlike conduct penalty on the Ravens bench moved the ball to the 5. Two plays later, Brady found Gronkowski for the touchdown, reducing the lead to 7 points. and tying Brady with Joe Montana for the most postseason touchdown passes.

After the kickoff, the ravens were out quickly, three-and-out, and the Patriots needed just three plays to tie the game at 28-all. On the quick drive, Brady had completions to Edelman and Vereen for 9 and 10 yards, respectively. Then, Brady he threw a lateral pass to Edelman, who then proceeded to throw a 51-yard touchdown strike to a wide-open Danny Amendola. This was Edelman's first career passing touchdown, tying the game at 28-28.

On the second play of the Ravens next drive, the Patriots snagged a turnover when McCourty intercepted Flacco at the Ravens 37. The Pats could not move the ball, and they chose to punt rather than attempt a 55-yard field goal.

The Ravens took off like inspiration incarnated. They zipped down the field with just over three minutes remaining in the third quarter, to the Patriots 7, in 16 plays. On third down, Daniels dropped a pass in the end zone from Flacco, thanks to excellent coverage by Patrick Chung, who was having a great comeback season, and the Ravens settled for a 25-yard field goal from Justin Tucker, taking a 31-28 lead fairly early in the fourth quarter.

On the next drive, Brady led the Patriots down the field, with the drive finishing with a 23-yard pass to LaFell with 5:21, giving the Patriots their first lead of the game, 35-31. With the pass, Brady set a new NFL record with 46 career postseason touchdown passes. He also set franchise single-game postseason records in passing yards (367) and completions (33).

On the next drive after the kickoff, the Ravens moved to the Patriots' 36-yard line. On 2nd-and-5, with 1:47 to go, Duron Harmon stepped in front of a Joe Flacco deep toss and took it in for the Patriots. New England took a knew three times and each time the Ravens called time-out. After the third knee and time-out, there were 14 seconds on the clock. The Patriots had to punt.

The Ravens were close enough for a Hail Mary and so it was. On the final play of the game Flacco's desperation heave was batted out of the end zone and was batted down to the ground at about the 5-yard line. This confirmed the Patriots' victory and sent them to their fourth consecutive AFC Championship Game.

The game was very intense as both teams were travelling on the road to the Super Bowl. Each team was trying to place big detours in front of the other. Tempers were seen and several skirmishes between Patriot and Raven players occurred. A highly noted controversy was quite visible when Ravens coach John Harbaugh accused the Patriots of using a formation that made unclear which receivers were eligible or ineligible, thereby causing confusion on the field.

The Patriots used this "strange" formation to gain a total of over 40 yards on their game-winning drive. Brady dismissed Harbaugh's comments in his postgame press conference. The NFL sided with the Patriots and agreed that the substitutions and plays by the Patriots were legal. There were similar formations were used by the Jaguars, the Lions, and the Bengals during the season. This was a great start to the playoffs for the Patriots.

AFC Championship Playoffs January 19, 2015

AFC Championship vs. Denver Broncos

	1	2	3	4	Total
Colts	0	7	0	0	7
Patriots	14	3	21	7	45

at Gillette Stadium, Foxborough, Massachusetts

This Conference Championship Game began at 6:50 PM on January 18, 2015 at Gillette Stadium, Foxborough Massachusetts. The weather was 51 °F, rain. There was a packed house of 68,756 at this Patriot home game. After a 12-4 regular season record, and the victory in the Division Playoffs, the New England Patriots soundly defeated the Indianapolis Colts in this game W (45-7).

Going into this game, the Colts were underdogs. The two teams had been like old shoes or a pair of shoes as they played so often. This would be the fourth time in just three seasons (the second time in the playoffs). The Patriots of course were looking to claim their sixth AFC Championship crown. The game conditions were not ideal with a downpour going on at Gillette. The weather gave nobody an advantage as both teams played in the same conditions.

The two teams started slowly with three-and-outs on their first drives of the game. As the Pats punted on their first drive, Josh Cribbs, the Colts return-man, muffed the punt. The ball bounced off his helmet and the Patriots' Darius Fleming recovered at the Colts 26. Five plays later, LeGarrette Montez Blount appeared to score on a 4-yard touchdown run. However, he was short. The official review showed that he was not in the end-zone. Knowing Blount as a key Pats weapon, most fans would expect, and they would get another try from Blount and this time, he did score from 1-yard out.

The Colts then put on a drive of 47 yards to the Patriots 34, but ex-Patriots Adam Vinatieri missed wide-right on his 52-yard field goal attempt. This gave the Patriots excellent field position at the Colts 47. They capitalized when Brady hit fullback James Develin for a 1 yd TD after a 30-yard catch by Vereen. The Pats had themselves a 14-0 lead after this late 1Q action.

The Colts punted after the kickoff and the Patriots began another gallop. This one was 44 yards to the Colts 26. This would not be a score as D'Qwell Jackson intercepted Brady's pass at the 1-yard line and returned it six yards. This time the Colts scored after a 93-yard 10-play drive assisted by a 36-yard catch by T. Y. Hilton. The Colts got in the end zone on a 1-yard scamper by Zurlon Tipton, making the deficit 7 points at 14-7.

The Patriots began their own drive, which went on for 65 yards to the Colts 3 but were stopped and they chose to settle for a 21-yard field goal by Gostkowski. This gave the Patriots a 17-7 lead. Andrew Luck took a knee and the game went to halftime.

It had been a fairly even ballgame during the first half, but the Patriots let it loose in the second half. After the kickoff, for example, they raced 87 yards in just 9 plays, with Brady hitting left tackle Nate Solder. He set up as an eligible receiver for the play, and they snagged a 16-yard touchdown out of the action thereby increasing their lead to 24–7. It was Solder's first career reception and touchdown.

The Patriots defense shut down Colt quarterback Andrew Luck for the entire half while Tom Brady and the Patriots offense continued to roll and roll up the scoring. After a Colts three-and-out, for example, the Patriots marched 62 yards in 8 plays. Brady hit Gronkowski with a 5-yard TD pass to make the lead 31–7. After four plays. Luck was intercepted by Darrelle Revis. It was Revis' third career playoff interception, and he returned it 30 yards to the Colts 13. On the very next play, Blount smashed through for 13 yards to the end-zone, his 2nd touchdown of the night. This laid the fate of the game in cement at 38–7.

When the Colts punted again, Edelman returned it 45 yards to the Colts 45. After a penalty added 5 more yards, the ball was on the colts' 40. It took 11 plays and over six minutes for the next touchdown from such a close distance. later, Blount literally burrowed through for his third touchdown of the night. This gave him 148 rushing yards for the game, second most in franchise history. On the next drive, Jamie Collins intercepted Luck. The next three drives were all three-and-outs before the Colts ran out the final 1:51 of clock tome.

Tom Brady made a record every play, or so it seemed. He extended his NFL record of playoff starts to 28, finished 23 of 35 for 226 yards three touchdowns and 1 interception. This was Brady's 7th career playoff game with 3 touchdowns, second only to Joe Montana's 9. Blount was once again the star for the Pats against the Colts, carrying the ball 30 times, a Patriots postseason record, for 148 yard and three touchdowns.

Continuing a trend of poor play versus the Patriots, Luck completed a bottomless 12 of 33 passes for 126 yards, with no touchdowns and 2 interceptions. For his career, Andrew Luck fell to 0–4 against the Patriots, including two playoff losses. They would lose 34-27 in the

2015 season. In those four games, the Patriots outscored the Colts 189–73. Andrew Luck had little luck on Gillette Stadium, throwing 9 career interceptions in three games played at Gillette Stadium.

Super Bowl XLIX February 1, 2015

	1	2	3	4	Total
Patriots	0	14	0	14	28
Seahawks	0	14	10	0	24

*** This goes down as one of the greatest Patriot games of all time ***

The Super Bowl XLIX kickoff was at 6:30 EST February 5, 2012. The weather was 66 degrees and the retractable roof was open. Led by starter Tom Brady, the Bill Belichick-led NE Patriots overcame the Seattle Seahawks in a tight match 28-24 at University of Phoenix Stadium in Glendale Arizona. before a packed house of 70,288. After a 12-4 regular season record, the Patriots played a great match with the New York Giants, winning the contest W (28-24) in a comeback effort.

The Patriots faced the defending-Super Bowl champion Seattle Seahawks in Super Bowl XLIX (49) 49. For the second year in a row the Seahawks boasted the #1 ranked defense (1st against the pass, 3rd against the run). This was the Patriots' first Super Bowl appearance since 2011, when they lost to the NY Giants. This was the stadium where the 18-0 Patriots lost to the Giants in Super Bowl XLII.

Boston Globe

Three plays in Super Bowl XLIX that the pundits at the Boston Globe believe really stand out as critical to the Patriots' victory over the Seahawks are as follows
:
1. **Julian Edelman 21-yard reception**
2. **Julian Edelman touchdown reception**
3. **Dont'a Hightower's tackle of Marshawn Lynch**

Julian Edelman scored the game-winning points on a three-yard touchdown pass play.

Julian Edelman is tackled by Kam Chancellor in the fourth quarter.

Julian Edelman's fourth-quarter touchdown provided the game-winning points.

Marshawn Lynch was kept out of the end zone on the Seahawks' second-to-last offensive play.

I enjoyed researching the Boston Papers to get the scoop the way it actually happened in 2015. This fine write-up from the Boston Globe at the time it was written gave New England fans enough of the Super Bowl that they felt they were there. Nice job Shalise Manza Young. She titled her article:

Patriots rally to beat Seahawks in Super Bowl

By **Shalise Manza Young** GLOBE STAFF FEBRUARY **02, 2015**

GLENDALE, Ariz. — The last time the New England Patriots played a Super Bowl in the Arizona desert, it was a most unlikely hero who made the play of the game, a play that broke the Patriots' backs.

This time the Patriots returned to the desert for Super Bowl XLIX, and it was again a most unlikely hero who made the play of the game, this time the play that delivered Lombardi Trophy No. 4 to New England.

The Patriots beat the Seattle Seahawks, 28-24, to reclaim the title of NFL champions thanks to an end-zone interception by undrafted rookie cornerback Malcolm Butler.

The interception capped an impressive second-half comeback by the Patriots, who seemed to be in control in the first half, only to rather quickly fall behind by 10 points in the third quarter.

But the improved defense, the one lauded all season as the best New England has fielded in a decade, once again shut out the opponent in the fourth quarter and the offense regrouped from some miscues to string together two fourth-quarter touchdowns.

Improbable comeback gives Patriots 4th title

Super Bowl MVP Tom Brady set multiple records in a thrilling finish.

"I couldn't be prouder of this team," said Bill Belichick, just the second coach in NFL history to lead his team to four Super Bowl victories, joining Chuck Noll. "These guys have been counted out many times through the course of the year by a lot of people, but they always believed in themselves and just kept fighting.

"This is a great team — a great group of competitors who never gave in, never lost their will. Mentally and physically, as tough of a group as I've been around, and I've been around some. These guys are really special."

Over the final nine games of their season, dating to their Nov. 23 win over Detroit, the Patriots' defense allowed just 12 fourth-quarter points, including final-frame shutouts of the Colts in the AFC title game and the Seahawks.

Conversely, Seattle hadn't surrendered more than 7 fourth-quarter points in a game since its Week 5 loss to Dallas.

"We knew it was going to be tough and we knew it was going to come down to minutes or even seconds in the ballgame because they are a great football team," defensive lineman Vince Wilfork said. "I'm a defensive guy — to win on a defensive note, that is the most amazing feeling you can have.

"I am so proud of this team, what we have done, the things we have been through, the ups and the downs, and we just stuck together."

Facing second and goal from the 1, the Seahawks made the stunning decision to pass the ball rather than hand it off to power back Marshawn Lynch. Russell Wilson (12 for 21 for 247 yards, two touchdowns, interception) threw the ball into traffic, and Butler, who a little more than a year ago was playing for West Alabama, stepped in front of the intended receiver, Ricardo Lockette, for the play of his young career.

Seattle coach Pete Carroll, whose team was trying to become the first back-to-back champion since the Patriots in 2003-04, took responsibility for the call to pass on second down, figuring they would run on third or fourth down.

Butler, who said the Patriots were the only team to offer him a contract, knew a pass was coming, crediting defensive coordinator Matt Patricia with getting his players ready.

"[Wilson] kept looking [toward the receivers], he kept his head still and just looked over there, so that gave me a clue," Butler said. "I just knew they were going to throw. My instincts, I just went with it, just went with my mind and made the play."

Butler has impressed the coaching staff and his teammates since the spring, and all of the New England defensive backs were singing his praises, saying the Mississippi native has been making plays in practice and in games since the day he arrived in Foxborough.

Butler's play came just moments after it seemed like the Patriots' championship dreams would be crushed by another miracle catch, as they were years earlier in this same building by the Giants' David Tyree.

Jermaine Kearse and Butler both rose for Wilson's sideline pass, and as both fell to the grass, the ball came down, hitting Kearse between the legs. It popped up, Kearse batted it up, and he was amazingly able to secure the ball. It never touched the ground, making it a legal reception.

"I felt like the game was on me if we lost," Butler said of Kearse's catch. "But we had another play."

Now with first and goal at the 5, Wilson handed off to Lynch, who picked up 4 yards. But on second down and just feet to the goal line, rather than give their Pro Bowl back the ball again, Seattle opted to have Wilson pass.

And there was Butler.

New England became the sixth franchise in NFL history to win at least four Super Bowls, joining the Steelers, Cowboys, Giants, Packers, and 49ers.

The Patriots also are the first team to come back from a 10-point second-half Super Bowl deficit and win.

The winning touchdown came with 2:02 to play, a 3-yard Tom Brady-to-Julian Edelman pass, Brady looking to his most trusted receiver when it mattered most. Edelman finished the game with nine receptions for 109 yards and the score.

Brady, the first quarterback to start six Super Bowls and who was chosen as the game's Most Valuable Player, set a slew of records in the win: his 37 completions (he was 37 for 50 for 328 yards, four touchdowns, and two interceptions) were a Super Bowl record; his 13 Super Bowl touchdown passes put him past his childhood idol, Joe Montana, who had 11; and he became the first quarterback in league history with 50 touchdowns in the postseason.

He is the sixth QB to throw four or more touchdowns in the Super Bowl but the first to have them go to four different receivers. Edelman, Rob Gronkowski, Danny Amendola, and Brandon LaFell were the lucky quartet.

"He's going to go down as the best quarterback to ever play this game," cornerback Darrelle Revis said of Brady. "He's clutch. He's clutch."

But Brady, who fought a cold and continued to hear questions about the team's alleged deflated footballs in the AFC Championship game all week and seemed more relieved than exhilarated when at his postgame news conference, gave the credit to every one of his teammates.

"It's just a lot of mental toughness. I think the whole team had it," he said. "Coach [Belichick] always says, 'Ignore the noise and control what you can control.' We had two great weeks of practice; that's what it took, and every situation that came up was important.

"Every third down that we made, every short-yardage, every red-area possession. That's what we were focused on, that's who we needed to be focused on, and that's how we got the victory."

Malcolm Butler's Interception in Super Bowl XLIX against the Seahawks in 2014 goes down as one of the greatest moments in Super Bowl history.

The Seahawks and Patriots are no strangers to big games. Both teams have been contenders for the past few years and know what it takes to win.

Naturally, when they met in Super Bowl XLIX, fans expected a gridiron battle. And boy, the Patriots and Seahawks did not disappoint! In the final seconds of the game, trailing 28 – 24, Russell Wilson attempted to throw the game winning TD, only to be intercepted on the goal line by Malcolm Butler.

Regardless of the controversy surrounding the play call, Butler made an outstanding read and willed his way to yet another Patriots Super Bowl victory.

2015 Bill Belichick #14

The 2015 New England Patriots football team competed in their fifty-sixth season of professional football and their forty-sixth season in the National Football League (NFL). The Patriots were led by Coach Bill Belichick in his sixteenth of eighteen seasons (so-far). Robert Kraft was the Patriot's owner. The Patriots record was 12-4 for the fourth year in a row and the team grabbed the #2 seed along with a first round playoff bye for the fifth year in a row. They entered the season as the defending Super Bowl Champions.

This year looked like it might be another 16-0 season. However, after going 10–0 to begin the season, the Patriots' first loss of the season came against the Denver Broncos in overtime in Week 12 (counting the bye week). The loss seemed to have an effect on the team's production after this. The Patriots would go on to lose four of their last six games, ultimately finishing the regular season with a 12–4 record for the fourth straight year.

In Week 14, the Patriots clinched their seventh straight AFC East division title. By way of this, they tied the 1979 Los Angeles Rams for most consecutive division titles. As the second seeded team in the AFC, they did secure a first-round bye for the playoffs and home-field advantage for their first playoff game.

In the divisional round of the playoffs, the Patriots beat the Kansas City Chiefs 27–20 to advance to the AFC Championship for the fifth straight year. However, they fell on the road to the eventual Super Bowl 50 champion Denver Broncos by just two points, 20–18.

Games of the 2015 Season

In the season and home opener on September 10, the Patriots defeated the Pittsburgh Steelers W (28–21) in Gillette Stadium. At Buffalo on Sept 20, the Patriots beat the Bills W (40–32) in Ralph Wilson Stadium. At home on Sept 27, the Patriots pummeled the Jacksonville Jaguars W (51–17) in Gillette Stadium. In week 4, there was a bye. In week 5, on Oct 11 at Dallas, the Patriots shipped the Cowboys W (30–6) at AT&T Stadium.

On Oct 18 at Indianapolis, New England defeated the Colts W (34–27) in Lucas Oil Stadium. On Oct 25 at home, the Patriots beat the New York Jets W (30–23) in Gillette Stadium. At home again on Oct 29, the Patriots thumped the Miami Dolphins W (36–7) in Gillette Stadium. Then, at home on Nov 8, the Patriots whipped the Washington Redskins W (27–10) in Gillette Stadium.

At New York, on Nov 15, the Patriots beat the Giants in a one-point match W (27–26) at MetLife Stadium. At home on Nov 23, the Patriots defeated the Buffalo Bills W (20–13) in Gillette Stadium. On Nov 29 at Denver, the Broncos beat the Patriots in OT L (24–30) in the Sports Authority Field at Mile High Stadium. On Dec 6, at home, the Philadelphia Eagles beat the Patriots L (28–35) in Gillette Stadium.

On Dec 13 at Houston, the Patriots broke their two-game losing streak and beat the Texans W (27–6) at NRG Stadium. On Dec 20, at home, New England beat Tennessee W (33–16) in Gillette Stadium. On Dec 27 at New York, the Jets beat the Pats in OT, L (20–26) in MetLife Stadium Recap. To wrap up the season at Miami on Jan 3, the Dolphins got the win on the Patriots L 10–20 in Sun Life Stadium. The next 2015-2016 Patriots game would be in the Divisional Playoffs.

The Divisional Playoffs January 16, 2016
Divisional Round vs. Kansas City Chiefs

	1	2	3	4	Total
Chiefs	3	3	7	7	20
Patriots	7	7	7	6	27

At Gillette Stadium, Foxborough, Massachusetts

This divisional playoff game began at 4:35 PM on January 16, 2016 at Gillette Stadium, Foxborough, Massachusetts. The weather was 38 °F, partly cloudy. There was a reasonably packed house of 66,829 at this Patriots home game. After a 12-4 regular season record, the Patriots squeaked by the Chiefs in this game W (27-20).

The Patriots would upset the Chiefs, who came into this game having won 10 in a row to end the regular season, and a playoff game at Houston the previous week. Ironically, the Patriots had won ten in a row at the top of the season. The game was a shootout, as both quarterbacks played well. The Patriots would lead for most of the game. The Chiefs mounted a brief come back later in the game to try to tie it, but the Patriots held them off and won 27-20. With the win, New England advanced to its 6th straight AFC Championship game, and it prepared to face Denver in the Conference Championship for the second time in 3 seasons.

AFC Championship Playoffs January 24, 2016

AFC Championship vs. Denver Broncos

	1	2	3	4	Total
Patriots	6	3	3	6	18
Broncos	7	10	0	3	20

at Gillette Stadium, Foxborough, Massachusetts

This Conference Championship Game began at 3:05 PM on January 24, 2016 at Sports Authority Field at Mile High Stadium in Denver, Colorado. The weather was 46 °F, mostly sunny. There was a packed house of 77,112 at this Broncos home game. After a 12-4 regular season record, and the victory in the Division Playoffs, the New England Patriots were defeated by the Denver Broncos in this game W (20-18). The Broncos advanced to the Super Bowl and became the Super Bowl Champions.

Denver had taken it on the chin in prior years in this game from the Patriots and this year, they stepped up to the challenge. They would lead the entire game, as their number 1 ranked defense outlasted Tom Brady and New England's number 1 ranked offense 20-18.

Towards the end of the game in a well-orchestrated last-minute comeback, the Patriots would score with 18 seconds left. Needing just two more points for the tie, they gave it their best shot. For the game. However, not all good happens without the best of luck.

Unfortunately, on this last play, Tom Brady's 2-point pass was intercepted, and the Patriots missed out on that necessary 2-point conversion. In extra point terminology, the point was no good. The Patriots would try an onside kick as a final attempt to salvage the game, but it wouldn't hold up, and the Broncos won.

They advanced to Super Bowl L (50). This would be the last time that Tom Brady and Peyton Manning would play each other, as Manning would retire the following season. Manning would ultimately end his career 3-1 against Brady in the AFC Championship game. Both are great talents and great competitors.

With the loss, the Patriots ended their season with an overall record of 13-5. But, they would be back with a vengeance the next season to win all the marbles.

2016 Bill Belichick #14

The 2016 New England Patriots football team competed in their fifty-seventh season of professional football and their forty-seventh season in the National Football League (NFL). The Patriots were led by Coach Bill Belichick in his seventeenth of eighteen seasons (so-far). Robert Kraft was the Patriot's owner. The Patriots record was 14-2, gaining two-more wins than in 2015. They earned the #1 seed along with a first round playoff bye for the sixth year in a row. They also gained home field advantage through the playoffs. The Patriots were not defending Super Bowl Champions when the 2016 season began but they were when it was over.

There was a lot happening in the 2016 season. The New England Patriots are a winning machine. They became the first team that originated from the American Football League to reach 500 franchise wins—regular season and playoffs. It happened in Week 12 with the win over the New York Jets.

In Week 15, the Patriots clinched their eighth straight AFC East division title, and in doing so surpassed the 1979 Los Angeles Rams for the most consecutive division titles. They were not finished.

In Week 17, the last win of the season over the Miami Dolphins, gave the Patriots home field advantage throughout the entire AFC playoffs and they ended the regular season with a league-best record of 14–2. As the Patriots had learned well in prior years, the home field advantage no longer offers an advantage when a team loses. SO, they kept winning.

With their win over the Houston Texans in the Divisional Round, the Patriots advanced to the AFC Championship Game for the sixth consecutive year, surpassing the 1977 Oakland Raiders for most consecutive appearances in conference championship games.

After their win over the Pittsburgh Steelers in the AFC Championship Game, the Patriots became the first organization to clinch a ninth Super Bowl berth. They surpassed the Pittsburgh Steelers, Dallas Cowboys, and Denver Broncos who are all tied at 8. IMHO, the Patriots with Bill Belichick and Tom Brady are amazing.

Furthermore, Bill Belichick broke the record for a head coach by coaching his seventh Super Bowl, breaking a tie with Don Shula. You may recall the "Deflategate" which cost Patriots starting quarterback Tom Brady a suspension for the first four games of the season due to his alleged role in the "Deflategate" scandal.

Under backup quarterbacks Jimmy Garoppolo and Jacoby Brissett, the team managed a nice 3–1 record during Brady's suspension. During the season, Bill Belichick moved into fourth place on the list for most wins as a head coach, and Tom Brady set the record for most wins by a starting quarterback (208 following the 2016-2017 Super Bowl win).

This year, the Patriots were 8–0 on the road, matching a feat they first accomplished in the 2007 season. They became the seventh NFL team to accomplish this feat.

The Patriots also set a record for the most pass attempts by a team without an interception to start a season, and, collectively, Garoppolo, Brissett, and Brady combined to set a single season record for fewest interceptions thrown by a team, with just 2. Considering three cooks in the mix, that is especially good.

Tom Brady also set the record for the best touchdown–interception ratio in a single season, with 28 touchdowns and 2 interceptions (a 14:1 ratio), breaking Nick Foles' mark of 27 touchdowns to 2 interceptions (13.5:1), set in 2013 while he was with the Philadelphia Eagles.

Meanwhile, the defense led the league for fewest points allowed (250) for the first time since the 2003 season. The Patriots were not only ready; they came through.

In Super Bowl LI, the team rallied from a 28–3 deficit – with 2:12 left in the third quarter – to win in overtime, with a score of 34–28.

Many of us stared at the TV in wonderment after it appeared that Atlanta had the game sewed up. This was the franchise's fifth Super Bowl title.

Super Bowl LI was the first Super Bowl that was decided in overtime and it was the first time the winner erased a deficit higher than ten points. I am still in awe of a guy who first sat out four games and then was solely responsible for their Super Bowl game victory.

This would also be a record fifth Super Bowl victory for the Brady-Belichick quarterback-head coach combo. For Tom Brady, this would be his fifth. With the Super Bowl win, he broke his tie with hall of fame quarterbacks Joe Montana and Terry Bradshaw who both have four Super Bowl wins each. Additionally, head coach Bill Belichick's fifth Super Bowl in 2016-2017 meant that he surpassed Hall of Fame coach Chuck Noll from Pittsburgh, for most wins in the Super Bowl by a head coach. Congratulations, Mr. Belichick. You are outstanding the old-fashioned way. You earn it! Please continue.

Games of the 2016 Season

In the season opener on September 11, 2016 at Arizona, the Patriots defeated the Cardinals W (23–21) in the University of Phoenix Stadium. Then, the following week in the home opener on Sept 18, New England defeated Miami W (31–24) in Gillette Stadium. At home again on Sept 22, the Patriots skunked the Houston Texans W (27–0) in Gillette Stadium. Then, on Oct 2, the Patriots lost their first game of the season after 3 straight wins L (0-16) against the Buffalo Bills at home in Gillette Stadium.

On Oct 9 at Cleveland, the Patriots whooped the Browns W (33–13) at FirstEnergy Stadium. Then at home on Oct 16 New England defeated Cincinnati W (35–17) in Gillette Stadium. On Oct 23 at Pittsburgh, the Patriots beat the Steelers W (27–16) at Heinz Field. In the Conference playoffs these two teams would again battle it out. On October 30 at Buffalo, the Patriots beat the Bills W (41–25) at

New Era Field bringing the record to 7–1. On Nov 6, in week 9, the Patriots drew a bye.

On Nov 13 at home, the Seattle Seahawks beat the New England Patriots L (24–31) in Gillette Stadium. At San Francisco on Nov 20, the Patriots beat the 49ers W (30–17) in Levi's Stadium. At New York, on Nov 27, the Pats beat the Jets W (22–17) in MetLife Stadium. At home on Dec 4, the Patriots defeated the Los Angeles Rams W (26–10) in Gillette Stadium.

On Dec 12, at home, the Patriots defeated the Baltimore Ravens W (30–23) in Gillette Stadium. At Denver, on Dec 18, the Patriots beat the Broncos W (16–3) in Sports Authority Field at Mile High Stadium in Denver Colorado. At home, on Dec 24, New England pasted the New York Jets W (41–3) in Gillette Stadium. In the season finale on Jan 1 at Miami, the Patriots squashed the Dolphins W (35–14) in Hard Rock Stadium.

The Divisional Playoffs January 14, 2017
Divisional Round vs. Houston Texans

	1	2	3	4	Total
Texans	3	10	0	3	16
Patriots	14	3	7	10	34

At Gillette Stadium, Foxborough, Massachusetts

This divisional playoff game began at 8:15 PM on January 14, 2017 at Gillette Stadium, Foxborough, Massachusetts. The weather was 28 °F, cloudy. There was a reasonably packed house of 66,829 at this Patriots home game. After a 14-2 regular season record, the Patriots solidly defeated the Texans in this game W (34-16).

On the way to a nice victory over the Texans, the New England Defense had a lot to say. First of all, they intercepted Houston three times. Meanwhile, the offense got its two cents in also as running back Dion Lewis scored three touchdowns – one rushing, one receiving and one kickoff return. The Patriots took this game and used it to advance first to the AFC Championship Game and second to the Super Bowl for the ninth time.

There was nothing small about the Pats offense on January 14 as big plays made the difference when New England took a 14–3 lead after just 6 offensive plays. Following a three-and-out from both teams, the Texans helped out the NE offense when defensive back A. J. Bouye committed a 30-yard pass interference infraction when trying to cover Chris Hogan. Up 14-3 at the time, this gave the Patriots a first down on Houston's 35-yard line.

QB Tom Brady got right in gear and completed two consecutive passes—the first to Hogan for 22 yards and the second to Lewis for a 13-yard touchdown completion. Houston was awakened and responded with a 62-yard drive in 14 plays. They did not reach pay-dirt but did score on Nick Novak's 33-yard field goal. On the kickoff, Lewis took the ball 98 yards right through all the defenders for a touchdown. This was the 1st kickoff return touchdown ever for the Patriots in postseason history.

Houston had trouble moving the ball and were forced to punt after just three plays. However, on the first play of the second quarter, Tom Brady helped them a bit too much by throwing a pass that went off the hands of Michael Floyd and was intercepted by Houston's Bouye. He returned the ball 7 yards to the Patriots' 27. Again, the Texans failed to get the ball into the end zone, but Novak kicked another field goal to make the score 14–6.

On the kickoff, Texans linebacker Akeem Dent forced and recovered a fumble from Lewis on the kickoff, giving Houston the ball back on the New England 12-yard line. This time, Houston had better luck and took it all the way, scoring on Brock Osweiler's 10-yard touchdown pass to tight end C. J. Fiedorowicz. This brought the score to 14–13.

After three series with a punt as the final outcome, Brady reached back and completed a 48-yarder to Julian Edelman giving New England a first down on the Houston 16. After a few plays it was first and goal from the 3-yard line, but the Pats got stopped and could not score a touchdown. Stephen Gostkowski came through with a chip shot field goal giving the Patriots a 17–13 lead at halftime.

After a series of punts which got the second half going, Brady seemed ready to take command. The All-Pro QB completed two passes to Edelman for 40 yards and one to Hogan for 22 yards before finding running back James White in the end zone for a 19-yard catch. This put New England up 24–13. Later in the third quarter, Devin McCourty's intercepted an Osweiler pass and New England had the ball on their own 44-yard line. They could not convert this into points.

After a few more punts, Brady threw an interception, snagged by Andre Hal. He took it just 6 yards to the Patriots' 34-yard line. However, Houston capitalized on the INT with Novak's third field goal on the second play of the fourth quarter, making it 24–16.

New England punted on their next drive. Osweiler's first pass after the punt was intercepted and returned 23 yards by Logan Ryan, providing the Patriots an opportunity with the ball on the Texans' 6-yard line. After a 5-yard run, Lewis took it in the extra yard on the next play giving the Patriots a 31–16 lead.

The Texans could not get a first down on their next try and when the Patriots got the ball back, they were off.43 yards in 10 plays for a Gostkowski field goal making the lead 34–16 with under 7 minutes left. Osweiler was intercepted again on Houston's final drive. Duron Harmon got the pick for New England.

Brady racked up 18 of 38 passes for 287 yards, two touchdowns and two interceptions. Lewis rushed for 41 yards, caught two passes for 23 yards and returned three kickoffs for 124 yards, and became the first player in NFL postseason history to score touchdowns by rushing, receiving and kick return.

Edelman added eight passes for 137 yards to his total and he also returned four punts for 24 yards. Hogan contributed four catches for 95 yards.

Osweiler threw 23 completions out of 40 passes for 198 yards and a touchdown, but he also had three interceptions. After their one-week bye prior to this game, the Patriots were pleased to advance to the AFC Championship Game for the sixth consecutive year, eclipsing the Oakland Raiders of 1973 to 1977 for most consecutive appearances in conference championship games. The record so far for the Pats was 15-2.

AFC Championship Playoffs January 24, 2017

AFC Championship vs. Pittsburgh Steelers

	1	2	3	4	Total
Steelers	0	0	0	9	17
Patriots	10	7	160	3	36

at Gillette Stadium, Foxborough, Massachusetts

This Conference Championship Game began at 6:40 PM on January 24, 2016 at Sports Authority Field at Mile High Stadium in Denver, Colorado. The weather was 41 °F, cloudy. There was a packed house of 66,829,112 at this Patriots home game. After a 14-2 regular season record, and the victory in the Division Playoffs, the New England Patriots defeated the Pittsburgh Steelers in this game W (36-17). The Patriots advanced to the Super Bowl and became the Super Bowl Champions.

The New England Patriots used this game to advance to familiar territory as their victory over Pittsburgh would give them their seventh Super Bowl game in the last 16 seasons under quarterback Tom Brady and coach Bill Belichick. They made the most of both games. In this Conference Championship, they piled up 431 yards and 26 first downs. Pittsburgh's offense was also firing on all cylinders but not getting the ball past the goal posts too often. Pitt amassed 368 yards, but their final score was just 17 points, eight of them on a single touchdown late in the game when the outcome had already been decided.

Meanwhile, the Steelers' rushing attack, that had been so critical to their earlier playoff wins, was set back on its heels because of an early injury to running back Le'Veon Bell. Bell finished the game with just 54 total yards on the ground.

When the game began, Brady got right into gear. On the game's opening drive, his 41-yard completion to Julian Edelman set up Stephen Gostkowski's first field goal (31-yards), giving New England a 3–0 lead less than two minutes into the game.

Following several punts, the Patriots went on an 80-yard, 11-play drive, the longest gain being a 26-yard catch by receiver Chris Hogan. Brady finished it off with a 16-yard TD pass to Hogan, for a 10–0 lead.

On the second play of Pittsburgh's next drive, Bell suffered his game-ending groin injury. His replacement DeAngelo Williams did his best but was clearly not the same talent as Bell. He caught two passes for nine yards and rushed four times for 25 yards, the last carry was a nice five-yard touchdown run to complete the 13-play, 84-yard drive early in the second quarter. Chris Boswell missed the extra point. The score then was 10–6.

New England fired right back with an 82-yard drive taking nine plays. The Pats scored on a Brady 34-yard TD pass to Hogan on a flea flicker play. Pittsburgh quickly moved the ball to the Patriots' 19-yard line, where Big Ben threw a TD pass to tight end Jesse James. Well, it was initially ruled a touchdown, but a replay determined that James was down on the 1-yard line.

It was a costly verdict for Pittsburgh. When play resumed, Williams was dropped for a one-yard loss by Dont'a Hightower and Patrick Chung. On second down, Williams was tackled for a three-yard loss by nose tackle Vincent Valentine. Pittsburgh was going backwards. On third down, Roethlisberger's pass was incomplete, so the team settled for Boswell's field goal, making the score 17–9.

In the second half, New England dominated. They buried the Steelers with four unanswered scores. After forcing Pitt to punt, New England drove 55 yards in nine plays, 24 of them coming on a catch by Hogan. Gostkowski finished the drive with a 47-yard field goal that put the Patriots up 20–9.

After another Pittsburgh punt, Brady uncorked a 39-yard completion to Hogan, which led to a one-yard touchdown by the bull, LeGarrette Blount, giving the team a 27–9 lead with 2:44 left in the third quarter.

On the first play after the kickoff, Pittsburgh coughed up the ball when Kyle Van Noy forced a fumble from Eli Rogers. It was recovered by linebacker Rob Ninkovich on the Steelers' 28-yard line. Brady took over and completed an 18-yard pass to Edelman on the next play, and eventually connected with him in the end zone for a 10-yard touchdown pass. Gostkowski missed the extra point, but the Patriots had already effectively put the game away, carrying a 33–9 lead going into the fourth quarter.

In the final period, the Steelers were able to get a drive going down to the New England 2-yard line. But, misfortune was the name of their game and the Steelers turned the ball over on downs.

Then after a Pats punt, Eric Rowe intercepted a pass from Roethlisberger and returned it 37 yards to the Steelers' 32-yard line, leading to another Gostkowski field goal that increased New England's lead to 36–9.

All that remained from this point on was an inconsequential Roethlisberger 30-yard touchdown pass to Cobi Hamilton and the subsequent 2-point conversion pass to Williams that made the final score 36–17.

Brady had a nice day passing. He completed 32 of his 42 passing attempts for 384 yards and three touchdowns. Hogan caught nine passes for 180 yards and two touchdowns, while Edelman had eight receptions for 118 yards and a touchdown. Roethlisberger threw for 314 yards, with a touchdown and an interception. The Patriots were smiling knowing they were on their way to the Super Bowl as a team for the ninth time.

Super Bowl LI February 5, 2017

	1	2	3	4	OT	Totals
Patriots	0	3	6	19	6	34
Falcons	0	21	7	0	0	28

*** This historic Super Bowl LI Comeback v Matt Ryan and the Falcons goes down as the top moment of all time in Patriot football.***

Any Patriot fan who was alive in February 2017, saw the greatest comeback game of all time.

I have been watching football since even before my older brother Ed, ignored my pleas when I was five years old at Meyers Stadium in Wilkes-Barre, PA at the annual Thanksgiving Day Game of Meyers v GAR on a blustery day in November. My feet were freezing and nonetheless I had no choice but to stay until the end of that game. That's how important football games are. Never in my life of watching football on TV or in a live stadium before or since then have I ever seen a game like the one on February 2017 -- Super Bowl LI. I don't think I'll ever see anything top that game in any sport.

I would suspect that Falcon supporters and Patriot haters would disagree, but Super Bowl LI is arguably the best game of the century. Considering the Patriots have played pro football for just 58 years as Boston and Now New England, that is a major statement.

The initial shock, the acceptance of a probable defeat, the denial of the impossible, and the comeback to top all comebacks—what more could a football fan ask for? What more could a football game offer?

After the first half, viewers in NRG Stadium and across the nation were simply stunned. The disciplined and dynamic Patriots were falling woefully short of stopping MVP Matt Ryan's offense. Matt

Ryan in the first half was performing like Tom Brady always performed.

Early into the third, the Falcons commanded a 28 – 3 lead, and they were unfaltering. I can recall the shocked pundits not believe they were actually saying that it was all but official in that the Falcons would earn their first title win. The Falcons were about to blow-out the Patriots, Tom Brady, and Bill Belichick too.

However, Tom Brady and the Patriots' defense found the grit to continue. They were not ready to quietly walk off the field without another Lombardi trophy. With an utter shutout and a record breaking performance (416 passing yards, most in a championship game), the Patriots forced the first ever overtime in a Super Bowl, and subsequently capped off their victory surge in the opening drive. It was truly an incredible game. To top off this recap, we use a great report by the Boston Globe. Thank them when you have a chance.

The Super Bowl XLIX kickoff was at 6:30 EST February 5, 2017. The weather did not matter as the game was played with the retractable roof closed. Led by starter Tom Brady, the Bill Belichick-led NE Patriots overcame the Atlanta Falcons in a tight match 34-28 at NRG Stadium in Houston Texas. before a packed house of 70,807. After a 14-2 regular season record, having won the Division and Conference, the Patriots played one of the greatest comeback matches in NFL history with the Atlanta Falcons, winning the contest W (34-28), gaining their fifth Super Bowl Conquest as a franchise.

Super Bowl LI: New England Patriots 34, Atlanta Falcons 28 (OT)

Despite the Falcons taking a 28–3 lead midway through the third quarter, the Patriots scored 25 unanswered points to tie the game at 28 with less than a minute left in regulation and take the game to the first overtime period in Super Bowl history. On the first possession of overtime, Patriots running back James White punched in the game-winning score to give his team a 34–28 comeback victory.

Each time the Patriots have been in a Super Bowl, I looked for the excellent Boston Globe's coverage of the game. I enjoyed researching the Boston Papers to get the scoop the way it actually happened in 2017. This fine write-up from the Boston Globe at the time it was written gave New England fans enough of the Super Bowl that they felt they were there. Nice job Jim McBride. He titled his article:

In a Comeback for the Ages, Patriots Beat Falcons in Heart-Pounding Super Bowl.

By Jim McBride GLOBE STAFF
FEBRUARY 6, 2017

HOUSTON — Case closed.

> Tom Brady cemented his legacy as the greatest quarterback in history Sunday night and he did it in the most dramatic fashion.
>
> The Patriots quarterback earned his fifth Super Bowl title and collected his fourth Super Bowl MVP as the Patriots staged the most incredible and improbable comeback in history of America's game, beating the Falcons, 34-28, in overtime at NRG Stadium.

The Photo next is by
STAN GROSSFELD/GLOBE STAFF

Danny Amendola scored a two-point conversion to tie the score at 28-28.

Erasing a 25-point second-half deficit, the Patriots scored 31 unanswered points against a Falcons team that played the fourth quarter as though they were waiting to be fitted for their rings rather than finishing their business on the field.

James White's 2-yard run in OT — the first in Super Bowl history — was the difference as the Patriots pulled off their second stunning Super Bowl victory in three seasons.

"This is unequivocally the sweetest," said team owner Robert Kraft after that long-awaited, awkward moment when commissioner Roger Goodell handed him the Vince Lombardi Trophy.

Brady was astoundingly brilliant in the second half, and put on a fourth-quarter performance that was incredible, even by his lofty standards.

For the record, Brady finished 43 of 62 for 466 yards and a pair of touchdowns. He hit White and Danny Amendola with fourth-quarter TD passes and they each converted 2-point conversions on the other's TD to tie the score at 28-28.

The Patriots won the toss in overtime and Brady carved up the gassed Falcons, driving 75 yards, capped by White's run.

"Yeah, they're all sweet," said Brady, when asked if this was the best, considering the Deflategate saga of the past two seasons.

"They're all different and this was just an incredible team and I'm just happy to be a part of it. It's just a great group of coaches and teammates and we overcame a lot of different things and it's all worth it."

It is the fifth Super Bowl title for the Patriots, who are now tied with the 49ers and Cowboys for the second most in NFL history (the Steelers have six).
All of New England's titles have come under the stewardship of the Kraft family, Bill Belichick, and, of course, Brady,

For two weeks, Belichick extolled the virtues of the Falcons' speed to anyone who would listen. Sunday night the 70,807 on hand and millions across the world found out just what the New England coach was talking about.

Atlanta blitzed the Patriots with 21 straight points, displaying tremendous speed and feverish quickness that left the favorites defenseless and helpless.

It felt over. Well, almost over.

The Falcons gave a preview of things to come on their first offensive play from scrimmage when Devonta Freeman gashed them for 37 yards.

The Patriots were able to put the clamps on the Falcons for the rest of the opening 15 minutes. Problem was, Brady and the offense couldn't sustain any momentum.

The one drive the Patriots showed life came at the end of the quarter, when a pair of passes to Julian Edelman — the second one for 27 yards on the first play of the second quarter — gave them a first down at the Atlanta 33. LeGarrette Blount, however, fumbled on the next play and the Falcons took advantage.

Matt Ryan led a surgical five-play, 71-yard drive that ended with Freeman's 5-yard zip around left end. He went in untouched. Ryan, the former Boston College star, hit Julio Jones for 19 and 29 yards before Freeman went the final 29 yards on three carries.

It marked the first time the Patriots had trailed in a game since Week 11 against the Jets.

After another three-and-out by the Patriots, the Falcons set up shop at their 38 after a 38-yard punt from Ryan Allen.

Ryan, looking every bit the league MVP that he had been voted the prior Saturday night, went back to shredding the Patriots defense. He hit Taylor Gabriel for 24 yards and Jones for a toe-tapping 18-yarder. Two plays later, Ryan dropped a beautiful 19-yard pass into tight end Austin Hooper's hands in the end zone to double the lead to 14-0.

The Patriots appeared poised to finally stop the hemorrhaging on the ensuing possession but again a turnover proved to be a killer.

After methodically marching from their 25 to the Atlanta 23 — aided by three defensive holding penalties — it appeared New England could still make a game of it.

That's when Robert Alford stepped in. Literally.

The cornerback cut in front a Brady pass intended for Danny Amendola and was off to the races for an 82-yard Pick-6 — with only a helpless and airborne Brady in his way.

It was a waste of an 11-play drive for New England.

The Patriots did mount an 11-play, 52-yard drive on their next possession, but it stalled when Martellus Bennett was called for holding, negating a White catch and run that would have put the ball inside the Atlanta 5.

Though Stephen Gostkowski would finally put the Patriots on the board with a 41-yard field goal, it was without a doubt the hollowest 3 points of the 2016 season.

Ryan was superb over the first 30 minutes, hitting on 7 of 8 passes for 115 yards. Brady was 16 of 26 for 184 yards and took two sacks. It was Brady's first multiple-sack game since Week 8 against Buffalo.

"We were down, some had some doubts [at halftime], we're only human," said Patriots defensive end Chris Long. "But we had enough guys pulling us along. Duron Harmon walked in and said, 'This is going to be the best comeback of all time.' And we completely believed that. And it was."

Nate Solder was a little blunter:

"I felt like I played like total poop," he said.

After trading three-and-outs to start the second half, the Falcons extended their lead to 28-3 when Ryan hit Tevin Coleman with a 6-yard swing pass touchdown. Gabriel was the star of the drive, hauling in catches of 17 and 35 yards.

Brady, who set a Super Bowl record with his 43 completions, rallied the Patriots when he got the ball back, driving 75 yards in 13 plays, capped by a 5-yard strike to White. Gostkowski doinked the extra point off the right upright and it was 28-9.

Gostkowski drilled a 33-yard field goal to pull the Patriots closer at 28-12 on the team's first possession of the fourth quarter, and two plays later, Dont'a Hightower got the ball back when he strip-sacked Ryan to hand the Patriots the ball at the Atlanta 25.

"Biggest play of the game," said Long.

Brady fired a 6-yard TD pass to Amendola and White scored on a 1-yard run to make it 28-20.

The tying drive — Edelman's incredible 23-yard catch the key — went 91 yards, matching New England's longest drive of the season. White finished it with a 1-yard run and Amendola caught the 2-point conversion. It was 28-28.

Ryan got the ball back and for the first time all night, he looked frazzled and overwhelmed, woefully misfiring on a third-down pass.

Once the Patriots won the OT coin toss, it was over.

White scores winning TD in OT. First time Super Bowl ever decided in OT

Writer Jim McBride of the Boston Globe can be reached at james.mcbride@globe.com. Follow him on Twitter @globejimmcbride. Thank Jim McBride for a great write-up that stirs up the emotion of the game and helps Patriot fans enjoy it over and over.

2017 Bill Belichick #14

The 2017 New England Patriots football team competed in their fifty-eighth season of professional football and their forty-eighth season in the National Football League (NFL). The Patriots were led by Coach Bill Belichick in his eighteenth of eighteen seasons (so-far). Robert Kraft was the happy defending Super Bowl Patriot's owner. The Patriots record was 13-3, gaining one less win than in 2016. They earned the #1 AFC seed along with a first round playoff bye for the seventh year in a row.

They also gained home field advantage through the playoffs. The Patriots were the defending Super Bowl Champions when the 2017 season began but, after a great season with fifteen total wins, they were not the champs when the season was over.

The defending Super Bowl champion New England Patriots entered the season feeling pretty invincible, having had a great 2016 season winning the Cigar, the rings, and all the marbles. They almost matched their excellent 14-2 showing with a fine 13-3 record in 2017. It was a Week 14 loss to Miami that set them back. Nonetheless, the Patriots again won the AFC Title. This was their 9th consecutive AFC East title, and it was their 15th of the last 17 seasons with Tom Belichick.

When they got their win over the Buffalo Bills in week 16, the Patriots had achieved their 8th consecutive 12-or-more win season stretching all the way from 2010, an NFL record. Their Week 17 victory over the New York Jets clinched their top seed in the AFC for the second straight year, thus, as noted, giving the Patriots home-field advantage throughout the entire AFC playoffs for the second year in a row. There was nothing at all for the Patriots to complain about, and nobody was complaining.

The Pats defeated the Titans in the Divisional Round 35–14, and they topped the Jacksonville Jaguars in the AFC Championship Game 24–20, grabbing their second consecutive AFC title. The game was their seventh consecutive AFC Championship appearance, adding onto their record from the previous year.

The win also made Tom Brady the oldest quarterback (40 years, 163 days) to win a playoff game, surpassing Brett Favre for the record. It looks to many like Brady is getting younger. He sure is enjoying football as is his compadre, Bill Belichick.

On top of all the other good things happening for the Patriots, this was also the second time they advanced to the Super Bowl two consecutive seasons since 2004. They faced the Philadelphia Eagles in a rematch of Super Bowl XXXIX.

This game—SB LII, also made the Patriots the only team in NFL history to appear in ten Super Bowls, and it gave the Patriots a chance to repeat as Super Bowl Champions for the second time in franchise history, and for the first time since 2004. In addition, they had the chance to tie the Pittsburgh Steelers for the record of most Super Bowl wins by a team in NFL history with 6.

Unfortunately, the win did not happen. Pointing to one cause, we would have to say it was because of a late strip-sack of Brady by Brandon Graham and a failed Hail Mary pass. The Eagles were playing at the top of their game with a substitute QB who had once been an Eagles star. This rebuilt team was molded to win by a young coach, Doug Pederson, who got the job done. The Eagles thus defeated the Patriots in Super Bowl LII by 41–33, ending their chance at a sixth Super Bowl title and resulting in their first Super Bowl loss since 2011.

The loss was devastating to the Patriots as it prevented New England from repeating their three-in-four Super Bowl run that they managed from 2001–2004. Also, with the loss, the Patriots tied the NFL record for most Super Bowl losses with five. Considering that the Patriots also have five big wins, that is not a bad record. The Patriots will be back in tact in 2018. I would expect a Belichick/Brady combo to be right up there ready to bring home all the marbles again. Don't you think?

In the home and season opener on September 7, Andy Reid's revitalized Kansas City Chiefs spoiled the party for New England by claiming a L (27–42) victory in Gillette Stadium. On Sept 17 at New Orleans, the Saints took it on the chin W (36–20) at the renamed

Mercedes-Benz Superdome. At home again on Sept 24, the Patriots squeezed out a win in a tight game against the Houston Texans W (36–33) in Gillette Stadium. On Oct 1 at home the Carolina Panthers edged out the Patriots L (30–33) in Gillette Stadium.

At Tampa Bay, on Oct 5, the Patriots got by the Buccaneers W (19–14) in Raymond James Stadium. Then, on Oct 15 at New York, the Patriots grabbed the win v the Jets W (24–17) in MetLife Stadium. At home on Oct 22, the Patriots again beat the Atlanta Falcons W 23–7, but in a more convincing fashion than in Super Bowl LI—in Gillette Stadium. At home on Oct 29, New England defeated Los Angeles W (21–13) in Gillette Stadium. On Nov 4, NE gained a bye week.

At Denver, on Nov 12, the Patriots thumped the Broncos W (41–16) in the Sports Authority Field at Mile High Stadium. At Oakland on Nov 19, the Patriots whooped the Raiders W (33–8) in Estadio Azteca (Mexico City). At home, on Nov 26 Miami took it on the chin from New England W (35–17) in Gillette Stadium. At Buffalo on December 3, the Patriots smashed the Bills W (23–3) in New Era Field.

At Miami on Dec 11, the Dolphins beat the Patriots L (20–27) in Hard Rock Stadium. At Pittsburgh, on December 17, in a close game, the Patriots beat the Steelers W (27–24) in Heinz Field. On Dec 24, at home, the Patriots hammered the Buffalo Bills W (37–16) in Gillette Stadium. At home, on Dec 31 in the final game of the season, the Patriots slammed the New York Jets W (26–6) in Gillette Stadium, giving New England a first place 13-3 record for the season. The Patriots did not have to compete in the Wild Card and so they had a rest week before the Divisional Championship playoffs began.

The Divisional Playoffs January 13, 2018
Divisional Round vs. Tennessee Titans

	1	2	3	4	Total
Titans	7	0	0	7	14
Patriots	0	21	7	70	35

At Gillette Stadium, Foxborough, Massachusetts

This divisional playoff game began at 8:15 PM on January 13, 2018 at Gillette Stadium, Foxborough, Massachusetts. The weather was 24 °F, clear & cold. There was a reasonably packed house of 65,878 at this Patriots home game. After a 13-3 regular season record, the Patriots solidly defeated the Titans in this playoff game W (35-14).

The Patriots reset their own club playoff record by sacking Marcus Mariota eight times for their second win in three career playoff matches against the Titans franchise. The Patriots held Titans RB Derrick Henry to only 28 yards on 12 carries the week after he went all-out for 156 yds against the Chiefs.

This was the third playoff game between the two teams, the first since 2003, with the Patriots in this meeting, holding a 2–1 advantage. They split the first two games, both in the Divisional round, including the first game against the Titans' predecessor, the Houston Oilers. Everybody in the stands and in the national audience knew this would be a good game.

New England racked up eight sacks, 438 yards, and 31 first downs as they advanced to their seventh consecutive AFC Championship game.

No game is decided by just a few plays. Midway through the first quarter, Tennessee put on a show by driving almost unimpeded 95 yards in 11 plays. In the end, it featured a 36-yard completion from Marcus Mariota to tight end Delanie Walker. Mariota got his arm back and tossed a 15-yard TD pass to Corey Davis, who made a great one-handed catch while scouting the back corner of the end zone. This put the up 7–0. The Patriots were undaunted, but they knew they were not leading.

New England came right back, with the master, Tom Brady completing five consecutive passes for 67 yards, the longest a 32-yard completion to Dion Lewis and the last pass at five-yards in shovel form to James White. This was a TD that tied the score.

After a Titans punt, Brady whipped off three consecutive passes for 28 yards as the team drove 48 yards in six plays to go up 14–7 on White's six-yard touchdown run with 9:20 left in the half.

When New England got the ball the next time, they were forced to punt after three plays. However, a neutral zone infraction penalty on Titans defensive back Brynden Trawick gave the Pats a 1st down. The Patriots were ready to sting the Titans on this second chance and they did.

They drove 91 yards in 16 plays to take a 21–7 lead on Brady's six-yard touchdown pass to Chris Hogan. Tennessee had not thrown in the towel and they then drove to the Patriots' 46-yard line; and on fourth-and-1, Derrick Henry tried to run for a first down, but defensive backs Malcolm Butler and Stephon Gilmore tackled him for no gain.

With 17 seconds left, the Pats were able to move the ball to the Titans' 35-yard line with time remaining, but Stephen Gostkowski, normally accurate, missed a 53-yard field goal attempt as time expired. In the first half alone, Brady completed 21 of 31 passes for 206 yards and two touchdowns. The Patriots were on the run to a victory.

In 3Q, the Titans Brett Kern's 40-yard punt from his own 16-yard line gave the Patriots good field position on their 44-yard line. On the next play, Brady completed a 27-yard pass to tight end Rob Gronkowski, and the team went on to increase their lead to 28–7 with Brandon Bolden's two-yard touchdown run.

The Titans got nothing done with the ball. The next time New England took over, they drove 90-yards in 15 plays. During the drive, the Pats faced only two third downs. Brady completed seven passes for 78 yards on the drive, the longest a 25-yard throw to Danny Amendola, and he finished it off with a four-yard touchdown toss to Gronkowski, making the score 35–7 with 10:22 left.

Before the end of 3Q, the Titans were able to make it 35–14 with Mariota's 11-yard touchdown pass to Davis on fourth down at the end of an 80-yard, 16-play drive.

Don't tell Tom Brady we know just how old he is; but he still operates like a kid on the field. At 40 years, 163 days, Brady became the oldest quarterback—this game.
He led his team to victory in a record-making postseason game, finishing the day 35-of-53 for 337 yards and three touchdowns.

Amendola caught 11 passes for 112 yards, while also returning three punts for 18 yards. Lewis rushed for 62 yards, caught nine passes for 79 yards, and returned a kickoff for 27 yards.[10]Linebacker Geneo Grissom and defensive tackle Deatrich Wise Jr. each had two sacks for New England.[10] Mariota completed 22 of 37 passes for 225 yards and two touchdowns.

This game set the NFL postseason record for the largest age difference between opposing quarterbacks: Brady was 40 and Mariota was just 24. Which of these QB's would you bet on?

AFC Championship Playoffs January 21, 2018

AFC Championship vs. Jacksonville Jaguars

	1	2	3	4	Total
Jaguars	0	14	3	3	20
Patriots	3	7	0	14	24

at Gillette Stadium, Foxborough, Massachusetts

This Conference Championship Game began at 3:05 PM on January 21, 2016 at Gillette Stadium, Foxborough, Massachusetts. The weather was 48 °F, clear & cool. There was a packed house of 65,

878 at this Patriots home game. After a 13-3 regular season record, and the victory in the Division Playoffs, the New England Patriots defeated the Jacksonville Jaguars in this game W (24-20). The Patriots advanced to the Super Bowl and lost the Super Bowl Championship to the Philadelphia Eagles in a tight match.

This marked the fifth playoff meeting between the two clubs with the Patriots now holding a 4-1 advantage. This was their second meeting in the AFC Championship Game, the Patriots winning in 1996 as well. The Pats overall record improved to 15-3.

There had been few conference championship games to feature a team from Florida in 15 years (the Super Bowl XXXVIIchampion Tampa Bay Buccaneers won the 2002 NFC championship game).

New England overcame a 10-point deficit in the fourth quarter to gain New England's 10th Super Bowl appearance.

On the opening drive of the Conference Championship game, Tom Brady fired off a 31-yard pass to Brandin Cooks and then a 20-yard pass to wide receiver Danny Amendola on fourth-and-1 as the team drove 62 yards in 10 plays to score an FG when Stephen Gostkowski connected on a 31-yard field goal.

Following a pair of punts, Jacksonville QB, Blake Bortles completed two passes to running back Corey Grant, collecting 44 total yards as the team drove 76 yards in seven plays to take a 7–3 lead on a four-yard touchdown pass to tight end Marcedes Lewis on the second play of the second quarter. Nothing happens without defense and offense.

The next time they got the ball, Bortles completed all four pass attempts for 47 yards. One of the passes was a 27-yard completion to Allen Hurns, as the Jaguars team drove 77 yards in 10 plays to score on Leonard Fournette's four-yard touchdown run, increasing their lead to 14–3.

The Patriots were not about to let some good fortune cost them the game. On the Jaguars' next drive, the Jags moved the ball to a third-and-7 on the Patriots' 47-yard line. Bortles then completed a 12-yard pass to Lewis that would have picked up a first down. The team was stuck for a delay of game and Bortles was then sacked by Adam Butler on the next play.

New England finally got the ball on their own 15-yard line with 2:02 left in the half, and they got their game going. They made it 85 yards in six plays – 47 yards of the total came from Jaguars penalties – to score on James White's 1-yard touchdown run. This cut the edge to 14–10.

You never know what will happen next in football. The next intercession came from Jacksonville safety Barry Church, who trying to do his best put a his helmet on a Patriots helmet in a hit on Patriots tight end Rob Gronkowski. Church got his team a 15-yard penalty, and Gronkowski was escorted off for medical testing that determined that he had suffered a concussion and could not return.

Jacksonville got the ball back with 55 seconds and all three timeouts remaining but chose to run out the clock and go to halftime, a choice that would later earn them criticism, as no team had deliberately run the first half clock out with more than 50 seconds left during the season.

Jacksonville got the second half kickoff and moved the ball 39 yards in nine plays, with 20 yards from a reception by fullback Tommy Bohanon. Josh Lambo finished the drive with a 54-yard field goal. This boosted the Jaguar lead to 17–10. The Jags were not finished.

Later in the period, the Jaguars advanced 66 yards in 11 plays. They got 18 yards on a completion from Bortles to Marqise Lee on third-and-3. On the second play of 4Q, Lambo scored with a 43-yard field goal, lifting the margin to a two-score differential at 20–10.

New England was not coming back, and it seemed like it might be all over for the Patriots. The game seemed to be slipping away from New England, particularly on their ensuing drive when linebacker Myles Jack forced and recovered a fumble from Dion Lewis on a trick play in which Amendola completed a forward pass to Lewis on the Jacksonville 33-yard line.

Thankfully for New England, their defense rose to the occasion and forced a three-and-out. They took the ball back on the Patriots' 15-yard line. Tom Brady was not giving up. He started the drive with an 18-yard pass to Cooks, and then he converted a third-and-18 with a 21-yard completion to Amendola on the 46-yard line.

From there, Mr. Brady completed passes to Phillip Dorsett for 31 yards and Amendola for 14 yards before finishing the drive with a nine-yard touchdown pass to Amendola. This brought the Pats to within three, 20–17.

As the game progressed, there was a pair of punts, including Ryan Allen's 35-yard kick, which pinned the Jaguars back at their own 10-yard line. The Jaguars lost one yard over their next three plays, and then Amendola returned Brad Nortman's 41-yard punt 20 yards to the Jacksonville 30-yard line with 4:58 left.

From there, New England put on a drive of 30 yards in five plays, culminating on Brady's four-yard touchdown pass to Amendola to take a 24–20 lead with 2:48 left.

After taking the ball back, Bortles' 29-yard completion to Dede Westbrook gave the Jaguars a first down on the Patriots' 38-yard line. But over the next two plays, Bortles threw an incompletion and then he fumbled the ball while being sacked by linebacker Kyle Van Noy.

Not everything looks good at first as Jacksonville tackle Cam Robinson recovered the fumble. However, the team lost nine yards on the play, bringing up third-and-19. After a four-yard pass to James O'Shaughnessy, Bortles' next pass was swatted away by Stephon Gilmore, causing a turnover on downs with 1:47 left. New England then got a key first down on third-and-10 with an 18-yard run by Lewis that let them run out the clock. Nobody had expected it at that point to go so well for the Pats.

Brady completed 26 of 38 passes for 290 yards and two touchdowns. He threw to whomever was open and Cooks was the top receiver of the game with six receptions for 100 yards, while Danny Amendola caught seven passes for 84 yards and two touchdowns. Amendola also returned two punts for 24 yards.

Van Noy had nine tackles – including five solo tackles – a sack and a forced fumble. Bortles completed 23 of 36 passes for 293 yards and a touchdown, while Fournette was the leading rusher of the game with 76 yards and a touchdown and Hurns was the Jaguars' leading receiver with six receptions for 80 yards.

The Patriots moved on to the Super Bowl v Philadelphia after playing this superb game, winning 24-20.

Super Bowl LII February 4, 2018

	1	2	3	4	Totals
Eagles	9	13	7	12	41
Patriots	3	9	14	7	33

At U.S. Bank Stadium, Minneapolis, Minnesota

The Super Bowl LII kickoff was at 6:30 EST February 4, 2018. The weather did not matter as the game was played indoors with the retractable roof closed. Led by starter Tom Brady, the Bill Belichick-led NE Patriots had the Eagles on the ropes at times but lost at the end of the game L (33-41) to the Philadelphia Eagles in a tight match 33-41 at US Bank Stadium, Minneapolis, Minnesota before a packed house of 67,212. After a 13-2 regular season record, having won the Division and the Conference championships, the Patriots played tough but could not come back despite a valiant Hail Mary attempt. The Eagles won their first Super Bowl Contest ever this year.

I enjoyed researching the Boston Papers to get the scoop the way it actually happened in 2018. This fine write-up from the Boston Globe at the time it was written gave New England fans enough of the Super Bowl that they felt they were there. Nice job Rachel G. Bowers. She titled her article:

Eagles stun Patriots in a Super Bowl LII thriller
Picture by *JIM DAVIS/GLOBE STAFF*

By Rachel G. Bowers GLOBE STAFF FEBRUARY 04, 2018

It was an offensive battle that set the record for most combined yards in an NFL playoff game — over 1,000 — as Tom Brady and Bill Belichick came up short of winning their sixth Lombardi Trophy.

"It's disappointing, but proud of the way we competed," Belichick said.
"We just came up a little bit short tonight. Tough way to end a lot of really good things that have happened this season. But that's what this game is about."

Eagles defeated the Patriots, 41-33, in Super Bowl LII on Sunday in Minneapolis.

"Today we had our opportunities. Never really got control of the game. Never really played on our terms. Just didn't make enough plays when needed to," Brady said.

"The Eagles played a better game today, they deserved to win. That's why they're the champs."

For the Eagles, it is their first Super Bowl win and first NFL championship since 1906 — and it came with backup quarterback Nick Foles—playing the game of his life, earning him MVP honors.

"I have the best players in the world," Eagles coach Doug Pederson said. "This is a resilient group."

Foles, playing in place of the injured Carson Wentz, completed 28 of 43 passes for 373 yards, three touchdowns, and an interception.

"I felt calm, we have such a great group of guys, such a great coaching staff, we felt confident going in," Foles said.

The play of the contest came at a time when Brady seemed poised to put together another game-winning drive. Trailing, 38-33, with just more than 2 minutes remaining, Brady and his offense took the field with 75 yards and the Philadelphia defense standing between them and a come-from-behind victory.

On the second play of the possession, defensive end Brandon Graham recorded the only sack of the game — and it was a strip-sack of Brady recovered by rookie Derek Barnett. The Eagles turned that into a field goal and an eight-point lead.

"Just kept going," Graham said on the field after. "We said we needed a play. We got one more opportunity; we were going to give it everything we got and I just so happened to get there. I'm just thankful because we got a team that's resilient. We going to stick around for a long time. We world champs, baby, and it feels so good.

"I'm just happy because we are world champs and we worked our butt off and everybody that doubted us, we world champs, baby, that's all I got to say."

"They made one good play at the right time," Brady said.

The Eagles' go-ahead touchdown with 2:21 remaining came on an 11-yard pass from Foles to tight end Zach Ertz that officials reviewed before ultimately upholding the call on the field.

"If they had overturned that [touchdown], I don't know what would have happened to the city of Philadelphia," said Ertz, who finished with seven catches for 67 yards and the touchdown.

Coin toss

The Eagles called tails and the coin came up heads. The Patriots chose to defer to the second half. Philadelphia will receive the opening kickoff.

Here is a look at the coin that was used for the coin toss:

1st quarter: Patriots 3, Eagles 3

The team that scores first in the Super Bowl is 34-17.

New England answered Philadelphia's opening possession with a 67-yard drive of its own, but it ended in much the same fashion: A field goal. Stephen Gostkowski made a 26-yarder to tie it up. Quarterback Tom Brady and the offense utilized their up-tempo attack and even caught the Eagles with too many men on the field. The Patriots covered the 67 yards in nine plays, two of which went for more than 15 yards. Brady targeted tight end Rob Gronkowski on third and goal from the 8-yard line, but cornerback Jalen Mills broke up the pass.

Running back James White and receiver Chris Hogan were the primary weapons on the possession with White getting three touches for 21 yards and Hogan getting two touches for 32 yards. Rowe was in coverage on both of the drive's third-down conversions. Of note: Rowe started over cornerback Malcolm Butler, who arrived late to Minneapolis as he was dealing with an illness.

1st quarter: Eagles 9, Patriots 3

It did not take long for Philadelphia to regain the lead. In fact, just three plays.

Quarterback Nick Foles found Alshon Jeffery for a 34-yard touchdown, but kicker Jake Elliott missed the extra point wide right. Cornerback Eric Rowe was in coverage on Jeffery.

The drive opened with Foles and Nelson Agholor connecting for 7 yards. Then LeGarrette Blount's 36-yard run set up the touchdown. So far, the Eagles have gained 149 yards, which is the fifth most ever in the Super Bowl. The 1994 49ers (193 yards) hold the record.

2nd quarter: Eagles 9, Patriots 3

Stephen Gostkowski's 26-yard field goal attempt hit the left upright and was no good. It would have capped a 74-yard drive and trimmed the Philadelphia lead.

On third and 2 from the 9-yard line, the Patriots ran a jet sweep to Brandin Cooks to the right end. But Cooks tried to hurdle safety Rodney McLeod, who corralled Cooks in the air and brought him to the ground for just a 1-yard gain.

Gostkowski, in his 12th season, has missed three other field goals in his postseason career: a 53-yarder against the Titans in this season's divisional round, a 44-yarder against the Ravens in the 2010 wild

card, and a 35-yarder against the Jaguars in the 2007 divisional round. The Patriots went 2-1 in those contests.
2nd quarter: Eagles 15, Patriots 3

LeGarrette Blount scampered 21 yards for a touchdown to cap a six-play, 65-yard drive and extend the Eagles' lead. Philadelphia attempted a two-point conversion, but Nick Foles and Alshon Jeffrey could not connect.

Three of the Eagles' six plays on the drive went for 19 or more yards: A 19-yard completion to Zach Ertz, a 22-yard completion to Jeffrey, and Blount's touchdown run. For the game, Philadelphia has notched eight plays of 15-plus yards, four plays of 20-plus yards, and two of 30-plus yards.

Blount so far has 58 rushing yards, a Super Bowl career-high, and the Eagles have 73 yards on the ground. The Eagles rushed for 100-plus yards 13 times in the regular season and went 12-1 in those games. They went 3-2 when held below 100 yards rushing.
Cooks ruled out

Patriots receiver Brandin Cooks was ruled out with a head injury after absorbing a big hit from Eagles safety Malcolm Jenkins early in the second quarter. Cooks, who has one catch for 23 yards, was slow to get up but walked off the field under his own power and went straight to the locker room.

2nd quarter: Eagles 15, Patriots 6

Stephen Gostkowski made a 45-yard field goal to cap a five-play, 48-yard drive by the Patriots.

The drive opened with a 46-yard catch-and-run by Rex Burkhead, but the Patriots could not sustain the momentum. Quarterback Tom Brady missed on two of his subsequent three pass attempts.
So far, Brady is 9-of-16 passing for 191 yards, the most of his career in a first half of a Super Bowl and the 10th most in Super Bowl history.

2nd quarter: Eagles 15, Patriots 12

Running back James White got loose for a 26-yard touchdown run, capping a seven-play, 90-yard drive and capitalizing on Duron Harmon's interception.

Stephen Gostkowski's extra point was wide left, his second miscue of the game.

White's touchdown was set up by a beautiful 43-yard throw from Tom Brady to Chris Hogan, their second-longest connection of the season.

The game's first turnover

Patriots safety Duron Harmon came up with a bobbled Nick Foles pass intended for Alson Jeffrey. The Patriots took over at their own 10-yard line

On first and 10 at the New England 43-yard line, Foles targeted Jeffrey inside the 5-yard line. But Jeffrey, who was covered on the play by his college roommate, Stephon Gilmore, could not come up with it and essentially batted it into Harmon's hands.
2nd quarter: Eagles 22, Patriots 12

Coach Doug Pederson and the Eagles gambled on fourth and goal from the 1-yard line and won.

On a trick play, running Corey Clement took a direct snap, handed off to tight end Trey Burton, who then tossed a 1-yard touchdown pass to Nick Foles. It came with just 34 seconds left in the second quarter. It was the sixth time in Super Bowl history that a team scored a touchdown when going for it on fourth down, and first since Emmitt Smith in Super Bowl XXVIII.

The touchdown capped a seven-play, 70-yard drive that included a 55-yard catch-and-run by Clement on third down.

3rd quarter: Eagles 22, Patriots 19

When in an offensive rut, go to Rob Gronkowski.
The Patriots opened the second half with an eight-play, 75-yard drive that ended on a 5-yard touchdown throw from Tom Brady to the big All-Pro tight end.

After making just one catch for 9 yards on five targets in the first half, Gronkowski was targeted five times on the drive, reeling in four catches for 68 yards and the touchdown.

Brady now has 344 passing yards, the eighth most in Super Bowl history. The record he set last year — 466 yards — is within reach.

Patriots safety Patrick Chung was injured on the possession but returned on the next defensive series.

3rd quarter: Eagles 29, Patriots 19

Quarterback Nick Foles threw a 22-yard pass to running back Corey Clement in double coverage to make it a two-score game. Clement's catch was reviewed by officials, who ruled the call on the field stands.

The touchdown capped an 11-play, 85-yard drive.

3rd quarter: Eagles 29, Patriots 26

Quarterback Tom Brady found receiver Chris Hogan for a 26-yard touchdown to again trim Philadelphia's lead. The touchdown finished off a seven-play, 75-yard drive.

Brady now has 404 yards passing and has connected with seven different receivers. For Hogan, who now has five catches for 125 yards, this is his first 100-yard game in the playoffs.

4th quarter: Eagles 32, Patriots 26

Jake Elliott connected on a 42-yard field goal to extend the Eagles' lead.

Elliott's attempt came after Marquis Flowers dropped Nelson Agholor for an 8-yard loss on third and 3.

The Eagles and Patriots have combined for more than 1,000 yards of offense, breaking the record for most yards in a Super Bowl. For Brady and Gronkowski, it was the 12th time they have connected for a touchdown in the postseason, tying Joe Montana and Jerry Rice for most by a quarterback/receiver.

The field goal capped an eight-play, 51-yard drive.

4th quarter: Patriots 33, Eagles 32

New England has its first lead in Super Bowl LII. It came on a 4-yard touchdown pass from Tom Brady to Rob Gronkowski, their second touchdown connection of the game.
It was a 10-play, 75-yard drive for the Patriots, who have found the end zone on all three of their second-half possessions.

4th quarter: Eagles 38, Patriots 33

Tight end Zach Ertz scored on an 11-yard touchdown pass from Nick Foles for the Eagles to retake the lead with just more than 2 minutes left in the game. Philadelphia's two-point attempt failed. Patriots safety Patrick Chung has been ruled out with a head injury.

4th quarter: Eagles 38, Patriots 33

The first sack of Super Bowl LII came at an inopportune time for New England.

Defensive end Brandon Graham came up with a strip-sack of Tom Brady with 2:21 left in the game. Rookie Derek Barnett recovered the fumble.

4th quarter: Eagles 41, Patriots 33

With 2:16 to play. When the Patriots had the ball, Brandon Graham drew cheers from Eagles fans as he sacked Tom Brady, who fumbled the ball. The ball was recovered by Eagles' Derek Barnett at the Patriots 31-yard line.

Philadelphia would then increase its lead after Elliott's 46-yard field goal, making the game score 41–33.

With seconds left, the Patriots were able to move the ball down to midfield. With just under 10 seconds remaining, Tom Brady gave it his best shot with a huge Hail Mary pass that would have sent the game into OT with a touchdown plus 2. However, the Eagles swarmed Gronkowski and the human blanket in the end zone caused a pass with a chance, to fall incomplete. This sealed the game and prompted a lot of happy sounds from Eagles and Eagles fans in the stadium and across the world. It was a heartbreaking experience for the Patriots who had come so close.

The 5-time Super Bowl champions were defeated by a score of 41-33. Nick Foles, a story unto himself this fall as The Little Engine That Could, was named Super Bowl MVP after the game. With this win, the Eagles finally won their first Super Bowl, and their first NFL title since 1960. The Patriots put up the good fight all year long.

And, then?

With Bill Belichick as the coach taking on Doug Pederson every year in a Super Bowl match, the games ought to be really good and nobody knows who will win. One thing is for sure. It is the Patriotss turn in 2018. Go Patriots!   Thank you for taking the time to enjoy this book about the best historical team in pro football today!

Other books by Brian Kelly: (amazon.com, & Kindle)

Great Moments in Philadelphia Eagles Football. The best from the Eagles from the beginning of football.
Great Moments in Syracuse Football The great moments, coaches & players in Syracuse Football
Boost Social Security Now! Hey Buddy Can You Spare a Dime?
The Birth of American Football. From the first college game in 1869 to the last Super Bowl
Obamacare: A One-Line Repeal Congress must get this done.
A Wilkes-Barre Christmas Story A wonderful town makes Christmas all the better
A Boy, A Bike, A Train, and a Christmas Miracle A Christmas story that will melt your heart
Pay-to-Go   America-First Immigration Fix
Legalizing Illegal Aliens Via Resident Visas Americans-first plan saves $Trillions. Learn how!
60 Million Illegal Aliens in America!!! A simple, America-first solution.
The Bill of Rights By Founder James Madison Refresh *your knowledge of the specific rights for all*
Great Players in Army Football Great Army Football played by great players..
Great Coaches in Army Football Army's coaches are all great.
Great Moments in Army Football Army Football at its best.
Great Moments in Florida Gators Football Gators Football from the start. This is the book.
Great Moments in Clemson Football CU Football at its best. This is the book.
Great Moments in Florida Gators Football Gators Football from the start. This is the book.
The Constitution Companion. A Guide to Reading and Comprehending the Constitution
The Constitution by Hamilton, Jefferson, & Madison – Big type and in English
PATERNO: The Dark Days After Win # 409. Sky began to fall within days of win # 409.
JoePa 409 Victories: Say No More! Winningest Division I-A football coach ever
American College Football: The Beginning From before day one football was played.
Great Coaches in Alabama Football Challenging the coaches of every other program!
Great Coaches in Penn State Football the Best Coaches in PSU's football program
Great Players in Penn State Football The best players in PSU's football program
Great Players in Notre Dame Football The best players in ND's football program
Great Coaches in Notre Dame Football The best coaches in any football program
Great Players in Alabama Football from Quarterbacks to offensive Linemen Greats!
Great Moments in Alabama Football AU Football from the start. This is the book.
Great Moments in Penn State Football PSU Football, start--games, coaches, players,
Great Moments in Notre Dame Football ND Football, start, games, coaches, players
Cross Country With the Parents A great trip from East Coast to West with the kids
Seniors, Social Security & the Minimum Wage. Things seniors need to know.
How to Write Your First Book and Publish It with CreateSpace
The US Immigration Fix--It's all in here. Finally, an answer.
I had a Dream IBM Could be #1 Again The title is self-explanatory
WineDiets.Com Presents The Wine Diet Learn how to lose weight while having fun.
Wilkes-Barre, PA; Return to Glory Wilkes-Barre City's return to glory
Geoffrey Parsons' Epoch... The Land of Fair Play Better than the original.
The Bill of Rights 4 Dummmies! This is the best book to learn about your rights.
Sol Bloom's Epoch …Story of the Constitution The best book to learn the Constitution
America 4 Dummmies! All Americans should read to learn about this great country.
The Electoral College 4 Dummmies! How does it really work?
The All-Everything Machine Story about IBM's finest computer server.
ThankYou IBM! This book explains how IBM was beaten in the computer marketplace by neophytes

Brian has written 154 books in total. Other books can be found at amazon.com/author/brianwkelly